DELIVERING PUSH

Delivering Push

Ethan Cerami

McGraw-Hill
New York • San Francisco • Washington, D.C. • Auckland
Bogotá • Caracas • Lisbon • London • Madrid • Mexico City
Milan • Montreal • New Delhi • San Juan • Singapore
Sydney • Tokyo • Toronto

McGraw-Hill

A Division of The ***McGraw-Hill*** *Companies*

1 2 3 4 5 6 7 8 9 0 DOC/DOC 9 0 2 1 0 9 8 7

P/N 012024-2
PART OF
ISBN 0-07-913693-1

The sponsoring editor for this book was Michael Sprague and the production supervisor was Sherri Souffrance. It was set in Century Schoolbook by Douglas & Gayle, Limited.

Printed and bound by R. R. Donnelley & Sons Company.

// Acknowledgements

Writing is certainly a solitary pursuit, but I couldn't have done it without abundant support from many people. First off, special thanks to Michael Sprague, my editor at McGraw-Hill. He successfully shepherded this project from initial thoughts to final production. And, he kept me on course when I missed my first deadline. No author could ask for a better, more knowledgeable editor.

Special thanks also go to Simon St. Laurent for introducing me to Michael in the first place, and inspiring me to actually put words to paper.

No acknowledgment would be complete without thanking three important teachers from New York University, who successfully took a liberal arts history major and made him into a computer scientist. Special thanks therefore go out to Susan Dickey, Arthur Goldberg, and Matthew Smosna. These three taught me just about everything I know about computers, and enabled me to write this book in the first place. Sadly, Professor Smosna passed away this last year, but I know that his spirit will live on in all of his many students.

Many thanks also go to the whole team at Cognitive Communications. Special thanks especially go to John Fine, the best damn boss I ever had. John and David Leveen, first got me started on push technology research, and then were gracious enough to put up with my part-time writing schedule. This book would not have been possible without their constant support.

I also wish to thank my entire family for providing constant support during the past five months. Special thanks to Mom, Dad, Nelli, Daryl and Carla.

And, lastly, special thanks go to all my supportive friends who put up with my schedule and kept me in good humor and good spirits. Special thanks go to Dooley, Liz, Dave, Jon, Sue, and Whitney.

To Helen K. Lindner (1914–1996)

CONTENTS

PART I

Overview of Push Technology

CHAPTER 1

Introduction to Push Technology

I see push creating almost a second Internet.

—Halsey Minor, CEO of c|net, Inc.

Push technology has been hailed as the next killer application of the Internet. Small start-up companies are scrambling to deliver their products to market. Broadcast and traditional print media companies, including CNN, ESPN, Time Warner, ABC, and the *New York Times* are rushing to create new push media content. Advertisers are hoping that they have finally found the Holy Grail for Internet advertising. And, the David and Goliath rivalry between Netscape and Microsoft has moved beyond the browser war to include a push-technology war. *Wired* magazine has even gone so far as to declare that the Web browser is dead, and push technology killed it.

But what exactly is push technology? At its heart, push technology (or *Webcasting*, as it is frequently called) represents a new model for the delivery of information across the Internet and intranets. The current model of Internet delivery consists of users pointing and clicking on Web pages. Users "pull" information from remote computers to their desktops. With push, users simply subscribe to "channels," and information is "pushed" automatically to their desktops. The information is constantly updated and tailored to meet the user's individual interests and preferences.

The push technology pioneer, PointCast, Inc., provides an ideal example of this new technology at work. Users throughout the world can connect to the PointCast Web site (`http:\\www.pointcast.com`) and download a free copy of the PointCast client software. To date, more than 1.7 million people have already done so.

After users download and install the software, they follow a step-by-step registration process. During this process, users are queried for a host of demographic information, which provides an invaluable wealth of information for potential advertisers.

After users are registered, they are prompted to subscribe to a group of channels. Current PointCast channels run the gamut from CNN and the *New York Times* to the *Seattle Times* and the *Boston Globe*. For each channel, users select specific topics that interest them. Subscribers to CNN, for example, can choose to receive news stories from a dozen news categories, including U.S. News, World News, Science and Technology, Health, and Travel. Subscribers to the Weather Channel can select weather reports for Tokyo and New York. Subscribers to the Companies Channel can select specific stocks to track. And subscribers to ZDNet can choose to follow news regarding software developments, the World Wide Web, Macintosh software, or even new game software.

Whenever the user's computer is idle, the PointCast software makes a network connection to the central PointCast server and checks for new information. Users can determine the frequency of these updates. And, if new information is available, the headline and the entire article text are downloaded automatically in the background. All articles then are cached locally on the user's hard drive.

At any point, users can start the PointCast viewer or choose to use PointCast as their default screen saver. The PointCast viewer displays a browser-like interface for viewing all channels and all new headlines (see Figure 1-1). The viewer also displays a multimedia-rich advertisement in one quarter of the screen. Users can click on any current headline to display the entire article text. And, because the article is cached locally, users do not experience a frustrating "world wide wait." In effect, PointCast provides news on demand. And, the news is tailored to the specific user's interest and is always available and up-to-date.

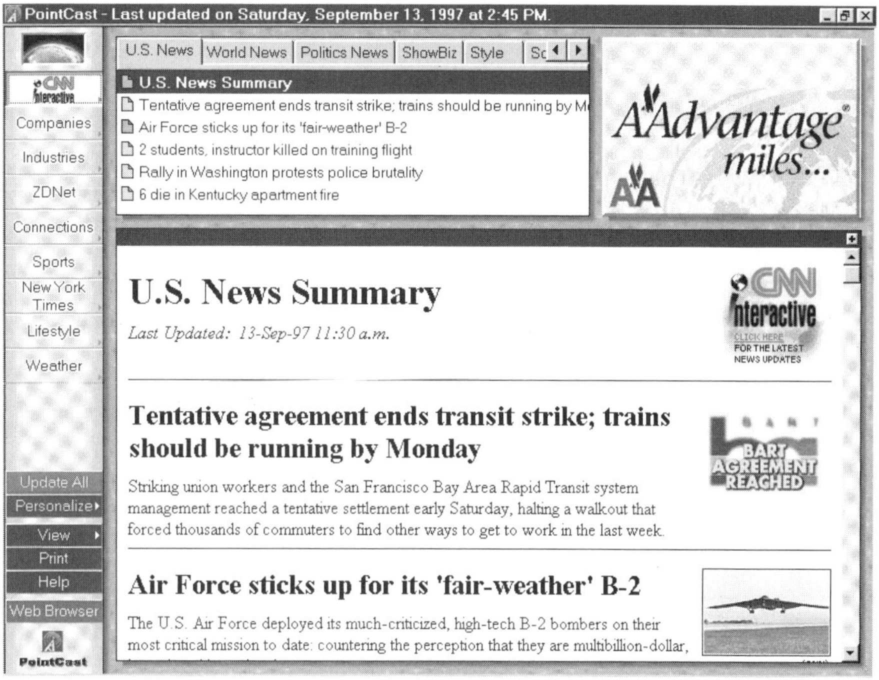

Figure 1-1
CNN on PointCast. Note the online advertisement in the upper corner.

For people who are tired of getting lost on the Web, this technology means a coherent and manageable mechanism for getting information. For companies and intranets, it means an efficient system for distributing timely corporate or market information to all employees or select groups of employees. And, for advertisers, this means a direct channel for marketing.

1.1 The Push Model

> ***Manually searching the Web is not a sustainable model, long term.***
>
> ***—Eric Schmidt, CEO, Novell, Inc.***

Regardless of the push product you choose, the basic push model remains the same. In fact, whether you use PointCast or any of the other market competitors, including BackWeb, Castanet, Intermind, Internet Explorer, or Netscape Netcaster, the basic model is quite simple:

Step 1: Users download the push client software. In the case of PointCast and BackWeb, this means that users must download and install a separate piece of software. In the case of Internet Explorer and Netscape Netcaster, push facilities come bundled with the browser, and no additional installation is required.

Step 2: Users complete a registration form: Most push products, including PointCast and Netcaster, gather basic demographic data regarding their subscriber audience. Users may be queried for their age, gender, ZIP code, professional occupation, or specific company information. This better enables push companies to attract and retain online advertisers.

Step 3: Users subscribe to channels. Most push products now include their own channel directories. PointCast has a built-in channel directory. Netscape and Marimba have an online Channel Finder guide. And Microsoft Internet Explorer now includes a list of premium channels directly embedded inside the browser. Subscribing to new channels usually is as simple as a single point and click. And, more and more, regardless of push platform, users can subscribe to new channels via their default Web browser.

Step 4: Users complete an individual profile. Most push content is tailored individually to meet users' interests and preferences. After users subscribe to a channel, they select the topics that interest them the most. Users may select from a predefined list of topics or type a series of keywords for important subject searches. Users then can store this *individual profile* locally on their machine or externally on the content provider's Web server.

Step 5: Channel providers create and tailor new content. Much like Web site designers who must create new content for Web pages, channel providers constantly need to gather new information and create new content (see Figure 1-2). Channel providers also need to categorize this new information to meet the set of individual preferences of their intended audience. Depending on the system involved, new content might include text, images, HTML, Java, ActiveX, Shockwave animation, video, and audio. Depending on the content, this information can be updated every week, every day, or every 30 minutes.

Step 6: Push client software automatically retrieves new information. Unfortunately, the term *push* can be highly misleading from a technical point of view. Most push servers do not actually broadcast or push information in the same way as television or radio transmitters. Instead, most push software works on a client polling model. (For further technical information on the client polling model, see Chapter 3, "A Technical Primer

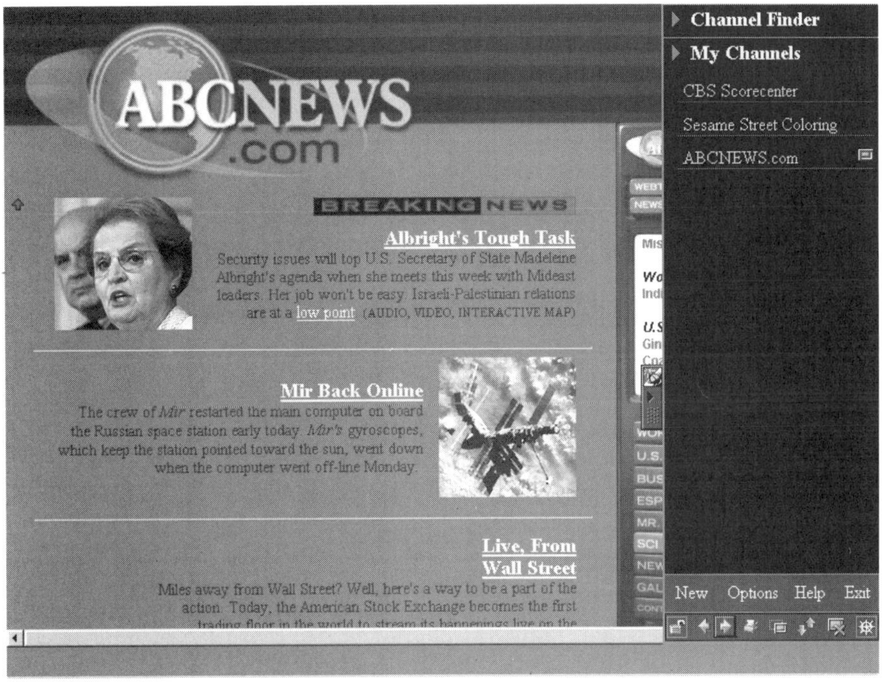

Figure 1-2
ABC News.com on Netscape Netcaster. News is constantly up-to-date and tailored for individual use.

on Push.") Push clients simply follow a preset schedule and periodically check the server for new information. When new information is available, that information is downloaded automatically in the background and stored on the user's local hard drive. This provides users with the illusion that their information is simply *pushed* to them. Nonetheless, the result is the same: Information is downloaded automatically instead of manually.

1.2 The New Lexicon

> **At first glance all this looks like revenge of the TV. It's back!**
>
> **—Kevin Kelly and Gary Wolf**
> **(*Wired* magazine)**

Despite the pitfalls of comparing new technologies to old ones, push technology has been compared repeatedly to traditional or cable television broadcasting. Push media companies therefore no longer refer to *Web pages*, *clients*, and *servers*. Instead, they refer to *channels*, *subscriptions*, *tuners*, *broadcasting*, and *narrowcasting*. Unfortunately, many of these new terms —even the term *push*—can be misleading from a technical point of view. The new lexicon does provide a coherent structure for understanding push technology from the user's point of view, however. (It also has been a very successful marketing tool for many push startup companies!)

Here is a quick primer on the new lexicon:

broadcast Instead of waiting for users to get information by pointing and clicking on Web pages, information is broadcast to all users. From a technical viewpoint, most push information is not actually broadcast in the same manner as television and radio. Because new information is downloaded automatically, though, it does have the appearance of traditional broadcasting.

channel Any set of data that is updated regularly. This information could be a set of financial news headlines, weather reports, or company announcements. This information also could be a constantly updated Java application channel, a QuickTime video, or a new signature file for the latest computer virus.

narrowcast With traditional and cable broadcasting, all viewers watch the same programs. Viewers certainly can change the channel or subscribe to new premium channels, but they cannot exercise control over the content on those channels. In contrast, push users can specify the topics that interest them the most and filter out the rest. Push broadcasters therefore can narrowcast specific stories to meet individual interests and preferences.

pull Any *manual* mechanism for getting information off the Web. Currently, this includes pointing and clicking on Web pages. Users click on a hypertext link and pull the associated HTML page, along with images and applets, from a remote computer to their desktop.

push Any *automatic* mechanism for getting information off the Web. From the user's perspective, *push* simply means that new information is delivered or retrieved automatically from a remote computer to the user's computer. No manual intervention is required. New information is updated periodically on a preset schedule.

subscription To get a print magazine every week, you simply fill out a subscription, and the magazine is pushed to you every week via the Post Office. In the push model, subscriptions work the same way: Users simply subscribe to specific channels, and the embedded software makes sure that they always receive new information and channel updates.

transmitter A transmitter is any computer that sends information to another computer. In traditional computer lingo, a transmitter is simply a *push-enabled server.*

tuner A tuner is any software application that constantly receives new information for a specific set of channels. In traditional computer lingo, a tuner is simply a *push-enabled client.*

1.3 The End of the Browser?

> **Order a headstone: The browser died on Wednesday.**
> **—Jesse Berst, "The Day the Browser Died"**
> ZDNet Anchor Desk, March 14, 1997

With all the media frenzy surrounding new Internet technologies, it has become increasingly difficult to separate the hype from reality. A February 24, 1997 cover story of *Business Week* hailed push technology as a fundamental new force destined to change the shape of the Internet. In fact, *Business Week* proclaimed that push technology has the potential to "tame the web, enhance corporate communication, spur digital commerce and provide one more jolt to the software Establishment."* A March 1997 *Wired* magazine article, "Kiss Your Browser Good-Bye," hailed push technology as the future of the Web: "The web browser itself is about to croak. And good riddance."†

But is the browser really dead?

No. The browser is far from dead. In fact, the browser still has many years of long-term growth. Traditional pull and new push technologies both have unique advantages and disadvantages. Consumers are likely to exploit the advantages of each. And, according to *PC Week*, this really isn't an *either or* proposition. The future of the Web will bring a melding of push and pull technologies. In fact, we are about to embark on a new era in which consumers use a combination of the two to get the information they need.

The traditional pull model of pointing and clicking on Web pages certainly has its distinct advantages. It puts users in control and gives them complete freedom to mine the vast resources of the net. Want to get some

---

*Cortese, Amy, "Webcasting: A Way Out of the Web Maze," *Business Week*, February 24, 1997.

†Kelley, Kevin and Wolf, Gary, "Push! Kiss your browser good-bye: The radical future of media beyond the Web," *Wired*, Issue 5.03, March 1997.

raw data on the United States-Japan trade deficit? Looking for the most recent photographs from the Hubble Space Telescope? More than likely, you are going to use pull—and will continue to use pull even when push has become as pervasive as today's browsers.

Pointing and clicking does have three distinct disadvantages, however. First, it can be extremely difficult to find the information you want. Second, there is no automatic method for getting Web page updates. And, third, users often experience frustrating download times for new Web pages. Fortunately, push excels at addressing each of these issues.

1.4 The Promise of Push

1.4.1 Organizing the Web

> **Sometimes I feel like I am browsing a gigantic maze. Help! I'm going in circles!**
>
> **—Lincoln Stein**
>
> **(*WebTechniques* magazine, on his latest ratings system for organizing the Web. Ratings include the Doodad Index, the Tutie-Frutie Index, and the Crass Commercialism Index.)**

One of the greatest promises of push is that it will help organize and tame the Web. Not all Web users enjoy foraging for themselves and frequently are left overwhelmed and lost. The latest Web search directories—including Yahoo! (`www.yahoo.com`), Lycos (`www.lycos.com`), and Excite (`www.excite.com`)—certainly are helpful. But, according to Marc Andreeson of Netscape Communications Corporation, "The Net for the first time is causing information overload." In fact, an estimated 150 million Web pages exist world wide, and this number could reach 1 billion by the year 2000.

With all these pages, new and even veteran Internet users can get lost and downright frustrated. *Wired* magazine calls this the "little-uttered secret" of the Web. And although *Wired* may have been premature in calling for the death of the browser, its description of this frustration is quite accurate:

> You don't know where the good stuff is, and when you land there, the signal is camouflaged by all the noise. Clicking becomes Russian roulette. Rolling your own is very rewarding, but often we'd like someone else to slip us a ready-made. Even though it may not be as nifty as the one we made. Or maybe because it's niftier and better made. As it is now, there is an audience of millions with high expectations, and they aren't being satisfied.*

For those users tired of getting lost, push provides an easy-to-understand custom-made delivery mechanism. Users simply fill out a set of interests and preferences. And, instead of roaming the vastness of the Internet, the Internet comes to them.

1.4.2 Delivering Time-Critical Data

The second great promise of push is the delivery of timely data. Currently, some Web pages provide notification of changes via e-mail. The online *JavaWorld* magazine, for example, enables users to subscribe to their e-mail notification system. When a new issue of the magazine arrives, all subscribers are e-mailed a new table of contents. Other Web sites partner with third-party software companies to provide automatic e-mail notification. Some software companies continuously check your company's Web pages, for example. Each page then is encrypted and compared to a small signature file. If the signature files do not match, e-mail is sent directly to all your subscribers to notify them that changes have been made. But, for the most part, users simply manually return to pages and check for new content. This is highly inefficient, because users may return and find no new content, or they may forget to return and miss vital information.

With push, new information is retrieved as soon as it is available or as often as the user requests. And, the user can sit tight knowing that the information is constantly up-to-date. This automatic update mechanism is highly desirable in many scenarios. The first scenario is the delivery of

---

*Kelley, Kevin and Wolf, Gary, "Push! Kiss your browser good-bye: The radical future of media beyond the Web," *Wired*, Issue 5.03, March 1997.

ultra time-critical data. Depending on the user's interests, this data might include financial information on the Dow Jones Industrial Average or specific company stock quotes. The data also might include the latest news headlines on U.S. politics or up-to-the-minute weather and traffic reports. And, for sports fanatics, it might include the current score for tonight's basketball game and its accompanying statistics.

Contrary to most media reports, however, push is not reserved exclusively for this ultra time-critical data. Only a subset of customers really wants information updated every hour. For these news junkies, push is a godsend. But, for the rest of us, knowing the current Microsoft stock price or the current Knicks-Heat basketball score is not critical, and getting constant updates can be distracting and overwhelming.

Most of us do want information updates anywhere between once a day and once a month, however. For the most part, this is not just raw data but news analysis or in-depth technical information. Or, it could include Web pages to which a user frequently returns. According to a recent survey, 50 percent of regular Internet users no longer surf. Instead, they find a subset of very useful Web pages and simply return to the same pages over and over again. These pages might include online magazines that are updated once a month, technical reports on the latest Internet technologies, or press releases from specific companies. These pages are ideal candidates for push. Why risk missing Web page updates when push can ensure that the changes are pushed automatically to you? And why return manually to a specific set of Web pages when push can deliver them to you on your own schedule?

1.4.3 Eliminating the World Wide Wait

> **Remote host contacted. Waiting for Reply.**
> **—Netscape Communicator**

Most Internet users, particularly home Internet users, have become increasingly frustrated with the "World Wide Wait." Users click on a hypertext link, and it may take several minutes before the new page downloads completely. Frustrating download times can result from several factors. The Web server may be slow or overwhelmed with too many simultaneous requests from other users. Internet routers may be overwhelmed with too much other traffic, and this traffic might include bandwidth-intensive information, such as audio or video. For home users or businesses not connected directly to the Internet, users simply may have a slow modem connection. Any of these factors, combined with the great number of new customers signing up for Internet accounts, can lead to very long download times.

Push technology certainly does not provide a magic bullet for solving Internet traffic or Internet routing. In fact, it probably will exacerbate most of the bandwidth and traffic problems currently associated with the net. But, because data is downloaded automatically, and this downloading usually is hidden from the user, users *perceive* a much faster response time. In the case of PointCast, Netcaster, and Microsoft's Active Channels, news articles are downloaded constantly and stored on the local hard drive (see Figure 1-3). When users want to view the contents of the article, they simply retrieve the article from the hard drive, and they perceive a very fast response time. Most push products also offer the option of automatic downloading overnight. This effectively delegates the push software to deal with frustrating waits, therefore sparing the user from experiencing them.

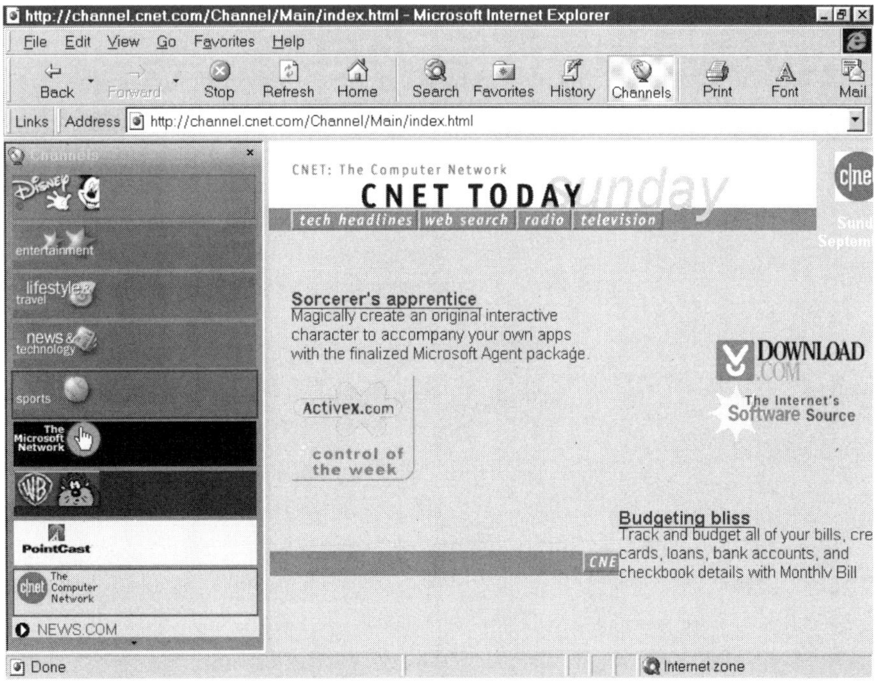

Figure 1-3 Internet Explorer Active Channels. Subscribing to new channels is a simple matter of pointing and clicking. IE 4.0 even includes a directory of premium channels built right into the browser interface.

1.4.4 Extending the Corporate Intranet

Currently, more than 96 percent of Fortune 500 companies are running or installing corporate intranets. The market for intranets is expected to reach $13 billion by 1999, up from $2.67 billion in 1996. And, intranets have proven to be a wise investment. Information is absolutely critical to compete effectively in today's marketplace, and intranets provide a scaleable, cross-platform mechanism for delivering and sharing information.

Intranets do have one major failing, however: Employees do not always return to the corporate intranet home page. And, no automatic mechanism exists to alert employees to important information that may have been posted on the intranet. When used wisely with existing intranets, push can provide just such a mechanism, however. And companies can provide an efficient mechanism for keeping all employees constantly up-to-date on company changes, economic conditions, and market competitors.

According to most industry analysts, businesses rather than consumers actually will provide the most lucrative markets for push technology. Companies already have the existing infrastructure—including direct connections to the Internet—and have time-critical information needs. In fact, according to *Business Week*, companies such as Amoco, NationsBank and Fruit of the Loom already are pushing industry news to their employees' desktops. These same companies also are setting up their own corporate channels to make sure that employees receive the latest announcements and corporate communiqués. General Motors even has started pushing training videos to its dealers.

1.4.5 Pushing Content and Software

If you can easily push news content, headlines, and articles, why not push software applications and Java applets as well? Marimba, Inc. and BackWeb, in fact, provide just such a mechanism for subscribing to both content and application channels. Users therefore can subscribe to the CBS Sports Ticker, for example, and not only receive updated sports

Figure 1-4
CBS Sports Ticker: Marimba's Castanet enables channel providers to push both content **and** software.

scores, but view the scores and news within the customized CBS Sports Ticker Java applet (see Figure 1-4). The applet remains on users' desktops in a small window and includes several options for immediate user customization.

Instead of manually installing thousands of programs on a local area network, push promises to provide automatic installation of new software applications. And, if the software application includes bugs or security flaws, software patches and upgrades can be pushed automatically to all employees overnight. *Information Systems* (IS) managers can feel confident that all employees are using the most up-to-date software applications.

As another example, McAfee Inc. already has started providing a push channel for its hugely popular VirusScan antivirus software program. According to McAfee, its *antivirus emergency response team* (AVERT) discovers approximately 200 new viruses per month. If IS managers are serious about keeping their networks virus-free, they need software patches for these viruses, along with detailed virus information. To provide this delivery mechanism, McAfee has teamed up with BackWeb, Inc. to create a push channel for virus updates. For a fee, companies can subscribe to the channel and automatically receive VirusScan software, virus signature updates, virus information library updates, news alerts, white papers, and technical notes. According to Bill Larson, McAfee's president, "timely VirusScan updates translate directly into superior protection." Marimba is hoping that its Castanet technology will provide similar functionality for Java applications.

1.4.6 Online Marketing and Advertising

> **It's like reaching through someone's TV screen when they're hungry and giving them popcorn.**
>
> **—Nancy Friedman**
>
> Marketing Director of Levi Strauss and Company, on the merits of push advertising*

Only a few years ago, it was almost considered a sin to allow any Web advertising. The Internet has its roots in federally funded research projects and academic collaboration. In this environment, the Internet was created specifically for noncommercial projects, including scientific research, academic exchange, and library archives. In fact, much of the funding for the Internet from the National Science Foundation specifically excluded any commercial activity and restricted Internet use to education and research only.

Since those early days, the Internet has grown at a phenomenal pace. And it certainly has moved away from its focus on research and education to business and electronic commerce. Businesses now account for the lion's share of new Internet domain names, and many companies are hoping to capture additional revenue from advertising and sales through their Web sites. Madison Avenue, however has been sorely disappointed with the success of Internet advertising. Because of restrictions on Web page real-estate, ads frequently are small. And because of restrictions in bandwidth, ads do not live up to their full multimedia potential and arguably are not as compelling as their television or even print counterparts.

Push provides a new venue for advertising, and it offers two distinct advantages over pull. First, push provides a much more effective mechanism for tracking and understanding online customers and their online behavior. During the registration process for PointCast and Netscape Netcaster, for example, users are asked a host of demographic questions concerning age, gender, and ZIP code. Most push companies do not release individual demographic records, but they do provide advertisers with aggregate demographic data. This data provides potential advertisers with a clear picture of their advertising audience. And, in most cases, this picture is more accurate than comparable surveys for print and television audiences. Most

---

*Bank, David, "How the Net is Becoming More Like Television to Draw Advertisers," *Wall Street Journal*, December 13, 1996.

push products also include automatic feedback mechanisms for logging user interest in specific companies or specific advertisements. Castanet, for example, includes specific HTML codes for tracking which advertisements users click and transmits this data back to the Castanet server.

The second advantage of push is the delivery of true multimedia advertising. When users point and click on a home page, bandwidth restricts the file size of ads. If the ad is too large, the transfer time is long, and the user is likely to click off the page before the full ad downloads. With push, all content is delivered in the background. This means that a push client could download a multimedia advertisement during the middle of the night, for example. When the user returns in the morning to check the latest news headlines, the advertisement is fully downloaded and ready to go. And, because bandwidth requirements have been distributed throughout the day, this advertisement can contain rich multimedia content, including audio, video, and true user interactivity.

These two advantages already have made push the darling of the advertising world. PointCast already boasts an average ad rate double the Web average. Levi Strauss and Company already has allocated a set of funds for push advertising, and Land's End has begun experimenting with electronic commerce through push. And that's not all. According to the Yankee Group, a Boston-based market research firm, push technology advertising will account for one-third of the $14 billion in Internet advertising, subscriptions, and retail revenues projected for the year 2000.

1.5 The Peril of Push

Push implies interruption and salesmanship. Pull implies choice.

—James Gleick
(New York Times)

Despite all these stunning attributes Push does have some disadvantages, however. And it certainly will not live up to all the hype surrounding it. Tony Davis, the former CEO of the push company Lanacom (recently acquired by BackWeb, Inc.) even started telling others that *push* actually stood for *people under the influence of software hype*. So, what is the downside of push?

1.5.1 When Push Comes to Shove

First and foremost of the downsides to push may be consumer unwillingness to have information pushed to them. Many customers already may be suffering from information overload and view push as an annoying nuisance that provides little added value. Push suddenly becomes shove. According to Denise Caruso of the *New York Times*, this could represent a potential backlash against Push: "Shoving it down our throats does not increase our capacity for information. If anything, it engages our gag reflexes."

It also is entirely possible that consumers will revolt against push advertising and turn off their push clients completely. This is essentially the billion-dollar question. How much online advertising are consumers willing to tolerate? And how much are advertisers willing to pay for it? Much like every other broadcast medium, however, the free market is likely to reach a happy equilibrium. In general, consumers are happy to view advertising in exchange for content that is free, accurate, reliable, or entertaining. And, in some cases, advertising even can be seen as a supplement to the content.

1.5.2 Bandwidth and Memory

Push also lays a large claim on bandwidth and computing resources. Push clients are constantly at work downloading new information off the Web. And because this information is being downloaded in the background, push content can include more multimedia-rich content. This translates into more frequent network connections and transfers of bigger multimedia files.

During off-peak hours, this can be a blessing, allowing networks to distribute their bandwidth load throughout the entire day. But, during peak hours, push easily can clog up computer networks and slow user response for all network applications. In fact, according to the market research firm Optimal Networks, almost one-fifth of corporate network traffic stems from push technologies, even though they are used only by 12 percent of users.

Such bandwidth issues may be even more critical for home users. According to Computer Intelligence, the vast majority of home PCs still runs at 14.4 kbits/s or less. And 82 percent of home PCs also have only 8M of RAM or less. Many of these PCs easily could be overtaxed by the multimedia requirements of new push content.

1.6 The Future of Push

Watch out for Bill.

—*Anonymous*

Determining the overall success of push is a difficult proposition. Intense market competition between software companies has dramatically shortened product-development time. We now work in *Web time*, and new software programs—bugs and all—are posted on the Internet as soon as they are ready. Software patches for bugs and security flaws usually are posted the same day. Within this environment, it can be very difficult to form objective assessments of new Internet technologies. In fact, the verdict is still out on Java, ActiveX, and dynamic HTML. And in much the same vein, the verdict is still out on push technology. Its overall success, however, does hinge on a number of critical factors.

First, how much information do users really want pushed to them? What kind of information will be pushed? And who will create this new content? Despite the technological glitz of the Web, content still is king. The quality, timeliness, and accuracy of content will determine whether consumers continue to subscribe to particular channels or stay hooked on push in general.

Another important factor is how much effort users are willing to expend to get push software. Here, Microsoft and Netscape have a distinct advantage over other push players. Their push products come bundled with their browsers, and users do not need to install separate push client programs. Smaller push players already have seen this writing on the wall and are working to incorporate their technology into the latest browsers. BackWeb, for example, is partnering with Microsoft to create a new version of its client program specifically tailored to Internet Explorer 4.0. And, Marimba has licensed its software to be included in Netscape's Netcaster software. If push requires installation of additional clunky software, most customers will run away in droves.

To be truly successful, it is paramount for the computer industry to agree on an open push standard. Part of the overall success of the Internet can be attributed to the open standards of *Transmission Control Protocol / Internet Protocol* (TCP/IP). And, part of the success of the Web itself certainly can be attributed to *Hypertext Transfer Protocol* (HTTP) and HTML. Standards provide companies with a specific reference point for the creation of new products and ensure that diverse computer systems and software can speak to each other in a common language. In the case of push, no such officially sanctioned standard yet exists; this means that much of the push software requires the use of diverse or proprietary languages. This necessity creates a significant barrier for the creation of new push content.

Currently, Microsoft is pushing to establish the *Channel Definition Format* (CDF) as an open standard. And, already approximately 30 other companies, including PointCast, have recommended and supported the CDF standard to the *World Wide Web Consortium* (W3C). Netscape has resisted supporting the CDF format, however, and is pushing its own channel format based on HTML and JavaScript. The result is that the two biggest push players are creating two entirely different systems. This means that most content providers will have to choose between the two systems. And, according to Jesse Berst of ZDNet, "that leads to the nightmare scenario of two incompatible Internets existing side-by-side." Ultimately, the final arbiter will be the World Wide Web Consortium, which has the ultimate authority for approving CDF as a Web standard. The W3C hopefully will reach a decision regarding CDF within the next year.

The final factor in the future of push will be company willingness to invest in next-generation push technologies. Ultimately, this also may hinge on investor willingness to fund new startup companies. In many ways, today's push technology is similar to the first Mosaic Web browser. Most companies have just released their first-generation push products. But, given time and money, push technologies certainly will advance technologically and will adapt to better meet consumer demands. In the future, for example, advances in IP multicasting may provide a less bandwidth-intensive means of pushing information. And, intelligent agent software may even provide a more accurate method of finding and filtering appropriate information.

SUMMARY

Push represents a new model for the delivery of information across the Internet and intranets. The current model of Internet delivery consists of users pointing and clicking on Web pages. Users *pull* information from remote computers to their desktops. With push, users simply subscribe to channels, and that information is *pushed* to their desktops. The information is constantly updated and tailored to meet each user's interests and preferences.

Push is not likely to dethrone the Web browser as the primary user interface to the Web. Instead, we are about to embark on a new era in which consumers use a combination of push and pull and get the information they need.

Push has four distinct advantages over pull. It promises to organize the Web into channels and bring the information to users. It ensures the delivery of time-critical data, eliminates frustrating download times, and provides an effective mechanism for Web advertising. These advantages can be leveraged to complement existing corporate intranets and provide for automatic software upgrades. Push disadvantages include the potential of information overload, customer annoyance with online advertising, and its large claim on bandwidth and computing resources.

The overall success of push probably will hinge on a number of economic and technical factors. The most important factors include the quality of content, industry support for the *Channel Definition Format* (CDF), and investor willingness to fund next-generation push technology products.

CHAPTER 2

Snapshot of the Push Market

Everywhere you look these days, new push products are hitting the market: BackWeb, PointCast, Netcaster, Marimba, Air Media, and Downtown. The list goes on, and the array of services provided by each of these products is dizzying. This book focuses on the four most prominent push applications: Netscape Netcaster, Microsoft Active Channels, PointCast, and Marimba's Castanet. But, in choosing your push platform, you also might want to check out the services provided by other products.

This chapter includes brief descriptions of 12 major push applications. Each push product described here includes an overall description of the product, the client platforms supported, hardware and software requirements, a sampling of premium channels, and an URL for additional information.

Before making a final decision on your push platform, it is recommended that you read this chapter first. Each push product claims a particular niche and might be more suitable for your overall push needs.

2.1 AfterDark Online

Berkeley Systems, Inc.
2095 Rose Street
Berkeley, CA 94709
(800) 757-7707
`http://www.afterdark.com`

Client Platforms: Windows 95, Macintosh
Current Release: Version 2.01
Price: Client software is free.
Hardware/Software Requirements:

- 5 M RAM
- 8 M free hard disk space
- Macintosh version requires Apple's Open Transport 1.1.1 communication software or MacTCP 2.0.6

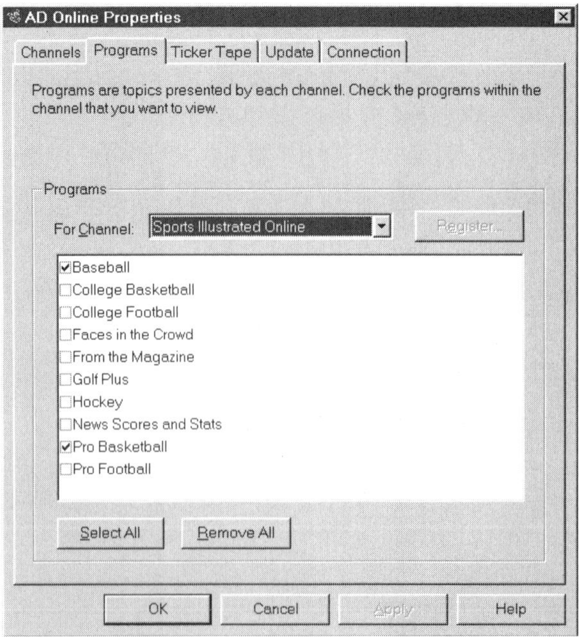

Figure 2-1
AfterDark Online is fully configurable, so you only receive the news that interests you the most.

Premium Channels:

DBC Financial News	*USA Today*
E! Online	The *Wall Street Journal* Interactive Edition
Sports Illustrated Online	ZDNet Computing Central

Description: AfterDark Online automatically retrieves news articles and displays them in a screen saver. The screen saver is visually compelling and easy to use. Just click on a news headline, and the article summary appears. Click again, and AfterDark opens your default Web browser with the full story.

AfterDark's premium channels are fully customizable. The *USA Today* channel, for example, lets you choose from several news sections: Front Page, Life, Money, News, Snapshot, Sports, Travel, Weather, and Web Traveler. The automatic update schedule is fully customizable (see Figure 2-2), and the screen saver works well offline.

In addition to AfterDark's premium channels, users can configure the screen ticker to display constantly updated stock quotes (you can track up to 25 companies) and sports scores.

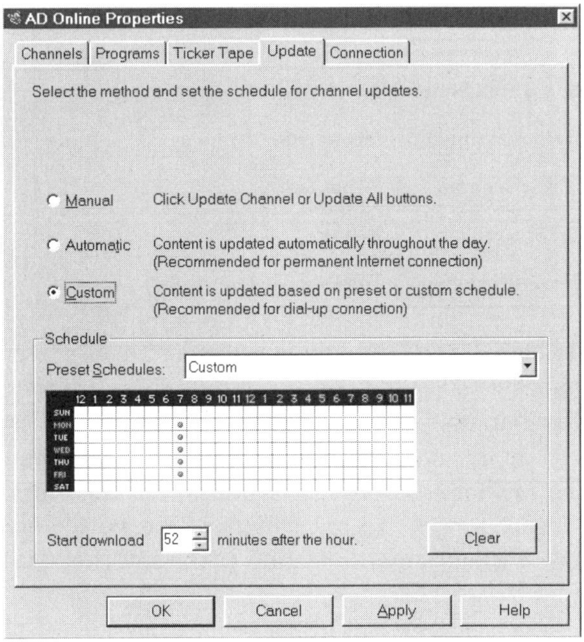

Figure 2-2
With AfterDark Online you can receive news updates as often as you want. Here, we can create a custom update schedule.

2.2 AirMedia

Air Media, Inc.
3501 Jamboree Road
Suite 400, South Tower
Newport Beach, CA 92660
(800) AIR-MEDIA
`http://www.airmedia.com`

Client Platform: Windows 95

Current Release: Version 2.0 (Version 2.1 currently is available in beta)

Price: NewsCatcher from Global Village Communication is approximately $100. You then purchase a monthly subscription: $5.95/month for the Premiere plan and $9.95/month for the Personal Premiere plan.

Hardware/Software Requirements:

- NewsCatcher from Global Village Communication
- Open serial port for NewsCatcher
- 16 M RAM
- 30 M free hard disk space
- CD-ROM

Premium Channels:

Business Wire	MovieLink
CBS SportsLine	Quote.com
CNN Interactive	Reuters
Knight-Ridder	Weather Channel

Description: AirMedia is perhaps the only "true" push application on the market today. Instead of relying on the Internet, AirMedia broadcasts new information to your computer via radio signals. The radio signals are picked up by your NewsCatcher antenna and immediately are displayed in the AirMedia scrolling marquees. You therefore can receive real-time stock quotes, sport scores, weather reports, and other news alerts immediately without any connection to the Internet.

If you opt for AirMedia's Personal Premiere plan, you get several added benefits. First, you can receive immediate notification of new e-mail messages. As soon as you receive a new e-mail message, AirMedia transmits a signal to your NewsCatcher, enabling you to receive e-mail notification even when not connected to the Internet. You can even opt to filter e-mail messages so that you are notified only of important messages. Second, you can enroll in AirMedia's Personal Portfolio plan. This enables you to track specific companies or receive immediate notification if stock prices rise or fall below a specified limit.

2.3 Astound WebCast

Astound, Inc.
3160 West Bayshore Road
Palo Alto, California 94303
1-(888)-4ASTOUND
`http://www.astound.com`

Client Platforms: Windows 95 and Windows NT

Price: The Channel Player is free. Check Web site for latest prices on Astound's channel-authoring tools.

Hardware/Software Requirements: Windows 95/NT Channel Player requires 8 M RAM (16 M recommended)

Figure 2-3
Astound WebCast includes a small multimedia window for displaying new Webcasts and a remote-control interface for controlling channel updates.

Premium Channels:	
ABC Tonight	Excite Live!
c|net News	*Golf* Online
Discovery Channel	*Sports Illustrated*
ESPNet	Yahoo News Headlines

Description: Astound WebCast includes two major components: client software (called the WebCast Live Channel Player (see Figure 2-3), which is used for receiving and playing Webcasts) and a series of authoring tools for creating new channels. Astound actually got its start with its multimedia authoring tools for business presentations and now is extending its presentation software to channel creation on the Web. Astound's WebCast multimedia presentations therefore are some of the most visually compelling on the market. The Astound Channel Player includes a small television remote control for flipping through subscribed channels, a small multimedia window for displaying Webcasts, and a built-in screen saver.

Astound's latest authoring tool, WebCast Professional, now includes tools for creating WebCast channels for Netscape Netcaster, Internet Explorer 4.0, and the Astound WebCast Channel Player. This includes built-in support for the *Channel Definition Format* (CDF) and dynamic HTML. In contrast to most push companies, Astound is attempting to market itself as both a Webcast platform and the leader in channel-creation tools

Figure 2-4 Astound WebCast Channels Directory.

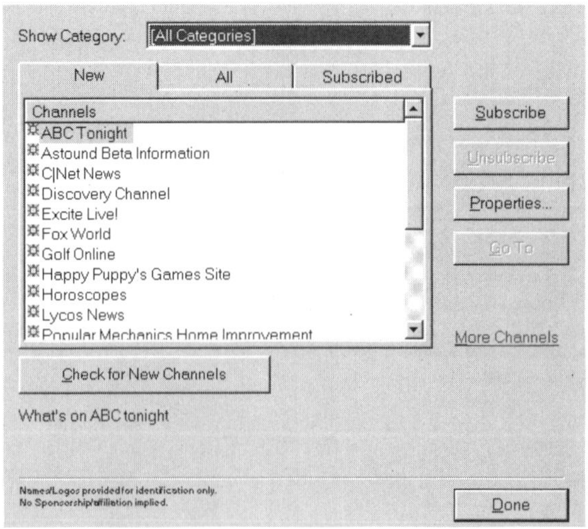

for other push platforms, including Netscape Netcaster and Internet Explorer.

2.4 BackWeb

BackWeb, Inc.
2077 Gateway Place, Suite 500
San Jose, CA 95110
(800) 863-0100
`http://www.backweb.com`

Client Platforms: Windows 95/NT, Windows 3.1, Macintosh, a Java-based UNIX client for Solaris, HP-UX, SGI
Server Platforms: Windows NT 3.5.1/4.0 and Sun Solaris 2.4 or higher
Current Release: Version 3.0

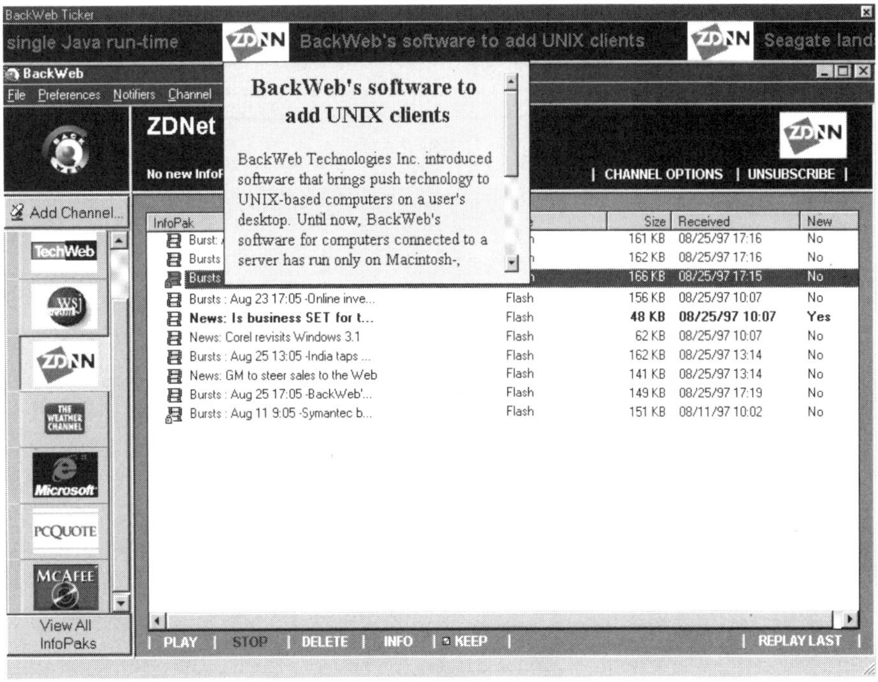

Figure 2-5
BackWeb 3.0 now includes a scrolling ticker. Just click on a headline, and the news summary immediately drops down.

Price: Client software is free; check Web site for latest price quotes on the BackWeb Server.

Hardware/Software Requirements for Client Software:

For Windows 95/NT 4.0 and Windows 3.1:

- 16 M RAM
- 4 M free hard disk space
- Netscape Navigator 2.0 or higher or Internet Explorer 2.0 or higher

For Macintosh:

- System 7.5 or higher
- 16 M RAM
- 3 M free hard disk space
- Netscape Navigator 2.0 or higher or Internet Explorer 2.0 or higher

Premium Channels:

CMP's TechWeb	Patricia Seybold Group
Commerce Net	PC Quote
House of Blues	the SoundBox
IBM	the *Wall Street Journal* Interactive Edition
Internet.com	Weather Channel
JAMtv	*Web Publisher* magazine
McAffee SecureCast	ZDNet
Modern Shopper	

Description: BackWeb is one of the most aggressive push companies to come out of Silicon Valley. Its flagship product is now in Version 3.0, and it is one of the most stable, efficient, and easy-to-use push applications on the market. Users can subscribe to dozens of possible channels, and channel contents are updated with BackWeb's incremental and very efficient Polite Agent update technology. Once downloaded, BackWeb updates can be displayed in a variety of formats:

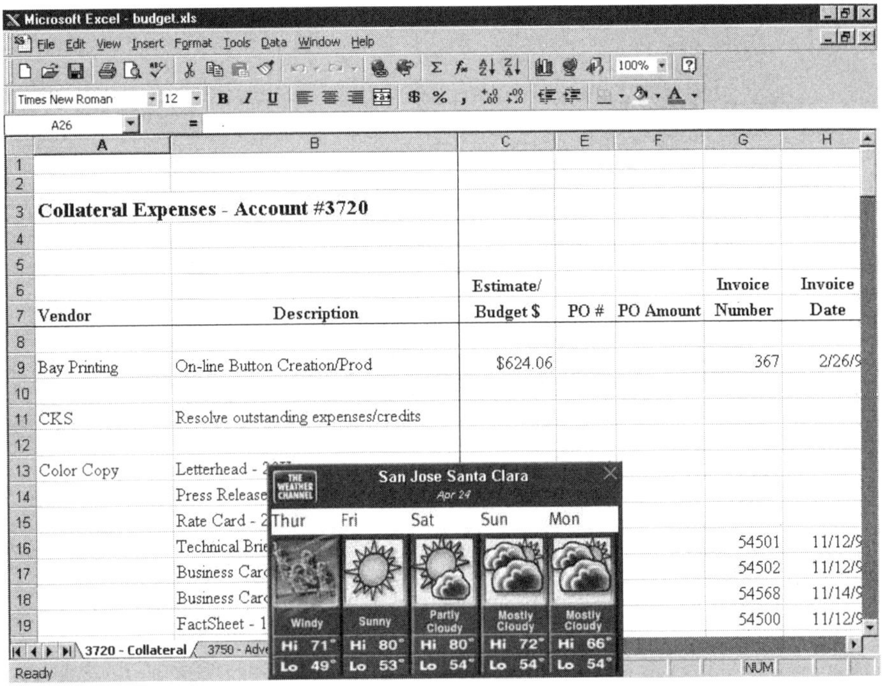

Figure 2-6 BackWeb Weather Flash. BackWeb distributes news updates and reports via InfoFlashes—small multimedia presentations that appear on the user's desktop.

BackWeb InfoFlashes: Small multimedia presentations that periodically pop up on the user's screen while working on other applications (see Figure 2-6). These flashes can include advanced animation presentations and audio clips, along with interactive buttons for obtaining more information.

Wallpapers and screen savers: You can subscribe to the Weather Channel, for example, and use a satellite image of current weather conditions as your default background image.

Ticker and onscreen announcer: BackWeb recently acquired Lanacom, a small push company that produces an onscreen scrolling ticker. The Lanacom Headliner is included in BackWeb 3.0 as an optional onscreen ticker. Click on a story in the ticker, and the article's summary immediately drops down.

To create new BackWeb channels, you need to purchase a separate BackWeb Server and a BackWeb Server console. New channels are created with a proprietary language called *BackWeb Authoring Language Interface* (BALI). The language includes its own BALI Editor and is used primarily for scripting multimedia presentations. BackWeb also includes a BackWeb Automation *software development kit* (SDK) for creating Web channels on-the-fly and for connecting automatically to legacy databases.

BackWeb also is designed to deliver software applications. This enables companies to automatically push software and software upgrades to employee computers. It also enables channel providers to push a large variety of content formats, including Java applications, Shockwave files, ActiveX controls, and native executables. Current software channels include Microsoft Internet Explorer 4.0 for automatic delivery of IE 4.0 upgrades; the McAffee channel for automatic delivery of its VirusScan software (see Figure 2-7); and Software InBox Direct for automatic delivery of freeware, shareware, and demonstration software.

A future version of BackWeb will be integrated tightly with Microsoft Internet Explorer 4.0 and the CDF.

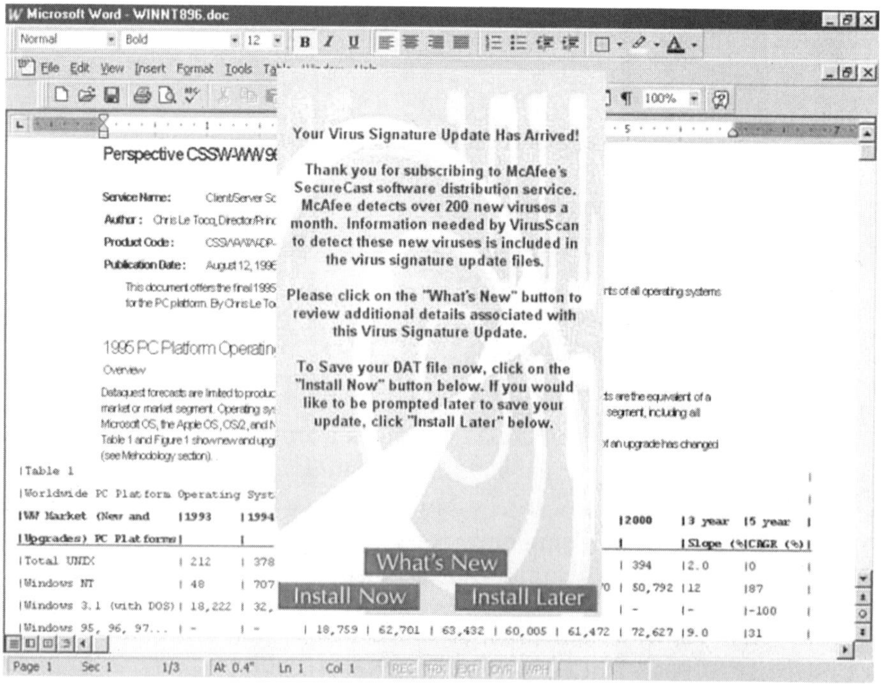

Figure 2-7
BackWeb enables content providers to push both content and software applications. McAffee, Inc. is one of the pioneers in distributing software upgrades for its antivirus software.

2.5 Diffusion IntraExpress

Diffusion, Inc.
321 Castro Street
Mountain View, CA 94041
(415) 237-8500
`http:\\www.diffusion.com`

Client Platforms: *See Description Below*

Server Platforms: The IntraExpress Server is available for Windows NT 3.51 and NT 4.0

Price: Call for latest price quotes.

Description: IntraExpress is tailored to meet the distribution needs of large corporations with mission-critical data. Unlike with most push products, IntraExpress users—including employees, clients, and customers—decide how they want to receive information updates. When the information is available, the IntraExpress Server follows the user preferences and uses any means to get the new information to the user: e-mail, fax, pager, network printers, Webcasting, or even the U.S. postal service. IntraExpress offers one of the most flexible distribution systems for delivering critical corporate information to the people who need it and offering it in a form of their choosing.

IntraExpress currently is partnering with a number of software companies—including Lotus Development Corporation to combine the functionality of Lotus Notes with IntraExpress; Tibco Inc. for the delivery of true IP multicast push; and BackWeb, Inc. for the delivery of Webcast channels.

2.6 Downtown

inCommon, Inc.
1875 South Grant Street, Suite 110
San Mateo, CA 94402
(415) 345-5432
`http://www.incommon.com`

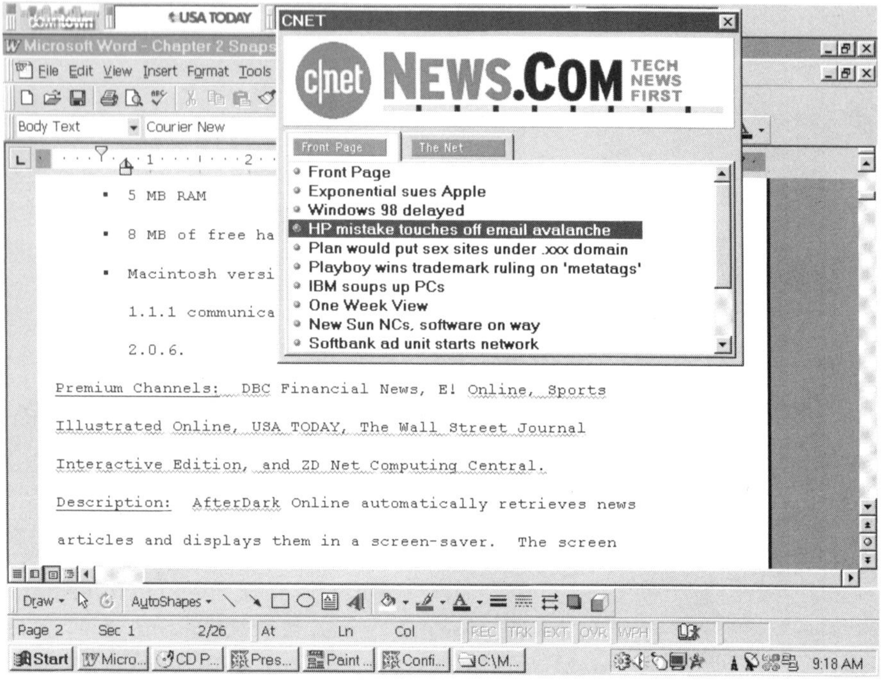

Figure 2-8 inCommon's push product Downtown.

Client Platforms: Windows 95, Windows NT 4.0, Windows 3.1 (forthcoming)

Current Release: Version 1.0

Price: Client software is free.

Hardware/Software Requirements:

- 16 M RAM
- 20 M free hard disk space
- Netscape Navigator 2.0 or higher, or Microsoft Internet Explorer 3.0 or higher

Premium Channels:

Astrology.net
Billboard Online
c|net news.com
CBS SportsLine
Los Angeles Times
Motley Fool
MovieLink
New York Times

Premium Channels:	
CMP TechWeb	*PC World* Online
Envirolink	*USA Today*
Excite	Yahoo!

Description: inCommon's Downtown push product automatically retrieves news articles and displays them in an onscreen ticker. New information and new articles are denoted with a green light. Click on the ticker, and you can view a full list of new articles. Click on an article, and Downtown launches your default Web browser and displays the already cached article. Downtown works online or offline.

Premiere channels are fully customizable. For the c|net news.com channel, you can select from seven news categories, for example. You also can customize the automatic update schedule (see Figure 2-9). And, in addition to premiere channels, you can direct Downtown to periodically monitor any Web site and push any changes to you.

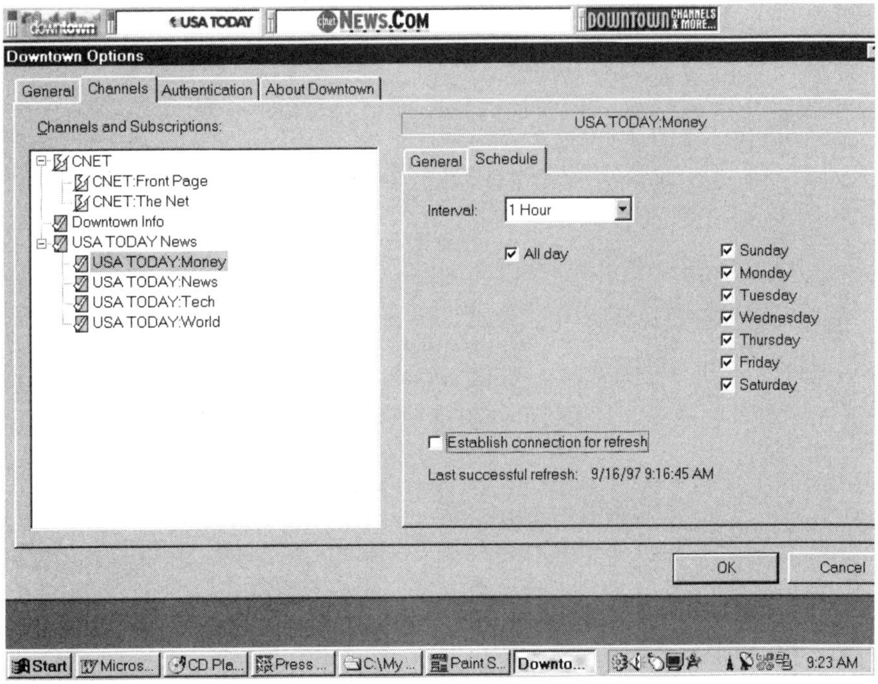

Figure 2-9 With Downtown, you can customize your channel contents and the update schedule.

2.7 Incisa

Wayfarer Communications, Inc.
2041 Landings Drive
Mountain View, CA 94043
(800) 300-8559
`http://www.wayfarer.com`

Current Release: Version 2.0
Client Platforms: Windows 95, Windows NT, Windows 3.1
Server Platform: Windows NT
Price: Pricing starts at $5000 for 100 seats, with discounts available for higher-volume purchases.
Premium Channels: *See Description*
Description: In contrast to most push products, Wayfarer's Incisa product focuses exclusively on the needs of corporate intranets. It therefore focuses on combining external news sources with internal news and legacy data, and it delivers information without advertisements.

The Incisa client application is a small desktop window that displays a rotating list of HeadLinks. *HeadLinks* are short headlines or summaries that are delivered as Macromedia Shockwave animations. Click on a HeadLink, and the full story appears on your default Web browser. The Incisa client maintains a persistent connection with the Incisa QuickServer, enabling the server to push new information as soon as it is available. This contrasts with the client-polling mechanism provided by most other push applications.

The Incisa Server includes a number of software components for gathering and filtering channel content. The NewsBridge enables companies to filter and search for business, industry, and competitor information. The DataBridge enables the automatic delivery of legacy data residing in corporate databases. The DataBridge, for example, can provide automatic updates on sales or inventory figures. The WebBridge monitors internal and external Web sites and automatically delivers updated content. And, the ReporterBridge enables you to publish news bulletins or create customized channels. This enables corporations to create multiple channels of information, such as channels devoted to sales, marketing, and human resources.

2.8 Intermind Communicator

Intermind Corporation
217 Pine Street
Seattle, WA 98101-1500
`http:\\www.intermind.com`

Client Platforms: Windows 95, Windows NT, Windows 3.1 (forthcoming: Macintosh and UNIX)

Current Release: Version 1.52

Price: Client application is free; to publish your channel, prices range from the most basic option ($195) to the most advanced customized option ($50,000).

Hardware/Software Requirements:

- Windows 32-bit support requires 16 M of RAM
- Windows 16-bit support requires 8 M of RAM

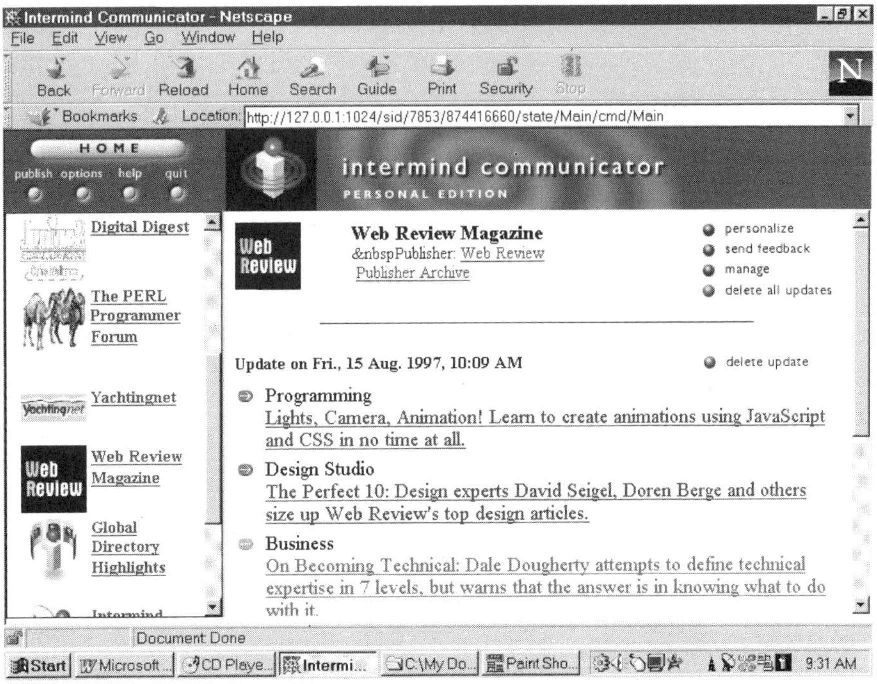

Figure 2-10 Intermind Communicator uses your default Web browser as its main interface.

- 6 M free disk space
- Netscape Navigator 2.0 or higher, or Microsoft Internet Explorer 3.0 or higher

Premium Channels:

Amnesty International	Macromedia
Computer World	Music Network USA
Edgar Online	PBS Online
Field & Stream	*The Sporting News*
Hot Wired	*Web Review*
Jupiter Communications	

Description: Intermind Communicator enables users to subscribe to more than 200 active channels. And, best of all, the entire Intermind interface is embedded directly inside your default Web browser (see Figures 2-10 and 2-11), and you have several configuration options that enable you to customize your display (see Figure 2-12). Just subscribe to a channel, and Intermind periodically checks the channel for new information. Users are notified of content updates with a small, nonintrusive dialog box or a color change in the Intermind taskbar icon (see Figure 2-13).

Intermind includes an easy-to-use publishing tool for creating your own channels. For intranet applications, Intermind also includes a dynamic publisher for pushing database content and complete support for Lotus Development Corporation's Domino.Broadcast.

2.9 Marimba Castanet

Marimba, Inc.
440 Clyde Avenue
Mountain View, CA 94043
(650) 930-5282
`http:\\www.marimba.com`

Client Platforms: Windows 95/NT, Macintosh, Solaris 2.X; the Castanet Tuner also is embedded inside Netscape's Netcaster, making it available to all 17 platforms supported by Netscape

Figure 2-11
The Intermind Channel Directory.

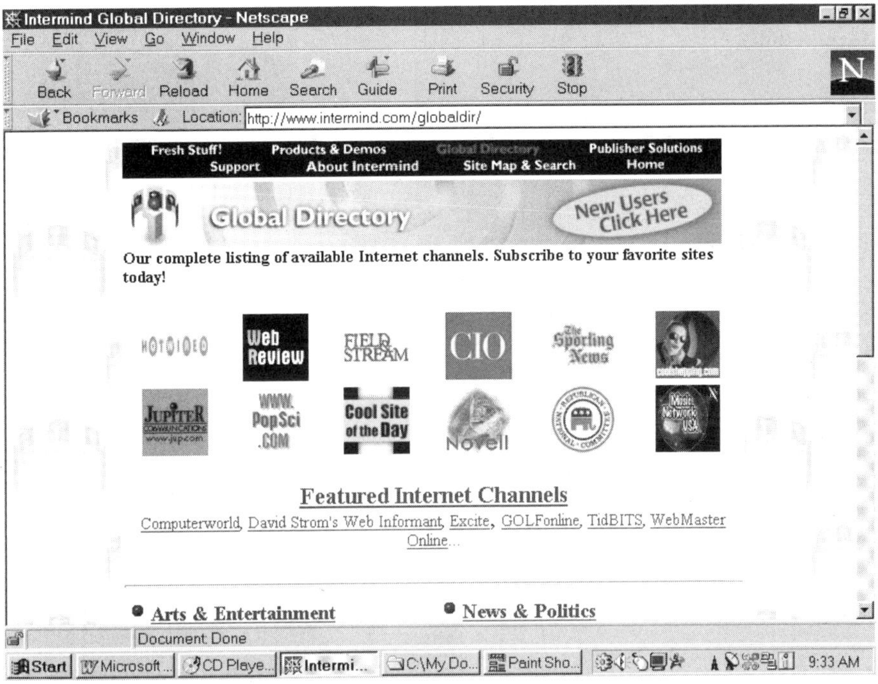

Figure 2-12
Intermind configuration options.

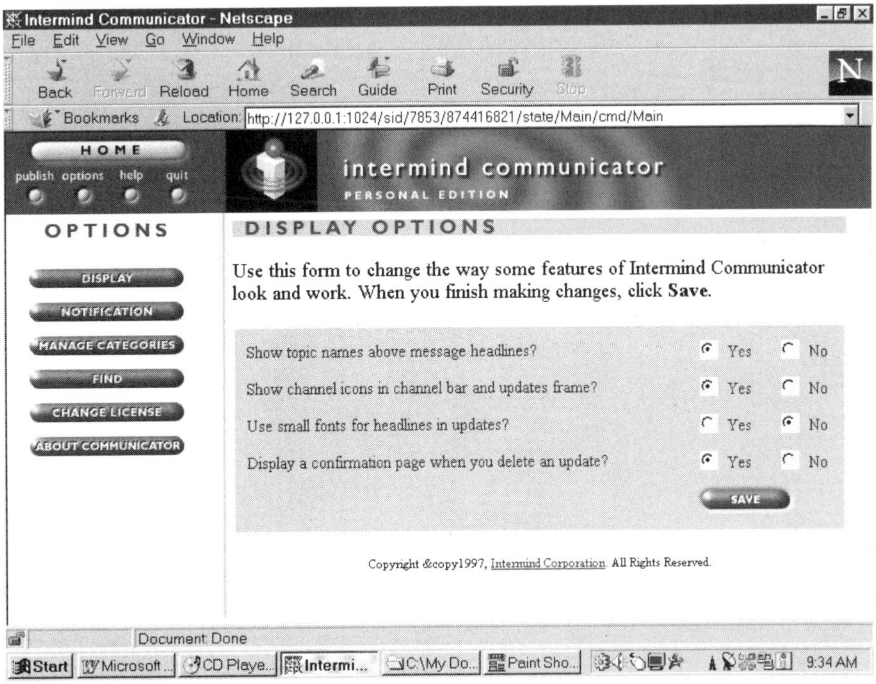

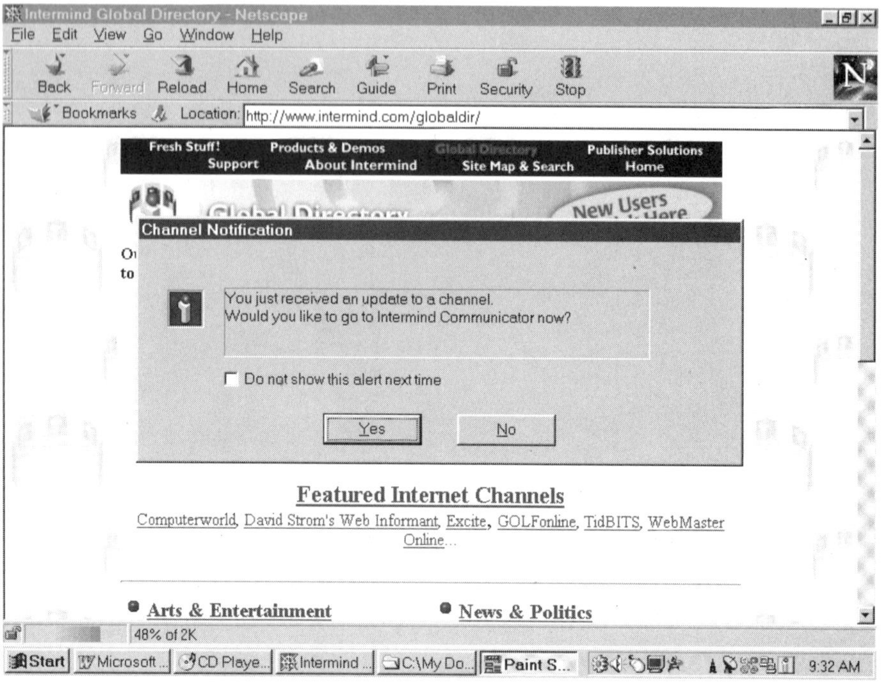

Figure 2-13 Users are notified of new channel updates via a dialog box or a change in color of the Intermind taskbar icon.

Server Platforms: Windows NT 4.0, Windows 95, Solaris 2.5 systems
Current Release: Version 1.1
Price: Castanet client Tuner software is free; Castanet Transmitters start at $995; check Web site for latest price quotes.
Client Tuner Software Requirements:

- 16 M RAM
- 10 M hard disk space

Premium Channels:

CBS SportsLine	Net-it Software
go2vision	Netmosphere Action Plan
HotWired talk.com	Pipe Live
MapQuest Interactive Atlas	Sesame Street
Mars Pathfinder WITS (Web Interface for Telescience)	Wall Street Web

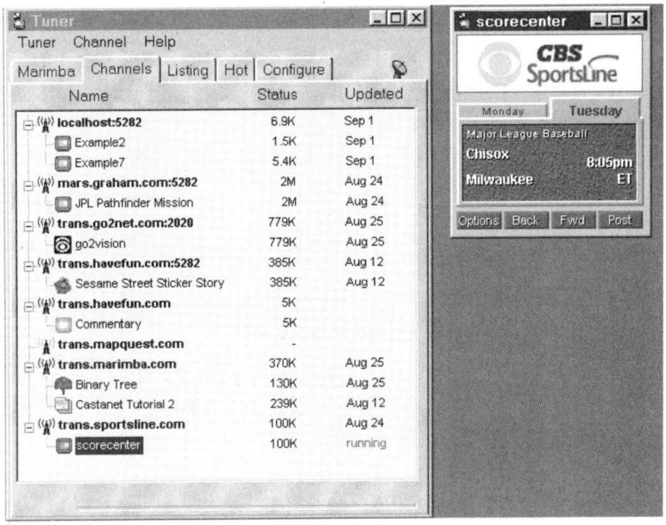

Figure 2-14 CBS SportsLine on Castanet. Castanet enables the distribution of both content and software applications.

Description: Castanet enables the delivery of both content and software applications, in the form of Java application channels (see Figure 2-14). This enables content providers to push full software applications and automatic software upgrades, along with changing news headlines or updated product information. At its core, the Castanet architecture is composed of two main software components: the Castanet Tuner, for receiving channel updates, and the Castanet Transmitter, a special server for broadcasting channel updates. The Castanet architecture includes a highly efficient differential update mechanism to cut down on network traffic between Tuners and Transmitters. The Castanet Tuner now is included in Netscape's Netcaster.

Castanet supports four basic types of channels:

HTML channels: Packaged HTML documents that are updated efficiently on a specified schedule.

Applet channels: Java applets that have been repackaged as channels. If you modify your applet code, the software update is pushed automatically to all your subscribers.

Presentation channels: Special channels created with Marimba's Bongo product. Bongo represents a Java-based GUI editor for easily creating presentations and user interfaces for Java application channels.

Application channels: Java channels that can automatically receive and display news updates, as well as automatically upgrade themselves when new software upgrades are available.

Castanet is geared primarily toward taking Java to the next level, enabling the wide distribution of Java application channels across the Internet and intranets. It therefore includes a host of software products to ensure widespread scalability, including a specialized Castanet Repeater, for managing push traffic across the Internet, and the Castanet Proxy Server, for managing push traffic through the corporate firewall.

Marimba recently released its Castanet UpdateNow software for the automatic deployment and installation of non-Java and Java applications, including those compiled in C, C++, and Visual Basic.

A full overview of Castanet is included in Part V, "Marimba Castanet Channels."

2.10 Microsoft Internet Explorer 4.0 Active Channels

Microsoft Corporation
`http:\\www.microsoft.com\ie`

Client Platforms: Windows 95/NT, Windows 3.1, Macintosh

Server Platforms: Active Channels can be broadcast from any standard Web HTTP Server

Current Release: Internet Explorer 4.0

Price: Client software is free.

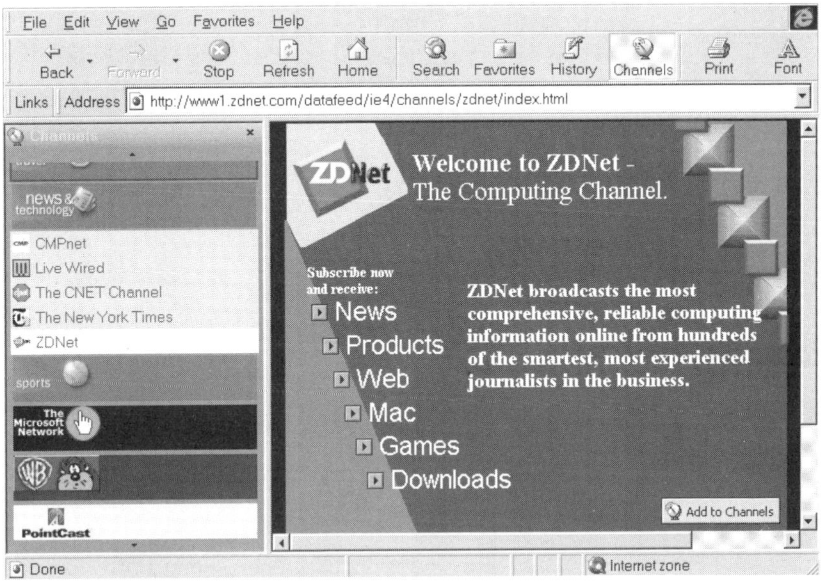

Figure 2-15 Internet Explorer 4.0's ZDNet channel.

Premium Channels:

CMPNet	MSNBC
CNET	*National Geographic*
Disney	*New York Times*
ESPN SportsZone	Warner Bros.
Hollywood Online	ZDNet
Live Wired	

Description: Microsoft has integrated its own push technology application into Internet Explorer 4.0. You can use Active Channels to subscribe to dozens of premium channels or to turn any regular Web site into a Web channel. At specified intervals, IE 4.0 checks the user's subscribed channels and downloads new content to the user's local hard drive. The Active Channel interface is built directly into the IE 4.0 interface and is integrated tightly with the IE 4.0 favorites menu. Even Microsoft's premium Channel Guide is built right into the browser.

After channel content is downloaded, subscribers can view it offline in a variety of formats: within Internet Explorer, within active desktop components (small Web pages that act as background applications), or within Internet Explorer's new HTML screen saver.

Active Channels is based on Microsoft's new proposed CDF, which is straightforward to learn and enables developers to quickly create their own channels. Channels then can be served from any standard HTTP Server. And, because you view Active Channels within Internet Explorer, Active Channels can include dynamic HTML, JavaScript, Java, and ActiveX components.

A full overview of Active Channels is included in Part III, "Microsoft Internet Explorer 4.0."

2.11 Netscape Netcaster

Netscape Communications Corporation
501 E. Middlefield Road
Mountain View, CA 94043

(415) 937-2555
product and sales information, corporate customers (7 a.m. to 5 p.m. PST)
(415) 937-3777
product and sales information, individual consumers (7 a.m. to 5 p.m. PST)
`http:\\home.netscape.com`

Client Platforms: Windows 95/NT, Windows 3.1, Macintosh, various flavors of UNIX; 17 platforms total

Server Platforms: Netcaster channels can be broadcast from any standard Web HTTP Server

Current Release: Version 1.0; included in Netscape Communicator 4.02 or later or the standalone Netscape Navigator 4.02 or later

Price: Netscape Communicator currently retails for $59.

Premium Channels:	
ABC News	HomeArts Network
CBS SportsLine	InfoSeek Industry Watch
CNET Channel	Red Herring Direct
CNNfn (see Figure 2-16)	Travelocity
Disney	*TV Guide* Online
Fast Company	ZDNet
Gartner Group Advisor	

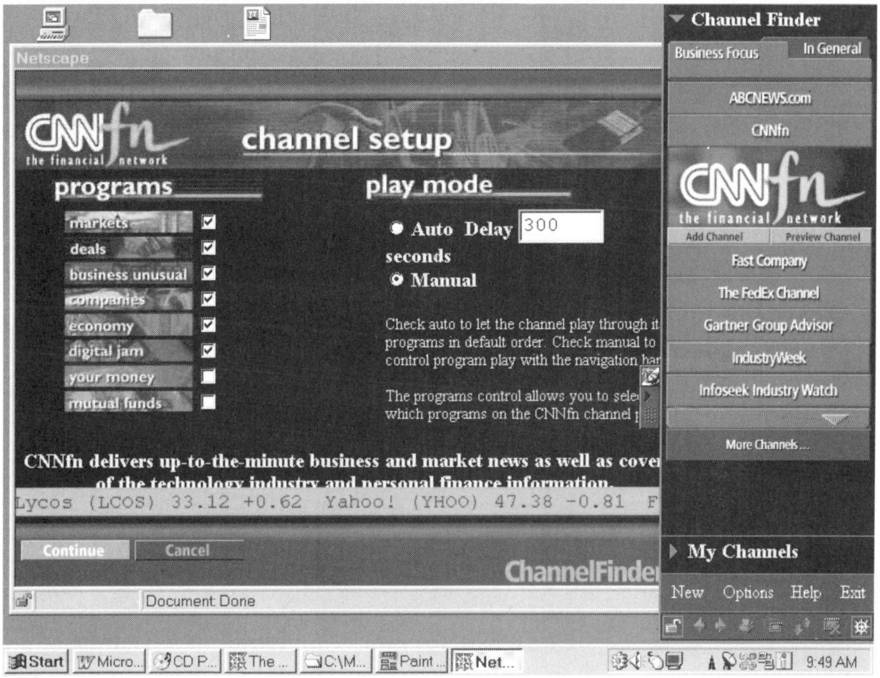

Figure 2-16
Netscape Netcaster's CNNfn channel.

Description: Netscape Netcaster comes as an integrated component of Netscape Communicator 4.0 and the standalone Netscape Navigator 4.0. With Netcaster, users can choose to subscribe to any of the dozens of channels provided by Netscape's built-in Channel Finder Guide. Users also can choose to subscribe to any regular Web site and to have Web site updates periodically pushed to them.

After the user subscribes to a channel, Netcaster periodically checks the Web site or channel and automatically downloads the updated contents to the user's local hard drive. This enables users to browse Web sites while not connected to the Internet. And, because you view Netcaster channels within Netscape Navigator, Netcaster channels can include dynamic HTML, JavaScript, Java, and other embedded objects, such as *Virtual Reality Modeling Language* (VRML) and *Portable Data Format* (PDF).

Netcaster currently does not support CDF. Instead, Netcaster channels are built entirely in HTML, JavaScript, and Java. And, it is relatively easy to convert an existing Web site into a Web channel with a few dozen lines of JavaScript code. No special server software is required.

Netcaster also includes a built-in copy of the Castanet Tuner. This enables Netcaster users to subscribe to Java application channels created with the Castanet architecture and enables the automatic installation and upgrading of both software and content.

A full overview of Netcaster is included in Part II, "Netscape Netcaster."

2.12 PointCast

PointCast, Inc.
501 Macara Avenue
Sunnyvale, CA 94086
(408) 990-7000
`http://www.pointcast.com`

Client Platforms: Windows 95/NT, Windows 3.1, Macintosh

Server Platforms: PointCast Connections works off any standard Web HTTP Server

Current Release: Version 2.0

Price: Client software is free.

Hardware/Software Requirements:

- 8 M RAM
- 10 M free disk space

Premium Channels:	
Boston Globe	Pathfinder
Chicago Tribune	*Seattle Times*
CMP TechWeb	*Star Tribune*
CNN	*Wall Street Journal*
Los Angeles Times	*WIRED News*
Miami Herald	ZDNet
New York Times	

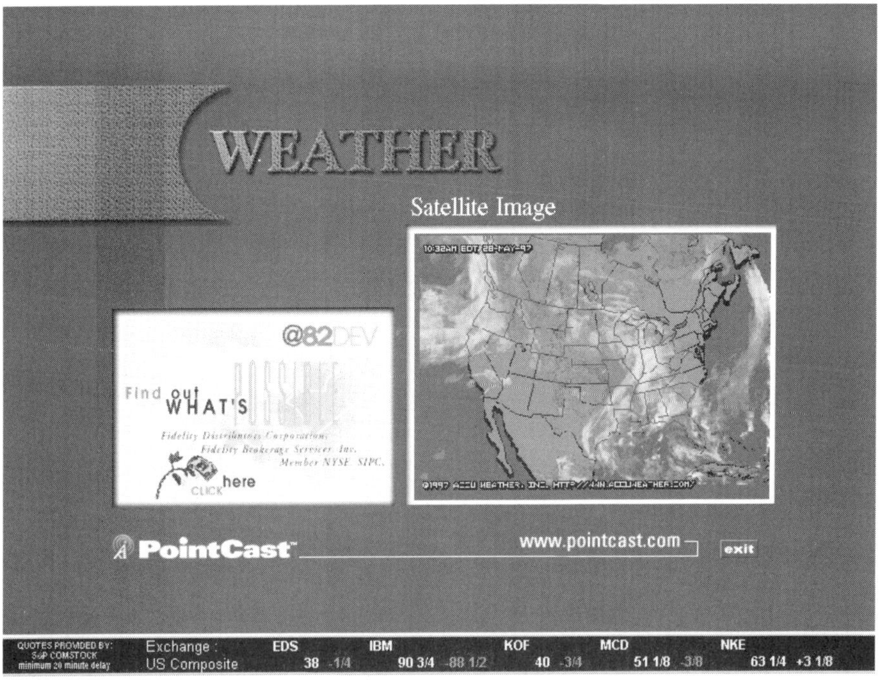

Figure 2-17 PointCast weather update.

Description: PointCast has been delivering push content longer than any other company. Its flagship product pioneered the entire field of push technology. Users simply subscribe to any of PointCast's multiple premium channels and automatically receive news updates on a specified schedule. News headlines and articles are displayed in the PointCast Channel Viewer (see Figure 2-18), the SmartScreen screen saver (see Figure 2-19), and the new scrolling ticker. Each channel is completely customizable so that you receive only the news that interests you the most.

Since its first product, PointCast has expanded its range of services considerably. The PointCast network now includes several versions, including the PointCast Business Network, the PointCast College Network, and the PointCast Government Insider Edition.

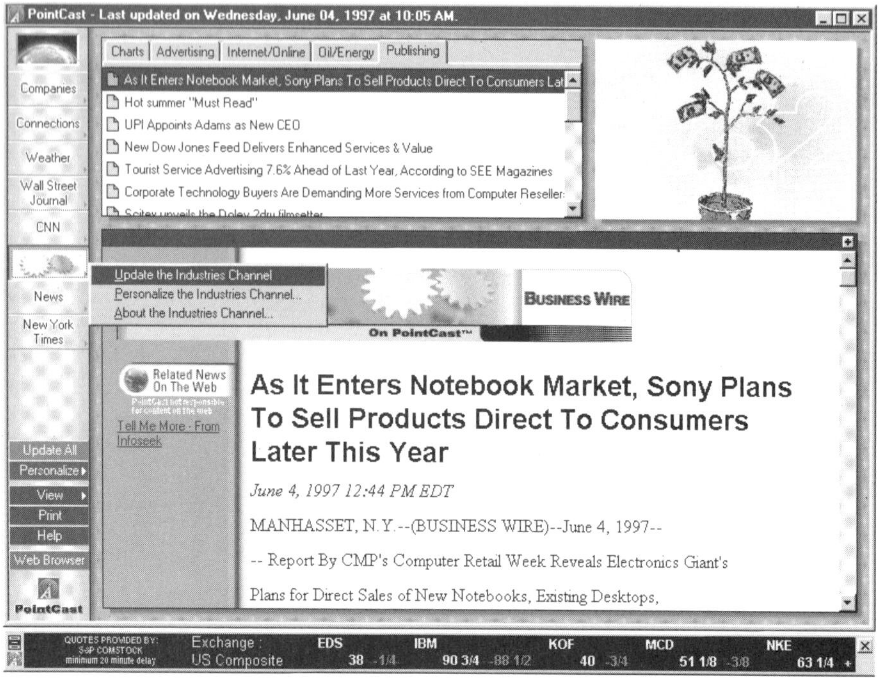

Figure 2-18
PointCast Channel Viewer.

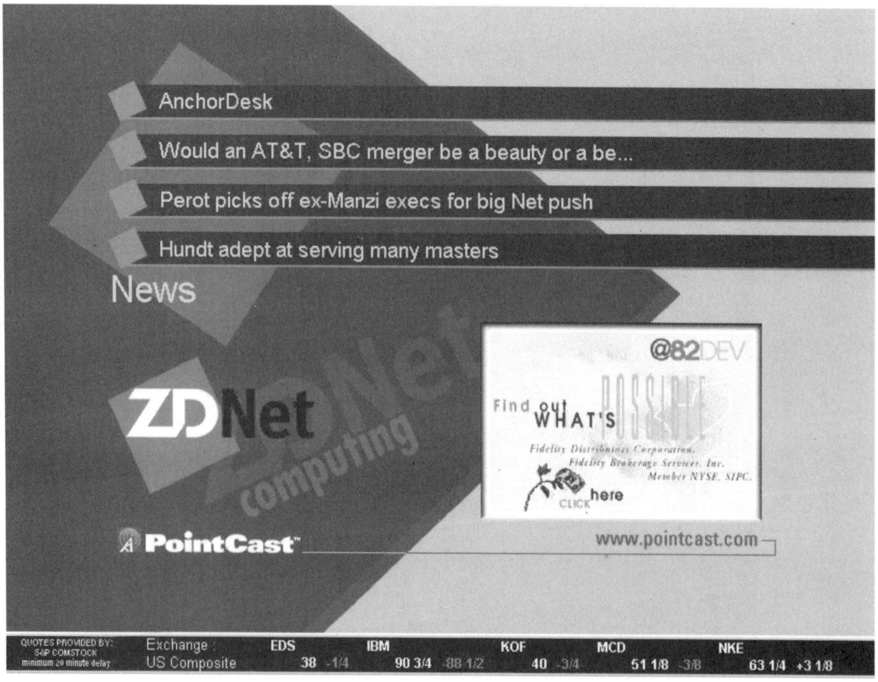

Figure 2-19
PointCast SmartScreen.

In the summer of 1997, PointCast decided to create the PointCast Connections Network, enabling PointCast users to subscribe to hundreds of possible new channels. With the PointCast Connections Network, any Web publisher can publish to the PointCast Network and automatically push news articles and customized animations.

To support the creation of new PointCast Connections channels, PointCast now includes the PointCast Connections Builder, an easy-to-use software application for creating new PointCast CDF channels, and the PointCast Studio, for creating custom animations and advertisements.

PointCast is hoping to capture more of the corporate intranet market by offering a number of corporate tools for managing internal push traffic. The PointCast I-Server and a new host of intranet administrative tools enable corporations to minimize push traffic through the corporate firewall and enable the creation of custom corporate channels.

A full overview of PointCast is included in Part IV, "PointCast 2.0 Connections Network."

CHAPTER 3

A Technical Primer on Push

Push just might qualify as one of the greatest misnomers in Internet terminology. The word *push* conjures up a specific image of one person or agent actively sending or manipulating a second, more passive agent. Most people who are introduced to push technology therefore have a very specific image of how push works. A client application sits passively on the user's desktop computer. When new information is available, the server application contacts all the clients and pushes the new data across the network. In fact, this is rarely how push works.

3.1 Good Old-Fashioned Pull

To understand how push really works, you must start with a solid understanding of how pull works. In the context of push, *pull* refers to any *manual* method of retrieving documents from the Web. Users simply point-and-click on a link, and the Web browser pulls the requested document from the specified server.

To communicate effectively, Web clients and servers agree to always follow the *Hypertext Transfer Protocol* (HTTP). HTTP is considered a *stateless* protocol, which means that the Web server does not need to store any information regarding the client requests. In comparison to most Internet protocols, HTTP is considered one of the easiest to implement.

Each time a user clicks on a link, the Web browser sends an HTTP request header. The request header consists of a specific HTTP command, a document address, and the HTTP version number. Consider this command, for example:

```
GET /index.htm HTTP/1.0
```

This command sends the HTTP command `GET`, requesting the transfer of the root `index.htm` file via HTTP, Version 1.0. Following the request header, the Web client may include additional information. It might identify the Web browser software, for example, or provide a list of document types (GIF, JPEG, and so on) the browser can process.

The server receives the client request, locates the specified file, and sends the file back to the client. The server response first includes a status line, consisting of the HTTP version number, a status code number, and a description of the status code. The following is a typical response header:

```
HTTP/1.0 200 OK
```

The `200` status code indicates that everything went OK—the requested file was located.

Immediately following the status line, the server sends a reply header with information about itself and about the requested document. For example, here is a complete server response:

```
HTTP/1.0 200 OK
Date: Sun, 21 Sep 1997 12:15:00 GMT
Server: NCSA/1.5.2
Last-modified: Sun, 21 Sep 1997 8:00:00 GMT
```

```
Content-type: text/html
Content-length: 3012
. . . document content follows
```

This tells you the date and time of the response, the server software, the document type (in this case, text/html), the size of the document (in this case, 3012 bytes), and the date the document was modified last.

In addition to the **GET** command, client applications may issue the **HEAD** command. A **HEAD** command returns the same document information as the **GET** command, but it does not return the actual file.

The **HEAD** command is particularly useful for monitoring and using cached documents. An HTML page may contain a large GIF image, for example. The first time the user visits the page, the browser stores a copy of the image in the user's cache. The next time the user returns, the browser first issues a **HEAD** command for the specified image. If the image has been modified since the last visit, the browser follows up with a **GET** command. Otherwise, the browser uses the cached image and immediately displays it to the user.

In "pulling" a single Web document, the Web browser first requests the actual HTML page (for example, **index.htm**). It then parses the entire page and extracts the URLs for all embedded images and objects. For each image or embedded object, the client makes a new HTTP request.

In HTTP 1.0, it is necessary to create separate HTTP requests for each HTML page, each image, and each embedded object. However, in Version 1.1, the client and server can maintain a single open connection and transfer multiple files at once. This cuts down on the overhead of multiple connections and can result in faster, more efficient network transactions.

3.2 Client Polling

So why delve into the specifics of HTTP and pull? Most push applications, in fact, are built entirely on HTTP. And, most push operations, in fact, are just automated pull.

Netcaster, Internet Explorer 4.0, Marimba, BackWeb, and PointCast all follow a model known as *request/reply* or *client polling*. Each time you subscribe to a new channel, the channel includes a recommended update schedule. You might subscribe to a stock ticker that is set to update every 30 minutes, for example.

At the specified update interval, your client application contacts the server and checks for updates. If new information is available, the channel update is sent, usually via HTTP. If no new information is available, the client application simply goes back to sleep and waits for the next update interval.

So push is nothing more than automated pull. But each push application has its own strategy for optimizing and downloading channel updates. Currently, three broad strategies are in practice: The Web-crawl approach, the CDF approach, and the proprietary-server approach.

3.2.1 The Web Crawl Approach

Netscape Netcaster and parts of Internet Explorer 4.0 follow an automated Web-crawl strategy. At the specified update interval, the client application requests the top-level Web page (usually, **`index.htm`**) in the Web channel. The client then parses this page and follows all the embedded links. It then continues to burrow deeper into the Web hierarchy until it reaches a specified depth (see Figure 3-1).

Most of the time, the Web-crawl approach consists of a series of HTTP **`HEAD`** commands. This enables the client application to identify the date the file was last modified without actually downloading it. If the file has not been modified since the last update, the client uses the already cached file. Otherwise, the client follows up with an HTTP **`GET`** command and downloads the new content to the user's hard drive.

The Web-crawl approach has the unique advantage of being built entirely on HTTP, and Web channels really are nothing more than regular Web pages. You therefore can easily convert any Web site into a Web channel, and you can use your existing HTTP Web server.

3.2.2 The *Channel Definition Format* (CDF) Approach

The second major approach to client polling is the CDF approach. The CDF approach currently is implemented by Internet Explorer 4.0 and the PointCast Connections Network.

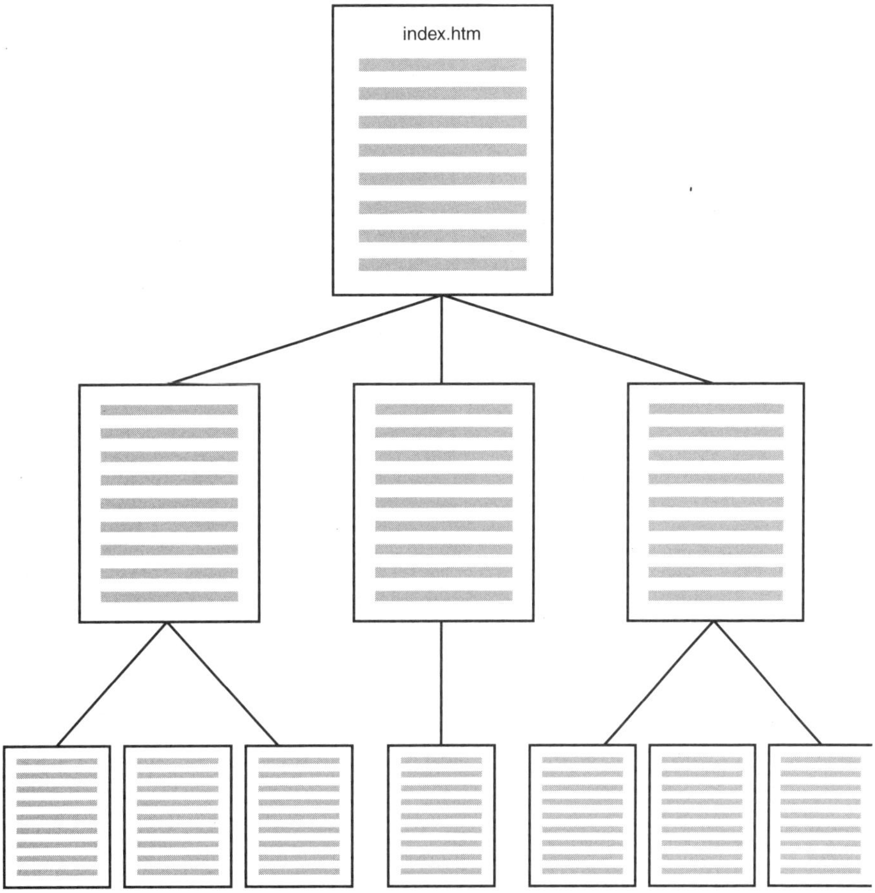

Figure 3-1
The Web-crawl approach. The client application burrows into the Web site until it reaches a specified depth.

The specifics of CDF are explored fully in Chapter 10, "Creating Active Channels," but here in a nutshell is how CDF works.

Instead of Web crawling an entire Web site, the client application first downloads a CDF file. Each CDF file provides a table of contents for an entire channel (see Figure 3-2). The file might indicate that the channel consists of six articles, for example. Each article is described in the CDF format (which is quite similar in syntax to HTML) and includes a name, short summary, and URL.

The client application parses the CDF file and then downloads each of the specified articles. Again, file transfers are done via HTTP, and the client application usually issues a **HEAD** command first so that it can take advantage of precached documents.

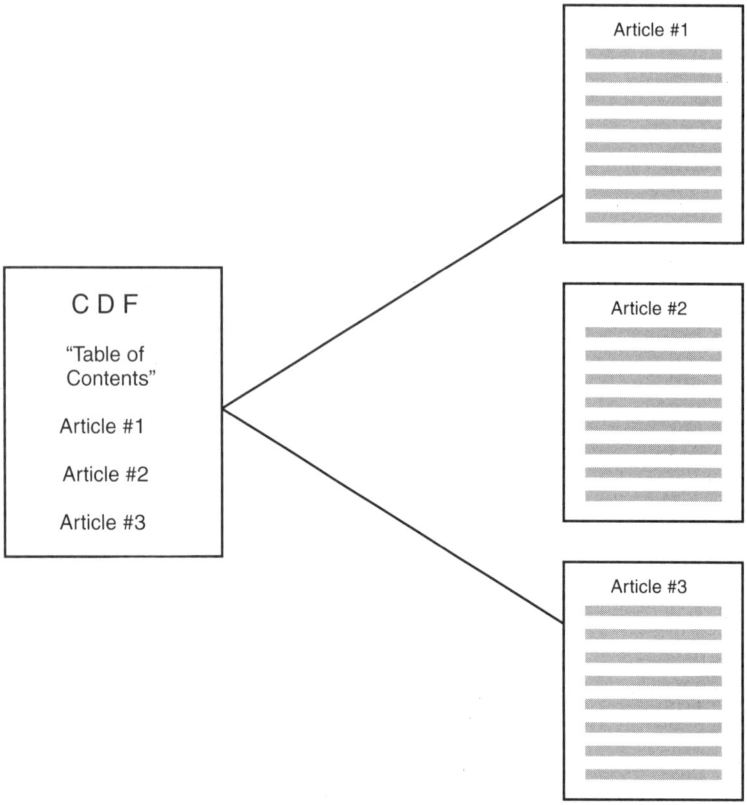

Figure 3-2
The CDF approach. CDF provides a table of contents for each channel. The client first parses the CDF file and proceeds to download all the indicated articles.

3.2.3 The Proprietary-Server Approach

The Web-crawl and CDF approaches are built entirely on HTTP and will work with any standard HTTP Web server. In contrast, the third approach to client polling requires the use of proprietary servers. This is the approach currently pursued by Marimba and BackWeb.

In the proprietary-server approach, the client application periodically checks back with a specialized server. In the case of Marimba's Castanet, the client Tuner application checks in with the specialized Castanet Transmitter application. The Tuner and Transmitter negotiate with one another, and the Transmitter sends a single differential update. Therefore, each Tuner receives only the files that have been updated since the last update, and the update occurs within a single network connection. This is similar to the Polite Agent technology provided by BackWeb.

The proprietary-server approach has the advantage of providing frequent and very efficient channel updates.

3.3 True Push

Currently, only two products on the market can qualify as true push. The first is the Incisa product from Wayfarer Communications, Inc. (see Chapter 2, Section 2.7). The Incisa QuickServer actually maintains connections with every single client application. When new data is available, it automatically pushes the data to the active clients. This is certainly a viable option for intranets, but the scalability immediately breaks down when you want to deliver to thousands of subscribers spread out across the Internet.

The second true push application is provided by AirMedia, Inc. (see Chapter 2, Section 2.2). In this approach, AirMedia literally broadcasts new information via radio waves, circumventing the Internet entirely.

As push matures, we are likely to see more applications that do implement true push. In particular, we are likely to see a number of applications that take advantage of IP multicast.

Today's *Internet Protocol* (IP) is essentially a unicast medium: Each packet of data has a single sender and a single recipient. With IP multicast, however, each single packet can be delivered to multiple addresses or groups of addresses. In the future, this is likely to be the most efficient method of delivering channel updates. And, it is likely to be a viable option for delivering multimedia applications, such as video conferencing.

As it is, however, IP multicast requires the installation of a new generation of Web routers and router software. This is certainly an option for local area networks and intranets. In fact, a number of companies, including Tibco, Inc., are hoping to capitalize on the corporate IP multicast market. But, it may take several years for wide scale deployment on the Internet. And, until that time, we are very likely to see more client-polling applications in all their various flavors.

SUMMARY

Push is primarily a marketing term meant to imply the automatic delivery of new information. From a technical perspective, however, push is really nothing more than automated pull. Each channel has its own update schedule, and at the specified update interval, the client application polls the server for new information. If new information is available, the client downloads the channel updates to the user's hard drive. Otherwise, it just goes back to sleep and waits for the next update interval.

Currently, three broad approaches exist to client polling: the Web-crawl approach, the Channel Definition Format approach, and the proprietary-server approach.

If you really want true push, try AirMedia's latest product. Or, stick around until IP multicast is implemented on a wide scale.

Online Resource

- IP Multicast Initiative `http://www.ipmulticast.com`. The source for information on IP multicast.

CHAPTER 4

Top 10 Tips for Creating Push Content

Creating your own push channels can be a large undertaking and a serious challenge. If you have experience creating Web sites, you can apply most of your knowledge to the creation of Web channels. HTML is still a standard. Java and JavaScript still are critical. Easy navigation and good Web design are paramount. And good, well-written content is still key. Your Web experience to date therefore is critical, and the more you know about Web site design, the more easily you can transition to push channels. The more successful your Web site, the better your odds at attracting new subscribers to your new channel.

Some specific challenges are unique to push, however. There are new technologies to learn. New Web standards to implement. New products to evaluate. New expectations concerning content. New expectations concerning the frequency of channel updates. New expectations concerning multimedia presentation and design.

The push medium is completely new. And, because this is an industry in its infancy, most content providers are slowly feeling their way through constant improvisation and improvement. Many of the major content providers now are in experimentation mode. CMP's TechWeb, HotWired, and ZDNet are perhaps three of the most ambitious channel providers in this new medium. And, each is now in the process of trying out new channel formats and presentations, as well as new channel content. Each one is hedging its bets on which push platform is likely to succeed. Tune into PointCast, Netcaster, or Microsoft's Active Channels, and you will see many of the same channels and the same channel providers.

As the push medium evolves, organizations are likely to develop new strategies concerning push content. But, after evaluating more than 12 push platforms over the past six months, I do believe there are a few kernels of truth to keep in mind. Some channels work, and others fail miserably. Regardless of the final push platform or push strategy you finally choose, keep these 10 important tips in mind.

4.1 Tip 1: Define Your Audience

The first step in creating a successful Web channel is to successfully define your audience. Who is likely to subscribe to your channels? Who are you hoping to attract? Are they corporate users with direct Internet connections? Home users with modem connections? What kind of information does this audience deem critical? The better you define your audience, the better you can attract and retain new subscribers. Try to focus your audience, and don't try to be all things to all audiences.

PointCast is a case in point in successfully defining a focused audience. PointCast specifically targets corporate professionals within mid-size to large companies. These users have direct Internet connections and specific information needs. PointCast therefore focuses on delivering business-critical information in a timely and accurate fashion. PointCast also focuses on creating a whole suite of corporate intranet tools for managing push traffic within corporations and creating corporate channels. Capitalizing on this market, PointCast now is expanding to target more specific niche markets with a new slate of products: the PointCast College Network, the PointCast Government Insider Edition, and its soon-to-be-released PointCast Network for Healthcare Professionals. PointCast knows its audience well, and its core strategy is translating into handsome profits.

4.2 Tip 2: Find Your Selling Point

What does your channel provide that no other channel provides? More important, what will your channel provide that your current Web site does not? What added value will users get by subscribing to your channel?

As you progress through each of the development chapters in this book, you quickly will realize that creating channels is not rocket science. You easily can convert your existing Web site into a Netcaster channel with a dozen lines of JavaScript code, for example. You easily can create a Microsoft Active Channel with a single CDF file. And, CDF is not much more complicated than HTML. But have you really created a Web channel? Technically, yes. Repackaging your existing Web site as a channel is a poor use of the medium, though. Most users are not likely to subscribe or maintain subscriptions to these repackaged or prepackaged Web sites.

To build a successful Web channel, you need to build it from the ground up. Focus on your unique selling point, and make sure that you consistently deliver it.

4.3 Tip 3: Pick One Push Platform and Then Hedge Your Bets

Everyone wants to know who is going to win the push war. Will the 800-pound gorilla, otherwise known as Microsoft, prevail? Will Netscape use its still considerable lead in the Web-browser market to dominate the push market? Or will both of these rivals be outwitted and outpaced by smaller competitors, such as BackWeb, Marimba, or PointCast? Which of these companies should we bet on, and for which platform should we choose to develop?

If you check any of the latest technology news Web sites, you will notice that most of the media tends to portray the push war as a zero-sum game: One company will emerge victorious, and the others will lose. But, in picking your push platform, there are in fact only two things that you can really count on. First, *no one really knows* who will win this competition. Second, this is not a zero-sum game. We are likely to see several push winners and several push losers. The success of Microsoft Active Channels does not, in fact, spell disaster for Netcaster.

My recommendation for picking a push platform is based on moderate risk taking. Select one major platform that you think best meets the needs of both your audience and your content. Develop this channel as your model channel, and take advantage of all the extra functionality and amenities offered by the platform you have chosen. But, after you have your channel up and running, start hedging your bets, and start developing for multiple platforms. Unfortunately, Web channels are not yet standardized, and writing for multiple push platforms requires extra work. However, this is currently the only option for reaching the broadest possible audience and hedging your bets against an uncertain future.

4.4 Tip 4: Focus on Content, Not Technology

Content is still king. More than any other factor, people will continue to subscribe to your channel because they find your content compelling, entertaining, or even vital to their jobs. Make this your *highest* priority.

When people ask me which push product I like the most, I usually joke that it's home delivery of the *New York Times*. It has the content I want, and it comes in a convenient, highly portable package. But the important point is that it has the *content* I want. And I consider its content timely, accurate, and well-written. The *New York Times*, in fact, has transitioned successfully to Web sites and Web channels specifically because it has chosen to focus on content rather than technology.

4.5 Tip 5: Develop a Realistic Update Schedule and Stick to It

How often do you plan on updating your channel? Every hour? Once a week? Once a month? Do you have the staff and resources to update your channel that frequently?

No matter what, pick a realistic update schedule and make it clear to subscribers. Users expect you to follow through on your commitment and quickly will unsubscribe if they find your information getting stale.

This is perhaps the most difficult transition from Web sites to Web channels. Most Web site designers are used to updating sites erratically —perhaps once a week or every six months. And, most Web site design shops simply are not ready to update channels more frequently. Like it or not, this usually requires additional staffers, writers, and programmers.

4.6 Tip 6: Create a Clean, Simple, and Elegant Design

Graphic design and clear navigation are critical for the success of your channel. So pick a simple design and make it consistent throughout. Do not require new skills of your users, and present a user interface that is both familiar and easy to use. Too many new channels have bizarre new scrollbars and nonintuitive interfaces that leave many new subscribers exasperated.

4.7 Tip 7: Don't Get Too Flashy

With all the new technology around, you probably want to include the flashiest graphics and coolest animations. Dynamic HTML is particularly in vogue these days. But don't go overboard. Don't let the flash overwhelm the content. Too many channels fall victim to glitz. Learn from their mistakes first.

4.8 Tip 8: Keep Track of Memory and Bandwidth

How long does it take your average user to update your channel? How much memory does your channel take up on the user's hard drive? Try as much as possible to keep channel updates both fast and small. Even if this is push, most users do not want to wait long for channel updates, and most users want to save room on their hard drives for other applications!

PointCast has a very specific limit that stipulates that Connections channel updates cannot occupy more than 150 kilobytes. Channel updates therefore are very frequent and very fast. But IE 4.0, Netcaster, and Castanet do not have any such built-in limits; you will need to keep track of them yourself.

4.9 Tip 9: Test, Test, Test

Testing makes perfect. Make sure that your channel downloads thoroughly before deploying. Make sure that it works online and offline. Test your channel on different operating systems. Test it with different system configurations. Test it with different Web browsers.

Push is still in its infancy, and unanticipated bugs arise quite frequently.

4.10 Tip 10: Monitor Your Progress

If you build it, they will come. But how do you know whether they actually came? Monitor your progress with some kind of logging mechanism. PointCast has free usage reports. Castanet has built-in logging support. And Active Channels and Netcaster channels can be monitored with regular HTTP Web server logging reports.

Watch your progress, and find out what users like and don't like. This is a flexible medium that might take several trial runs before you hit it right.

PART II

Netcaster

CHAPTER 5

Introduction to Netscape Netcaster

Amid much fanfare, Netscape introduced its eagerly awaited Netcaster product during the summer of 1997. Formerly code-named Constellation, Netcaster is a full-featured and easy-to-use push product that provides four main features:

- Channel subscriptions
- Automatic downloading of channel contents
- Offline browsing
- Support for advanced application channels using Marimba's Castanet technology

Netcaster marks Netscape's first foray into push technology. Given its huge installed base in the browser market, though, Netscape is likely to be a major player in the push market. According to the most recent surveys, Netscape still retains 60–70 percent of the browser market. And, according to Netscape, it has distributed more than 55 million copies of Navigator and currently supports more than 17 different operating systems. These facts alone make Netscape a major push player.

Netscape originally was caught off guard by push technology and some of its smaller Silicon Valley competitors. It was particularly caught off guard by the success of PointCast. But Netscape now clearly recognizes the importance of push and is trying desperately to leapfrog ahead of the competition. In particular, it is investing heavily in new technology and forming strategic partnerships with existing push companies, including Marimba, Inc. Netscape also is busy garnering strategic partnerships with large media companies, including Time Warner, ABC News, c|net, and CNNfn.

In its ongoing competition with Microsoft, Netscape is banking on Netcaster to give it an edge over Internet Explorer 4.0. Gone are the days when browsers merely enabled users to surf the Web. Today's fourth-generation browsers now include an entire suite of programs for communicating and collaborating over the Internet. Communicator 4.0 and Internet Explorer 4.0 now include programs for e-mail, newsgroups, conferencing, and calendaring—and now, Netscape and Microsoft are including competing push products.

Netcaster does not support the *Channel Definition Format* (CDF) originally proposed by Microsoft and supported by PointCast, however. Instead, Netcaster is based entirely on the existing standards of HTML, JavaScript, and Java. And, according to Netscape, CDF is unnecessary, untested, and fundamentally flawed. Regardless of the exact rationale for Netscape's decision, it leaves Web developers with a fundamental problem. When creating Web channels, should you support CDF, should you support Netscape's standard, or should you support both? The browser war clearly has expanded to include a push war, and we are likely to see a great deal of hype from both companies concerning which implementation is better.

This chapter and the two that follow introduce Netcaster both from a user's perspective and from a developer's perspective:

- This chapter provides an overview of Netcaster and the Netcaster architecture. Specifically, you will look at the main features of Netcaster and contrast those with other push products. You also will take a behind-the-scenes look at how Netcaster works. And, finally, you will look at some of the potential future directions for Netcaster.

- Chapter 6, "Using Netscape Netcaster," provides a how-to guide for using Netcaster. Specifically, it covers the various methods for subscribing to Web channels, updating channel contents, and manipulating Webtops. You also will look at several configuration options for channels and Netcaster itself.
- Chapter 7, "Creating Netcaster Channels," provides a hands-on tutorial for building your own Netcaster channels. With less than a dozen lines of JavaScript code, you easily can convert your existing Web site into a Web channel. Chapter 7 introduces the Netcaster *Application Programming Interface* (API) and JavaScript 1.2 code necessary for creating channels. You also will explore several tips for ensuring browser and version compatibility for Netcaster channels.

5.1 Netcaster Features

As a component of Communicator 4.0, Netcaster enables users to combine the traditional pull technique of pointing-and-clicking on Web pages with the automatic push mechanism for continuous channel updates. Using Netcaster, you easily can subscribe to channels or existing Web sites and receive automatic channel updates as often as you want. And, current Netcaster channels already provide a diverse range of information—from business and financial news to sports scores and children's programming. Before delving into the mechanics of Netcaster, however, take a look at its main features.

5.1.1 Netcaster Channels

Netcaster users access a Web channel first by subscribing to it. With Netcaster, users can choose from a variety of subscription methods. They can opt to use the built-in Netscape Channel Finder for premium channels. They can visit an existing Web site and click their Subscribe button (creating this Subscribe button is the focus of Chapter 7). Or, they can choose to turn any existing Web site into a Web channel and have it automatically downloaded on a preset schedule. No matter which method a user follows, Netcaster always ensures that channel contents are refreshed constantly and are continuously up-to-date.

5.1.2 Offline Browsing

After Web channel content is downloaded, it is stored on the user's hard drive. This enables users to view the complete channel content even when not connected to the Internet. Users can schedule their laptop to download the latest news from ABC News at 6 a.m. every morning, for example. The news is stored automatically on the user's hard drive and is available offline for the user's 7:30 a.m. commute. This can be ideal for home users with slow modems or frequent travelers with laptops.

5.1.3 Complete Support for HTML, JavaScript, and Java

At its heart, Netcaster is doing nothing more than automatically downloading regular Web pages. Thus, anything that can be displayed within a Netscape Navigator 4.0 browser can be displayed as a Netcaster channel. Netcaster therefore fully supports HTML 3.2, JavaScript 1.2, and Java 1.1. This capability enables content developers to easily reuse or reformat existing content. Netcaster also provides complete support for any Netscape plug-in document format, such as QuickTime movies, MPEG movies, *Portable Data Format* (PDF), or even *Virtual Reality Modeling Language* (VRML).

5.1.4 Premium Channels

In partnership with a number of major media companies, Netscape has created the Netcaster Channel Finder. The Channel Finder helps users easily find premium Web channels and usually represents the user's first extensive exposure to Netcaster. The current roster of premium channels includes ABC News, *Wired* magazine, CBS Sports, c|net, CNNfn, and dozens more.

5.1.5 Webtops

Webtops are full-screen Web pages without any of the normal "chrome" elements usually present in the Navigator window. These chrome elements include the main menu across the top, the button bar, and the Bookmark and URL Location bar. By hiding the chrome elements and attaching itself to the bottom application layer, Webtops enable full-screen, fully immersive Web page experiences. When combined with the latest JavaScript 1.2 features, content providers can create their own user interfaces entirely from scratch. And, because the Webtop remains "glued" to the bottom application layer, content providers can display their content consistently in the user's workspace or even create new user operating environments.

5.1.6 User Customization

Netcaster enables complete user and company-wide customization. Most important, users can decide how frequently a channel will update, how much hard drive space to allocate for any given channel, and whether their channels will run in regular or Webtop mode. Through Netscape's Mission Control software, system administrators can set company-wide settings for Netcaster. System administrators can presubscribe users to particular channels, for example, such as an internal or corporate Netcaster channel. Or, system administrators can control the schedule and frequency of all channel updates, giving companies greater control over their push traffic.

5.1.7 Support for Castanet Channels

Netcaster includes built-in support for Marimba Castanet channels. In 1996, Marimba, Inc. created the Castanet architecture to enable the automatic downloading and updating of Java applets and channels. To use a particular application, users simply subscribe to the channel and receive automatic software upgrades. When they want to use the application, the application already is on the local hard drive, and no additional network connections are required.

Each copy of Netcaster includes a built-in copy of the Castanet Tuner, and users no longer are required to download a separate tuner application. Netcaster users also have complete freedom to subscribe to any of the more than 100 existing Castanet channels. The Castanet architecture and more detailed examples are more fully described in Part V, "Marimba Castanet Channels."

5.2 How Netcaster Works

5.2.1 Netcaster as Crossware

In addition to marking Netscape's first foray into push technology, Netcaster also marks Netscape's first full-scale example of crossware. *Crossware* is Netscape's newest term for creating cross-platform Web applications that run on any existing operating system. Crossware also specifically refers to cross-platform applications that adhere to the Internet standards of HTML, JavaScript, and Java. In pursuing crossware, Netscape is hoping to continue its long-term goal of *write once, run anywhere*.

Netcaster itself is written entirely in HTML, JavaScript, and Java. The main user interface is written in dynamic HTML, for example, which enables drop-down menus, option dialog boxes, and mouse rollovers. The Channel Finder also is written in dynamic HTML, with the list of premium channels being served directly from the Netscape Server. The Web crawl engine for automatically retrieving content updates and managing the user cache is written entirely in Java.

According to Netscape, the crossware nature of Netcaster cut more than five months in internal development efforts, specifically because there was no need to port the application to different operating system platforms. And, Netcaster now runs on all 17 of the platforms supported by Netscape, making it the most widely available push technology.

Unfortunately, the crossware nature of Netcaster leaves it open to the current disadvantages of Java as a programming language. Specifically, Netcaster can be slow.

According to James Gosling, Vice President of JavaSoft and the original creator of Java, Java still runs twice as slow as native applications written in the C programming language. This means that it can take you at least twice as long to download a Web page in Netcaster as it would to download the same page in a regular Navigator window. No doubt, Java performance will increase steadily in the future, but for now, it leaves Netcaster at a performance disadvantage when compared to other push products. Specifically, it leaves Netcaster at a serious performance disadvantage when compared to PointCast and Microsoft Internet Explorer, both of which are written in native code and are optimized for the Windows 95/NT operating systems.

Developments to Watch: Improving Java Performance

Java has become the leading programming language of the Internet. It runs on any operating system. It includes built-in security. And it can rival the object-oriented facilities of C++. Sun Microsystems and Netscape also have diligently improved the functionality of Java. In the spring of 1997, Sun released Java 1.1 and introduced Java Beans, a structure for creating reusable and interchangeable Java components. Netscape and Sun now are jointly supporting the *Java Foundation Classes* (JFC), a new set of components for creating advanced *graphical user interfaces* (GUIs).

Since its inception, the greatest criticism leveled against Java is that it performs slowly. To ensure complete platform independence, Java originally was optimized for portability rather than performance. Hence, most users notice a significant performance difference between Java applications and native applications written in C or C++. In fact, even the most recent *Just-in-Time* (JIT) compilers from Microsoft, Symantec, and Sun still run at half the speed of C.

So, are we stuck with slow Java?

Not likely. Sun is busily preparing the next generation of Java and promises significant performance improvements. By the end of 1997, Sun also plans to ship its Hot Spot Virtual Machine. The Hot Spot technology includes significant compiler optimization and may enable Java to run as fast as C++. And, according to Jon Kannegaard, Vice President of software products at JavaSoft, the Hot Spot technology finally will “eliminate the tradeoff between performance and portability.” Microsoft also is busily upgrading its Virtual Machine to provide significant performance improvements on the Windows 95/NT platform.

In conjunction with Hot Spot, Sun has made significant business deals for the creation of Java chips. Already, Toshiba, Samsung, Mitsubishi, and NEC have signed on to build general-purpose Java chips. And the chips, whether used independently or as add-on processors promise to deliver superior Java performance.

Hold on to your hats!

5.2.2 Automatic Web Crawl

Each time Netcaster updates a channel, it follows an automatic Web-crawl algorithm. First, Netcaster retrieves the top-level HTML page. It then parses and retrieves each of the embedded hypertext links. It continues to burrow deeper, one level at a time, until it reaches the maximum depth set by the user.

When Netcaster reaches the maximum depth, it returns to the top-level page and proceeds to download all the embedded images in the Web site hierarchy. And, after it successfully retrieves all the images, it starts all over again and retrieves all the embedded objects, including Java applets. By retrieving the text first, Netcaster ensures that users always retrieve the most critical information.

In retrieving each page or each page element, Netcaster first checks the date it was last modified. The last modified date is a standard component of the *Hypertext Transfer Protocol* (HTTP), enabling Web browsers to cut down on network use and employ existing cached pages. If the page was modified recently, Netcaster retrieves it. If the page has not been modified since Netcaster last retrieved it, Netcaster uses the existing cached page. This cuts down on bandwidth use and significantly speeds channel updates.

Note that when performing its automated Web crawl, Netcaster follows each and every link on the page. This contrasts with the CDF, which enables you to specify which links to follow. This can result in significant performance considerations, because Netcaster does not differentiate between internal links to the existing Web site and external links to other Web sites. If your top-level channel page includes a link to another Web site and you are set to retrieve three levels of information, for example, Netcaster may spend an inordinate amount of time retrieving a Web site that you do not control.

To take advantages of Netcaster's automatic Web-crawl capabilities, you therefore need to pay special attention to the hierarchy of your channel. Specifically, you want to include your most important and updated information in the top two levels of your hierarchy. You also want to minimize the number of links to external links. These and other channel tips are explored in Chapter 7.

5.2.3 Caching Capabilities

As each page is downloaded, Netcaster stores content in a cache directory on the user's hard drive. From the developer's perspective, it is important to note that the Netcaster cache is completely separate from the regular Navigator cache. This can be a mixed blessing and contrasts with the single-caching capabilities provided by Internet Explorer 4.0.

In Netscape Navigator and Internet Explorer, cached files are maintained by a *least recently used* (LRU) algorithm. When the cache becomes full, the files that were used most recently are protected. Files that haven't been accessed in a long time are deleted automatically. This manages to save hard drive space while protecting the user's most important and frequently accessed files.

In contrast, the Netcaster architecture uses a garbage-collection mechanism for managing the cache. If the user still is subscribed to a given channel, the top-level page and all its associated links are protected. If the user unsubscribes or the hierarchy changes so that a page is left dangling or is inaccessible, the page and all its links are deleted automatically.

The dual cache has the advantage of the Netcaster channel contents always being available and protected as long as the user remains subscribed to the channel. The disadvantage is that Communicator can store two identical copies of the same Web site—one copy for Navigator and one copy for Netcaster. This wastes hard drive space and can result in user confusion over which copy is more up-to-date.

5.3 Assessing Netcaster

How does Netcaster stack up against the competition? No objective assessment would be complete without a complete discussion of its several weaknesses. But Netcaster does include a number of significant strengths, and it is likely to hold its own against Microsoft and PointCast.

5.3.1 Netcaster Strengths

Easy to use. Netcaster supports an intuitive user interface for subscribing to and managing channels. The main control looks similar to a television remote control and easily slides off the screen when not in use. The Channel Finder provides an easy-to-use interface for subscribing to premium channels.

Easy to develop. Netcaster channels are built entirely from HTML, JavaScript, and Java. This enables existing Web sites to reuse or repackage existing content for use within new Web channels. It also enables organizations to leverage the existing skill set of their current development team without requiring a major investment in additional training.

Cross-platform capabilities. Netcaster runs on all 17 operating systems supported by Netscape Communicator, from Macintosh and Windows 95/NT all the way to UNIX and IBM mainframes. This makes it the most widely available and accessible push product with the largest online audience.

Compelling content. In the push marketplace, content is still king. And Netscape has allied itself with a number of major media providers to provide compelling content for Netcaster users. Time Warner, ABC News, CNN, SportsLine, and Hearst New Media already are onboard, and more are likely to arrive soon. The more compelling the premium content, the more likely users will stick with Netcaster.

Basic and advanced channel capabilities. Netcaster supports both regular Netcaster channels and advanced Castanet channels from Marimba, Inc. This capability enables content providers to deliver both content and sophisticated Java applications over the net.

5.3.2 Netcaster Weaknesses

Slow performance. The Netcaster Web-crawl program is written entirely in Java. This results in significantly slower performance when compared to the update mechanisms provided by PointCast and Internet Explorer, both of which are written in native code.

Separate application interface: The Netcaster interface is completely separate from the Navigator interface. Depending on your point of view, this could be a strength or a weakness. But Internet Explorer 4.0 does provide a more cohesive and integrated interface for traditional Web surfing alongside newer channel-subscription capabilities.

No support for CDF. Netscape claims that Netcaster supports all the functionality of CDF with the existing standards of HTML, JavaScript, and Java. But, by withholding support for CDF, Netscape has made the developer's job more difficult, requiring developers to learn the new Netcaster API *and* CDF if they want to support both Netscape and Microsoft channels. Should the *World Wide Web Consortium* (W3C) support CDF as a standard, Netscape has promised to implement it. But there may be a lag between the W3C approval and Netscape's own implementation, and this could give Microsoft and PointCast an edge.

5.4 The Future of Netcaster

As the push market heats up and Microsoft and Netscape continue their intense rivalry, we are likely to see a continuing evolution in Netcaster's capabilities. With Communicator 4.0, Netscape is introducing its new *Smart-Update* capability. By simply clicking on a few links, users now can easily add new Communicator components or features. And Netscape no doubt will exploit the Smart-Update technology to provide its customers with ongoing updates to Netcaster.

But what do the engineers at Netscape have in store for future releases of Netcaster? Netscape is holding its cards close, but we probably will see two major developments: the *Open Profiling Standard* (OPS) and increased support for digital convergence.

5.4.1 *Open Profiling Standard* (OPS)

In May 1997, Netscape—along with Firefly Inc. and Verisign Inc.—introduced the OPS and submitted it to the W3C. Netscape is hoping that OPS soon will become an Internet standard and plans to include OPS as a standard component of both Navigator and Netcaster.

With OPS, Web sites and Web channels will be able to offer individually tailored content based on a user's personal profile. As a base, this personal profile will include a unique ID, demographic information (country, ZIP code, age, and gender), and contact information (name, address, phone, and e-mail address.) In the future, OPS may include support for credit card numbers or e-cash accounts and could provide a vitally needed component for electronic commerce. Using Verisign's encryption technology, this information will be encrypted and digitally signed on the user's hard drive, ensuring both security and privacy.

When a user first visits a home page or subscribes to a channel, the channel can request the user's personal profile. Users have the option of releasing all, part, or none of their personal profile. By analyzing the profile, content providers can build demographic databases of their audience or track the number of new customers without requiring new users to complete a lengthy and often redundant registration process. In addition, Web channels can collect information regarding a user, including special interests or preferences, and store that information in the user's personal profile. When the user returns to the page or receives a channel update, this information can be used to create individually tailored content.

OPS represents a significant advance over current profiling mechanisms, most of which are based on persistent cookie technology. OPS already has garnered support from more than 60 organizations, including American Express, IBM, Oracle, and Sun Microsystems. One month after its introduction, Microsoft announced its support for OPS, and we are likely to see competing implementations provided by Microsoft and Netscape.

5.4.2 Digital Convergence

Only a few years ago, most pundits were predicting a vast information superhighway and a universe of 500 channels. The buzzwords were *interactive television*, *video on demand*, *home shopping*, and *digital convergence*. And the cable, telephone, and television giants were scrambling to create optical fiber networks and large test beds for interactive television. None of these companies counted on the Internet, though, and most interactive television projects have been completely derailed or shut down, usually in favor of developing new Internet projects. In fact, the Internet has become the de facto standard for online interactivity and electronic commerce.

Interactive television and digital convergence still remain a dream for many. And, in the medium- to long-term future, Netcaster itself may be adapted to provide rudimentary interactivity for television sets. At the Third Annual Netscape Developers Conference held during the summer of 1997, Netscape provided a quick sneak peak at such plans.

In conjunction with Intel's Intercast technology, broadcasters now can embed HTML and other data into television or cable signals. The signal is delivered directly to the PC where the video, audio, and HTML are separated and decoded. Netcaster theoretically could provide a front end for viewing and interacting with these information-rich channels. And, at the developer demonstration, Netcaster was used to view a televised baseball game. The center of the screen included a view of the television broadcast, while an HTML ticker scrolled along the bottom of the screen with current sports statistics.

By clicking on specific baseball players, Netcaster followed the embedded URLs and automatically displayed precached information. Clicking on the pitcher, for example, popped up a small window with individual player statistics. By clicking on the scrolling ticker, users could access more in-depth information or updates on other games in progress. Voilà. Interactive television! Stay tuned . . .

SUMMARY

Netcaster marks Netscape's first foray into the push technology market. As the leading Internet browser maker, Netscape is likely to emerge as a major player in the push market, and we are likely to see a continuing evolution in Netcaster's capabilities.

Netcaster itself is built entirely in dynamic HTML, JavaScript, and Java. It provides a number of important features: easy channel subscriptions; automatic channel updates; offline browsing; complete support for HTML, Java, and JavaScript; support for fully-immersive Webtop experiences; premium content through the Netcaster Channel Finder; complete user and enterprise-wide customization; and support for advanced Java channels through Marimba's Castanet technology.

The main strengths of Netcaster are ease of use, ease of channel development, cross-platform support for 17 operating systems, compelling content through partnerships with media providers, and support for Castanet channels. Its main weaknesses are slow performance, a separate application interface from Navigator, and a lack of support for the CDF.

With Communicator's new Smart-Update mechanism, users easily can add new components and features as they become available, and Netscape is likely to exploit this mechanism to provide automatic upgrades for Netcaster. The most likely new feature of Netcaster will include support for the OPS. OPS will better enable Web channel designers to create individually tailored content based on a user's personal profile. In the medium- to long-term future, we may see additional functionality for interactive television.

Online Resources

- Netcaster *Frequently Asked Questions* (FAQ)

  `http://home.netscape.com/inf/comprod/products/communicator/netcaster_faq.html`

  The Netcaster FAQ is a good place to start for a general overview of Netcaster's main features. The FAQ also includes a detailed discussion of Netscape's decision to forgo support for the CDF.
- Netscape Web Site **`http://www.netscape.com`**

For ongoing product updates and hints about future developments, be sure to check out the Netscape Web site. Netcaster is a rapidly evolving application, and Netcaster 2.0 is probably just around the corner.

- Netscape's White Paper of Developing Crossware

  `http://developer.netscape.com/library/wpapers/crossware/index.htm`

  Still not sure what crossware means and want to get a sneak peak at how Netcaster was built? Check out Marc Andreesen's white paper on crossware and the networked enterprise.

- CNET's Browsers.com **`http://www.browsers.com`**

  For the latest product and beta releases from Microsoft and Netscape, be sure to check out c|net's browsers.com. In addition to providing fast downloads for the latest products, browsers.com includes an ongoing comparison of Netscape Navigator 4.0 and Microsoft Internet Explorer 4.0, with detailed commentary on their push products.

- OPS Frequently Asked Questions

  `http://developer.netscape.com/ops/opsfaq.html`

  What is the Open Profiling Standard? How will OPS work? Why is OPS important? What kind of information will be stored in personal profiles? Are personal profiles secure? Check out the FAQ.

CHAPTER 6

Using Netscape Netcaster

Netscape's Netcaster is easy to use and already has won industry praise for providing one of the best user interfaces to a push technology product. Expanding on the analogy of Internet broadcasting, the Netcaster interface actually was built to resemble a television remote control. By clicking on a small tab, you can slide the control into place or discreetly slide it off the screen when not in use. And, to view new content, you simply change the channel. With the possible exception of Webtops (which take a little time to get used to), new users should be comfortable with Netcaster in less than an hour.

6.1 Getting Started

6.1.1 Netcaster 1.0

In August 1997, Netscape released the first consumer version of Netcaster 1.0. Netcaster now is included as a standard component of Netscape Communicator. Netscape Communicator includes a full suite of Internet applications, including Netscape Navigator 4.0 and facilities for e-mail, newsgroups, real-time conferencing, and HTML authoring. Late in August, Netscape decided to unbundle its browser and offer a standalone version of Netscape Navigator 4.0. The standalone version does not include any of the extra applications provided by Communicator, but it does include Netcaster.

NOTE: *Note that Netcaster works only with Netscape Communicator 4.02 or higher. Check the Netscape Web site (`http:\\home.netscape.com`) for the latest downloads for your operating system.*

6.1.2 Launching Netcaster

To launch Netcaster, you first must launch Netscape Communicator or the standalone Netscape Navigator.

- From within Communicator, choose Communicator from the main menu and choose Netcaster.
- From within the standalone Navigator, choose Window from the main menu and choose Netcaster.

By default, Netcaster appears on the right side of your screen, and the default Netscape channel opens.

6.2 Subscribing to Channels

6.2.1 The Netcaster Interface

Borrowing from the metaphor of television and broadcasting, the Netcaster interface looks very much like a television remote control (see Figure 6-1). You use the control to subscribe to and view your channels. On the left side, the interface includes a black tab for hiding and showing the control. Click on the tab, and the interface slides off screen and frees up valuable screen real-estate space; click on the tab again, and the control slides back into place. This is one remote control you are not likely to lose!

6.2.2 The Channel Finder

The Channel Finder is Netscape's directory of premium channels (see Figure 6-2). Netscape is working hard to recruit new channel providers, and

Figure 6-1 The Netcaster interface.

Figure 6-2 The Channel Finder. Check here for the newest and coolest channels.

the Channel Finder already includes dozens of new channels—from ABC News and CBS SportsLine to CNET and *Wired* magazine.

Subscribing to new channels via the Channel Finder is extremely straightforward:

1. Click on the Channel Finder tab.
2. Select a channel category. The Channel Finder is currently broken into two categories: one for business and another for general channels.
3. Select the channel of your choosing. You are presented with a small graphical logo of your channel, along with options for adding or previewing the channel (see Figure 6-3).
4. Click the Add Channel option.
5. Complete the membership registration. If this is your first time subscribing to one of Netscape's premium channels, you need to complete the online registration form. You are asked to supply your name, mailing address, and e-mail address. You also are asked to fill out an online survey about your company and profession.

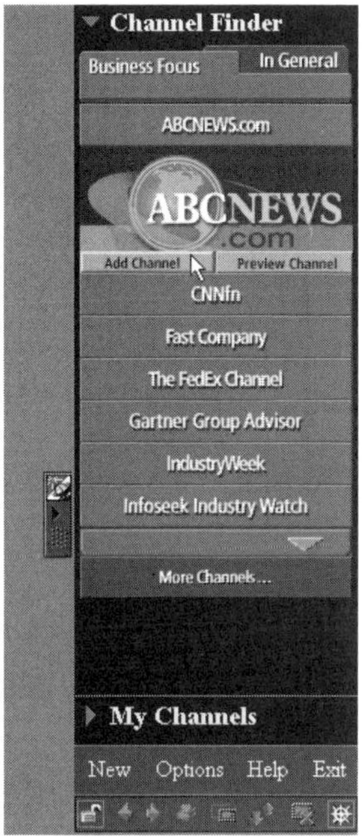

Figure 6-3 Subscribing to a channel via the Channel Finder. Just click the Add Channel button to complete the subscription process.

6. After completing the registration process, you are presented with the Channel Properties dialog box (see Figure 6-4). Channel providers can set recommended default values for display and cache properties, but you can override any of these settings (see Section 6.4, "Setting Channel Properties"). To accept the channel's default properties, click OK.

6.2.3 Viewing a Channel

After you subscribe to your channel, click the My Channels tab. The My Channels page includes a list of all your currently subscribed channels (see Figure 6-5).

To receive your first batch of content, right-click on the channel and choose the Start Update option. (Macintosh users should Control-click the channel and choose the Start Update option.) You immediately see a red line moving back and forth, indicating that Netcaster is busy download-

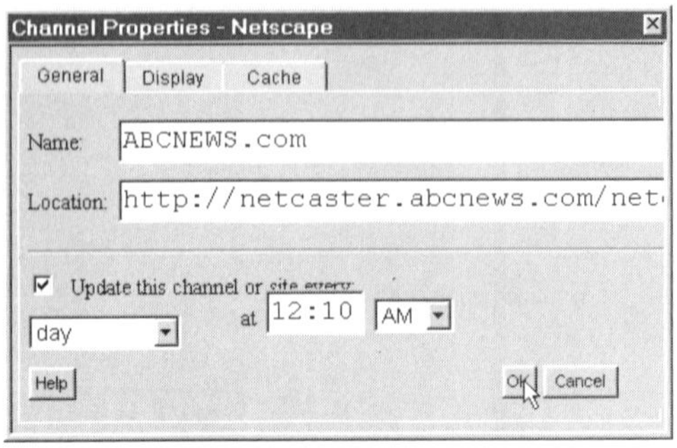

Figure 6-4
The Channel Properties dialog box. Each time you subscribe to a new channel, you can override the schedule, display, and cache settings recommended by the channel publisher. To accept the publisher's recommendations, just click OK.

ing your channel. You can choose to view your channel content as it is being downloaded or to wait until the entire content is retrieved. In either case, just click the channel name, and Netcaster opens a new Navigator window or Webtop and displays the channel's content.

6.2.4 The My Channels Interface

There are a few important elements to note in the My Channels interface. First, you may see a small glowing dot to the left of your channel:

- Green indicates that new content is available.
- Red indicates a network error. The channel content could not be downloaded properly.

Second, you may see a small rectangular screen icon. (See the ABC News.com channel in Figure 6-5.) This indicates that your channel is set to display in Webtop mode. If the Webtop is activated, the icon has a green glow. (See Section 6.3, "Working with Webtops," for more information on Webtops.)

Figure 6-5
The My Channels interface. Channels set for Webtop mode are denoted with the small screen icon to the right.

6.2.5 Automatic Updates

At specified intervals set by the channel provider, Netcaster checks for and downloads new content. If new content is available, the green indicator light appears in the My Channels interface. Note that Netcaster must be running in order to retrieve automatic updates. If Netcaster is not running at the scheduled update time, or if your are currently in offline mode, Netcaster simply waits until the next update interval.

You also have the option of manually updating your channels at any time. Just right-click the channel and choose Start Update.

To cancel a channel update in progress, right-click the channel and choose Stop Update.

6.2.6 Deleting Channels

To delete your channel at any time, right-click the channel and choose Delete.

6.3 Working with Webtops

6.3.1 Webtops Defined

A *Webtop* is a borderless Web page that remains on your screen underneath all other application windows. The Webtop is always visible and enables you to view channel updates while working on other applications (see Figure 6-6).

Netscape is positioning Webtops as a direct competitor to Microsoft's Active Desktop Components, now available as part of Internet Explorer 4.0. Netscape also is positioning Webtops as a way for content providers to create an immersive experience for users, where the content *is* the interface. When in Webtop mode, the normal Navigator interface is hidden, and content providers have free reign to create their own user interfaces from scratch. This "kiosk" mode functionality is something that many Web designers have wanted for a long time.

No one is quite sure whether users will find Webtops useful and entertaining or just plain annoying, however. One of the main disadvantages of Webtops is that it completely obscures your regular Windows 95/NT desktop along with all your useful program shortcuts. This alone can be enough to convince you not to use Webtops. Others, however, may find that Webtops provide added value that a regular browser widow cannot match. Luckily, Netcaster can accommodate both groups by giving you complete control over Webtops.

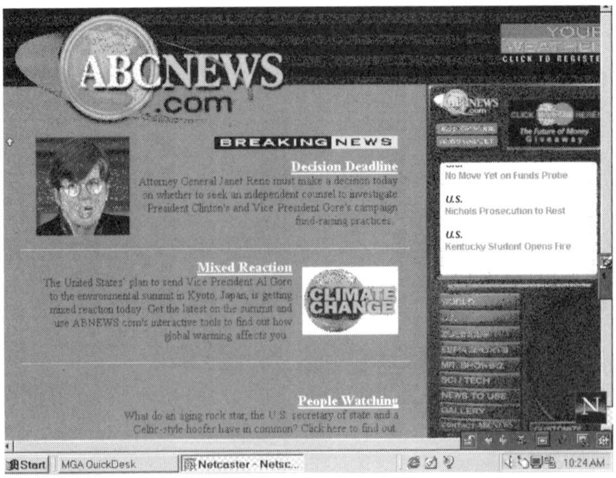

Figure 6-6
The ABC News.com Webtop.

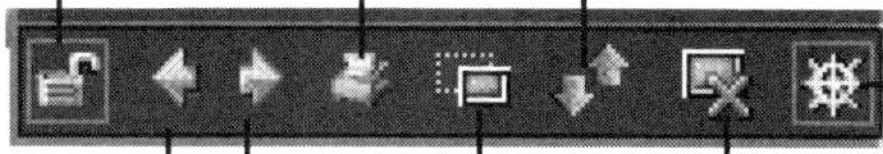

Figure 6-7
When in Webtop mode, Netscape displays the Webtop control bar.

6.3.2 Webtop Controls

When in Webtop mode, a small Webtop control bar appears in the lower right hand of your screen (see Figure 6-7).

Use the control bar to manipulate the currently displayed Webtop:

Security: Displays security information regarding the currently displayed page.

Back: Takes you to the previous Webtop page.

Forward: Takes you to the next Webtop page.

Print: Prints the current Webtop.

Desktop/Webtop: Toggles the operating system between desktop and Webtop mode. When in desktop mode, the Webtop is hidden and the user's regular desktop icons appear.

Front/Back: Moves the Webtop to the back (its default position), behind all other application windows, or to the front, in front of all other application windows.

Close the Webtop: Closes the current Webtop.

Open a New Navigator Window: Opens a new Navigator window on top of the Webtop.

TIP: *If you want to disable the Webtop functionality of a particular channel and would rather display the channel within a regular Navigator window, you can change its display properties. Right-click on the channel and choose Properties. Then click on the Display tab and select the Navigator Window option.*

6.4 Setting Channel Properties

When you first subscribe to a channel, you can override the default settings recommended by the channel provider. Or, you can change these settings at any time by right-clicking on a channel and choosing Properties.

6.4.1 Setting the General Channel Properties

The general properties determine the name, location, and update schedule for your channel (see Figure 6-8). You can change the name of a specified channel, but you should never change its default location.

You also can customize Netcaster to retrieve automatic updates as often as you want, and you can even specify the exact day and time for updates.

To set the automatic update schedule, make sure that you select the Update This Channel or Site Every ___ option. If you do not want any automatic updates, deselect this option and update your channels manually.

Currently, you have seven options for your update schedule: every 30 minutes, every hour, every two hours, every three hours, every 12 hours, once a day, and once a week. If you choose a daily or weekly update schedule, you are prompted for the exact time and/or date.

6.4.2 Setting the Display Properties

The display properties determine the look and feel of your channel (see Figure 6-9). You can choose to display your channel within a regular Navigator window or in Webtop mode.

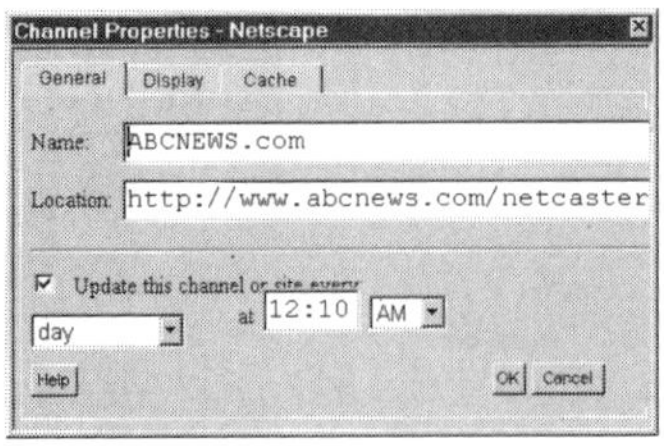

Figure 6-8
General Channel Properties.

6.4.3 Setting the Cache Properties

When Netcaster updates a channel, it automatically stores channel contents in the Netcaster cache on the user's hard drive. Each channel has two specific cache properties (see Figure 6-10). The first property tells Netcaster the number of levels to retrieve. Every Netcaster channel is composed of a series of Web pages that link to another set of Web pages. These pages include their own links in a somewhat hierarchical structure (see Figure 6-11). When Netcaster updates a channel, it first retrieves the top-level home page. This is considered Level 1. It then parses the entire page and follows all the embedded links. These Level 2 pages then are saved to the cache. And, if the user desires, Netcaster can keep traversing deeper and deeper into the Web page hierarchy.

Figure 6-9
Display Properties.

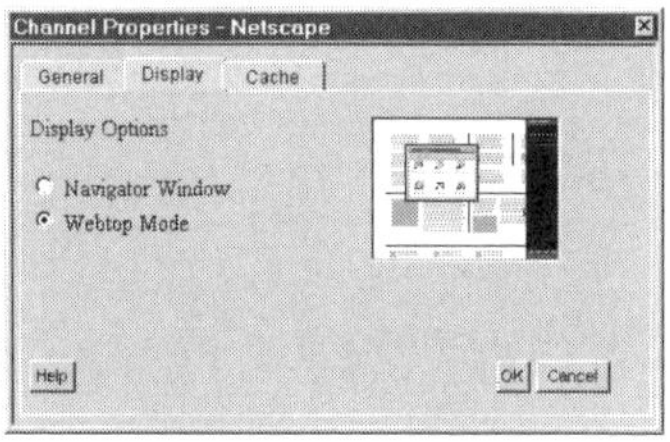

Figure 6-10
Cache Properties.

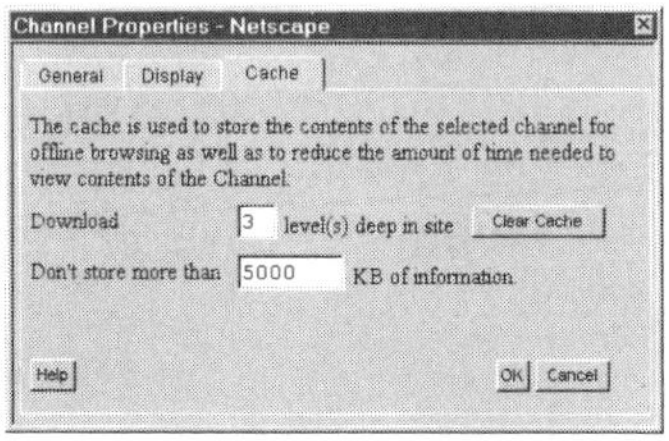

Figure 6-11
The Web Channel hierarchy. Each channel is composed of one main page, with links to a hierarchy of other pages.

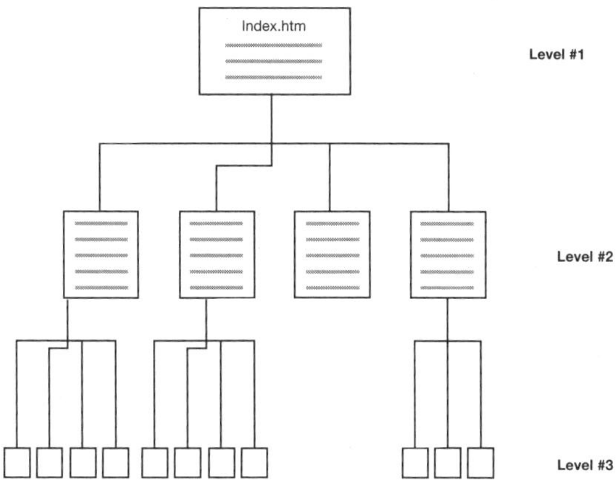

The second property places an upper limit on the amount of disk space reserved for channel updates. This restricts your channel memory requirements to a specified kilobyte target and prevents your hard drive from being swamped with channel data. (Note: Clicking the Clear Cache button here erases all content files related to this channel.)

Setting your cache properties can be a difficult decision and involves several tradeoffs. If you burrow too deep into a Web hierarchy and set a high maximum cache target, your computer can spend an inordinate amount of time downloading new files. It also can quickly swamp your hard drive. On the other hand, if you don't dig deep enough and set a low maximum cache target, you will not download all the information you need. This can eliminate many of the speed benefits of caching and defeat the entire purpose of subscribing to a channel in the first place. It also can get quite frustrating if you are planning on doing most of your browsing offline.

6.5 Subscribing to Web Sites

As one of its great strengths, Netcaster enables you to subscribe to any existing Web page—essentially turning any Web page into a Web channel. After it is set up with your preferences, Netcaster repeatedly downloads your designated Web page and all its links, just like a regular Netcaster channel. You then can browse through these pages when not connected to the Internet.

To subscribe to an existing Web site, follow these steps:

1. Click the New button. The Channel Properties dialog box appears.
2. Enter the channel's name.
3. Enter the channel location. This is the top page URL of the Web site you want to retrieve.
4. Set the update schedule. You can schedule updates as often as you want. The default is once every 12 hours.
5. Set the display properties. You can turn any Web site into a Webtop or confine it to a regular Navigator window (default).
6. Set the cache properties. By default, Netcaster downloads two levels of information and places a 5000-Kbyte cache limit.
7. Click OK.

6.6 Subscribing to Castanet Channels

6.6.1 What Is Castanet Again?

Marimba's Castanet technology provides a revolutionary new method for distributing software and content over the Internet. Unlike regular Netcaster channels, which mainly deliver content, Castanet channels can deliver both content and applications in the form of Java application channels. For a full description of Castanet, see Part V, "Marimba Castanet Channels."

6.6.2 Subscribing to Castanet Channels

Every copy of Netcaster includes a built-in Castanet Tuner for subscribing to Castanet channels. Subscribing to Castanet channels is nearly identical to subscribing to regular Netcaster channels. The Netscape Channel Finder includes both Netcaster and Castanet channels side by side.

When working with Castanet channels, there are only a few minor differences to note:

- When you first subscribe to a Castanet channel, you are not given the opportunity to override the schedule, display, or cache properties (see Figure 6-12).
- After the contents of the channel are downloaded, you can modify the channel's schedule. If the channel displays HTML pages, you

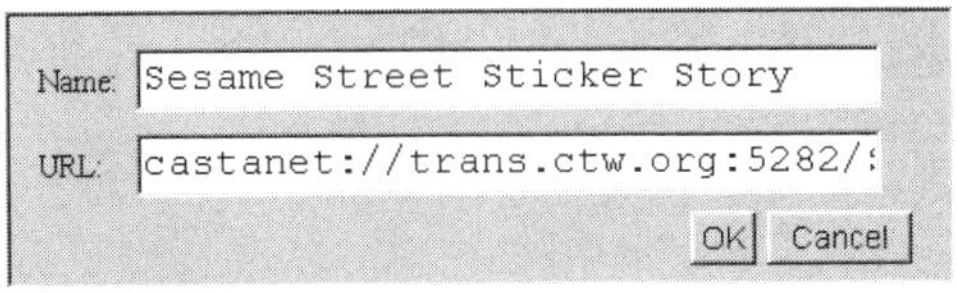

Figure 6-12
Subscribing to a Castanet channel is nearly identical to subscribing to regular Netcaster channels.

can set its display properties (regular or Webtop). You may not modify the cache properties, however; the cache is fixed by the channel provider.

- When you view or launch a Castanet channel, your Castanet channel application appears in a Java applet window.

If you want to just try out a simple Castanet channel, try subscribing to the Sesame Street Coloring Book Channel (see Figure 6-13). The channel is available in the Channel Finder and downloads in just seconds.

6.6.3 The Marimba Channel Guide

For a complete listing of Castanet channels, it is best to go directly to the source. Marimba's Channel Guide is located at `http:\\www.marimba.com\channels`. Just click any of the channel icons to initiate a channel subscription.

Figure 6-13 The Sesame Street Coloring Book Channel—Castanet at work.

6.6 Configuring Netcaster

To configure Netscaster, click the Options button.

6.6.1 Layout Options

Under Layout Options, you can choose to place Netcaster on the right or left side of your screen (see Figure 6-14). You also can choose to automatically hide the Netcaster window. This option automatically hides the Netcaster window when you launch or view a new channel.

6.6.2 Setting a Default Webtop

Under Layout Options, you can choose to display a default Webtop. Just choose a channel from the pull-down menu of subscribed channels. This Webtop opens automatically each time you launch Netcaster.

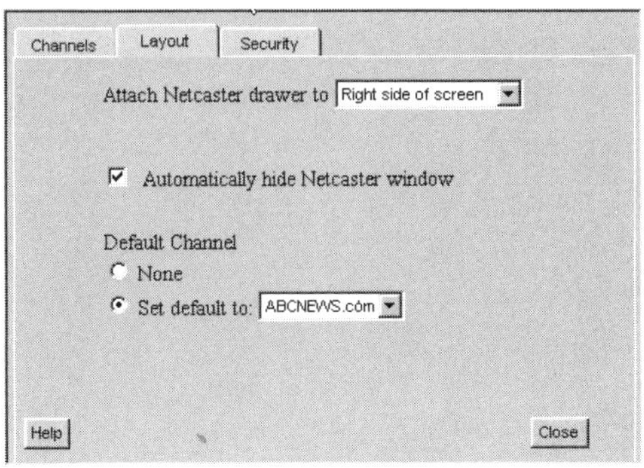

Figure 6-14
The Netcaster Layout options.

6.6.3 Security Options

All the Netcaster security options relate to Castanet channels. You can choose to disable any one of the following:

Castanet cookies: Each Castanet Tuner has a unique identification string or *cookie*. Each time the Tuner requests a channel update, the Tuner sends its identification string, enabling the channel publisher to separate the number of hits for updates from the number of actual subscribers.

Castanet logging: The Castanet architecture includes a number of sophisticated mechanisms for tracking user behavior and providing feedback to channel providers. The exact nature of these logging capabilities varies from channel to channel, but it may include any of the following: tracking user interest in online advertising, recording results of user surveys, tracking user interest in new software features, and logging specific user suggestions regarding content or software.

Castanet profiling: In addition to the logging capabilities, Castanet includes a sophisticated structure that enables users to personalize and customize their channel experience. With profiling, you can select a list of companies to track, for example, or select a list of news topics that interest you most. These profile options are sent back to the channel provider, and your channel then is modified on-the-fly.

As you set each of these options, you should be aware of the tradeoffs. Enabling any one of these options does open you up to possible online abuses, including invasion of privacy. The truly paranoid therefore are wise to disable all these feedback options. However, disabling these options also prevents you from taking advantage of the many advantages offered by Castanet, including built-in support for customization and personalization.

SUMMARY

Netcaster is easy to use, and most users should be comfortable with its use in less than an hour. Just launch Netcaster and browse the Channel Finder to get started. When you first subscribe to a channel, you are given the option of overriding the default settings specified by the channel provider. This capability gives you complete control over the look and feel of channels, the frequency of updates, and the hard disk space devoted to channel contents. Happy netcasting!

Online Resources

- c|net Broswer Tips and Tricks

  `http://www.cnet.com`

  c|net runs a series on browser tips and tricks. Check out the latest tips on Communicator 4.0 and Netcaster.

- Marimba Channel Guide

  `http://www.marimba.com/channels`

  For the most comprehensive list of Castanet channels, go directly to the source. New channels are added all the time.

CHAPTER 7

Creating Netcaster Channels

This chapter explores the steps necessary for creating your own Netscape Netcaster channels. Fortunately, Netscape has made our task quite simple and straightforward. You do not need any special Web server software. You do not need much programming experience. And, best of all, you easily can convert your existing Web site into a Web channel. If you are familiar with HTML and JavaScript, you should be up and running in a few hours.

Before beginning this chapter, make sure that you are familiar with the material presented in Chapters 5, "Introduction to Netscape Netcaster," and 6, "Using Netscape Netcaster."

7.1 JavaScript 1.2

This chapter assumes that you have some working knowledge of JavaScript. *JavaScript* is a portable language for embedding small programs into HTML documents. And, despite its name, it actually bears little resemblance or connection to the Java programming language created by Sun Microsystems. JavaScript was created by Netscape and has since been supported by Microsoft's Internet Explorer. JavaScript actually was originally called LiveScript and was cleverly renamed in the wake of Java's huge popularity.

With each new release of Navigator, Netscape has included an updated version of JavaScript. Navigator 2.0 includes JavaScript 1.0. Navigator 3.0 includes JavaScript 1.1. And, with the release of Netscape Communicator, Netscape is including JavaScript 1.2. JavaScript 1.2 includes several added features for channel creation and dynamic HTML. And, the more you know about JavaScript in general, the sooner you can take advantage of these newest features.

If you are completely unfamiliar with JavaScript, you probably should take some time out right now to learn the basics. Throughout this chapter, I have included a number of JavaScript tips. These tips illustrate several key JavaScript concepts, including event handling and JavaScript's object-oriented facilities. If you are an experienced JavaScript programmer, you safely can skip these sections. But, if you are new to JavaScript, you might find these sections quite helpful.

7.2 Creating Netcaster Channels

7.2.1 Overview

As a developer, you easily can convert your existing Web site into a Web channel by including a simple Subscribe button and a dozen lines of JavaScript code. After the end user clicks the Subscribe button, your Java-

Script code interfaces with the Netcaster API and initiates the subscription process.

Here, then, is our first example. Listing 7-1 includes HTML and JavaScript code for subscribing to the ABC News.com channel. Take a moment to review the code before we examine the program in detail.

Listing 7-1
Basic Netcaster Channel

```
<!- Basic Netcaster Channel ->
<HTML>
<SCRIPT LANGUAGE="JavaScript">
function addChannel() {
   nc = components["netcaster"];  // Access Netcaster
                                  // API
   import nc.getChannelObject;    // Import Channel
                                  // Methods
   import nc.addChannel;
   var chan = getChannelObject(); // Get preinitialized
                                  // Channel Object
   chan.url = "http://netcaster.abcnews.com/netcaster/webtop/
  webtopreal.html";
   chan.name = "ABC News";        // Set Channel Name
   chan.intervalTime = 720;       // Update Channel
                                  // every 12 hours
   chan.maxCacheSize = 5120000;   // Set Max Cache Size
                                  // to 5,000 KB
   chan.depth = 3;                // Burrow 3 levels
   chan.mode= "webtop";           // Set display mode
                                  // to webtop
   chan.type=1;                   // Type = HTML Channel
   addChannel(chan);              // Add Channel to
                                  // Netcaster
 }
</SCRIPT>
<BODY>
<FORM>
<INPUT TYPE=BUTTON VALUE="Subscribe to ABC News!"
  onClick="addChannel();">
</FORM>
</BODY>
</HTML>
```

JavaScript Tip: The `onClick()` Event Handler

Like many modern programming languages, JavaScript includes an event-driven programming mode. At any point during program execution, a number of events may occur. These events could include system errors, such as an inability to locate a given URL, or time-out signals to control animation speed. These events also could include user actions, such as clicking a button or adding text to an HTML form. To process events, JavaScript includes *event handlers*. When the given event occurs, program execution passes automatically to the appropriate event handler.

The **`onClick()`** event is one of the most commonly used JavaScript constructs. As an extension to HTML, an **`onClick`** event can be associated with any of a number of HTML components, including buttons, checkboxes, and radio buttons. The following HTML code creates a button, for example, that displays a short message after being clicked:

```
<HTML>
<HEAD><TITLE>Sample OnClick Event Page</TITLE></HEAD>
<BODY>
<FORM>
<INPUT TYPE="button" VALUE="Click here!" onClick="alert
('Ouch!');">
</FORM>
</BODY>
</HTML>
```

After the user clicks the button, the code between the matching quotation marks is executed. In this case, the **`alert`** function is called with a text string. The **`alert`** function displays the given text string in a small dialog box, as shown in Figure 7-1.

NOTE: *To try out the sample code in Listing 7-1, make sure that Netcaster already is running when you attempt to subscribe. If Netcaster is not running, you receive a JavaScript alert informing you that* **`getChannelObject()`** *is not a function. We will fix this problem in Section 7.3, "The Add Channel Wizard."*

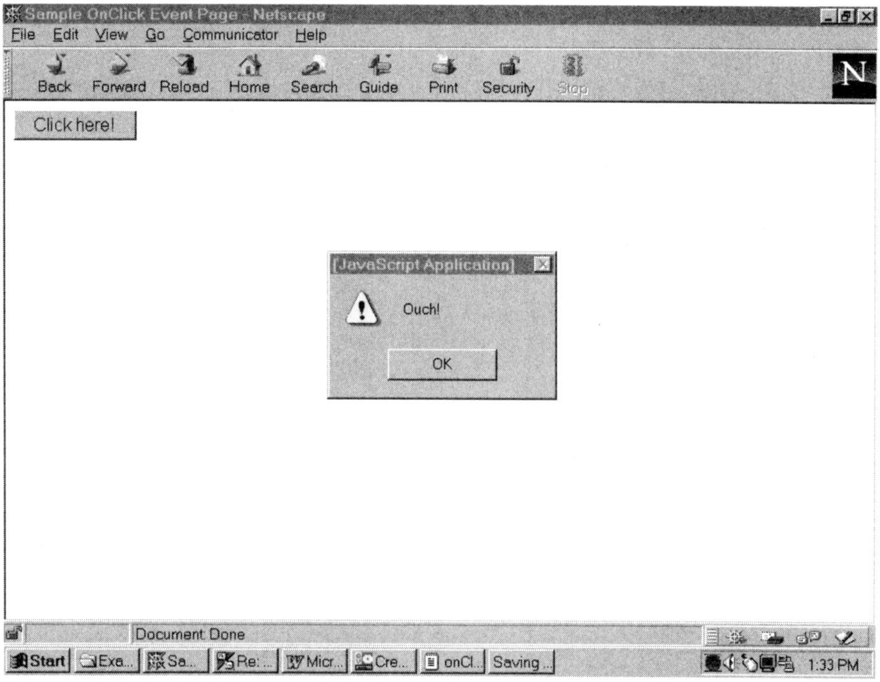

Figure 7-1
Displaying an alert

First note that line 21 creates a simple HTML form button. After the user clicks the button, the **`onClick`** event handler calls the **`addChannel()`** function.

The second important point to note is that the JavaScript code in the **`addChannel`** function interfaces with the Netcaster API. Developers interface with the Netcaster API first by requesting a preinitialized channel object. If you are not familiar with object-oriented programming, simply think of a JavaScript channel object as a "black box" that contains all the settings for your channel. After you have a channel object, you can set its primary properties, including name, location, and update schedule. Then you can add the channel to the list of My Channels.

7.2.2 Accessing the Netcaster API

What, then, is the Netcaster API, and how do you access it? The first three lines of the **`addChannel`** method in Listing 7-1 set the groundwork:

```
5      nc = components["netcaster"];// Access Netcaster API
6      import nc.getChannelObject;   // Import Channel Methods
7      import nc.addChannel;
```

Even if you are a veteran JavaScript programmer, these lines will look new to you. Line 5 requests the component or library associated with Netcaster. In fact, the components array is a new JavaScript 1.2 feature that allows programmers to access the other software components provided by Netscape Communicator. In the future, this array may allow programmers to access the Messenger mailbox, Collabra's discussion groups, or Netscape's Conference software. But, for now, Netcaster is the only registered element of the components array.

Lines 6 and 7 also are likely to look unfamiliar. The Netcaster component includes two main methods: **`getChannelObject`** and **`addChannel`**. To access these methods, each one must be imported explicitly with the JavaScript **`import`** statement. This, too, is an entirely new construct and is required by JavaScript's new security model.

7.2.3 The `getChannelObject` Method

After you successfully import the Netcaster component, you can create a new channel by calling the Netcaster **`getChannelObject`** method. This method returns one complete channel object, preinitialized with default settings. And, after you have a channel object, you can set its general, schedule, cache, and display properties.

7.2.4 General Required Properties

The Netcaster channel object has only two required properties: name and URL. The name identifies your channel and appears in the user's list of My Channels. The URL points to the top-level HTML page of the channel. The following two lines set the name and location of the ABC New.com channel:

```
9      chan.url ="http://netcaster.abcnews.com/netcaster/webtop/
       webtopreal.html";
10     chan.name = "ABC News";          // Set Channel Name
```

The Netcaster Object

The Netcaster object enables programmers to interface with the Netcaster API. The Netcaster object defines three public methods:

Method: `activate()`

Argument: None

Description: Launches Netcaster. Note that Netcaster must be running in order to process new channel subscriptions.

Example:

```
components["netcaster"].activate();
```

Method: `addObject()`

Argument: `channelObject`—A variable representing a channel object previously returned by the `getChannelObject` method.

Description: The `addChannel` method completes the subscription process by adding the channel specified in the `channelObject` parameter to the user's My Channels list.

Example:

```
components["netcaster"].addChannel (channelObject);
```

Method: `getChannelObject()`

Argument: None

Returns: A Netcaster channel object.

Description: Returns a new channel object, preinitialized with default values.

Example:

```
var chan = components["netcaster"].getChannelObject();
```

7.2.5 Schedule Properties

As a channel publisher, you can set a recommended update schedule for your channel. But, remember that users always have the option of overriding your recommended schedule.

The `intervalTime` property specifies the schedule for automatic channel updates, in minutes. An `intervalTime` of 30, for example, schedules a channel update every 30 minutes. An `intervalTime` of 720, as shown in

Required Channel Properties

Property: `name`

Specifies: User-visible name of the channel.

Syntax: `channelObject.name = "string";`

Parameters: `channelObject` is a variable representing a channel object previously returned by the `getChannelObject` method. `string` is a string representing the name of the channel.

Description: The `name` property identifies the channel. After the channel is added, the name appears on a tab in Netcaster's My Channels list. The `name` property is required and must be set before the channel object can be passed as a parameter with the `addChannel` method call.

Example:

```
var nc = components["netcaster"];
import nc.getChannelObject;
import nc.addChannel;
var chan = nc.getChannelObject();
chan.name = "The Super News Channel";
```

Property: `url`

Specifies: URL of the channel.

Syntax: `channelObject.url = "string";`

Parameters: `channelObject` is a variable representing a channel object previously returned by the `getChannelObject` method. `string` is a string representing a complete URL address for the channel.

Description: The `url` property points to the top-level HTML page of the channel. The `url` property is required and must be set before the channel object can be passed as a parameter with the `addChannel` method call.

Example:

```
var nc = components["netcaster"];
import nc.getChannelObject;
import nc.addChannel;
var chan = nc.getChannelObject();
chan.url = "http://www.supernews.com";
```

Listing 7-1, schedules a channel update every 12 hours. Special negative **intervalTime** values also are reserved for predefined times: −3 is every 30 minutes, −4 is every hour, −5 is daily, and −6 is weekly.

Theoretically, Netcaster should be able to handle any **intervalTime** down to the minute. But, in its current incarnation, Netcaster really only accepts the following restricted values:

Time Period	intervalTime	Reserved Negative Value
30 minutes	30 minutes	−3
1 hour	60 minutes	−4
2 hours	120 minutes	
3 hours	180 minutes	
12 hours	720 minutes	
daily		−5
weekly		−6

These are the exact values that correspond to the pull-down schedule options in the Netcaster interface. If you enter an **intervalTime** outside of these defaults, Netcaster tries to round up or down to the nearest default value. An **intervalTime** of 750 minutes therefore is rounded down to 720 minutes or 12 hours. Note that you might encounter some unpredictable results, however. If you set **intervalTime** to 15 minutes, for example, Netcaster erroneously rounds up to 12 hours! And, if you enter 1400 for a 24-hour daily update, it is rounded down to 12 hours! It therefore is advisable to always stick with the default values recommended here.

If you choose to set a daily or weekly update schedule, it is possible to set the exact day and time for channel updates. By default, daily updates occur at 12:00 a.m.; weekly updates occur at Sunday 12:00 a.m. You can override these default times by setting the **absoluteTime** property. The **absoluteTime** value enables you to set the exact time and day, in minutes after Sunday at midnight.

To set a channel update for Monday at 6:00 a.m., for example, you add the number of minutes for Monday (1440 minutes past Sunday midnight) plus the number of minutes for 6:00 a.m. (360) = 1800:

```
chan.intervalTime = -6;
chan.absoluteTime = 1800;
```

Channel Schedule Properties

Property: **`absoluteTime`**

Specifies: Absolute download time for the channel content.

Syntax: `channelObject.absoluteTime = time`

Parameters: `channelObject` is a variable representing a channel object previously returned by the `getChannelObject` method. `time` is an integer value representing the absolute time for downloading, in minutes after midnight on Sunday.

Description: `absoluteTime` sets the exact time for channel updates. `absoluteTime` is used only if `intervalTime` has been set for daily (−5) or weekly (−6) updates.

For daily updates, `time` represents the absolute time, in minutes after midnight. Acceptable bounds for daily events are 0–1339 minutes. This represents a time range of 12:00 a.m. through 11:59 p.m.

For weekly updates, `time` represents the absolute time, in minutes after midnight on Sunday. Acceptable bounds for weekly events are 0–10,079 minutes. This represents a time range of Sunday 12:00 a.m. through Saturday 11:59 p.m.

To set a channel update for Monday at 6:00 a.m., for example, you add the number of minutes for Monday (1440 minutes past Sunday midnight) plus the number of minutes for 6:00 a.m. (360) = 1800.

Example:

```
nc = components["netcaster"];
import nc.getChannelObject;
var chan = getChannelObject();
// Update channel every Monday at 6:00 am
chan.intervalTime = -6;
chan.absoluteTime = 1800;
```

Property: **`intervalTime`**

Specifies: Download interval time for the channel.

Syntax: `channelObject.intervalTime = period`

Parameters: `channelObject` is a variable representing a channel object previously returned by the `getChannelObject` method. `period` is an integer value representing the interval period, in minutes, or one of the special negative values.

Description: **intervalTime** sets the Netcaster schedule for automatically updating channel contents. The period denotes number of minutes between each update. The **intervalTime** property is optional. Special negative values represent predefined times—−3 is every 30 minutes, −4 is every hour, −5 is daily, and −6 is weekly.

When **intervalTime** is set to −5 (daily) or −6 (weekly), you can set the exact time and date for channel updates with the **absoluteTime** property.

Example:

```
var nc = components["netcaster"];
import nc.getChannelObject;
var chan = nc.getChannelObject();
//  Update every 60 minutes
chan.intervalTime = 60;
```

Table 7-1 provides an easy conversion chart for converting weekdays to number of minutes.

7.2.6 Cache Properties

As a channel publisher, you can set a number of recommended default values for your channel's caching mechanism. Listing 7-1, for example, sets two important cache properties:

Table 7-1

The **absoluteTime** Property: Converting Weekdays to Number of Minutes

Day	Value
Sunday	0
Monday	1440
Tuesday	2880
Wednesday	4320
Thursday	5760
Friday	7200
Saturday	8640

```
chan.maxCacheSize = 5120000;    // Set Max Cache Size
                                // to 5,000 KB
chan.depth = 3;                 // Burrow 3 levels
                                // deeps
```

If you recall the subscription process outlined in Chapter 6, both these properties should be familiar to you. **depth** represents the number of levels to retrieve in the Web hierarchy. This can be a value between 1 and 99. **maxCacheSize** represents the maximum hard drive allocation for the channel, in bytes. **maxCacheSize** can be any value between 1 and 1,047,527,424 (approximately 1 gigabyte).

In Listing 7-1, we set our channel to retrieve three levels of the Web site and allocated 5000 Kbytes of hard drive space.

As noted in Chapter 6, setting the **depth** and **maxCacheSize** properties can be a difficult decision and involves several tradeoffs. If you set **depth** to burrow deeply into a Web hierarchy and allocate a large cache, your subscribers will spend an inordinate amount of time downloading new files. This wastes time, bandwidth, and hard drive space. On the other hand, if you don't dig deep enough and set a low maximum cache target, users will not download all the information they need. This can eliminate many of the speed benefits of caching and defeat the entire purpose of subscribing to a channel in the first place.

As you build your channels, you might need to experiment with these parameters to meet the specific needs of both your content and your audience. To limit the bandwidth necessary for your channel, it is recommended that you start out with **depth** set to 2 or 3. Anything higher is likely to require long channel updates. It also is recommended that you place your most important news and information on the first two levels of your Web site. This ensures that users have easy access to your most important information without making additional network connections.

Note that the Netcaster interface also includes an **estCacheSize** property. This property currently is not implemented in Netcaster 1.0 but will be included in later versions.

7.2.7 Display and Channel Type Properties

Listing 7-1 now has only two remaining properties:

```
chan.mode= "webtop";      // Set display mode to webtop
chan.type=1;              // Type = HTML Channel
```

Channel Cache Properties

Property: depth

Specifies: Link hierarchy depth of the channel to be downloaded into the cache.

Syntax: `channelObject.depth = value`

Parameters: `channelObject` is a variable representing a channel object previously returned by the `getChannelObject` method. `value` is an integer value between 1 and 99.

Description: The `depth` property represents the number of levels to retrieve in the Web hierarchy. This can be a value between 1 and 99. If depth is set to 1, Netcaster simply retrieves the top page in the Web hierarchy; if `depth` is set to 2, Netcaster retrieves the top page plus all the links referenced in the first page, and so on.

Setting the `depth` property does involve some tradeoffs. If `depth` is set too high, Netcaster spends an inordinate amount of time digging into the given Web site, which wastes time and hard drive space. If `depth` is set too low, Netcaster retrieves only a small subset of the Web site, requiring users to make additional network connections to retrieve important information.

Example:

```
var nc = components["netcaster"];
import nc.getChannelObject;
var chan = nc.getChannelObject();
//  Set depth to 3 levels
chan.depth = 3;
```

Property: maxCacheSize

Specifies: Maximum cache size for the channel.

Syntax: `channelObject.maxCacheSize = size`

Parameters: `channelObject` is a variable representing a channel object previously returned by the `getChannelObject` method. `size` is an integer value between 1 and 1,047,527,424 representing the estimated cache size in bytes.

Description: `maxCacheSize` represents the maximum amount of hard disk space required to store the channel's contents on the client's computer. Values are represented in bytes.

Setting the **maxCacheSize** property does involve some tradeoffs. If **maxCacheSize** is large, Netcaster spends an inordinate amount of time digging into the given Web site, which wastes time and hard drive space. If **maxCacheSize** is small, Netcaster retrieves only a small subset of the Web site, requiring users to make additional network connections to retrieve important information.

Example:

```
var nc = components["netcaster"];
import nc.getChannelObject;
var chan = nc.getChannelObject();
//  Set maximum cache size to 1 MB
chan.maxCacheSize = 1048576;
```

The **mode** property sets the display mode of your channel. Possible values are **"webtop"** and **"window"**. Here, we set the ABC News channel as a Webtop.

In future versions of Netcaster, you will be able to set recommended coordinates and dimensions for Webtops and windows. Specifically, the Netcaster API will include four methods: **topHint**, **leftHint**, **widthHint**, and **heightHint**. Currently, these properties are not implemented in Netcaster 1.0 but are included in the sidebar for future reference.

7.2.8 The addChannel Method

With all the channel's properties set, we can proceed to add the channel to the user's list of subscribed channels. To do this, we call the **addChannel** method of the Netcaster object:

```
addChannel(chan);                      // Add Channel to
                                       // Netcaster
```

By calling **addChannel**, Netcaster initiates the subscription process. The user is prompted to set the channel's settings and to confirm or cancel the subscription.

If you haven't done so already, try out the example and make sure that everything is in working order.

Channel Display and Type Properties

Property: mode

Specifies: Display mode of the channel.

Syntax: `channelObject.mode = "string"`

Parameters: `channelObject` is a variable representing a channel object previously returned by the `getChannelObject` method. `string` is one of the two strings: `window` or `webtop`.

Description: `mode` sets the onscreen appearance of your channel. If the value of `string` is `window`, Netcaster opens the channel into a regular Communicator window. If the value of `string` is `webtop`, Netcaster opens the channel into a chromeless window locked to the backmost layer of the user's display.

Example:

```
var nc = components["netcaster"];
import nc.getChannelObject;
var chan = nc.getChannelObject();
//  Set to webtop mode
chan.mode = "webtop";
```

Property: type

Specifies: Type of channel.

Syntax: `channelObject.type = integer`

Parameters: `channelObject` is a variable representing a channel object previously returned by the `getChannelObject` method. `integer` is one of the two integers: 1 for Netcaster channels and 2 for Castanet channels.

Description: Identifies the type of channel. Currently, there are only two types of channels: 1 for regular HTML Netcaster channels and 2 for Castanet channels.

Example:

```
var nc = components["netcaster"];
import nc.getChannelObject;
var chan = nc.getChannelObject();
//  Set to Netcaster HTML Channel
chan.type = 1;
```

Method: `heightHint`

Specifies: Preferred height of the channel window.

Syntax: `channelObject.heightHint = value`

Parameters: `channelObject` is a variable representing a channel object previously returned by the `getChannelObject` method. `value` is an integer value representing the number of pixels.

Method: `leftHint`

Specifies: Preferred horizontal position of the channel window relative to the left edge of the display.

Syntax: `channelObject.leftHint = value`

Parameters: `channelObject` is a variable representing a channel object previously returned by the `getChannelObject` method. `value` is an integer value representing the number of pixels.

Method: `topHint`

Specifies: Preferred vertical position of the channel window relative to the top edge of the display.

Syntax: `channelObject.topHint = value`

Parameters: `channelObject` is a variable representing a channel object previously returned by the `getChannelObject` method. `value` is an integer value representing the number of pixels.

Method: `widthHint`

Specifies: Preferred width of the channel window.

Syntax: `channelObject.widthHint = value`

Parameters: `channelObject` is a variable representing a channel object previously returned by the `getChannelObject` method. `value` is an integer value representing the number of pixels.

7.3 The Add Channel Wizard

7.3.1 Ensuring Browser Compatibility

The example in Listing 7-1 does a good job of explaining the fundamentals of the Netcaster API. But, unfortunately, this example also includes a number of pitfalls that can trip up potential subscribers. Unless the subscriber is using the latest Netscape Communicator 4.02 or higher and Netcaster is running when the user attempts to subscribe, our JavaScript code panics and displays a series of errors. Here are the specific pitfalls that may occur:

- If Netcaster is not running when users subscribe to the channel, users receive a JavaScript alert informing them that `getChannelObject()` is not a function. This occurs because the Netcaster API is available only when Netcaster is installed and running.
- If the subscriber is using an earlier version of Navigator, such as 3.0 or lower, the browser is unable to access the Netcaster API and produces a series of errors.
- If the subscriber is using Internet Explorer, our JavaScript code produces a whole other series of errors instead of pointing users to additional options, such as a CDF Active Channel.

The example in Listing 7-1 therefore is far from ideal for actual deployment on the Internet. Too many users are likely to receive complicated JavaScript errors and assume that your channel simply does not work.

7.3.2 Getting the Add Channel Wizard

How do we address the pitfalls that arise from Listing 7-1? The simple answer is to use the Netscape Add Channel Wizard (`http://developer.netscape.com`). The Add Channel Wizard provides a simple interface for creating Netcaster channels from scratch without any knowledge of JavaScript. And, the JavaScript code created by the Add Channel Wizard includes built-in testing for the pitfalls outlined earlier.

JavaScript Tip: Creating and Using Functions

Functions are one of the most important tools for creating manageable and readable code. They enable programmers to take a large, often complex program and break it up into small, focused building blocks. These building blocks usually refer to a group of related statements and are easier to debug, modify, and maintain.

To define a JavaScript function in its simplest form, you can use the following syntax:

```
function function-name ( ) {
// function body here
}
```

The following function prompts the user with a short greeting:

```
     function userMsg () {
     alert ('Hi There!');
}
```

To activate a function, you write out the function name, followed by matching parentheses. The HTML code that follows, for example, associates the **onClick** event handler with the **userMsg** function defined here. Note that the **userMsg** function is declared inside the **<SCRIPT>** tags, whereas the **onClick** event handler simply is defined within the **<INPUT>** HTML tag:

```
<HTML>
<HEAD><TITLE>Sample Function Page</TITLE></HEAD>
<SCRIPT>
function userMsg () {
     alert ('Hi There!');\}
</SCRIPT>
<BODY>
<FORM>
<INPUT TYPE="button" VALUE="Click here!"
onClick="userMsg();">
</FORM>
</BODY>
</HTML>
```

7.3.3 Using the Add Channel Wizard

The Add Channel Wizard presents a series of form pages to identify and set your channel's properties (see Figures 7-2 through 7-5). Follow the pages and set your channel's name, location, schedule, cache, and display properties. After you complete the channel properties, the Wizard creates a customized JavaScript program that you can cut and paste into a separate HTML document.

Figure 7-2
Netcaster Add Channel Wizard, screen 1

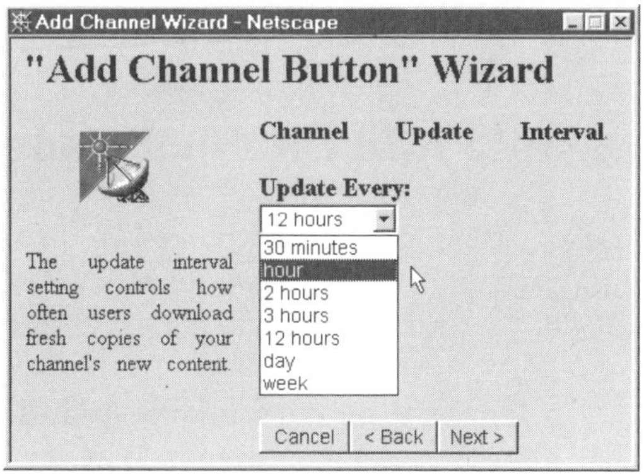

Figure 7-3
Netcaster Add Channel Wizard, screen 2

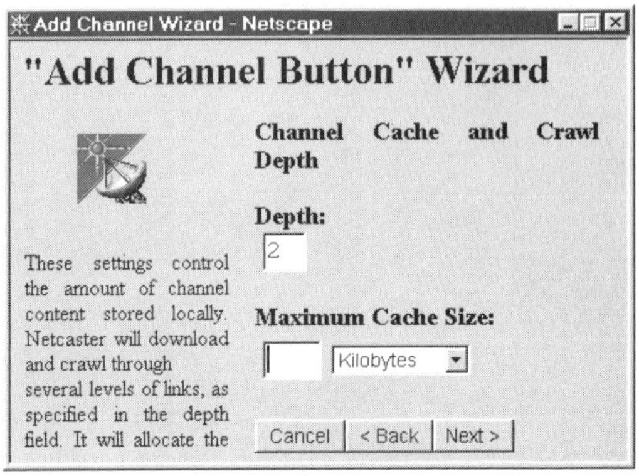

Figure 7-4 Netcaster Add Channel Wizard, screen 3

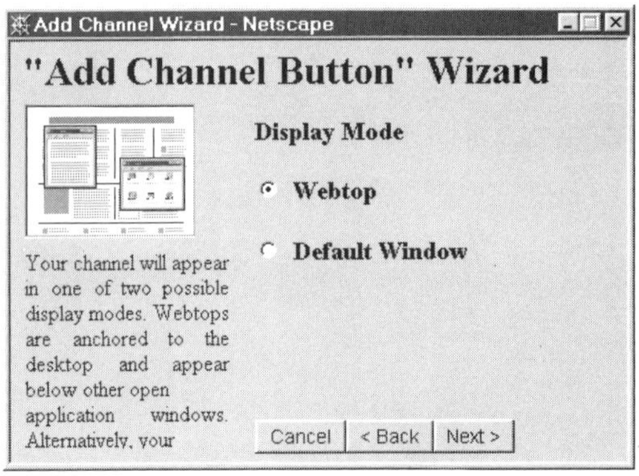

Figure 7-5 Netcaster Add Channel Wizard, screen 4

7.3.4 Sample Add Channel Code

The JavaScript code created by the Channel Wizard is quite instructional. And, if you do not end up using the Wizard, its JavaScript code still can serve as a model for dealing with the potential pitfalls described in Section 7.3.1.

Listing 7-2 includes the output from the Add Channel Wizard for our ABC News channel. Take a moment to look at the code before we examine it in detail.

Here are the highlights of the Add Channel Wizard code:

First, lines 72–75 add the Netcaster GIF image for attracting new subscribers.

Second, after the user clicks the Netcaster GIF image, the **addChannelAPI** function is called. But, if you look closely, you will notice two **addChannelAPI** functions (lines 4 and 50). JavaScript has strict conventions regarding the interpretation of JavaScript versioning. Any browser that implements JavaScript will execute statements embedded inside a **<SCRIPT LANGUAGE="JavaScript">** tag. But only Netscape Communicator 4.0 will execute statements embedded inside a **<SCRIPT LANGUAGE="JavaScript 1.2">** tag.

Therefore, if the user is running Netscape Communicator 4.0, the second **addChannelAPI** function (line 50) is called, and the subscription process proceeds. If, on the other hand, the user is using Netscape Navigator 3.0 or earlier, or any version of Internet Explorer, the first **addChannelAPI** function (line 4) is called. This function opens a new window with information on downloading Netscape Communicator. You could modify this URL to point to a custom download page with additional information regarding CDF Active Channels, if any.

Third, the **netcasterSniffer** function (lines 33–49) checks to make sure that Netcaster is installed and running. If Netcaster is not running,

JavaScript Tip: Setting Object Properties

In object-oriented programming languages, every object has a set of internal variables and a set of methods or functions. In JavaScript, these internal variables usually are referred to as *properties*. The JavaScript document object, for example, contains a number of properties that correspond to the currently displayed HTML document. Among its many properties are **bgColor**, to indicate the current background color, **fgColor**, to indicate the current text color, and **alinkColor**, to indicate the color of hypertext links.

To read or write an object's property, you use the following syntax: **[object].[property]**. The **.** operator is an accessor method for reading and writing property values. To set the current background color to black, for example, you would type the following:

```
document.bgColor = "000000";
```

To display the current background color within an HTML document (possibly for debugging purposes), you would use this syntax:

```
document.write (document.bgColor);
```

Listing 7-2: The Add Channel Wizard Output

```
<SCRIPT LANGUAGE="JavaScript">
function needNetcaster() {
window.open("http://netcaster.netscape.com/finder/nee
  _netcaster.html","need_netcaster","width=500,height=4
  0,titlebar=yes,toolbar=no,location=no,directories=no,
  status=yes,menubar=no,scrollbars=yes");}
function addChannelAPI() {
   needNetcaster(); }
</SCRIPT>
<SCRIPT LANGUAGE="JavaScript1.2">
   var chanURL = http://netcaster.abcnews.com/
netcaster/webtop/
webtopreal.html";
   var chanName = "ABC News";
   var chanIntervalTime = 720;
   var chanMaxCacheSize = 5120000;
   var chanDepth = 3;
   var chanActive = 1;
   var chanMode = "webtop";
   var chanType=1;
   var getChannelObject = null;
   var addChannel = null;
   var nc = null;
   var ncActive = 0;
   var poller = null;

function activateNetcaster() {
   nc.activate();
}
function pollActive() {
   if (nc.active) {
      ncActive=1;
      setTimeout(addChannelAPI,10000);
      clearInterval(poller);
   }
}

function netcasterSniffer() {
   if (!components["netcaster"]) {
      alert("This page requires the Netcaster
      component.");
      needNetcaster();
   }
   else {
      nc = components["netcaster"];
      if (nc.active == false) {
            activateNetcaster();
```

Listing 7-2: Continued.

```
42                  poller=setInterval(pollActive,500);
43            }
44            else {
45                  ncActive = 1;
46                  addChannelAPI();
47            }
48        }
49    }
50    function addChannelAPI() {
51        if (ncActive == 0) netcasterSniffer();
52        else {
53            nc = components["netcaster"];
54            import nc.getChannelObject;
55            import nc.addChannel;
56            var chan = getChannelObject();
57            chan.url = chanURL;
58            chan.name = chanName;
59            chan.intervalTime = chanIntervalTime;
60            chan.maxCacheSize = chanMaxCacheSize;
61            chan.depth = chanDepth;
62            chan.active = chanActive;
63            chan.mode=chanMode;
64            chan.type=chanType;
65            addChannel(chan);
66        }
67        ncActive = 0;
68    }
69    function clikImg() {}
70    </SCRIPT>
71    <TABLE><TR><TD ALIGN="CENTER">
72    <A HREF="#" onClick="addChannelAPI(); clikImg();
         return(false);">
73    <IMG NAME="ncnowimage"
      SRC="http://home.netscape.com/inserts/images/
      ncnow.gif" WIDTH=117 HEIGHT=55 BORDER=0 ALT="Add ABC
      News Now!"><br>
74     Add ABC News Now!
75     </a></td></tr></table>
76     </script>
```

it launches it with the Netcaster **activate()** method. But, because Netcaster can take several seconds to load up, the code also includes a **pollActive ()** function (lines 25–31). This function checks the active property of Netcaster every half second and proceeds with the subscription process when Netcaster is fully initialized.

7.4 Potential Pitfalls

With your JavaScript code in hand, you may be tempted to immediately deploy your Netcaster channel. But, before you do begin deployment, pay close attention to the potential pitfalls described in this section.

7.4.1 Page Aliases and Server Redirection

Netcaster 1.0 has serious difficulties dealing with page aliases and server redirection. Page aliases represent a shorthand mechanism for identifying URLs. A user may enter the URL `http://www.acme.com`, for example. The Acme sever receives this request and understands that if no specific file is requested, it is required to return the default page alias `index.htm`. The server therefore returns the HTML file associated with the complete URL: `http://www.acme.com/index.htm`.

Unfortunately, Netcaster 1.0 cannot discern the difference between the page that is requested originally and the page that actually is returned by the server. In parsing the top-level page of a Web channel, for example, Netcaster extracts the URL for `http://www.acme.com`. Netcaster then retrieves the URL. For each page in the Web hierarchy, Netcaster places the URL in a special cache directory table. But, because of page aliasing, Netcaster stores the full URL, `http://www.acme.com/index.htm`, in the cache table.

Later, when the user is viewing the channel contents, the user clicks on the link for `http://www.acme.com`. Netcaster searches for a match in the cache table but does not find an exact match. It therefore proceeds to make additional networks connections to download the already cached page!

Netcaster Properties

Property: `active`
Returns: True if the Netcaster component is installed and running.
Syntax: `components["netcaster"].active`
Property: `componentVersion`
Returns: Version number of the component.
Syntax: `components["netcaster"].componentVersion`

This exact sort of error can occur with server redirection. Server redirection occurs when a server receives a specific URL request but decides to forward the request to another URL address. A user may try to connect to `http://www.acme.com`, for example, and be directed to `http://server1.acme.com`. Most of the time, this process is completely hidden from the user. But, again, Netcaster fails because it indexes the HTML page by the URL returned by the server redirect, not the URL originally requested.

Both these bugs are quite serious and can completely eliminate many of the offline and speedy cache capabilities provided by Netcaster. Future Netcaster releases certainly will include bug patches, but for now, the solution is actually quite simple:

- Do not use page aliases. Check all the URLs in your Netcaster HTML channel, and check for page aliases. Replace any page aliases with the full filename. Change anything of the form `http://www.acme.com`, for example, to `http://www.acme.com/index.htm`.
- Do not use server redirection in any of your Netcaster HTML documents.

7.4.2 Embedded JavaScript Code

During its Web crawl, Netcaster downloads any HTML documents with JavaScript code or any separate JavaScript (`.js`) files. But, it will not execute any of the JavaScript code until the user decides to view the channel. Therefore, if your JavaScript code includes any reference to opening URLs or retrieving images, there is a very good chance that these URLs and images will not be precached by Netcaster.

When Netcaster executes the JavaScript code, it attempts to locate the cached URLs or images. More often than not, however, it fails to find the items and is required to make additional network connections. This is more than likely to drive your offline and laptop subscribers completely nuts!

Fortunately, there is a simple trick for resolving this issue. Suppose that you have the following simplistic `getHelp` function in your top-level HTML page:

```
function getHelp () {
      window.open ("http://www.acme.com/help/index.htm");
}
```

Netcaster dutifully downloads the JavaScript function but postpones its execution. But, because it postpones execution, Netcaster has no foreknowledge that it needs to download the **help.htm** file. Your offline and laptop users have just been stranded without help.

You can trick Netcaster into downloading the help file by including it as an invisible link in your top-level HTML page:

```
<A HREF="http://www.acme.com/help/help.htm"></A>
```

No text here

When Netcaster encounters this tag, it downloads the file to the user's cache, but it does not display it or any possible links. When the JavaScript code is executed, the help file is immediately at hand.

For each URL referenced within your JavaScript code, you should include one of these invisible links. This is particularly important if you are performing any sort of image rollover. When the user's cursor is over a particular graphic, you might want to swap graphics files. But, you must make sure that the images are resident in the Netcaster cache.

7.4.3 Embedded Java Applets

You must exercise caution when embedding Java applets. Most Java applets consist of multiple Java class files. The main class file is indicated in the **applet** tag:

```
<applet code = "Game" width = 400 height = 400>
</applet>
```

The browser first executes this class file and then dynamically downloads the remaining class files. In this case, the browser first loads the **Game** class file and then dynamically loads the **Player** and **Monster** class files.

Again, Netcaster dutifully downloads the `Game` class. But it postpones execution until the user launches the channel. And, because it has postponed execution, it has no way of knowing which additional class files it needs. If your applet also requests specific image or sound files, Netcaster remains unaware of these requests as well. Your subscribers again are left with either no applet or additional network connections.

Again, the solution is quite simple. Your can place each class file and each Java resource file (including images and sounds) in an invisible tag. Or, you can place your entire Java program within a single *Java archive* (JAR) file. Placing your program in a JAR file is usually the best option, because it ensures that your applet has everything it needs to work properly. And, channel updates are much more efficient, because JAR files are compressed zip files and are sent in a single TCP/IP connection.

SUMMARY

Creating Netcaster channels is simply a matter of accessing the new JavaScript 1.2 Netcaster API. The Netcaster API includes two important methods: **`getChannelObject`** and **`addChannel`**. You use **`getChannelObject`** to receive a preinitialized channel object. You then set your channel's properties, including schedule, cache, and display properties. And, after the channel is initialized with the proper settings, you call the **`addChannel`** method to add the channel to the user's list of subscribed channels.

As you develop your Netcaster channels, beware of the potential pitfalls. First, make sure that your JavaScript code fails gracefully when run by a browser other than Netscape Communicator 4.0. Second, include specific error-checking code to make sure that Netcaster is indeed installed and running. To avoid both these pitfalls, it is highly recommended that you use Netscape's Add Channel Wizard. Third, avoid page aliasing and server redirection. And, fourth, make sure that your JavaScript programs and Java applets work successfully while in offline mode.

Online Resource

- Netcaster Developer's Guide
  `http://developer.netscape.com/library/documentation/netcast/devguide/contents.htm`. The definitive reference for building Netcaster channels. Check here for updates to the Netcaster API.

PART III

Microsoft's Active Channels

CHAPTER 8

Introduction to I.E. 4.0 Active Channels

Microsoft's Internet Explorer 4.0 represents a significant software upgrade. And it is perhaps one of the most eagerly anticipated pieces of software since Windows 95. At stake is not just the future of Web browsing software (and the future of Netscape), but Microsoft's entire gamble to capture the Internet software and content markets.

Internet Explorer 4.0 also represents more than just an upgrade to the Web-browsing capabilities of IE 3.0. In fact, IE 4.0 is an upgrade to the entire Windows 95/NT operating system.

This upgrade was described best by one reviewer as the search for the "unified field theory." For years, Einstein toiled away searching for a way to unify the diverse fields of gravity and electromagnetism, hoping to find a single, simple equation to connect the two. Unfortunately, he failed and, in his darkest moments of research, found himself in the "agony of mathematical torment." *

In contrast, the makers of IE 4.0 have toiled away searching for a way to unify the world of the personal computer with the world of the Internet. The ostensible goal is to present one unified view for browsing documents on the PC and browsing documents downloaded off the World Wide Web. It's all just data, after all, and you should be able to access your office memos from your hard drive just as easily as you access trade figures from Hong Kong.

Whether Microsoft has succeeded in this goal is open to debate. And we are likely to see a continually evolving strategy, particularly with the upcoming release of Windows 98.

But, after all, this is a book about push. And, leaving aside all the other new features, let's begin with an overview of IE 4.0's built-in push capabilities.

8.1 IE 4.0 Push Features

The primary push feature of Internet Explorer 4.0 is complete support for *Channel Definition Format* (CDF) channels (henceforth also known as *Microsoft Active Channels*). We therefore begin our detailed discussion of IE 4.0 features with an overview of Web site subscriptions versus Active Channel CDF subscriptions.

8.1.1 Web Site Subscriptions

Much like Netscape Netcaster, Internet Explorer enables users to subscribe to any existing Web site. And, much like Netcaster, users can customize their own update schedule and specify the number of levels to retrieve in the Web hierarchy.

*Ashley Dunn, "Internet Explorer 4.0: The Unified Field Theory," *New York Times*, April 16, 1997.

At the specified update interval, Explorer performs an automated Web crawl on the specified Web site and downloads new information. To speed up channel updates, Explorer downloads only new information that has been modified since the last update.

The primary advantage of Web crawling is that any Web site easily can be converted to a Web channel. And, content providers can reuse much of their existing content.

8.1.2 Active Channel Subscriptions

In contrast to Web site subscriptions, CDF-enabled Active Channels provide a more coherent structure for delivering channel contents. The particulars of creating CDF channels are discussed in Chapter 10, "Creating Active Channels." But, for now, let us examine CDF from the end-user perspective.

Each time a user subscribes to an Active Channel, Explorer downloads a CDF file. This CDF file provides Explorer with all the necessary information pertaining to this channel, including its name, description, and update schedule. The CDF file also includes a table of contents detailing all the articles that are included within the channel.

Explorer parses the CDF file, downloads the specified articles, and displays the CDF table of contents (see Figure 8-1). From an end-user perspective, CDF therefore provides a coherent framework for browsing or reading a channel. From a channel-developer perspective, CDF provides a coherent framework for organizing channel content. And, from a technical perspective, CDF provides an easy means of circumventing the (often long) downloads associated with Web crawling.

8.1.3 Complete User Customization

IE 4.0 is completely customizable for both corporate users with direct Internet connections and home users with modems. For each channel, users can opt to follow the recommended update schedule provided by the channel publisher or to create their own customized schedule.

Users also have complete control over the notification and download options associated with each channel. Each time new information is downloaded, Explorer displays a small red gleam on the Favorites pull-down menu. But users also have the option of receiving channel updates via

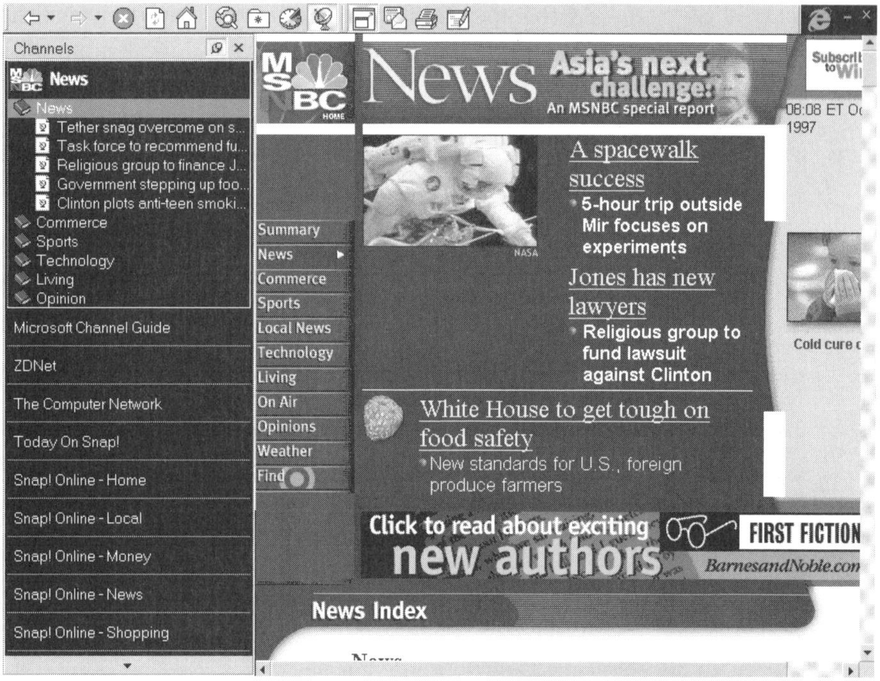

Figure 8-1
Explorer displays the CDF table of contents directly inside the Active Channel bar for easy user navigation.

e-mail. And users have complete control over the amount of information downloaded during each channel update. They can specify a maximum hard drive allocation for each channel, for example, or specify the types of content (images, Java applets, ActiveX controls, and so on) that are downloaded automatically. By limiting the hard drive allocation to a minimum and restricting content types to HTML and GIF images, it is possible to speed up channel updates while ensuring the delivery of the most critical data.

8.1.4 Offline Browsing

After channel contents are downloaded to the user's hard drive, they are available for offline browsing. You therefore can browse your favorite Web sites and channels without being connected to the Internet. This is particularly useful for home users with slow modem connections or road warriors with laptop computers.

8.1.5 Complete Support for HTML, Java, and ActiveX

The articles specified in the CDF file table of contents are just regular Web pages. You therefore can push anything that normally would appear within the IE 4.0 browser: dynamic HTML, Java, VBScript, JavaScript, or ActiveX components. The tools and skills you have developed for Web pages are available immediately for your new Web channels.

8.1.6 Premium Channels

Every major push platform has lined up its own roster of premium channels. Microsoft is no exception and already has announced broad support from more than 250 content providers. Here is just a sampling of premium channels currently being offered or under development:

AudioNet
CBS SportsLine
CMPNet
CNET
CNN Interactive
CNNSI
Condenet
Discovery Channel Online
Disney Online
Dun & Bradstreet's and Lycos' Companies Online
ESPN SportsZone
Forbes
Fortune Online
Hollywood Online
Intuit-Quicken Financial Network
iVillage

Microsoft Investor

MSNBC

MTV Networks

National GeographicNew York Times

People

PointCast

Snap Online

Time Online

Universal Press Syndicate

The *Wall Street Journal* Interactive Edition

Warner Bros. Online

Wired Digital

ZDNet

8.1.7 Active Desktop Components

One of the newest features provided by Internet Explorer 4.0 is the active desktop component. *Active desktop components* are small Web pages that are "glued" to the background of the user's desktop. Desktop components therefore are always visible, even when Explorer is not running and can display news headlines or scrolling tickers. When integrated with CDF, these desktop components can display continuously refreshed content and represent an effective medium for delivering real-time (or near real-time) data.

Already, a number of content providers have deployed their own desktop components, enabling users to stay on top of the latest news. The CNET News desktop component, for example, displays the latest technology headlines in a small, simple-to-use format (see Figure 8-2).

8.1.8 Channel Screen Saver

PointCast first started delivering news via its hugely popular screen saver. And Microsoft would like to follow PointCast's lead on this front. Not only can you display channels directly on your desktop with active desktop components, but, you also can display your channels as screen savers.

Figure 8-2 The CNET active desktop component delivers late-breaking technology news.

The Explorer screen saver simply displays an HTML page. But, with the introduction of dynamic HTML, the HTML screen saver can put on quite a show. And, when integrated with CDF, the screen saver content can be refreshed continuously with new information.

8.1.9 Auto-Authentication

Finally, Explorer 4.0 includes built-in support for auto-authentication. This capability enables users to subscribe to premium Web sites or channels that require registration and/or payment. The *New York Times* Web site, for example, requires a username and password. Users can supply their username and password ahead of time, and Explorer forwards the logon information when it contacts the site for channel updates.

8.2 Assessment of IE Push Capabilities

Explorer is definitely here to stay, and it is a good, solid product. But it also certainly has its share of weaknesses. Here is my most objective assessment of IE's push capabilities.

8.2.1 IE's Push Strengths

Easy to use. The subscription capabilities of IE 4.0 are straightforward and easy to use. Subscribing to a Web site is nearly identical to adding it to your Favorites menu, and Explorer includes a built-in Channel Subscription Wizard. The built-in directory of premium channels also makes it extremely easy for new users to get started.

Easy to develop. If you know HTML, you can learn CDF in a few hours. Netscape claims that Netcaster channels are far easier to create, because developers do not have to go through the trouble of learning CDF. But Netscape still requires you to learn the new Netcaster API. The bottom line is that both platforms require you to learn something new. The Netcaster API is not complicated, and neither is CDF. And regardless of the platform, you still can leverage your existing HTML, Java, and JavaScript skills.

CDF works. CDF is an effective format for organizing channel contents and is usually much more efficient than Web crawling. If Microsoft gains approval from the World Wide Web consortium, CDF may become *the* standard for push, and Microsoft will lead the way.

Complete channel customization. Users can view channel contents when and how they want. Channel developers have the option of developing regular Web channels, active desktop components, or HTML screen savers.

Compelling content. As has been stated several times in this book, content is still king. The more content providers you can line up behind your push platform, the more viable the platform itself. Microsoft has racked up an impressive list of 250 premium content providers who are busy deploying new channels.

8.2.2 IE's Push Weaknesses

Windows-centric. Internet Explorer 4.0 was designed primarily for Windows 95/NT. Most of the operating system integration—including active desktop components—is available only for Windows 95/NT and is not available in the Macintosh or UNIX versions.

Inability to push software applications. In its current incarnation, Explorer can handle content, embedded Java applets, and embedded ActiveX components. But it does not provide the automatic delivery and installation of Java applications, such as that provided by Netcaster and Marimba. Microsoft is planning to deliver applications via CDF, but this is not implemented currently.

SUMMARY

Internet Explorer 4.0 includes a full line of built-in push features. The most prominent of these features is complete support for Active Channels, created in the *Channel Definition Format* (CDF.) Explorer also includes support for Web site subscriptions to any existing Web site, offline browsing, active desktop components, and a built-in HTML screen saver.

IE 4.0's push capabilities are quite impressive. Its main strengths include a user-friendly interface with a built-in Subscription Wizard, complete channel customization, and a roster of more than 250 premium content providers. On the flip side, many of IE's newest features are available only on Windows 95/NT and not on Macintosh or UNIX. And, Explorer cannot match the Java-based push capabilities of Netcaster and Marimba's Castanet.

Online Resources

- `http://www.microsoft.com/ie/press/whitepaper/pushwp.htm`

  Webcasting in Microsoft Internet Explorer 4.0 White Paper

  Provides a general overview of IE 4.0 push capabilities, along with a detailed comparison between IE 4.0 Active Channels and Netscape Netcaster.

CHAPTER 9

Using IE 4.0 Active Channels

If you have spent any time working with Internet Explorer 4.0, you probably have already subscribed to at least one Active Channel. But, in case you haven't, this chapter lays out the basics on subscribing and managing Active Channels and Web site subscriptions. It also lays out the basics on using the Microsoft active desktop and the new HTML screen saver. If you are planning to develop your own CDF Active Channels, you probably should take the time to review this chapter and learn the basics from the end-user perspective.

9.1 Subscribing to Active Channels

9.1.1 Subscribing to Premium Channels

Getting started with Active Channels is quite simple. You have three ways to get started:

- You can click the Channels icon on the Windows taskbar (see Figure 9-1).
- You can launch Internet Explorer and click the Channels icon on the main button bar (see Figure 9-2).
- You can use the built-in Active Channel desktop component (refer to Figure 9-1). This component is installed automatically if you choose the Web integration options during IE 4.0 installation.

Figure 9-1 Getting started with Active Channels.

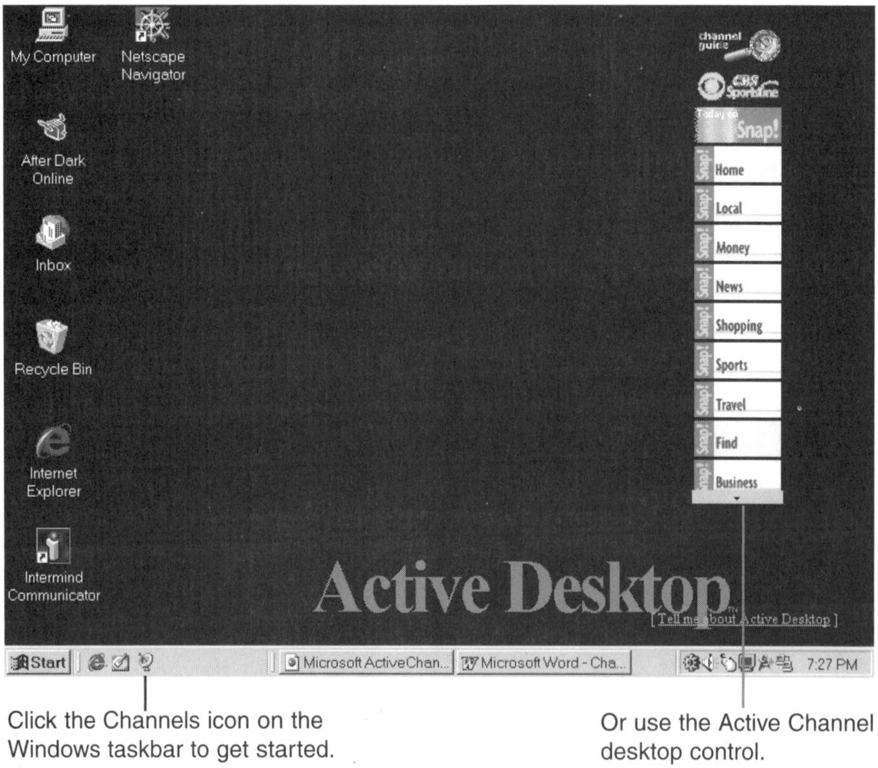

If you follow either of the first two options, your browser opens with a listing of channels on the left-hand side of the screen (see Figure 9-3). This listing is known as the *Active Channel bar* and includes a listing of premium Web channels and Web sites. At the very top of the Channel bar, you will see an icon for the Microsoft Active Channel Guide. Click the Channel Guide icon to navigate to Microsoft's directory of premium channels. As of this writing, the Channel Guide includes five categories of channels: News & Technology, Sports, Business, Entertainment, and Lifestyle & Travel. New categories certainly will be added in the near future. And, the Channel Guide sports a visually compelling interface complete with dynamic HTML, making it extremely easy to browse and search for new channels.

Figure 9-2 Internet Explorer's main button bar.

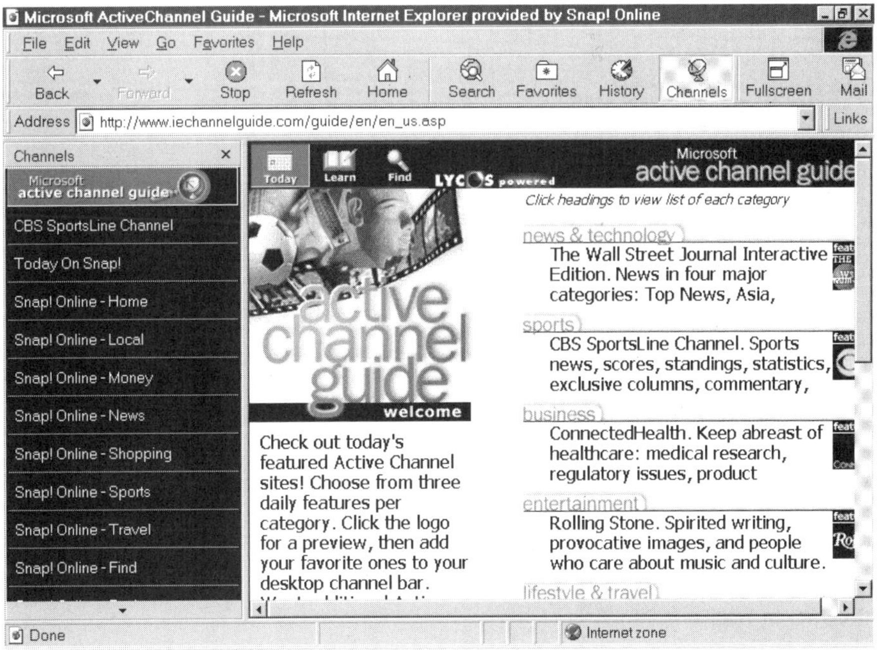

Figure 9-3 The Active Channel bar appears on the left-hand side of the browser window.

From within the Channel Guide, simply follow the onscreen instructions for subscribing to new channels. Each channel has its own preview or summary page. Some channels may require registration; other channels may also offer a menu of channel options. Each channel has its own Add Active Channel button (see Figure 9-4).

After you click the Add Active Channel button, Explorer downloads a *Channel Definition Format* (CDF) file with complete information on the channel contents. This file includes the recommended update schedule and a complete index of articles referenced in the channel (creating this CDF file is the subject of Chapter 10, "Creating Active Channels").

After the CDF file is downloaded (CDF files are extremely small and download in seconds), Explorer launches the Active Channel Subscription Wizard—a multistep guide for customizing your Active Channels.

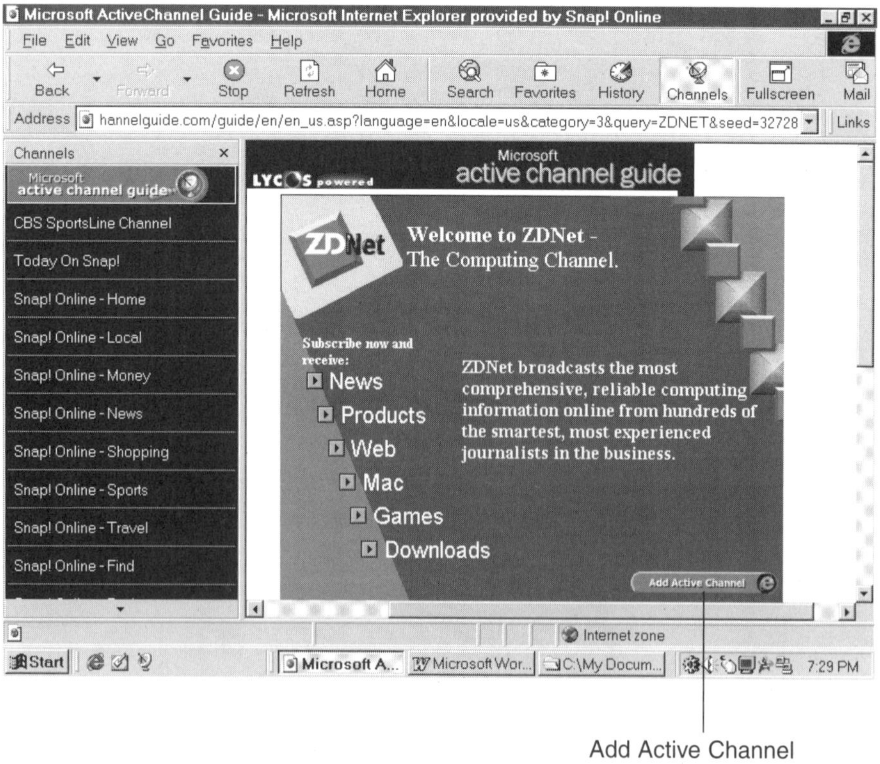

Figure 9-4 Just click the Add Active Channel button to subscribe.

9.1.2 The Subscription Wizard

The first screen in the Subscription Wizard offers three options (see Figure 9-5):

- You simply can add this channel to your Channel bar but not subscribe to it. The Active Channel bar contains a listing of all your favorite channels and Web sites, regardless of whether you are subscribed to them.
- You can subscribe to the channel and choose to be notified of channel updates. This means that Explorer periodically downloads the channel's CDF file but does not download any of the referenced articles.
- You can subscribe to the channel and tell Explorer to download the updated channel contents. This means that Explorer periodically downloads the channel's CDF file and all specified articles. This is the default option.

Simply select an option and click OK. That's all there is to it! Explorer also offers great flexibility in customizing channels. If you want to customize your channel, click the Customize button, and Explorer continues with the Subscription Wizard. The customization options are outlined in the following section.

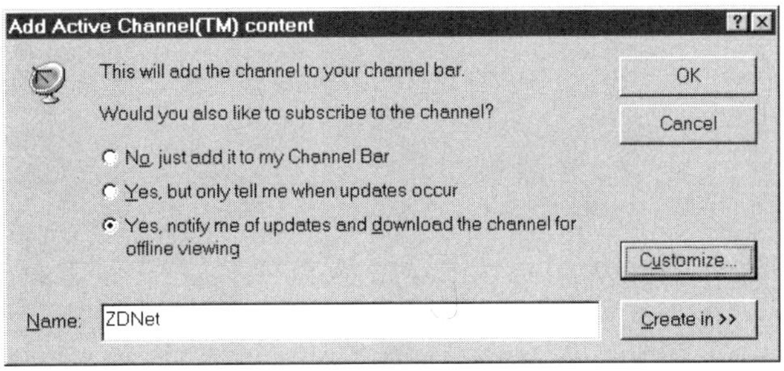

Figure 9-5 The Active Channel Subscription Wizard.

9.1.3 Download Options

The first customization page in the Subscription Wizards deals with automatic download options (see Figure 9-6). The choices here are quite simple. You can download the channel home page (meaning the Channel CDF file plus the channel home page), or you can download all the new channel content. In the latter case, Explorer downloads the CDF file along with all the articles referenced in the CDF file and stores them on your local hard drive.

The option you choose really depends on the type of information you are seeking. If you want to be notified only of new information but don't want to spend too much time downloading the channel contents, the first option is usually a good bet.

9.1.4 E-Mail Notification Options

The next customization page deals with e-mail notification (see Figure 9-7). At the specified update interval, Explorer checks your channel subscriptions and downloads new information. If new information is available, Explorer displays a small gleam on the Favorites pull-down menu (see Figure 9-8). But, you also have the option of receiving updates via e-mail. Click Yes here to receive e-mail updates, and click the Change Address button to set the correct e-mail address. You also might have to set the correct e-mail server name (SMTP) and consult your system administrator for the proper settings.

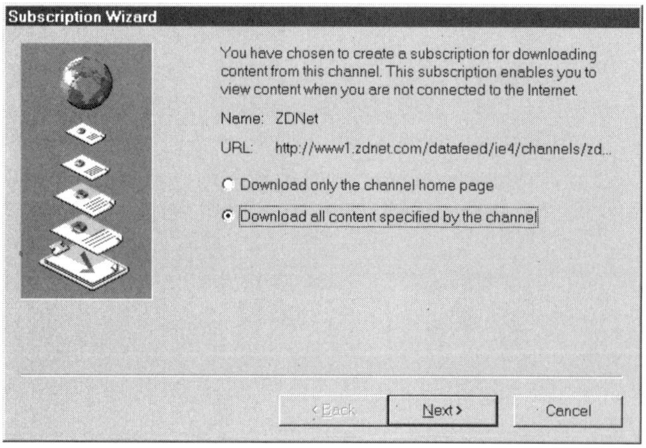

Figure 9-6
Setting download options.

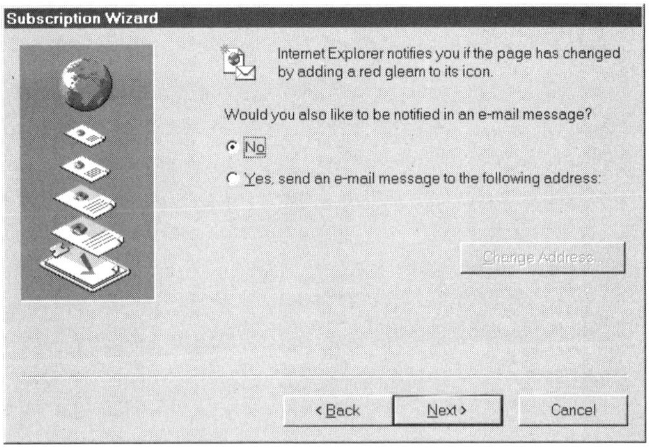

Figure 9-7 Setting e-mail options.

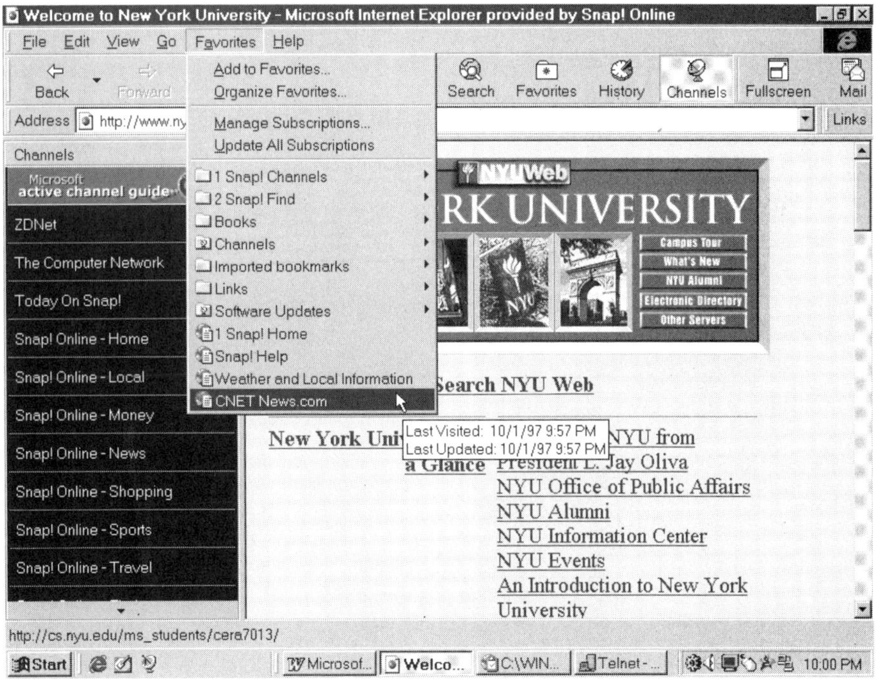

Figure 9-8 When updated information is available, Explorer displays a small gleam on the Favorites pull-down menu. If you hold your mouse cursor over the channel, you can find out when the channel was updated and when you last visited it.

9.1.5 Schedule Options

The final customization options concern the automatic update schedule (see Figure 9-9). Just like every other push product, each channel in Internet Explorer gets its own update schedule. Explorer makes every attempt to follow this schedule and download new information.

Here, you have two basic options: auto-schedule and manual update. If you select Scheduled, you can choose from several default options: daily, weekly, or monthly updates. Or you can choose to follow the channel publisher's recommended update schedule. If you choose this option, the recommended schedule appears in the small text box at the bottom of the Subscription Wizard. You can see in Figure 9-9 that the ZDNet is set to check for updates every day at 1:00 a.m.

You also can create entirely new update schedules. Simply select a predefined update schedule (daily, weekly, or monthly) and click the Edit button. Or, just click the New button to create a new schedule from scratch. In either case, another customization screen appears (see Figure 9-10). This page enables you to define the exact specifics of the frequency of your channel update. If you are creating a new weekly update schedule, for example, you can specify the exact day of the week, along with the exact

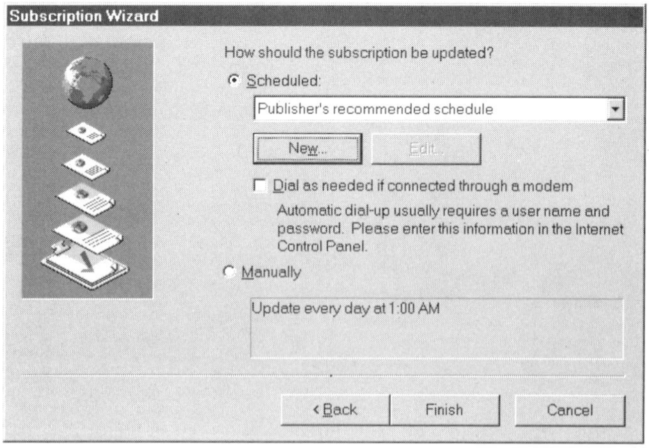

Figure 9-9 Setting schedule options.

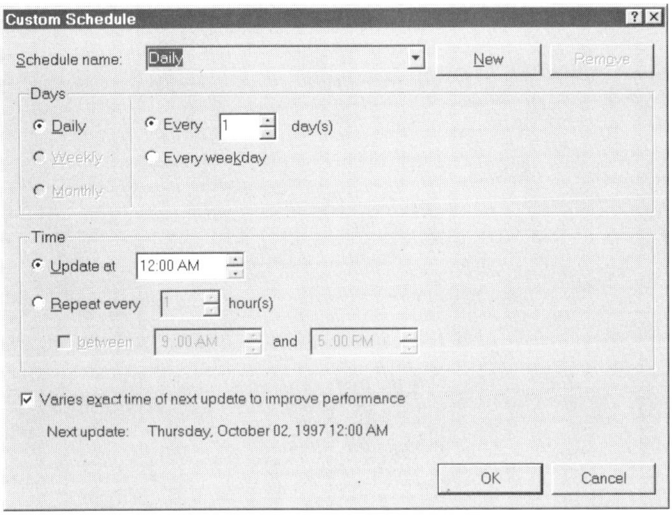

Figure 9-10
Creating a customized schedule.

time. You also can specify that the channel be updated at specified intervals during a certain time range. You can update your channel every hour between 9 a.m. and 5 p.m., for example.

You certainly can create any number of custom schedules for each Active Channel. But, if you are connected via modem, your computer then may start dialing up and disconnecting repeatedly throughout the day. The best option is to pick one custom schedule and set all your Active Channels to that one schedule. That way, all channels are updated at once on the same schedule.

If you do opt for an automated schedule and are connected to the Internet via modem, you have the option of allowing unattended channel updates. If you click this option (refer to Figure 9-9), Explorer connects to your *Internet service provider* (ISP) and downloads new information. But, in order for this to work properly, you must supply Internet Explorer with your logon and password information. You can supply this information in the Explorer Configuration Panel, which is located on the Windows Control Panel (see Figure 9-11).

As a last option, you always can choose to eliminate the auto-scheduling capabilities inherent in Explorer and choose the manual update option. (Manual updating is covered in Section 9.2.3, "Updating Channel Contents.")

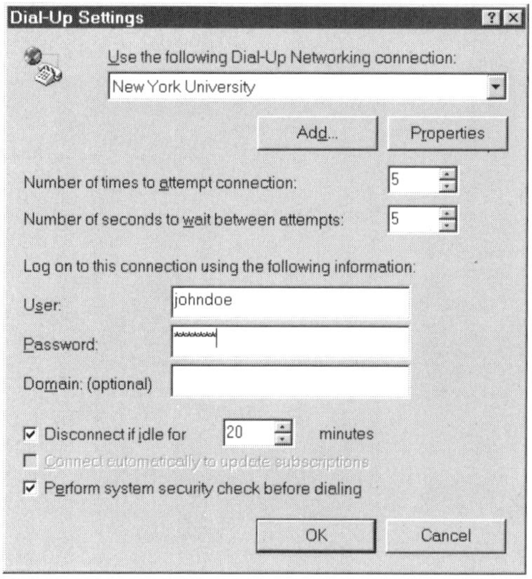

Figure 9-11 Entering your logon name and password for unattended channel updates in the Explorer Configuration Panel..

9.2 Managing Active Channels

9.2.1 Working in Full-Screen Mode

After you complete the Subscription Wizard, Explorer downloads your channel contents. Explorer switches to full-screen mode and displays the first cover page associated with your channel (see Figure 9-12).

Working in full-screen mode is just slightly different than working in a regular browser window. The first difference is that if you move your browser to the left-hand side of the screen, the Active Channel bar slides into place. If you then move your mouse cursor off the Channel bar, it slides back offscreen.

If you want to close the Channel bar completely, click the x icon in the upper right corner. But, if you want to keep the Channel bar from sliding onscreen and offscreen, click the push-pin icon (refer to Figure 9-13). This anchors the Channel bar to the desktop and aligns the current Web page exactly to the right of the Channel bar. Anchoring the Channel bar is usually the best option for viewing channel contents.

Figure 9-12
Full-screen mode.

NOTE: *If you don't like the full-screen mode and want to return to regular Web mode, you always can click the Full Screen / Normal Screen toggle switch on the button bar.*

9.2.2 Channel Navigation

After you subscribe to a new channel, you will notice that its logo appears in the Active Channel bar. Simply click the logo to view the channel contents. You'll see the listing of channel articles directly within the Channel bar and the default cover page associated with the channel.

If you subscribe to the ZDNet channel, for example, you will notice six categories of information: News, Products, Web, Mac, Games, and Download. Click on any of these items, and Explorer displays the article to the right. It also is possible that channel contents may be organized hierarchically within folders. The CNET channel, for example, includes folders of information on News.com, CNET Online, and CNET TV. Click on any one of these folders, and Explorer displays the HTML articles contained in the folder (see Figure 9-13). Creating this type of newsfolder and channel hierarchy is the subject of Chapter 10, Section 10.2, "Creating CDF Folders."

TIP: *If you hold your mouse cursor over any of the channel icons, newsfolders, or HTML arcles, additional summary information may appear in a Windows ToolTip box (see Figure 9-14).*

TIP: *You can rearrange the order of your channels simply by dragging-and-dropping each channel logo.*

The push pin icon anchors the channel bar to the left-hand side of the screen.

Figure 9-13 The CNET channel navigation.

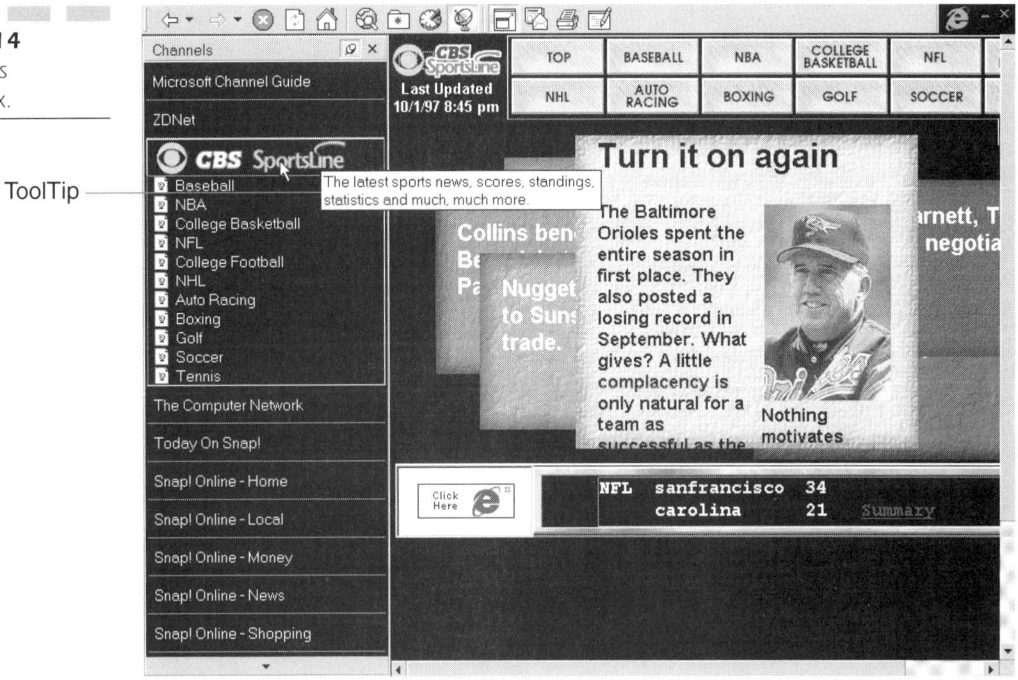

Figure 9-14 A Windows ToolTip box.

9.2.3 Updating Channel Contents

If you have set your channel to use the auto-schedule, Explorer downloads new content without requiring any user intervention. If you want to manually update your channel, select Manage Subscriptions from the Favorites menu. Explorer opens a new window and displays a listing of all your subscribed Active Channels and Web site subscriptions. To update an individual subscription, right-click on the item and choose Update Now (see Figure 9-15).

If you want to manually update all your channels at once, choose Update All Subscriptions from the Favorites menu.

9.2.4 Managing Channel Properties

At any time, you may modify your channel's download, notification, or schedule properties. Again, choose Manage Subscriptions from the

Favorites menu. Then right-click on the channel and choose the Properties option. Explorer displays a three-page customization Control Panel (see Figure 9-16). On the Subscription tab, you will see a complete summary of your channel's properties. You then can click on any of the other

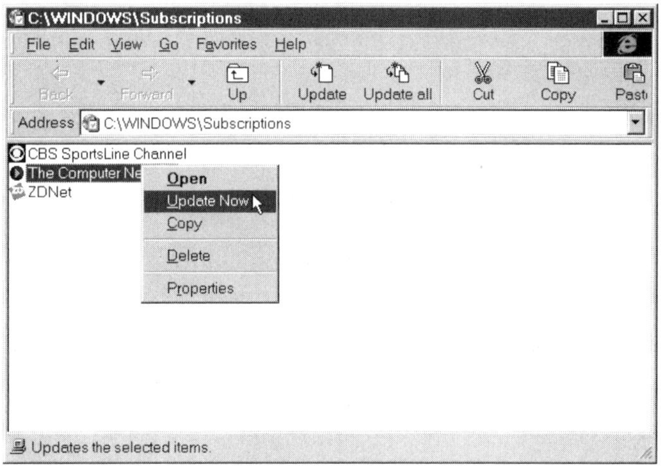

Figure 9-15 Managing subscriptions.

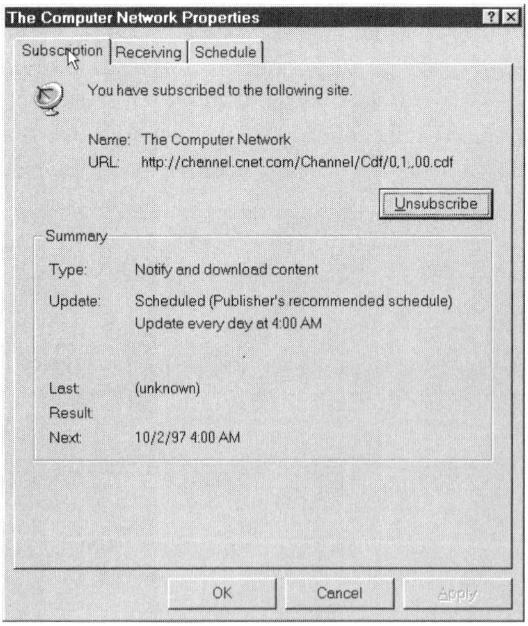

Figure 9-16 Modifying channel properties.

tabs to modify your customization. Most of these customization options are identical to the options described in Section 9.1, "Subscribing to Active Channels;" advanced customization options are detailed below.

9.2.5 Setting a Logon Name and Password

Some Active Channels require registration and/or payment and may require a logon name and password. If so, select the Receiving tab and click the Login button. Then enter your username and password.

9.2.6 Advanced Download Options

If you have directed Explorer to automatically download channel content, but you want fine-grained control over what is downloaded, select the Receiving tab, and click the Advanced button. The Advanced Download Options page appears, which offers several options (see Figure 9-17):

Items to Download: You can choose what type of content is downloaded. Specifically, you can choose to download or deny downloading for images, sound and video, or ActiveX controls and Java applets. If

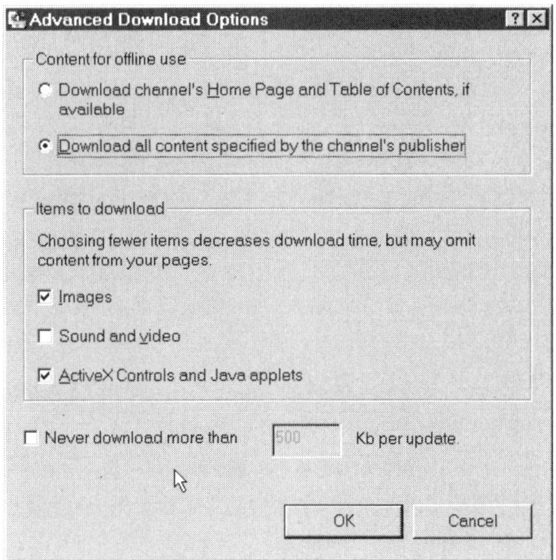

Figure 9-17 Modifying channel properties by specifying advanced download options.

you choose to omit any of these items, channel updates may occur faster, but you are denied the benefits provided by each individual item.

Never Download More Than ___ Kb per Update: You can set a maximum hard drive allocation for each channel update. This prevents your hard drive from getting swamped with large channel updates. Specify your maximum hard drive allocation in kilobytes.

9.2.7 Unsubscribing Channels

To unsubscribe a channel (but keep it on your Active Channel bar), follow the earlier directions for modifying your channel's properties. Then click the Unsubscribe button on the Subscription page (refer to Figure 9-16). To remove the channel from the Channel bar, right-click the channel's icon and choose Delete.

9.3 Subscribing to Web Sites

9.3.1 Web Site Subscriptions

You certainly can subscribe to Active Channels, but Internet Explorer 4.0 also enables you to subscribe to any existing Web site. And, just like Active Channels, Explorer periodically checks the designated Web site and downloads the changes to your local hard drive.

Subscriptions to Web sites are integrated tightly with the Explorer Favorites menu. Just like in IE 3.0, the Favorites menu includes all your favorite Web sites, but in IE 4.0, some of these Web sites may be subscriptions.

9.3.2 The Web Site Subscription Wizard

To subscribe to a Web site, first navigate to the Web site location. Then choose Add to Favorites from the Favorites menu. The Add Favorite dialog box appears, where you can confirm that you want to add the page to your list of favorites. You also can enter the Web site name or place the site in a specific Favorites folder (see Figure 9-18).

You have three subscription options:

- You can add this site as a regular favorite and choose not to subscribe.
- You can subscribe to this site and receive notifications when the page is updated.
- You can fully subscribe to this site, receive update notifications, and automatically download new content.

You also can choose to customize your Web site subscriptions. If you click the Customize button, Explorer launches another Subscription Wizard that is very similar to the Active Channel Subscription Wizard described earlier. You can set your notification options, as well as a customized update schedule.

There are only two differences between the Active Channel Wizard and the Web Site Subscription Wizard. The first difference is that you immediately have the option of setting a logon name and password. Logon names are required only for certain restricted or pay-per-visit sites (see Section 9.2.5, "Setting a Logon Name and Password"). The second difference concerns the Web-crawl or download parameters for channel contents.

TIP: *To customize your Favorites folders or create new categories, choose Organize Favorites from the Favorites menu.*

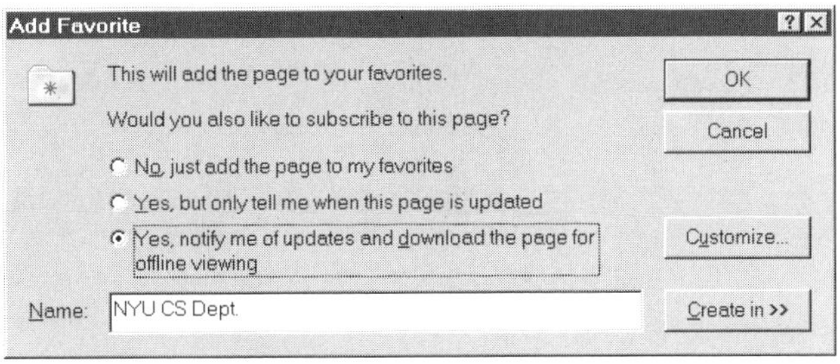

Figure 9-18
Using the Web Site Subscription Wizard.

9.3.3 Web-Crawling Options

Just like Netscape Netcaster, Internet Explorer performs an automatic Web crawl on subscription sites. This means that Explorer first retrieves the top-level page, usually `index.html`, and then follows all the embedded links. It continues to burrow until it reaches the level limit set by the user.

The first customization page in the Subscription Wizard enables you to control how much of the specified Web site is downloaded (see Figure 9-19). You have two options here:

- Download this page.
- Download this page and pages linked to it.

If you choose the Download this page and pages linked to it option and click the Next button, you are prompted for the number of levels to retrieve (see Figure 9-20). Unless you want to spend an inordinate amount of time downloading new information, it is recommended that you set the number of levels to 2 or 3.

9.3.4 Updating Web Site Subscriptions

If you have set your subscription schedule to use auto-scheduling, Explorer downloads new content automatically—just like Active Channels

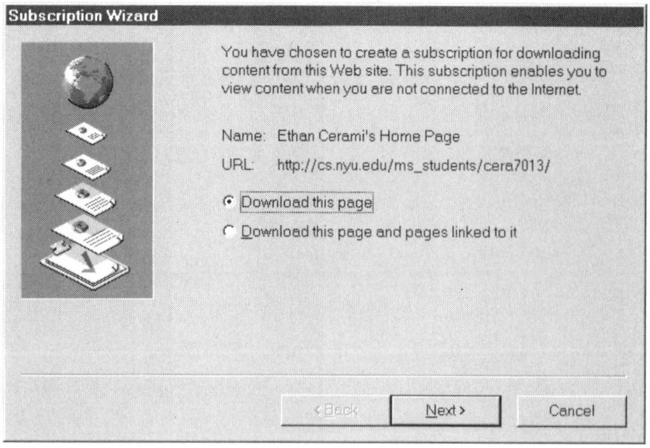

Figure 9-19 Selecting download options in the Web Site Subscription Wizard.

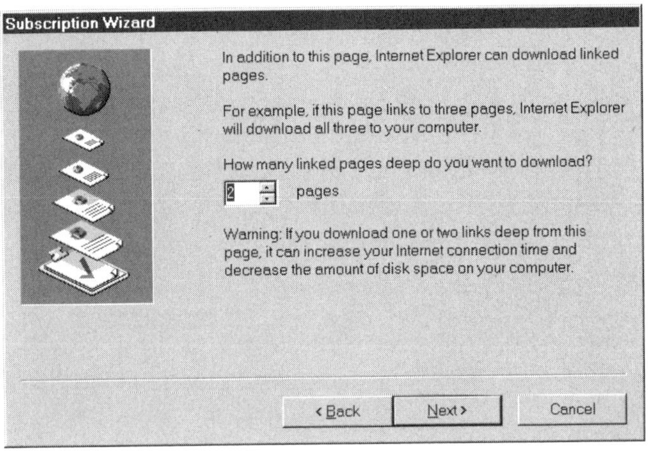

Figure 9-20 Setting Web-crawl options in the Web Site Subscription Wizard.

—and does not require any user intervention. If you want to manually update your Web site subscriptions, choose Manage Subscriptions from the Favorites menu. Then right-click an any individual subscription and choose Update.

You also can right-click on any subscription to modify its properties or delete the subscription entirely.

9.4 Working Offline

Working offline could not be easier. Simply choose Work Offline from the File menu, and Explorer uses only precached items or precached channels and refrains from making additional network connections. While in offline mode, the mouse cursor indicates whether the specified HTML link is precached. If the item is not precached, you see a small "no" icon (a small circle with a bar through it). If you then click on a noncached item, Explorer gives you the option to return to online mode or to stay offline (see Figure 9-21).

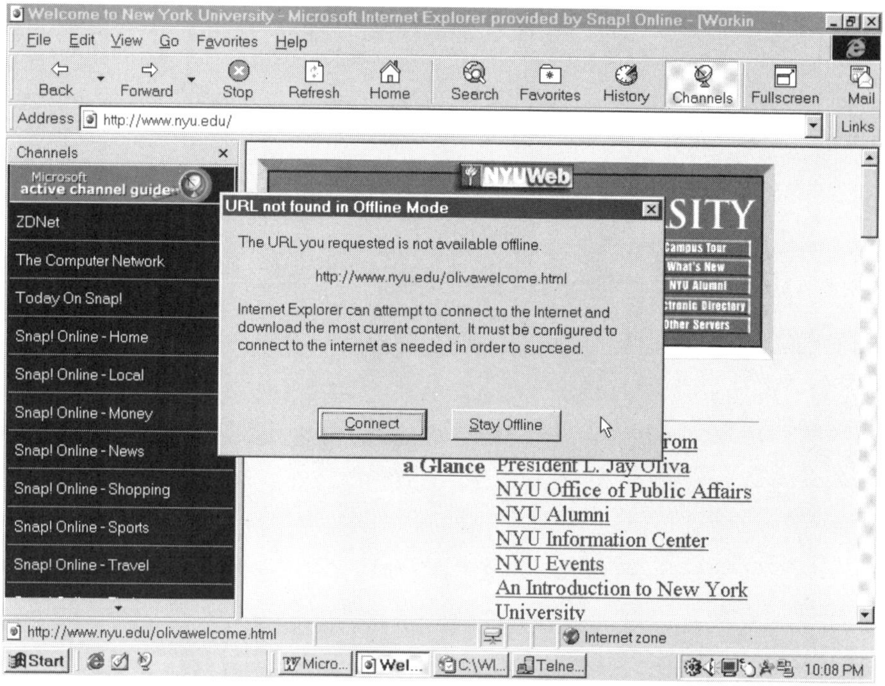

Figure 9-21
Working offline.

9.5 Working with Active Desktop Components

If you opted to install the Web integration components of IE 4.0, you have immediate access to the newest active desktop components. Desktop components are one of the best new features of IE 4.0 and are extremely easy to use.

9.5.1 Launching the Active Desktop

To activate the active desktop, choose Settings from the Windows Start menu. Then choose View as Web Page from the Active Desktop submenu (see Figure 9-22).

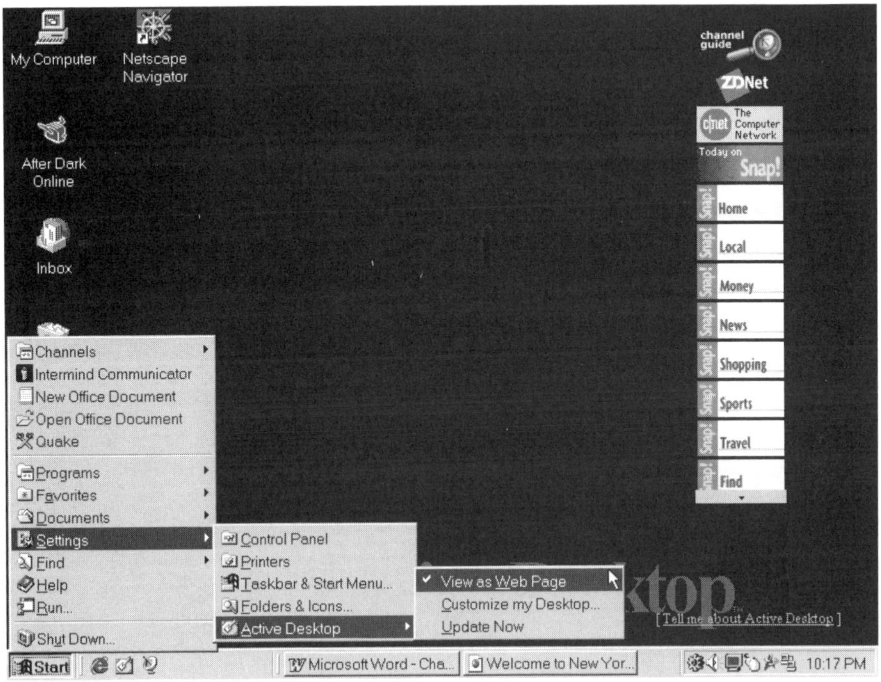

Figure 9-22 Launching the active desktop.

9.5.2 Adding New Desktop Components

If you want to get a quick start with new desktop components, visit the Microsoft IE 4.0 Gallery at

```
http://www.microsoft.com/ie/ie40/gallery/
```

The gallery has sample components from some of the leading content providers, including c|net News.Com, ESPN SportsZone, CBS Sports Center, and the Microsoft Investor Ticker. Just follow any of these links, and Explorer downloads and installs the new component. Figure 9-23 shows a screen shot of the ESPN SportsZone and c|net News.Com components.

TIP: *You can customize the subscriptions to your desktop components just like any other channel. Just click the Customize Subscription button during installation (see Figure 9-24).*

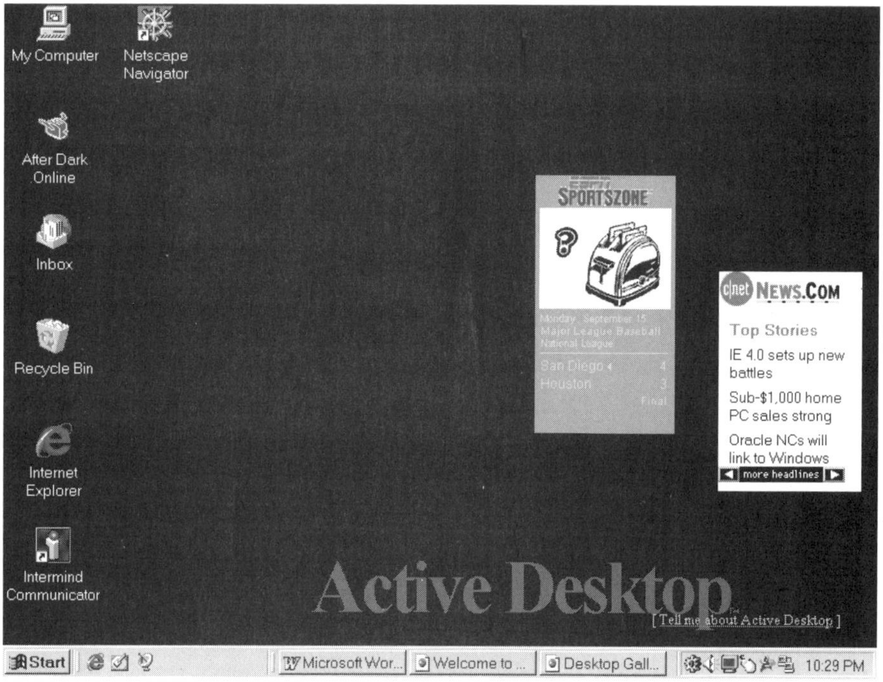

Figure 9-23
c|net News.Com and ESPN SportsZone desktop components.

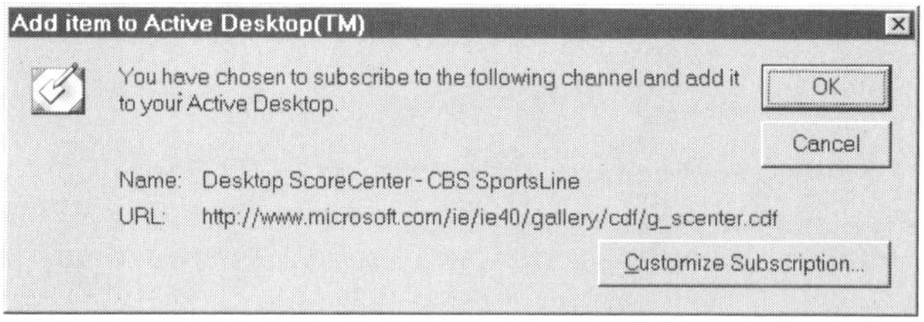

Figure 9-24
Click the Customize Subscription button to customize the component's subscription properties.

9.5.3 Customizing the Active Desktop

To customize the active desktop, choose Settings from the Windows Start menu. Then choose Customize My Desktop from the Active Desktop submenu. From there, you can enable or disable any individual desktop component (see Figure 9-25).

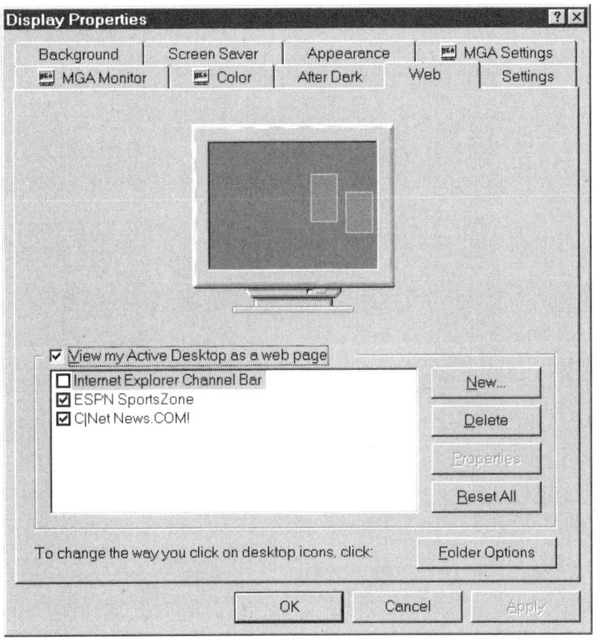

Figure 9-25 Customizing the active desktop.

9.5.4 Updating Desktop Components

Each desktop component follows its own update schedule, just like any other channel. To manually update your components, choose Settings from the Windows Start menu. Then choose Update Now from the Active Desktop submenu.

TIP: *You can manage your desktop component like any other Active Channel or Web site subscription. Just choose Manage Subscriptions from the Favorites menu. You then can update the component or modify its properties.*

9.6 Working with the Channel Screen Saver

Last, but not least, we have the IE 4.0 Channel screen saver. To activate the HTML screen saver, right-click on any empty area of the Windows desktop and choose the Properties option. Then click on the Screen Saver tab (see Figure 9-26). From the list of available screen savers, choose the Channel Screen Saver option.

If you click the Settings button on this tab, you can further customize the screen saver. You can choose which HTML pages to display, how long each page is displayed, and whether background sounds are enabled (see Figure 9-27).

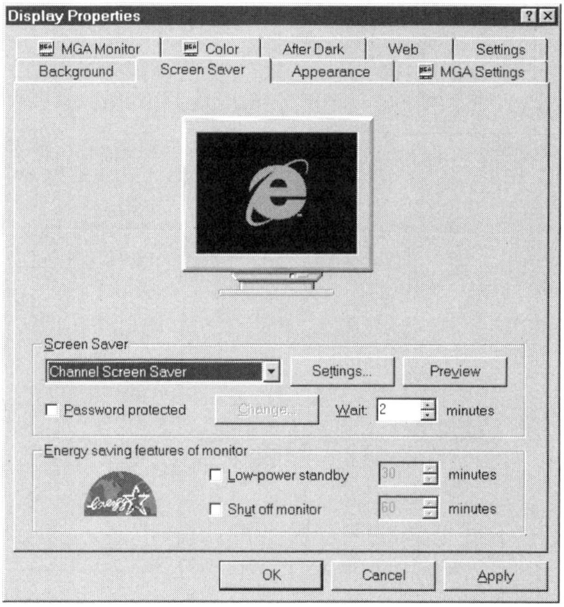

Figure 9-26 Setting up the Channel screen saver.

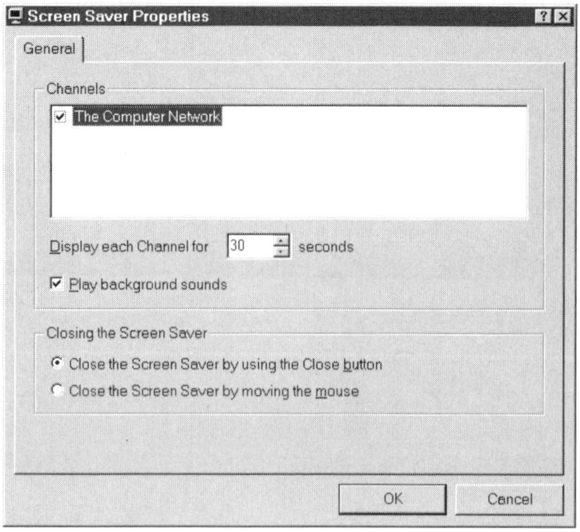

Figure 9-27 Customizing the Channel screen saver.

SUMMARY

Internet Explorer 4.0 represents a big jump up from IE 3.0. Just covering all the new IE 4.0 features could fill an entire book. This is a book about push technology, though, so this chapter covered only the push capabilities built right into IE 4.0. We started with an overall discussion of subscribing to Active Channels. Fortunately, Microsoft has made this an easy, painless process with its new Channel Subscription Wizard. The Wizard guides you through the complete customization of your subscriptions, including the setting of notification, download, and schedule options.

Internet Explorer 4.0 also enables you to subscribe to any existing Web site. Just like Active Channels, Explorer checks these sites and downloads new contents to your local hard drive. Subscribing to Web sites is integrated tightly with the Explorer Favorites menu, which includes its own Web Site Subscription Wizard.

Last, we examined the active desktop components and the HTML screen saver. Both these new features exhibit Explorer's best attempt to tightly integrate the operating system with the Web browser and represent two new innovative modes for viewing channel content.

CHAPTER 10

Creating Active Channels

This chapter explores the steps necessary for creating your own Active Channels. As was noted several times in previous chapters, Microsoft Active Channels are built in the new *Channel Definition Format* (CDF). If you already are well versed in HTML, CDF should be quite easy to pick up. In fact, CDF has much of the same feel as HTML. But, whereas HTML is used to lay out text and graphical elements within a Web page, CDF is used to hierarchically organize and describe sets of HTML pages. And, with the power and flexibility of CDF, you easily can create new dynamic channels to reach your customers over the Internet or your employees over the corporate Intranet.

This chapter starts out with the most basic examples of CDF and then moves on to more advanced topics. We'll begin with an overview of the most important CDF tags for describing a channel table of contents. Then, we'll look at the CDF options for the channel update schedule. Along the way, we will create a sample, fictional channel, known as the New York Arts Channel.

After we cover the basics, we will move on to more advanced topics. One of the great strengths of CDF is the capability to create topical folders within channels. You easily can create a news channel, for example, with special interest folders for Business, Technology, Politics, and Entertainment. A second great strength of CDF is that Internet Explorer supports several mechanisms for displaying your channel contents. You can display your channel in a regular Web browser, as an active desktop component, or as an HTML screen saver. Each of these options gives channel providers a rich array of possibilities. And, the more options you have, the greater flexibility you have in attracting new subscribers.

10.1 Basic CDF

10.1.1 Cutting to the Chase

Itching to try out your first CDF example? Let's cut to the chase. The code in Listing 10-1 describes a complete sample channel.

Listing 10-1 creates a fictional channel called the New York Arts Channel. The channel provides subscribers with the latest arts and entertainment news in New York City. This is the first edition, and it currently includes only three sections: Theatre Reviews, Dance Reviews, and Film Reviews. (Note: the URL **www.nychannel.com** does not really exist; it is used here only for purposes of explanation.)

10.1.2 Who's Afraid of XML?

At a glance, the example in Listing 10-1 looks suspiciously similar to HTML. In fact, there is a good reason for the family resemblance. CDF and HTML are both offspring of two meta-languages known as *Extensible Markup Language* (XML) and *Standard Generalized Markup Language* (SGML).

Listing 10-1:
Example 1

```
<?XML version="1.0"?>
<!DOCTYPE Channel SYSTEM "http://www.w3c.org/Channel.dtd">

<CHANNEL HREF="http://www.nychannel.com/index.html">
    <TITLE>The New York Arts Channel</TITLE>
    <LOGO HREF="http://www.nychannel.com/nyarts.gif" STYLE="image" />
    <LOGO HREF="http://www.nychannel.com/nyarts.ico" STYLE="icon" />
    <ITEM HREF="http://www.nychannel.com/theatre.html">
        <TITLE>Theatre Reviews</TITLE>
        <ABSTRACT>Broadway, Off Broadway, and Off-off Broadway
        Reviews</ABSTRACT>
    </ITEM>
    <ITEM HREF="http://www.nychannel.com/dance.html">
        <TITLE>Dance Reviews</TITLE>
        <ABSTRACT>The New York International Fringe Festival opens
        this week.
        </ABSTRACT>
    </ITEM>
    <ITEM HREF="http://www.nychannel.com/film.html">
        <TITLE>Film Reviews</TITLE>
        <ABSTRACT>Don't miss the Full Monty!</ABSTRACT>
    </ITEM>
</CHANNEL>
```

Understanding the sordid details and history of both XML and SGML can be a brave undertaking. Fortunately, to understand CDF, you need to know only a few facts.

First, XML is actually a simplified version of SGML. For you, that basically means that CDF is just about as simple as HTML.

Second, XML represents a new language for classifying and organizing data on the Web. As it exists now, HTML merely organizes elements of data *within* a Web page. But XML represents an attempt to organize and catalog sets of data across the Internet. In fact, the future may include many new XML applications, including more efficient methods of cataloging Internet libraries, encrypted electronic payment schemes, and even standards for the exchange and transfer of patient medical records.

Third, XML is considered a *meta-language*, meaning that it is used to describe new languages. And CDF is an application of XML. In fact, CDF is currently the *only* XML application supported by Internet Explorer 4.0.

As the Web continues to grow, we are likely to see many more applications of XML. And, unlike HTML, which is limited to a set group of tags or elements, XML provides the flexibility to create a near limitless number of new languages and applications.

This may sound well and good, but how does all this relate to our first example? Check out the first two lines:

```
<?XML version="1.0"?>
<!DOCTYPE Channel SYSTEM "http://www.w3c.org/Channel.dtd">
```

Line 1 identifies our code as an XML document. Currently, we are using XML 1.0. XML has not actually been approved by the World Wide Web Consortium, and Version 1.0 has not even been completed yet. But this tag provides us with insurance for future releases of XML. When XML 2.0 comes along, our code will still work.

Line 2 identifies the document type of our code—in this case, identifying our document as a channel or CDF file. The `Channel.dtd` file represents a *document type definition* (DTD) file. DTD files describe the exact syntax, rules, and grammar for each particular application of XML. And, in this case, the `Channel.dtd` file contains all the information necessary for parsing and creating CDF channel files.

In the future, we may see a whole host of new XML applications. The `<!DOCTYPE>` tag therefore allows us to identify which particular XML application we are referencing.

Because CDF is the only XML application supported by Internet Explorer 4.0, and XML currently is only in Version 1.0, you can entirely omit the first two lines of code. By default, Internet Explorer just assumes that you are creating a CDF file, and your channel will run just fine. But, as XML takes off, and we see more and more XML applications, these first two lines will be increasingly necessary. And, as an insurance policy against new XML developments, it is highly recommended that you always include them. Fortunately, you need these same two lines for every new CDF file, so you can just cut and paste.

10.1.3 The <CHANNEL> Tag

Next up, the `<CHANNEL>` tag. Here, we return to more familiar territory. Just like HTML, every CDF element has both a start tag that begins with the open angle bracket (`<`), such as `<CHANNEL>`, and an end tag that begins with the open angle bracket followed by a backward slash (`</`), such as `</CHANNEL>`. Anything between the start and stop tags is considered data or content.

The **<CHANNEL>** tag defines a new channel. Anything between the start **<CHANNEL>** tag and the end **</CHANNEL>** tag is considered a *child* element of the channel. As we shall soon see, these elements could include logos, articles, titles, abstracts, or even other channels.

Just like HTML, each CDF tag also can have a set of specified attributes. In HTML, for example, you can create a very simple table with the **<TABLE>** tag, but if you want to create a table with borders, you set the **BORDER** attribute: **<TABLE BORDER=YES>**.

The same idea applies to CDF elements, and the **<CHANNEL>** tag includes its own attributes. In our first example, we set the channel **HREF** attribute. This attribute is nearly identical to the **HREF** attribute used in HTML anchor tags—for example, **<A HREF="http://www.yahoo.com">**. Here, though, **HREF** refers to the cover page of your channel. When users first subscribe to a channel, the cover page is the first to appear. In our case, we simply point to the default New York Arts home page, **http://www.nychannel/index.html**. If you do not want a cover page, simply omit the **HREF** tag.

NOTE: *It is highly recommended that you include the complete* **http://** *prefix prior to any URLs. It also is highly recommended that you include the full path and filename for all referenced URLs. Instead of setting an* **HREF** *attribute to* **www.nychannel.com**, *for example, set it to* **http://www.nychannel.com/index.html**.

The <CHANNEL> Tag

Description: Defines a channel.

Syntax:

```
<CHANNEL
HREF="url"
>
...Channel "Child" Elements go here...
</CHANNEL>
```

Parameter: **HREF="url"** specifies the cover page URL of the channel. Internet Explorer opens this location when the user first launches the channel. This attribute is optional.

The specification for the <CHANNEL> tag is included in the sidebar on page 171. The complete CDF specification is included on the CD-ROM that accompanies this book. The latest CDF specification also is available online at **http://www.microsoft.com/standards/**.

10.1.4 The <LOGO> Tag

If you have spent any time working with Active Channels, you probably have noticed that each channel gets its own individualized logo in the Active Channel bar. You also may have noticed that each channel has its own icon in the Favorites pull-down menu.

As a channel developer, you can create your own logos and icons with the <LOGO> tag. Unlike other push products, most notably PointCast, your logos can appear directly alongside Microsoft's premium content providers. In other words, your channel has a fair shot at sharing the spotlight.

The <LOGO> tag has two attributes: **HREF** and **STYLE**. **HREF** indicates the URL of your graphics file. **STYLE** represents one of two options:

IMAGE: The graphical image that is placed in the Channel bar. The image must be an 80×32 pixel GIF. The top-left pixel indicates the background color if the user expands the Channel bar beyond 80 pixels wide.

ICON: The icon that appears in the Favorites pull-down menu. The image must be 16×16 pixels large in GIF or Windows ICO format.

For our first example, I created one simple GIF log and reused an existing icon from the Windows operating system:

nyarts.gif 

nyarts.ico: 

With the <LOGO> tag, we have set the **nyarts.gif** image as our Channel bar image and the **nylogo.gif** image as our pull-down icon (see Figure 10-1).

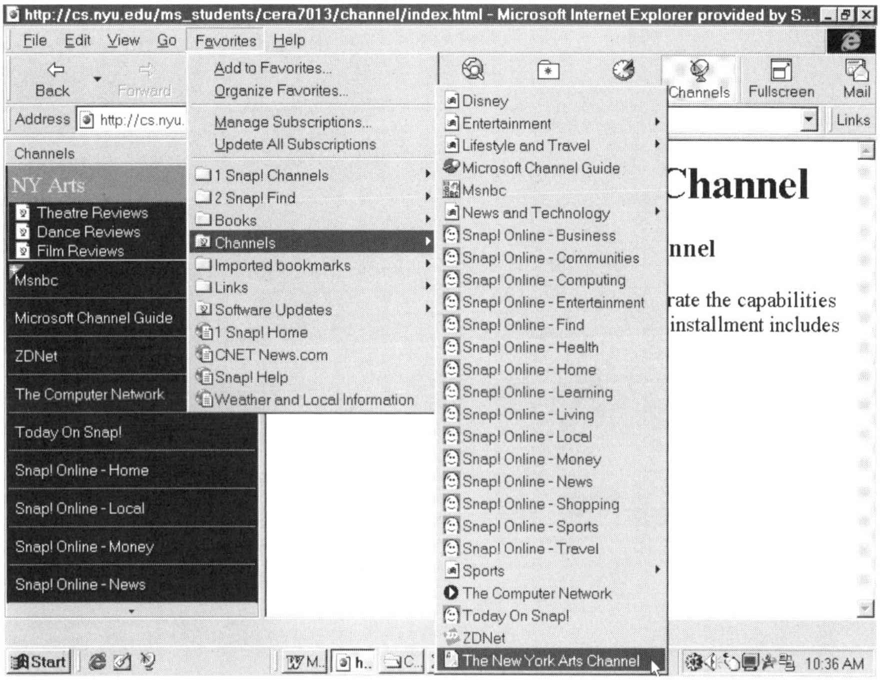

Figure 10-1 The New York Arts Channel. The first edition includes theatre, dance, and film reviews. Each item referenced in the CDF file appears on the Channel bar. The image logo appears in the Active Channel bar, and the icon logo appears on the Favorites pull-down menu.

The <LOGO> Tag

Description: Specifies an image that can be used to represent a channel or channel item.

Syntax:

```
<LOGO
HREF="url"
STYLE="ICON" | "IMAGE"
/>
```

Note: No end tag is associated with this element!

Parameters: `HREF="url"` is a required parameter. It specifies the URL associated with the channel logo or icon.

`STYLE="ICON" | "IMAGE"` where `"IMAGE"` specifies an 80×32 GIF image, which appears in the Explorer Active Channel bar. `"ICON"` specifies a 16×16 image in GIF or Windows ICO format. The icon image appears in the Explorer Favorites drop-down menu.

```
<LOGO HREF="http://www.nychannel.com/nyarts.gif" STYLE="image" />
<LOGO HREF="http://www.nychannel.com/nyarts.ico" STYLE="icon" />
```

Note that no end tag is associated with the `<LOGO>` tag, and *you must end the `<LOGO>` tag with a `/>`*. Ending the `<LOGO>` tag with just a `>` is a common error, but your CDF file will be rendered completely useless!

TIP: *You can use the Microsoft Icon Editor to create icons. The Icon Editor is available with the Windows 95 Resource Kit at* **http://www.microsoft.com/windows95/info/win95reskit.htm**

Several shareware icon editors also are available at **http://www.windows95.com/apps/icons-edit.html**

10.1.5 The <ITEM> Tag

Each CDF channel contains a series of items or articles. These articles represent the news, information, or content that is the heart of your channel. Usually, these articles point to simple HTML documents on your existing Web server. But they just as easily could point to HTML articles with embedded Java applets, ActiveX controls, dynamic HTML, or Macromedia Shockwave or Flash files. Or, they easily could point to Active Server Pages or CGI scripts for database access and customized information.

The `<ITEM>` specification is included in the following sidebar. Just like the `<CHANNEL>` tag, we have an `HREF` attribute that indicates the URL of the selected article. For example, our first article references theatre reviews:

```
<ITEM HREF="http://www.nychannel.com/theatre.html">
    <TITLE>Theatre Reviews</TITLE>
    <ABSTRACT>Broadway, Off Broadway, and Off-off Broadway
    Reviews</ABSTRACT>
</ITEM>
```

Anything between the start `<ITEM>` tag and the end `</ITEM>` tag is considered a *child* element. Usually, this is reserved for the item's title and abstract.

The <ITEM> Tag

Description: Defines an item or article in a channel. Items usually refer to standard HTML pages.

Syntax:

```
<ITEM
HREF="url"
>
… Item "child" elements, including Title and Abstract go here…
</ITEM>
```

Parameter: `HREF="url"` specifies the article's URL. Explorer displays this location when the user selects the article. There must be exactly one **HREF** attribute for each **ITEM** element.

10.1.6 The <TITLE> Tag

Pure and simple, the **<TITLE>** tag does just what it says. It assigns a title to its parent element. This parent element might be a channel or an item.

In the case of a channel, the **<TITLE>** tag designates the overall name of the channel:

```
<CHANNEL HREF="http://www.nychannel.com/index.html">
        <TITLE>The New York Arts Channel</TITLE>
…
</CHANNEL>
```

This title appears on the Favorites pull-down menu (refer to Figure 10-1).

In the case of an item, the **<TITLE>** tag designates the title of the parent article:

```
<ITEM HREF="http://www.nychannel.com/theatre.html">
     <TITLE>Theatre Reviews</TITLE>
…
</ITEM>
```

The <TITLE> Tag

Description: A text string representing the title of the channel or item.
Syntax: `<TITLE>Title Text Here</TITLE>`

When the channel is selected in the Channel bar, the article titles are listed for the user's perusal (refer to the Active Channel bar in Figure 10-1).

10.1.7 The <ABSTRACT> Tag

The **<ABSTRACT>** tag provides a short abstract or summary of the item. When the user holds the mouse cursor over an article's title, the abstract appears in a small Windows ToolTip box (see Figure 10-2). This provides the user with a little bit of extra information to help determine whether it is worthwhile to follow the link.

We can try to convince subscribers to read our review of the film "The Full Monty," for example:

```
<ITEM HREF="http://www.nychannel.com/film.html">
        <TITLE>Film Reviews</TITLE>
        <ABSTRACT>Don't miss the Full Monty!</ABSTRACT>
</ITEM>
```

Although the **<ABSTRACT>** tag usually is used for items, it just as easily can be used for channel elements:

```
<CHANNEL HREF="http://www.nychannel/index.html">
       <TITLE>The New York Arts Channel</TITLE>
       <ABSTRACT>Theatre, Dance, and Film Reviews. We bring
       the Big Applet to you.</ABSTRACT>
...
</CHANNEL>
```

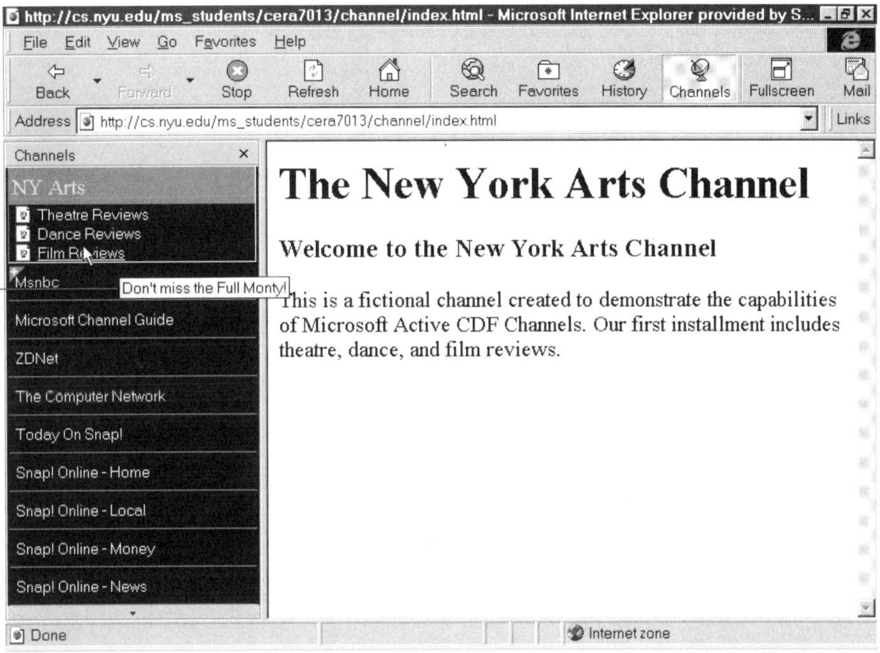

Figure 10-2 The **<ABSTRACT>** tag text appears in a Windows ToolTip box.

When the user holds the mouse cursor over the channel's logo, the abstract message appears as a ToolTip. Without an abstract element for your channel, the ToolTip displays the **HREF** attribute for your channel instead, providing little if any extra information for the end user. It therefore is always recommended that you include an abstract for your channel.

The <ABSTRACT> Tag

Description: A text string representing a description or summary of the associated channel or item element. Explorer displays the abstract text in a Windows ToolTip box.

Syntax: `<TITLE>Abstract Text Here</TITLE>`

10.1.8 Adding an Update Schedule

Before deploying our New York Arts Channel, let's add an update schedule. CDF channels can be updated as often as you want. However, remember that users always have the final say on customizing their channel schedules.

The New York Arts Channel will be updated once every 24 hours. So, we must add the following CDF code:

```
<SCHEDULE>
      <INTERVALTIME DAY="1"/>
</SCHEDULE>
```

By default, this code directs Explorer to check the channel contents once every 24 hours exactly at 12:00 a.m. The complete code appears in Listing 10-2.

Adding an update schedule is simply a matter of adding a **<SCHEDULE>** tag with an embedded **<INTERVALTIME>** tag. The **<SCHEDULE>** tag can include optional start and end dates. **INTERVALTIME** indicates the frequency of channel updates, whether in days, hours, or minutes. For example, here is another possible update schedule:

```
<SCHEDULE StartDate="1997-09-01" EndDate="1998-09-01">
        <INTERVALTIME MIN="30" />
</SCHEDULE>
```

This schedule updates the channel contents once every 30 minutes and is valid for one year, beginning on September 1, 1997 and ending on September 1, 1998. If you choose to indicate a start and stop date, dates must be indicated in the ISO 8601 format (**YYYY-MM-DD**). For example, October 3, 1998 must be represented as **1998-10-03**.

In addition to the **INTERVALTIME** property, it is possible to specify a specific time range when updates should ideally occur. Suppose that the New York Arts Channel is updated once a day, and the new edition is published at 10 a.m. every morning. Ideally, we want our subscribers to get the most current update as soon as it is available. For this, we can use the **<EARLIESTTIME>** and **<LATESTTIME>** tags:

```
<SCHEDULE StartDate="1997-09-01" EndDate="1998-09-01">
      <INTERVALTIME DAY="1" />
      <EARLIESTTIME HOUR="10" />
      <LATESTTIME HOUR="12" />
</SCHEDULE>
```

The <SCHEDULE> Tag

Description: Defines the channel update schedule. Starting at midnight on **STARTDATE**, channel updating occurs once within each consecutive timer interval specified by the **INTERVALTIME** child element.

Syntax:

```
<SCHEDULE
STARTDATE="date"
ENDDATE="date"
>
...
</SCHEDULE>
```

Parameters: **STARTDATE="date"** is the date when the schedule will start to apply. The date must be written in ISO 8601 format (**YYYY-MM-DD**). If this attribute is omitted, the schedule will start to apply on the current day. **ENDDATE="date"** is the date when the schedule will expire. This date also must be written in ISO 8601 format.

The <INTERVALTIME> Tag

Description: Determines the frequency of channel updates. The days, hours, and minutes are totaled to determine the length of the interval.

Syntax:

```
<INTERVALTIME
DAY="n"
HOUR="n"
MIN="n"
/>
```

Parameters: **DAY="n"** is the number of days between each scheduled update. For example, **DAY="1"** updates once a day. **HOUR="n"** is the number of hours between each scheduled update. For example, **DAY="12"** updates once every 12 hours. **MIN="n"** is the number of minutes between each scheduled update. For example, **MIN="30"** updates once every 30 minutes.

The <EARLIESTTIME> Tag

Description: Specifies the earliest time offset within a repeating interval that the channel is updated. The days, hours, and minutes are totaled to determine the offset value.

Syntax:

```
<EARLIESTTIME
DAY="n"
HOUR="n"
MIN="n"
/>
```

Parameters: `DAY="n"` specifies the first day within `INTERVALTIME` that the schedule can be updated. `HOUR="n"` specifies the first hour within `INTERVALTIME` that the schedule can be updated. Hours are denoted by a 24-hour clock. `MIN="n"` specifies the first minute within `INTERVALTIME` that the schedule can be updated.

The <LATESTTTIME> Tag

Description: Specifies the latest time offset within a repeating interval that the channel is updated. The days, hours, and minutes are totaled to determine the offset value.

Syntax:

```
<LATESTTIME
DAY="n"
HOUR="n"
MIN="n"
/>
```

Parameters: `DAY="n"` specifies the latest day within the `INTERVALTIME` that the schedule can be updated. `HOUR="n"` specifies the latest hour within the `INTERVALTIME` that the schedule can be updated. Hours are denoted by a 24-hour clock. `MIN="n"` specifies the latest minute within the `INTERVALTIME` that the schedule can be updated.

This tells Explorer to update the channel once a day. At the earliest, it should attempt to get the update at 10 a.m. At the latest, it must get the update by noon. By offering a window of opportunity, Explorer attempts to randomize the exact time of update. This prevents the Web server from being swamped with thousands of update requests at exactly 10 a.m. Note that the `HOUR` attribute is a 24-hour clock; for example, 6 p.m. is represented as 18.

Listing 10-2 shows the example in Listing 10-1 with an update schedule added.

10.2 Creating CDF Folders

10.2.1 Newsfolders

Most newspapers and periodicals are organized along topical interests—World News, National News, Local News, Business, Sports, Arts & Leisure, and so on. Sometimes, these sections are subdivided. Business may be subdivided into Investing, Real Estate, and Technology. Most people are used to getting their news in this fashion and don't want to spend a lot of time scanning articles to find the topics that interest them. Fortunately, CDF provides just the right navigational mechanism that readers want.

10.2.2 Embedded Channels

As noted in Section 10.1.3, "The `<CHANNEL>` Tag," anything between a start `<CHANNEL>` tag and an end `</CHANNEL>` tag is considered a child element of the channel. Most of the time, these are abstract, title, or item elements. But you just as easily can embed a channel within another channel. The subchannel then becomes a newsfolder, which can include its own set of articles.

Listing 10-3 provides an example of subchannels. In it, we expand our New York Arts Channel to include three topical folders: Theatre Reviews, Dance Reviews, and Film Reviews. Each folder, in turn, has its own set of

Listing 10-2: Example 1 with Update Schedule

```
<!-  The New York Arts Channel  ->
<!-   Example #1 Channel Definition Format ->
<?XML version="1.0"?>
<!DOCTYPE Channel SYSTEM "http://www.w3c.org/Channel.dtd">

<CHANNEL HREF="http://www.nychannel.com/index.html">
    <TITLE>The New York Arts Channel</TITLE>

    <ABSTRACT>Theatre, Dance, and Film Reviews. We bring
    the Big Applet to you.</ABSTRACT>

    <SCHEDULE>
        <INTERVALTIME DAY="1"/>
    </SCHEDULE>

    <LOGO HREF="http://www.nychannel.com/nyarts.gif" STYLE="image" />
    <LOGO HREF="http://www.nychannel.com/nyarts.ico" STYLE="icon" />
    <ITEM HREF="http://www.nychannel.com/theatre.html">
       <TITLE>Theatre Reviews</TITLE>
       <ABSTRACT>Broadway, Off Broadway, and Off-off Broadway
       Reviews</ABSTRACT>
    </ITEM>
    <ITEM HREF="http://www.nychannel.com/dance.html">
       <TITLE>Dance Reviews</TITLE>
       <ABSTRACT>The New York International Fringe Festival opens
       this week.
       </ABSTRACT>
    </ITEM>
    <ITEM HREF="http://www.nychannel.com/film.html">
       <TITLE>Film Reviews</TITLE>
       <ABSTRACT>Don't miss the Full Monty!</ABSTRACT>
    </ITEM>
</CHANNEL>
```

articles. The Film Review section, for example, has articles on "The Full Monty" and "The Game." Take a look at the code now before we examine it in detail.

Listing 10-3 is very similar to Listings 10-1 and 10-2. We have created a channel with the same title, abstract, update schedule, and images. But, instead of embedding three articles within the channel, we now have three embedded subchannels. Each embedded subchannel has its own URL and its own set of items.

We have created a Film Review subchannel, for example, that contains two articles:

Listing 10-3: Embedded Channels

```
<!-  The New York Arts Channel  ->
<?XML version="1.0"?>
<!DOCTYPE Channel SYSTEM "http://www.w3c.org/Channel.dtd">

<CHANNEL HREF="http://www.nychannel.com/index.html">
    <TITLE>The New York Arts Channel</TITLE>
    <ABSTRACT>Theatre, Dance, and Film Reviews. We bring the Big
    Applet to you.</ABSTRACT>

    <!- Set Channel Update Frequency to Daily  ->
    <SCHEDULE>
       <INTERVALTIME DAY="1"/>
    </SCHEDULE>

    <!- Set Image/Logo Images ->
    <LOGO HREF="http://www.nychannel.com/nyarts.gif" STYLE="image" />
    <LOGO HREF="http://www.nychannel.com/nyarts.ico" STYLE="icon" />

    <!- Create Theatre Review Folder ->
    <CHANNEL HREF="http://www.nychannel.com/theatre.html">
       <TITLE>Theatre Reviews</TITLE>
       <ABSTRACT>Broadway, Off Broadway, and Off-off Broadway
       Reviews</ABSTRACT>
       <ITEM HREF="http://www.nychannel.com/alligator.html">
          <TITLE>Alligator Tales</TITLE>
          <ABSTRACT>Opening this week at the Manhattan Theatre
          Club</ABSTRACT>
       </ITEM>
       <ITEM HREF="http://www.nychannel.com/tango.html">
          <TITLE>Forever Tango</TITLE>
          <ABSTRACT>Created and directed by Luis Bravo, now playing at
          the Walter Kerr Theatre</ABSTRACT>
       </ITEM>
    </CHANNEL>

    <!- Create Dance Review Folder ->
    <CHANNEL HREF="http://www.nychannel.com/dance.html">
       <TITLE>Dance Reviews</TITLE>
       <ITEM HREF="http://www.nychannel.com/nature.html">
          <TITLE>Furies of Nature</TITLE>
          <ABSTRACT>A blend of modern and West African dance
          techniques.</ABSTRACT>
       </ITEM>
       <ITEM HREF="http://www.nychannel.com/indrani.html">
          <TITLE>Indrani:  Dances of India</TITLE>
          <ABSTRACT>This week only!</ABSTRACT>
       </ITEM>
    </CHANNEL>

    <!- Create the Film Review Folder ->
    <CHANNEL HREF="http://www.nychannel.com/film.html">
```

Listing 10-3: Continued.

```
        <TITLE>Film Reviews</TITLE>
        <ABSTRACT>Don't miss the Full Monty!</ABSTRACT>
        <ITEM HREF="http://www.nychannel.com/monty.html">
            <TITLE>The Full Monty</TITLE>
            <ABSTRACT>Six unemployed steel workers decide to
            go all the way.</ABSTRACT>
        </ITEM>
        <ITEM HREF="http://www.nychannel.com/game.html">
            <TITLE>The Game</TITLE>
            <ABSTRACT>Michael Douglas receives a most
            unusual birthday gift.</ABSTRACT>
        </ITEM>
    </CHANNEL>
</CHANNEL>
```

```
<!- Create the Film Review Folder ->
<CHANNEL HREF="http://www.nychannel.com/film.html">
     <TITLE>Film Reviews</TITLE>
     <ABSTRACT>Don't miss the Full Monty!</ABSTRACT>
     <ITEM HREF="http://www.nychannel.com/monty.html">
          <TITLE>The Full Monty</TITLE>
          <ABSTRACT>Six unemployed steel workers decide to
          go all the way.</ABSTRACT>
     </ITEM>
     <ITEM HREF="http://www.nychannel.com/game.html">
          <TITLE>The Game</TITLE>
          <ABSTRACT>Michael Douglas receives a most unusual
          birthday gift.</ABSTRACT>
     </ITEM>
</CHANNEL>
```

By default, your channel folders are displayed in the Active Channel bar. Each subchannel gets its own icon (which resembles a book), and users can click on the book to dig deeper into the channel hierarchy (see Figure 10-3).

Theoretically, there is no limit to the number of embedded channels, but it really is not recommended that you include more than two levels. Microsoft also recommends that you include no more than eight articles in each folder.

The only trick to creating embedded channels is to make sure that every embedded channel has both a start `<CHANNEL>` tag and an end `</CHANNEL>` tag. When you start creating multiple levels of channels, it can become difficult to keep track. And, unfortunately, if you neglect one end `</CHANNEL>` tag, Internet Explorer merely alerts you that it **Failed**

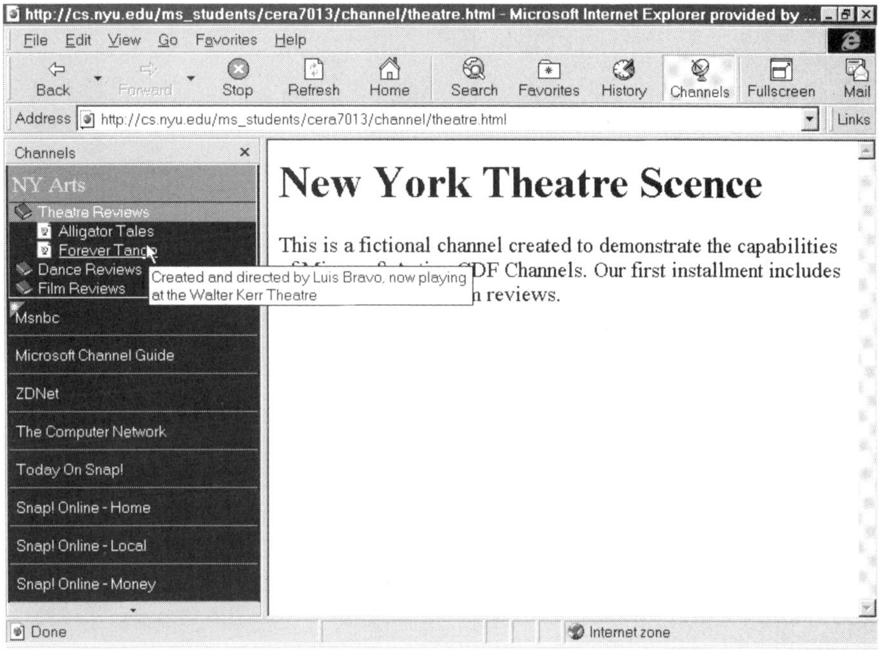

Figure 10-3
The New York Arts Channel, with folders for Theatre, Dance, and Film Reviews.

`to open or parse the channel definition file`, without even giving you an inkling of what the problem might be. The best method of keeping track of start and end tags is to ensure consistent indentation.

10.2.3 More Icons

Each channel folder appears with a tiny book icon, and each article appears with its own default icon (refer to Figure 10-3).

If you are ambitious enough to create your own set of icons, you easily can replace the default images with the **`<LOGO>`** tag. The **`<LOGO>`** tag can refer to a parent channel or item element. We can replace the default article icon with our New York Arts icon, for example (see Figure 10-4):

```
<ITEM HREF="http://www.nychannel.com/alligator.html">
        <LOGO HREF="http://www.nychannel.com/nyarts.ico"
        STYLE="icon" />
        <TITLE>Alligator Tales</TITLE>
        <ABSTRACT>Opening this week at the Manhattan
        Theatre Club</ABSTRACT>
</ITEM>
```

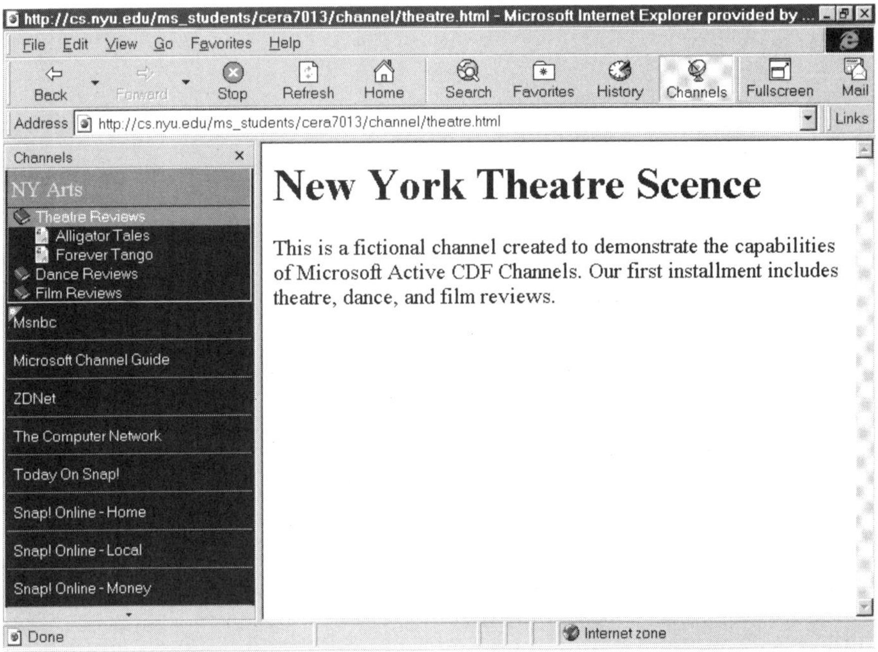

Figure 10-4
Use the **<LOGO>** tag to create your own icons.

10.3 Extra! Extra! Get Your Channel Here!

After you create your CDF files and all the referenced HTML articles, you can start attracting new subscribers. To enable users to subscribe to your channel, you simply include a link to the completed CDF file, as in this example:

```
<A HREF="nyarts.cdf">Subscribe now!</A>
```

You also might want to include the Microsoft Add Channel GIF image. A copy of the image is available online at

```
http://www.microsoft.com/ie/images/addchannel.gif
```

10.4 Creating Active Desktop Components

10.4.1 Planning for Your Desktop Component

Turning your existing channel into a desktop component is a straightforward process. You only need to add a few more CDF tags. Creating an effective desktop component that users will keep on their screen requires a lot of additional work, though. Before you embark on creating a desktop component, you might want to ask yourself or your organization a few questions:

- What added benefit can a desktop component provide that my current channel offering does not provide?
- What kind of information am I delivering? What information is most critical and time-sensitive for my audience?
- Does my desktop component complement and connect to my existing channel or Web site?

  The most successful components provide short headlines or summaries, for example, and link back to the existing Web site.
- How often will my content be updated?

  A desktop component that updates once a week is not likely to keep users riveted. Most components update every half hour or hour.

  Does my organization have the resources to provide that kind of update schedule?
- Is my component visually compelling and eye-catching?

  More often than not, you will find yourself working with dynamic HTML, Java, and ActiveX to create a compelling user interface.
- Does my component effectively make the most of its onscreen real-estate?

  Because desktop component real-estate is quite limited, you might want to consider various techniques for creating screen tickers or rotating headlines.

- Does my component work offline?

  Components appear on the user's screen as soon as the operating system boots up and when not connected to the Internet. You therefore need to make sure that your Java applets or ActiveX controls can work offline with or without new updated data. Most users are not likely to keep components that display arcane Java error messages!

10.4.2 Creating Desktop Components: The <USAGE> Tag

In contrast to creating a compelling user interface and then providing a steady stream of content, setting up a desktop component is extraordinarily simple. Along with the CDF specification, Microsoft has included a number of CDF extensions specifically tailored for the Internet Explorer active desktop.

You use the **<USAGE>** tag to denote the onscreen appearance of your channel. By default, your channel and its associated articles have their **`USAGE`** element set to **`Channel`**, meaning that they will be displayed within the Active Channel bar. To create an item as a desktop component, you override its default value and set **`USAGE`** to **`"DesktopComponent"`**.

The program in Listing 10-4 creates a desktop component for our New York Arts Channel (see Figure 10-5). This is certainly not the most useful desktop component, but covering the dynamic HTML and Java necessary for creating compelling components is beyond the scope of this book.

With the **<USAGE>** tag, Microsoft has added three Internet Explorer specific tags: **`OPENAS`**, **`WIDTH`**, and **`HEIGHT`**. **`OPENAS`** is used to denote the onscreen appearance of the desktop component, allowing you to display HTML pages or images (GIFs or JPEGs). By default, **`OPENAS`** is set to HTML.

`WIDTH` and **`HEIGHT`** are used to denote the onscreen dimensions of your component in pixels. Microsoft believes that smaller is better and recommends that components occupy a maximum size of 200×200 pixels. But Internet Explorer does not enforce any size restrictions, and your component can occupy the entire screen. Note that currently, no method exists for specifying the location of your component. Location is determined by

The <USAGE> Tag

Description: Indicates how an item should be used.

Syntax:

```
<USAGE
VALUE = "Channel" | "Email" | "DesktopComponent" |
     "NONE" | "Screensaver"
>
```

Parameters:

`VALUE="Channel"` These items appear in the Explorer Active Channel bar. This is the default behavior when no **USAGE** element appears under an item.

`VALUE="Email"` These items are e-mailed when the channel content is updated.

`"NONE"` The item will be downloaded but will not appear anyway. Primarily used for caching hidden or future documents.

`"DesktopComponent"` These items are displayed as active desktop components. If you choose this option, you must set the **OPENAS**, **HEIGHT**, and **WIDTH** parameters.

`"ScreenSaver"` These items are displayed in the Internet Explorer HTML screen saver.

Listing 10-4: Creating an Active Desktop Component

```
<!- Sample Active Desktop Component ->
<?XML version="1.0"?>
<!DOCTYPE Channel SYSTEM "http://www.w3c.org/Channel.dtd">

<CHANNEL>
      <TITLE>The New York Arts Channel Desktop
      Component</TITLE>
      <ITEM HREF="http://www.nychannel.com/desktop.html">
            <USAGE VALUE="DesktopComponent">
                  <OPENAS VALUE="HTML" />
                  <WIDTH VALUE="400" />
                  <HEIGHT VALUE="200" />
            </USAGE>
      </ITEM>
</CHANNEL>
```

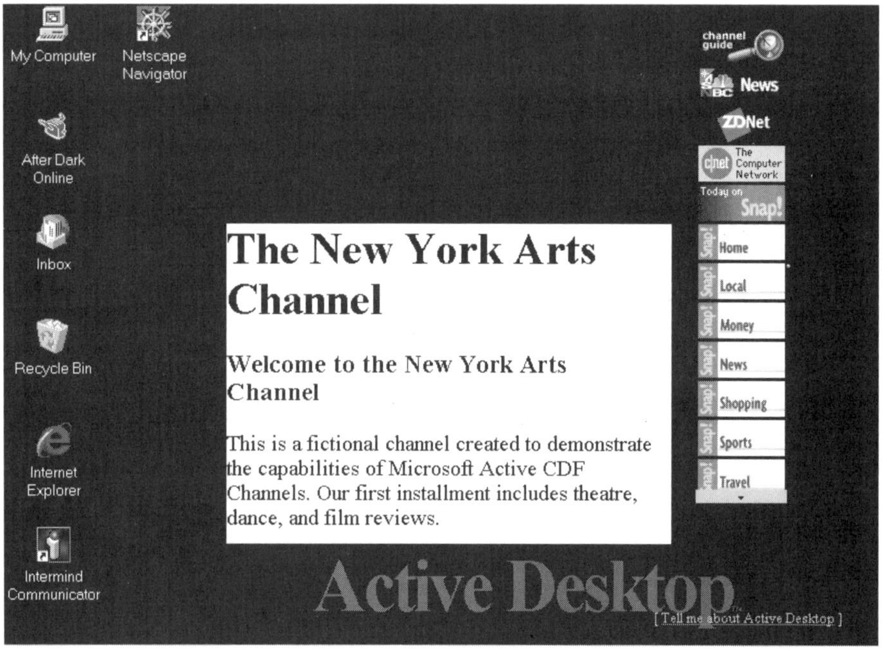

Figure 10-5 The New York Arts desktop component.

Internet Explorer and is based on the number and size of existing desktop components. If things get too crowded, components may be layered on top of one another.

10.5 Creating Channel Screen Savers

If you can create an active desktop component, you can just as easily create an HTML screen saver. Just create an item that points to a dynamic HTML page and set its <USAGE> to "ScreenSaver". Again, the easy part is writing the CDF. The hard part is creating a visually compelling screen saver that makes the most of your content and dynamic HTML.

Listing 10-5 provides sample CDF code for the New York Arts Channel screen saver.

The <OPENAS> Tag

Description: Indicates the content type of the active desktop item specified in the item element.

Syntax:

```
<OPENAS
VALUE = "HTML" | "IMAGE"
/>
```

Parameter: `VALUE="HTML"|"IMAGE"` specifies the content type of the active desktop item. The default is `"HTML"`. `IMAGE` can refer to GIF or JPEG images.

The <HEIGHT> Tag

Description: Indicates the height, in pixels, of the active desktop item specified in the item element.

Syntax:

```
<HEIGHT
VALUE=<"pixels">
/>
```

Parameter: `VALUE="pixels"` is a required parameter. It specifies the height of the active desktop item.

The <WIDTH> Tag

Description: Indicates the width, in pixels, of the active desktop item specified in the item element.

Syntax:

```
<WIDTH
VALUE=<"pixels">
/>
```

Parameter: `VALUE="pixels"` is a required parameter. It specifies the width of the active desktop item.

Listing 10-5: The New York Arts Channel Screen Saver

```
<!- Sample Active Desktop Component ->
<?XML version="1.0"?>
<!DOCTYPE Channel SYSTEM "http://www.w3c.org/Channel.dtd">

<CHANNEL>
	<TITLE>The New York Arts Channel</TITLE>
	<ITEM HREF="http://www.nychannel.com/screensaver.html">
		<USAGE VALUE="ScreenSaver"></USAGE>
	</ITEM>
</CHANNEL>
```

Normally, you will not want to create a screen saver by itself. Instead, you can embed a screen saver item into the rest of your channel CDF file. You could include the screen saver item in Listing 10-5 as the final element in the CDF file from Listing 10-3, for example.

SUMMARY

The Channel Definition Format is a new file format for describing channel contents. You can think of your CDF file as a single document that contains everything pertaining to your channel: its title, its update schedule, its logos, and a complete table of contents describing the individual articles that comprise your channel content.

CDF is very similar in syntax to HTML. Every CDF start tag, for example, has a corresponding end tag. And CDF tags have their own sets of special attributes.

The best way to learn CDF is to learn from examples. This chapter therefore provided several coded examples for our fictional CDF channel, the New York Arts Channel. We started out with the most basic CDF example with three sample articles and then moved on to adding an update schedule. We then explored subchannels and created three newsfolders for theatre reviews, dance reviews, and film reviews. As a final exercise, we explored two new formats for displaying channel contents: active desktop components and dynamic HTML screen savers.

Online Resource

- CDF 101: Creating a Simple Channel **http://www.microsoft.com/workshop/prog/ie4/channels/cdf1-f.htm**. George Young, from Microsoft Corporation, sets out the basics.

PART IV

The PointCast Network

CHAPTER 11

Introduction to PointCast

Founded in 1992, PointCast is the original pioneer of push technology. In February 1996, while most companies were focusing on the Web and Web browsers, PointCast developed a novel approach to delivering information. Instead of pointing and clicking on Web pages, users were encouraged to subscribe to channels. Channel content then was downloaded seamlessly in the background and displayed in rich multimedia screen savers. And PointCast decided to give away all its software for free in the hopes of generating profits from advertising revenue.

The idea struck a chord with users and has propelled PointCast to the front ranks of Web development companies. Today, in fact, PointCast can boast a market audience of more than 1 million subscribers. And, because most of these subscribers use PointCast at work in medium- to large-size companies, the average household income of PointCast viewers is more than $80,000. With this lucrative advertising audience, PointCast now can boast advertising rates that are double the industry average.

PointCast has been so successful that in March, 1997, it was reported that Rupert Murdoch's News Corp. offered a $400 million buy-out. Most analysts, including Hambrecht & Quist, however, estimated that the company was worth far more—perhaps as much as $750 million. PointCast executives rejected Murdoch's offer, preferring instead to take the company public in the very near future.

PointCast now is in an intensely competitive marketplace. Its original model for information delivery has spawned an entire market of push technology products. PointCast now competes with Netscape, Microsoft, Marimba, and a host of smaller push companies.

In its drive to maintain a lead over its competitors, PointCast has opted for a multitiered strategy of premium content, technological innovation, open standards-based Webcasting, targeted audiences, and corporate management tools.

11.1 Premium Content

PointCast is a firm believer that content is king, and it has pressed hard to expand its roster of premium content providers. In February, 1996, PointCast supported only a few premium channels, including the *LA Times* and the *Boston Globe*. Since then, it has gone on to add channels for CNN (see Figure 11-1), CNNfn, CMP, the *New York Times*, and the *Wall Street Journal*. And, more are on the way. Here is the complete roster of current PointCast premium channels:

Boston Globe	*Los Angeles Times*	Sports
Chicago Tribune	Mercury Center	*Star Tribune*
CNN	*Miami Herald*	*Tampa Tribune*

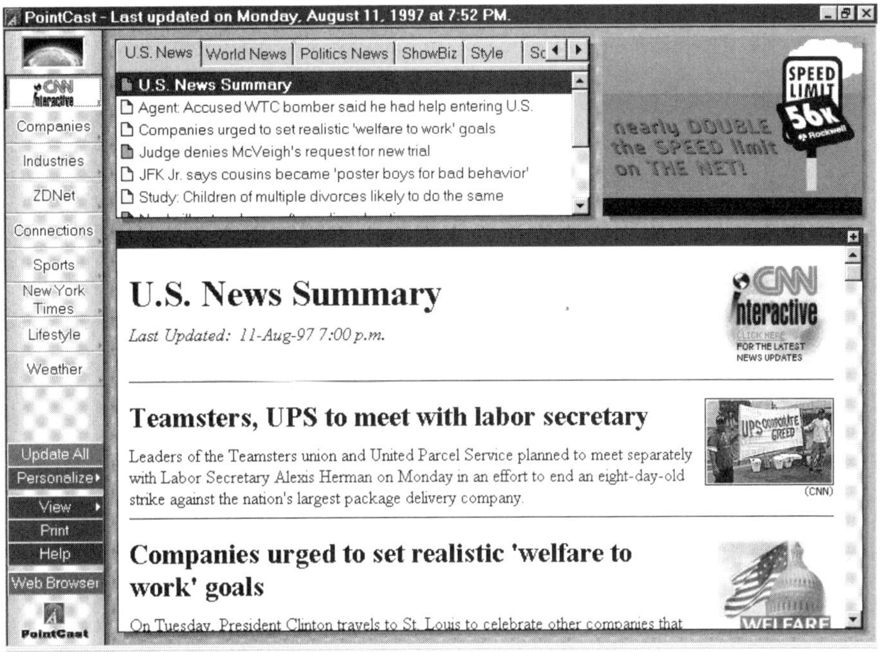

Figure 11-1 CNN on PointCast. PointCast has worked hard to expand its offering of premium content providers.

- CNNfn
- Companies
- Health
- Hot Coco
- Industries
- Lifestyles
- *New York Times*
- News
- Pathfinder
- *Philadelphia* Online
- *Seattle Times*
- TechWeb
- *Wall Street Journal*
- Weather
- *WIRED* News
- ZDNet

11.2 PointCast 2.0

As Microsoft and Netscape delivered their first-generation push products, PointCast released PointCast 2.0, which is a significant software upgrade. PointCast 2.0 is one of the most stable and easy-to-use push technology products today.

With PointCast 2.0, users can do the following:

- Subscribe to PointCast's premium channels
- Receive automatic and seamless channel updates in the background
- Customize the update schedule to meet their needs and optimize bandwidth performance
- Personalize channels to receive specific news topics, company information, and weather forecasts
- Display news headlines in PointCast's patented SmartScreen screen saver or scrolling ticker
- Browse through articles while offline

For complete details on how to use PointCast 2.0, see Chapter 12, "Using PointCast 2.0."

11.3 PointCast Connections Network

With PointCast 2.0, PointCast also heralds the introduction of PointCast Connections. In prior versions of PointCast, users were restricted to subscribing to PointCast's premium channels, such as CNN and the *New York Times*. But, with PointCast Connections, any Web publisher can publish on the PointCast Network.

Connections is based entirely on existing Web standards, including HTTP, HTML, and the proposed *Channel Definition Format* (CDF). This means that anyone can publish a channel without special server software.

PointCast Connections is the company's first attempt to open the PointCast Network beyond its core of premium content providers. As such, it also represents a serious effort to compete with the open Webcasting facilities provided by Netscape's Netcaster and Microsoft's Active Channels.

By agreeing to follow the Channel Definition Format, PointCast is following a potentially lucrative but potentially dangerous partnership with Microsoft. In fact, PointCast was one of the earliest supporters of

Microsoft's CDF proposal and has worked out several strategic partnerships with Microsoft. The first of these agreements enabled PointCast to tightly integrate Internet Explorer within the PointCast Channel Viewer. And, in the second agreement, Microsoft agreed to advertise and distribute PointCast channels through the Microsoft Active Channel technology. This eventually could turn into a complicated dance of cooperation and competition, and PointCast is likely to remain wary of Microsoft's overall Internet strategy.

11.4 Targeted Audiences

In an effort to capture lucrative niche markets, PointCast has expanded the PointCast Network to target specific industries, regions, and professions. The first of these is a Japanese edition of PointCast, created in cooperation with the *Asahi Shimbun*, Japan's leading daily newspaper. A PointCast Asia is also in the works; its goal is to deliver national and local news from Southeast Asia and Greater China in both English and Chinese.

PointCast also is busy creating niche markets for United States audiences. The first of these, the PointCast Network Government Insider, will deliver targeted news and information to federal employees, military personnel, and government contractors. Specific channels include defense news, legislative news (including bill status and committee schedules), and a channel devoted to government executives.

On the heels of the Government edition, PointCast is creating the PointCast HealthCare Insider, which targets healthcare professionals. Channels will include medical news, journal reports, topical channels on subjects such as allergy or cancer, and channels devoted to specific healthcare professions, such as nursing and pharmacology.

Last, but not least, PointCast also is targeting younger audiences with the PointCast College Network. The Network will include content from *Billboard* magazine, University Wire, E! Online, and the Music Zone, as well as resources for academic research, graduate school information, and internship opportunities. The network also will include tools for broadcasting internal campus news, such as class schedules and event calendars, and even for creating extranet channels for alumni.

These initiatives are part of PointCast's continued strategy to focus on specific audiences and deliver timely information to niche markets. The more targeted and relevant the information, the more likely users will maintain subscriptions. And the more likely PointCast will capture advertising revenue.

11.5 Corporate Management Tools

PointCast's original and most lucrative market remains corporate employees with dedicated connections to the Internet. PointCast has strategized to further focus on this market and the lucrative intranet business by delivering a set of corporate tools for managing PointCast data throughout the corporate enterprise.

When PointCast shipped its first version of the PointCast Network software, the most common criticism was its huge bandwidth requirements. In fact, PointCast swamped many corporate networks, forcing some *Information Systems* (IS) departments to ban PointCast entirely. To alleviate this problem, PointCast released the corporate I-Server in the spring of 1997.

The *I-Server* acts as a proxy server for PointCast data. It basically checks the PointCast central broadcasting facility at regular intervals, caches the latest news updates, and then relays this information to clients within the local area network. It thereby can reduce PointCast data through the corporate network by as much as 80 percent.

The I-Server also provides facilities for creating intranet and extranet channels. Corporate channels can deliver secure information to employees, including company announcements, human resources information, industry-specific news, and competitor information. And all this information can appear alongside business information from PointCast's premium content providers.

As this books goes to press, PointCast is busy creating a new suite of corporate tools for controlling employee access to the PointCast Connections Network. These tools will enable IS managers to set mandatory, recommended, or optional channels, as well as to filter for office-appropriate content.

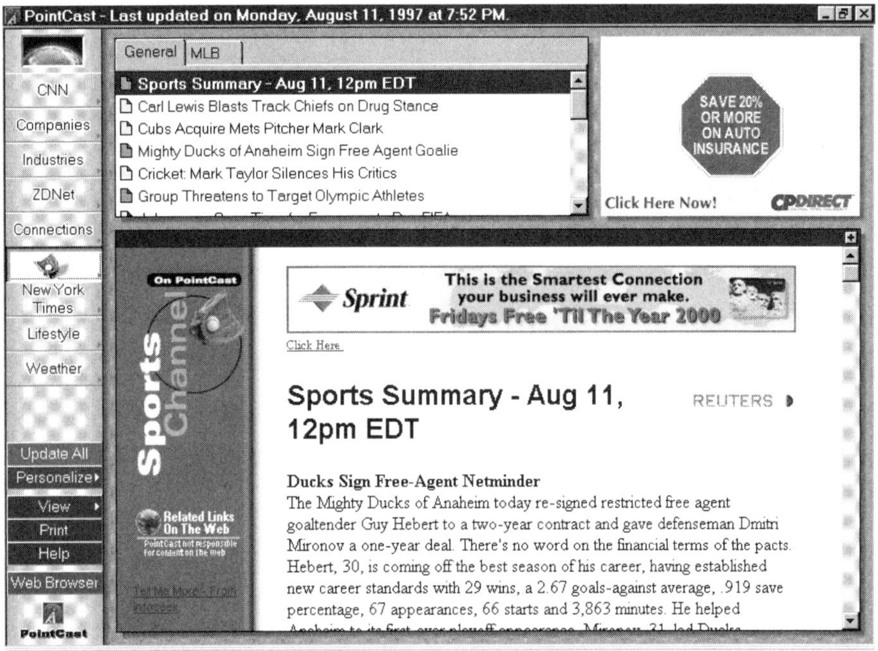

Figure 11-2 Sports updates. Looking for today's scores? The latest sports statistics?

11.6 Assessing PointCast

PointCast has been in the push technology business longer than anyone. As such, it still retains a technological lead over its closest competitors, while also succeeding in delivering the most wide-ranging and up-to-date news and information. Its strengths are quite considerable:

- PointCast 2.0 is the only major second-generation push application on the market. It is fast, stable, and easy to use.
- PointCast's premium content providers provide reliable, timely, and accurate news and information.
- The PointCast client software offers significant customization, including the capability to personalize news channels and display news content on the PointCast SmartScreen or ticker (see Figure 11-3).
- The PointCast I-Server provides a complete suite of tools for managing push traffic within the enterprise and creating secure corporate channels.

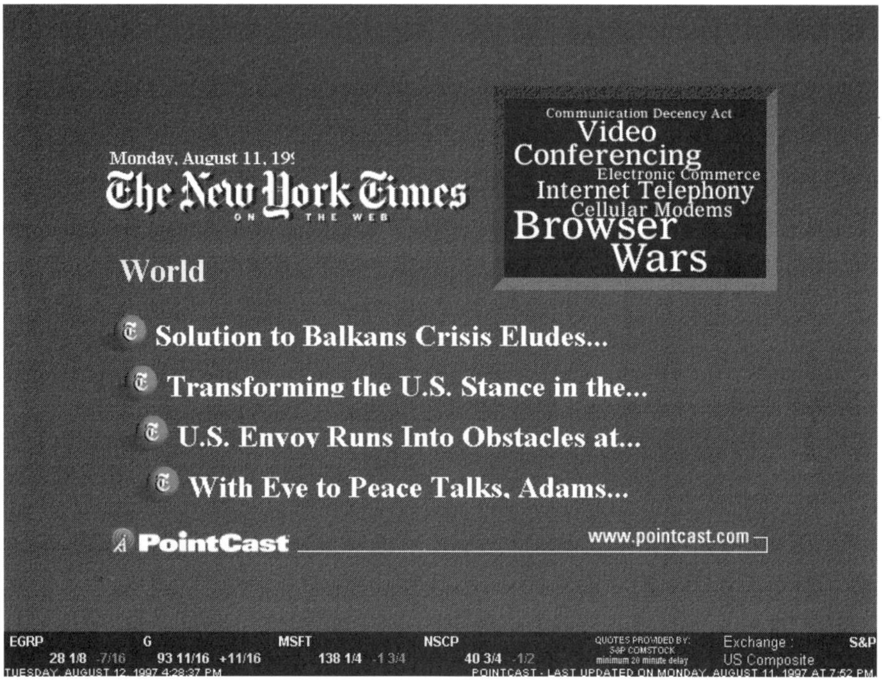

Figure 11-3 The PointCast SmartScreen presents dynamic news and advertisements.

- PointCast has a broad market audience of more than 1 million subscribers, including broad access to business professionals.

The PointCast Connections Network also offers significant advantages:

- Capability to Webcast from any Web server with no special server software required
- Complete support for the *Channel Definition Format* (CDF)
- Easy-to-use channel-creation tools, including the PointCast Connections Builder (see Chapter 13, "Creating PointCast Animations") and the PointCast Studio for creating custom animations (see Chapter 14, "Creating PointCast Animations")
- Support for subscription- or fee-based channels
- Corporate tools for managing channel subscriptions and a filter for office-appropriate content

The only significant disadvantage of the PointCast Connections Network is its inability to broadcast software applications, including Java applets (see Chapter 13, Section 13.3.3, "Formatting Article Contents").

SUMMARY

PointCast is the original pioneer of push technology. Since its inception, PointCast has followed a strategy of delivering targeted information to corporate employees with direct connections to the Internet and making a profit through advertising revenue.

PointCast also has pursued a multitiered strategy of providing premium content, including CNN, the *New York Times*, and the *Wall Street Journal*; targeting audiences with new international initiatives in Asia and new domestic initiatives in government, healthcare, and academia; providing corporate management tools, including the I-Server for managing push traffic and creating secure corporate channels; and supporting open standards-based Webcasting through the PointCast Connections Network, enabling anyone to publish on the PointCast Network. Recently, PointCast released Version 2.0 of its flagship product, which is one of the most stable and easy-to-use push technology applications on the market.

Online Resource

- PointCast Web Site

  `http://www.pointcast.com`

  Check here for product updates and press releases.

CHAPTER 12

Using PointCast 2.0

PointCast 2.0 is one of the most easy-to-use and stable push technology applications on the market today. If you have used previous versions of PointCast, you should be quite happy with the significant improvements of 2.0:

- Native 32-bit support for faster performance on Windows 95/NT
- Improved bandwidth use—by as much as 55 percent for most major channels
- Tight integration with Microsoft Internet Explorer 3.0 and 4.0
- Single-channel updates
- A completely customizable screen ticker
- Enhanced 90-day stock price charts
- New user interface for marking news articles as read, unread, or protected
- Complete support for the PointCast Connections Network

12.1 Installation

12.1.1 System Requirements

Windows 95/NT PointCast 2.0 currently requires the following system requirements:

- PC/AT 486/33 compatible or higher
- 8 Mbytes RAM
- 10 Mbytes free hard drive space
- Direct or dial-up connection to the Internet
- 256-color mode or higher

12.1.2 Installing PointCast

The PointCast 2.0 client is available at no charge from the PointCast Web site at **http://www.pointcast.com**. A copy of the software also is available on the CD-ROM at the back of this book. To begin installation, just double-click on the PointCast self-extracting executable file.

12.1.3 Registration and Setup

During the installation process, PointCast guides you through a five-step Registration and Setup Wizard:

1. Review the PointCast licensing agreement.
2. Enter your registration information, including your e-mail address, country, ZIP code, age, and gender. PointCast uses this information to create an aggregate demographic profile of the entire PointCast audience but will not release your individual profile information to advertisers.
3. You can elect to join a PointCast review panel and provide PointCast with user feedback.
4. Specify your Internet connection (see the following section).
5. Specify a default Web browser (see section 12.1.5, "Choosing a Web Browser").

NOTE: *If you are upgrading from a previous version of PointCast, your registration and channel-subscription information is maintained and automatically ported over to 2.0.*

12.1.4 Specifying Your Internet Connection

You have three main options for an Internet connection:

Direction connection (nonmodem): This applies to most medium- to large-size businesses or educational institutions with direct Internet connections.

Windows 95/NT dial-up (modem): This applies to most home users with a modem. Click the Configure Connection button to select a previously configured Internet connection. If you have not already configured a connection, click the Windows Start button, choose Accessories, and then choose Dial-Up Networking.

Other modem service: Some *Internet service providers* (ISPs) supply their own Internet connection software. Check your ISP documentation or contact your ISP for further help.

12.1.5 Choosing a Web Browser

PointCast includes its own built-in Web browser, but it also can be integrated with your default Internet Explorer or Netscape Navigator browser. When you initially view article contents in the PointCast Channel Viewer, the articles are rendered by the built-in PointCast browser. But, when you follow links within articles, you can choose to have these articles rendered by PointCast, Internet Explorer, or Netscape Navigator.

If you choose to use the PointCast browser, note that it does have some limitations; the most serious is a lack of support for Java. And, if you choose to use Netscape, it is launched as an external application and so is not tightly integrated with the PointCast Channel Viewer. The best option usually is to select Internet Explorer, because it appears in the Channel Viewer and includes complete support for Java.

12.2 Orientation

After you complete the PointCast installation and registration process, launch PointCast from the Windows Start menu. Then click the Update All button to receive your first batch of news.

12.2.1 The User Interface

The PointCast Channel Viewer interface consists of five panels (see Figure 12-1):

Figure 12-1 The PointCast Channel Viewer.

- The control bar for selecting channels. This includes options for updating, printing, and personalizing channel contents, as well as options for launching your Web browser and getting help information.
- The Channel Content interface for selecting topics and news articles. Each channel is divided into a number of tabbed folders, and each contains a list of current news articles.
- The Article Viewer for displaying the currently selected article. You can maximize the article view by clicking on the plus (+) sign in the upper right corner.
- The Advertisement window for broadcasting the current multimedia advertisement. Just click on the ad to retrieve additional information.
- The screen ticker for displaying a scrolling list of the current news headlines.

By default, you are subscribed to a number of channels, including CNN, ZDNet, Companies, Industries, Weather, Sports, Lifestyle, and Connections.

12.3 Working with Articles

12.3.1 Viewing Articles

To view an article, select a channel in the control bar, select a news topic, and click on the article. Remember that you can maximize the Article Viewer by clicking on the plus (+) sign in the upper right corner and then return it to its original size by clicking the minus (−) sign.

12.3.2 Marking Articles

New articles appear in yellow. Older articles that you have read appear in gray. To mark an article as read or unread, right-click on the article and choose your setting (see Figure 12-2).

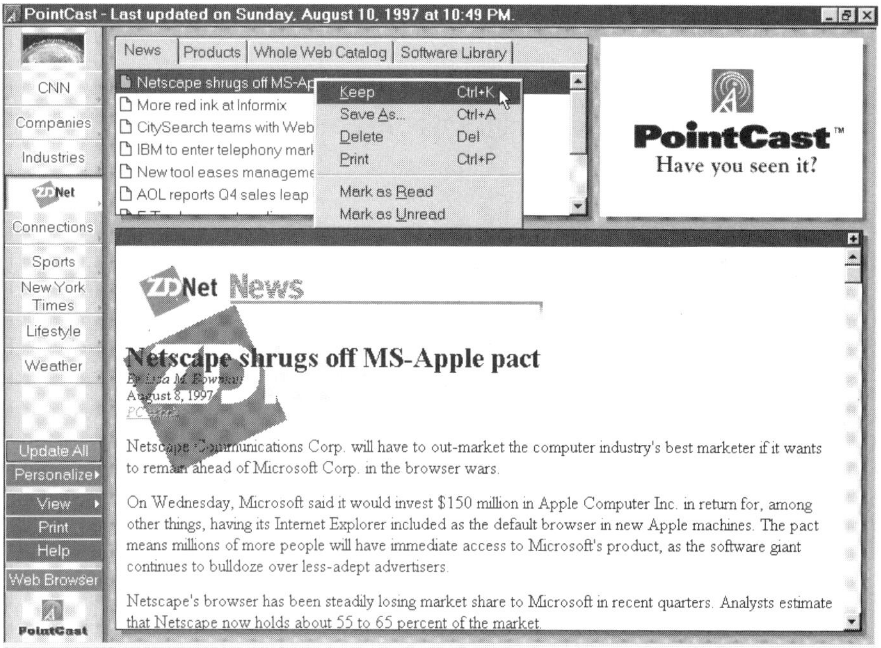

Figure 12-2 Working with articles. By right-clicking on an article, you can keep, save, print, or delete it. You also can mark it as read or unread.

12.3.3 Keeping and Saving Articles

Each topic folder can hold up to 25 articles at any one time. When this limit is reached, older articles are purged as new ones are downloaded. To protect an article from deletion, you can elect to keep or protect it. Just select the article by right-clicking it and choose Keep. Articles that have been marked for keeping are displayed with a small floppy disk icon; those articles are protected from deletion until you choose to manually delete them.

PointCast offers the option of saving articles to your hard drive. Again, select the article by right-clicking it and choose Save As. You can save your article in HTML or text format.

12.3.4 Printing Articles

To print the contents of an article, click the Print button on the control bar. Or, right-click the article and choose Print.

12.3.5 Deleting Articles

Older news articles are deleted automatically to save hard drive space. Nonetheless, you have the option of manually deleting articles. Select the article by right-clicking it and choose Delete. There is no method of restoring deleted files.

12.4 Working with Channels

12.4.1 Adding/Removing Channels

You can subscribe to a maximum of nine premium channels. To add or remove channels, click the Personalize button and select Add/Remove channels. The Add/Remove Channels dialog box appears (see Figure 12-3). Available channels are listed on the left, and selected or subscribed chan-

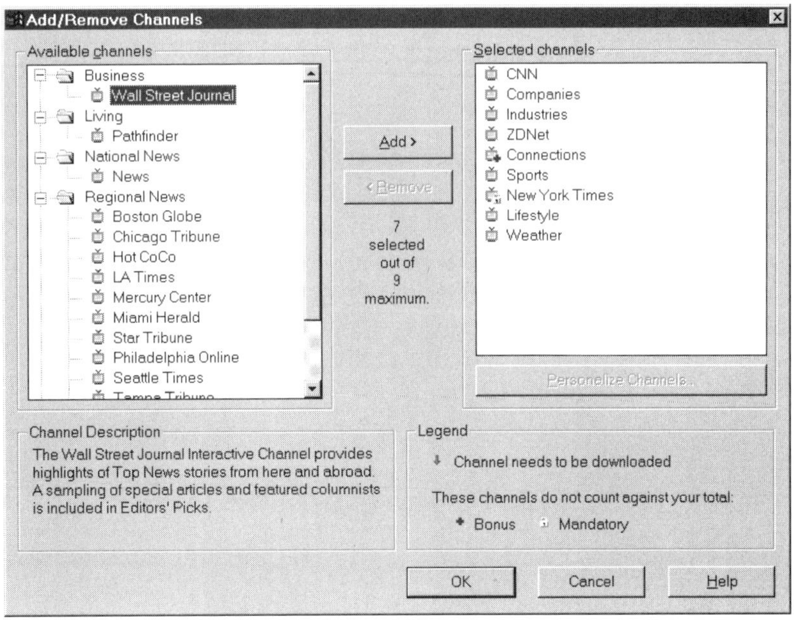

Figure 12-3 The Add/Remove Channels dialog box.

Table 12-1
Current PointCast Channels

Boston Globe	*Chicago Tribune*
CNN	CNNfn
Companies	Health
Hot Coco	Industries
Lifestyles	*Los Angeles Times*
Mercury Center	*Miami Herald*
News	*New York Times*
Pathfinder	Philadelphia Online
Seattle Times	Sports
Star Tribune	*Tampa Tribune*
TechWeb	*Wall Street Journal*
Weather	*WIRED* News
ZDNet	

nels are listed on the right. Channel descriptions appear in the lower left corner.

To add a channel, select its title in the list of available channels and click Add. To remove a channel, select its title in the list of selected channels and click Remove.

Note that some channels are marked as mandatory; these are denoted with a yellow padlock icon. Mandatory channels usually are based on region and cannot be removed. On the East Coast, for example, the *New York Times* is a mandatory channel. Bonus channels with a blue plus (+) icon denote optional new channels; for now, the only optional new channel is the Connections channel. Table 12-1 shows the current PointCast channels.

12.4.2 Changing the Order of Channels

You can change the order of your channels by clicking-and-dragging channels up or down on the control bar.

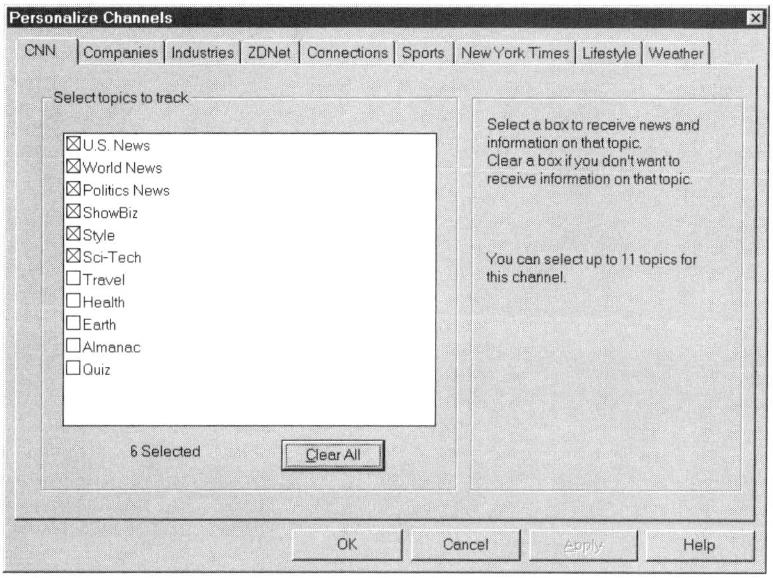

Figure 12-4 Personalizing your channels. In the Personalize Channels dialog box, you can add or remove topics for each channel; just click on the topics that interest you.

12.4.3 Personalizing Channels

To personalize your channels, click Personalize on the control bar and select Personalize Channels. Or, right-click on a channel on the control bar and choose Personalize.

The Personalize Channels dialog box appears, as shown in Figure 12-4. Here, you can add or remove topics for each channel. Just click on the topics that interest you. You can choose up to 11 topics for the CNN channel, for example—from U.S. News and World News to ShowBiz to Travel to Health.

12.4.4 The Companies Channel

The Companies Channel displays 90-day stock-price information and press releases for publicly held companies. Press releases are issued by Business Wire and PRNewsWire.

You can personalize the Companies Channel to track up to 25 companies. Right-click on the Companies Channel and select Personalize the Companies Channel. Then enter the company ticker symbol and click

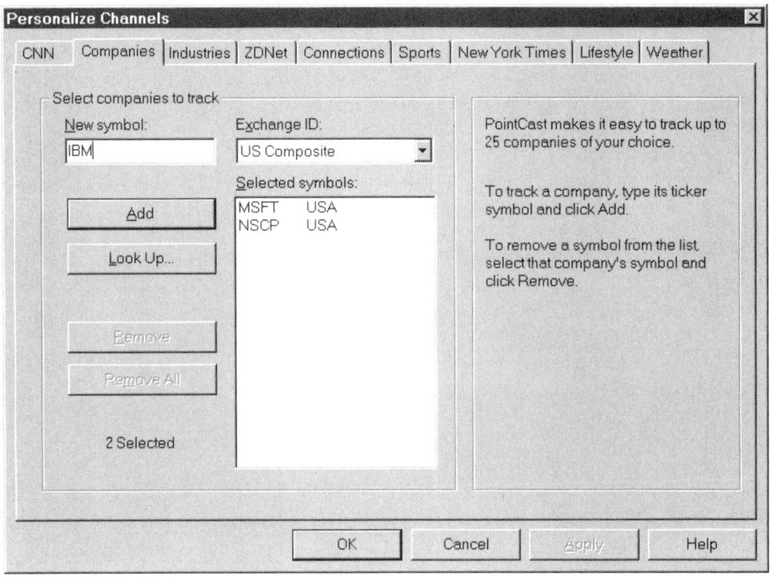

Figure 12-5 Personalizing the Companies Channel. You can track up to 25 companies, and if you don't remember a company's ticker symbol, you can just look it up.

Add. If you do not know the ticker symbol, you can look it up by clicking the Look Up button (see Figure 12-5).

Note that the 90-day stock charts are interactive. Hold your mouse cursor over the chart, and you can receive details on stock open, close, high, low, and volume information (see Figure 12-6).

12.4.5 The Weather Channel

The PointCast Weather Channel provides weather forecasts, maps, and satellite images on the latest weather conditions. Forecasts are displayed in a scrolling window at the top of the screen, and maps are displayed in the lower quarter of the screen (see Figure 12-7). You can pause the scrolling forecast window by clicking and holding the mouse button. Or, you can change the speed and direction of the scroll by clicking the window, moving the mouse up or down, and then releasing the mouse button. To magnify the maps and satellite images, just point-and-click.

You can personalize the Weather Channel to receive up to 50 city forecasts and up to 10 regional maps. Right-click the Weather button and select Personalize the Weather Channel. To add new forecasts, select the Forecasts radio button, double-click on a region, select a city, and click Add (see Figure 12-8). Follow the same procedure for maps.

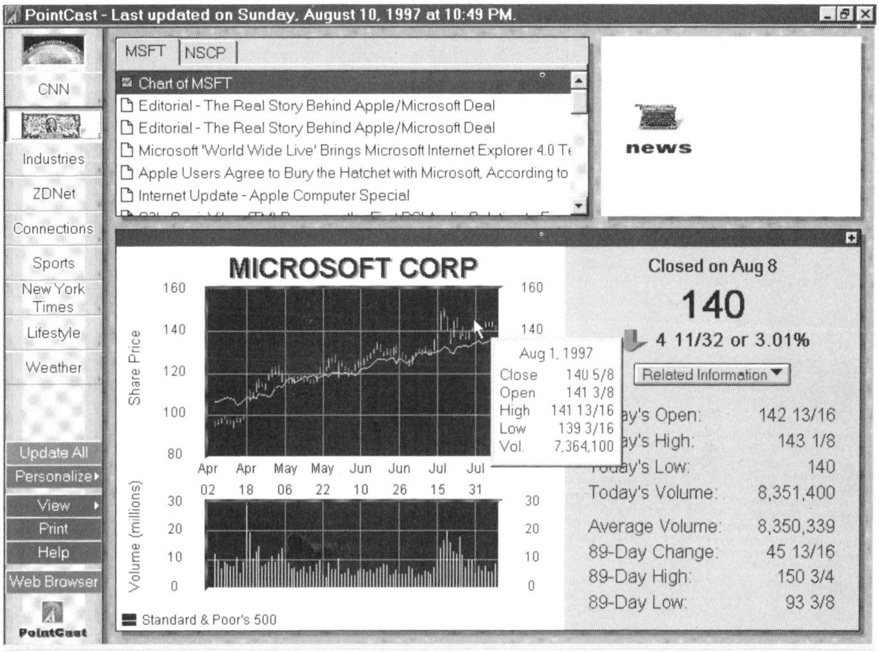

Figure 12-6 The Companies Channel includes interactive 90-day stock charts plus the latest press releases from Business Wire and PRNewsWire.

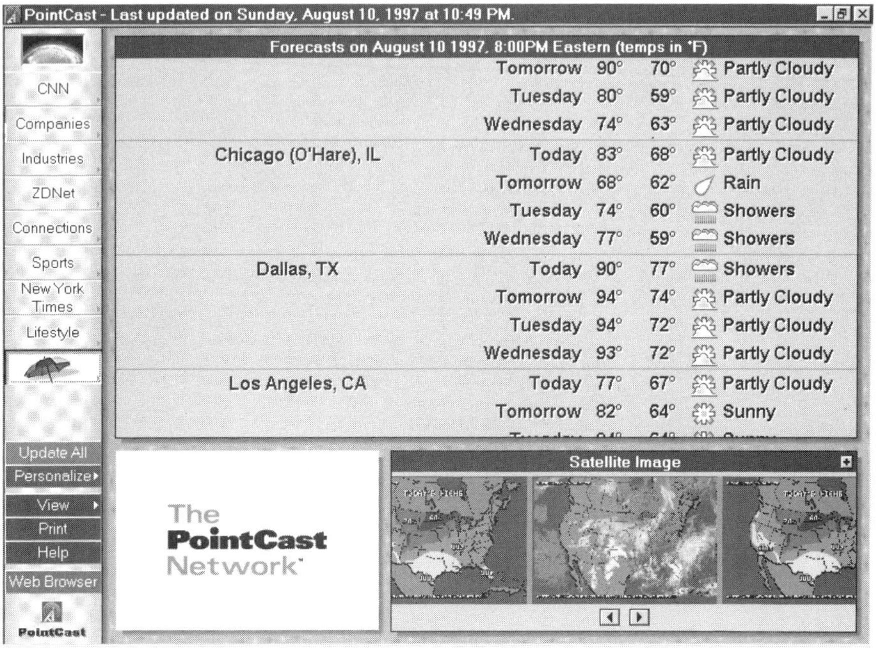

Figure 12-7 The Weather Channel provides weather forecasts, maps, and satellite images on the latest weather conditions.

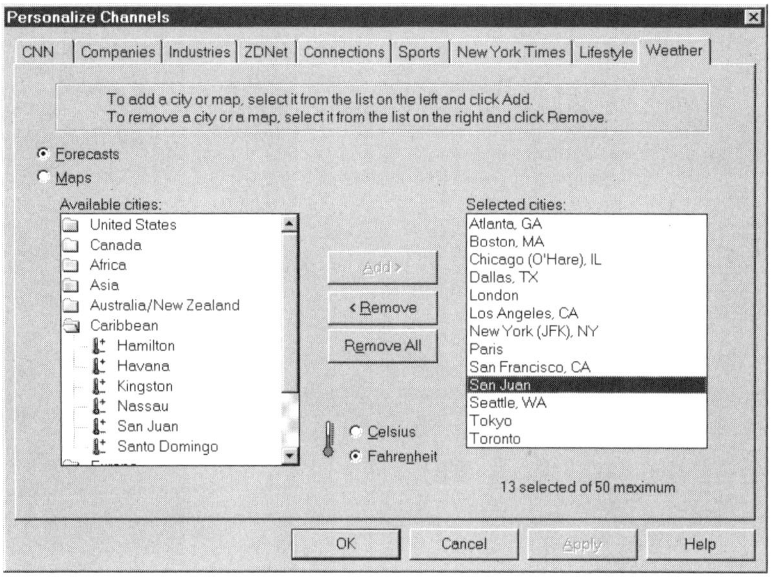

Figure 12-8 Personalizing the Weather Channel; you can receive up to 50 city forecasts and up to 10 regional maps.

You also can choose to display temperatures in Celsius or Fahrenheit.

12.5 Updating Channel Contents

To set or change your automatic update schedule, click Personalize, select Application Settings, and select the Update tab. PointCast supports four options for channel updates:

All Day Schedule: Updates to PointCast occur throughout the day. This option is best if you already are connected directly to the Internet. Updates occur whenever your computer is idle for more than 10 minutes, and approximately every half hour.

Limited Schedule: Updates occur at lunch time, and before and after regular business hours. Updates therefore never occur during the regular business hours of 9 a.m. to noon and 1 p.m. to 5 p.m.

Custom Schedule: You create your own customized schedule for channel updates. You can set the exact time and day of week for each update.

Manual Update: PointCast is updated only when you manually choose to do so. This is probably the best option for home users with modems.

NOTE: *You always can stop a channel update by clicking the Stop button.*

TIP: *You can manually update all your channels by selecting Update All. Or, you can update individual channels by right-clicking the channel on the control bar and selecting Update the xyz* Channel.

12.6 Working with the PointCast SmartScreen

In addition to the PointCast Channel Viewer, PointCast includes the SmartScreen screen saver. Whenever your computer is idle for a period of time, the SmartScreen kicks in and displays a multimedia-rich screen saver with headlines, article summaries, and advertisements (see Figure 12-9).

To set up the SmartScreen, click Personalize, select Application Settings, and select the SmartScreen tab. Here, you can set SmartScreen as your default screen saver and set the idle time in minutes. You also can choose an activation corner to manually start the screen saver.

While the SmartScreen is running, you can pause it at any time by pressing Alt. PointCast provides two options for exiting:

Option 1: The SmartScreen closes when you click anywhere on the SmartScreen background. Mouse-cursor movements alone do not close the screen saver.

Option 2: The SmartScreen closes with any mouse-cursor movement. If you want to view an article's contents, you first must hold down the Alt key and point.

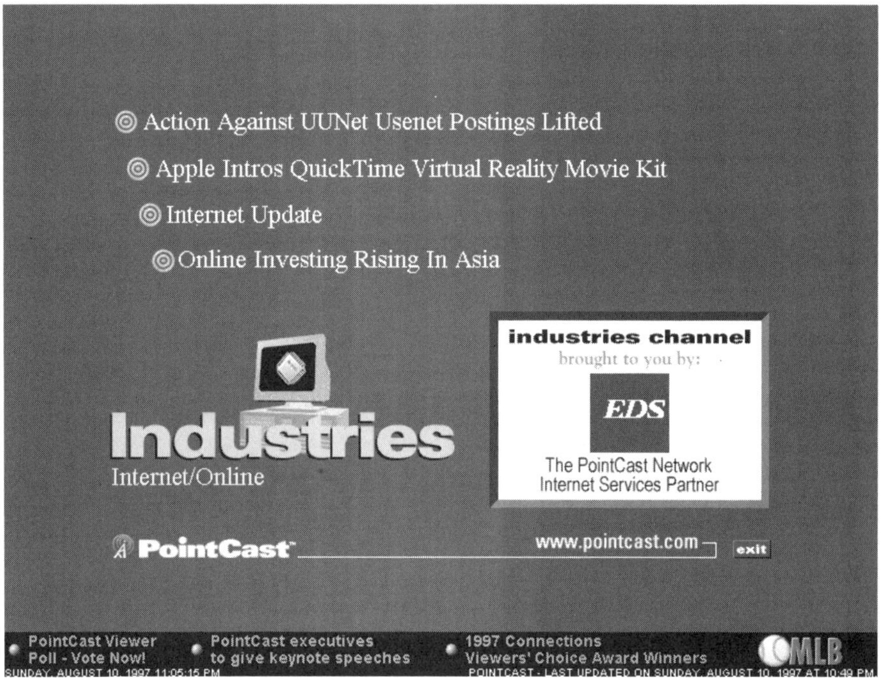

Figure 12-9
The PointCast SmartScreen replaces your regular screen saver with dynamic headlines, article summaries, and multimedia advertisements.

TIP: *You now can password protect the SmartScreen. In Windows 95/NT, right-click on any empty area of the desktop and choose Properties. Then select the Screen Saver tab and select Password Protected. You are prompted to supply and verify a password.*

12.7 Working with the Screen Ticker

The PointCast screen ticker provides a scrolling list of news headlines from your current list of subscribed channels. When open, the ticker always is displayed as a top-level application, so you can view it while working in other applications (see Figure 12-10).

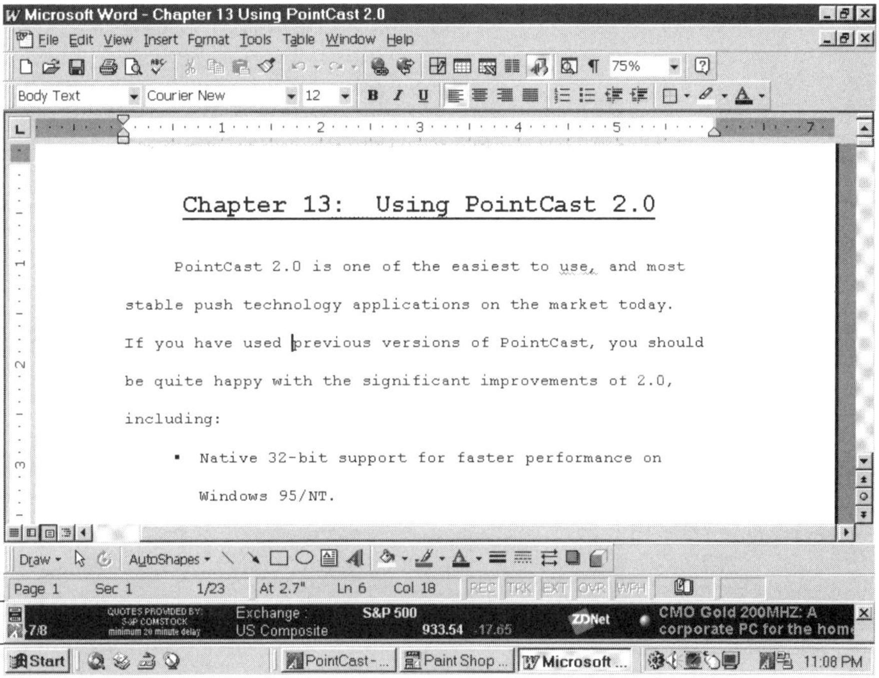

Figure 12-10 You can view the screen ticker even when working in other applications.

12.7.1 Showing/Hiding the Ticker

To display the ticker, click View and choose Show Ticker. To later hide the ticker, click View and choose Hide or click the x icon in the upper right corner of the ticker.

12.7.2 Selecting an Article

To view an article's contents, double-click on its headline. The article opens in the PointCast Channel Viewer.

12.7.3 Setting Ticker Direction and Speed

You can pause the scroll at any time by clicking on the ticker and holding down the mouse button. You can change the speed and direction of the scroll by clicking on the ticker and throwing the hand icon to the right or left.

12.7.4 Setting the Ticker Location

The ticker can be located at the top or bottom of the screen. To set the location, click on the Ticker Options box in the upper left-hand corner of the ticker and select Move Ticker to Top or Move Ticker to Bottom.

12.7.5 Personalizing the Ticker

You can personalize the ticker to display headlines for a specific subset of subscribed channels. Click on the Ticker Options box, select Personalize Ticker, and select the channels you want to include.

12.8 Working with Connections Channels

By far, the greatest new feature of PointCast 2.0 is the PointCast Connections Network. Prior to Version 2.0, viewers were restricted to subscribing to PointCast's premium channels, such as CNN or the *New York Times*. But, with 2.0, you now can subscribe to hundreds—perhaps thousands—of additional channels through the Connections Network. Table 12-2 shows some of the channels available through this subscription.

If you are considering creating your own PointCast channel, the PointCast Connections Network will enable you to reach your potential audience.

12.8.1 Adding/Removing Connections Channels

You can subscribe to a Connections channel in two ways. The first method is to search the PointCast/Excite Connections directory. The second is to

Table 12-2

Some of the channels available through Connections Network.

Fidelity	Knight Ridder	Telecomworldwire Inkling
Forbes	M2	TimeCast
Fujitsu	MCI	Toshiba
IBM	Microsoft CarPoint	*U.S. News & World Report*
Inc. Online	Microsoft Expedia	Virtual Vineyards
iVillage About Work	Oracle	*Worth* Online
iVillage Parent	Progressive	
Soup	Networks	

visit an existing Web site with a PointCast channel and simply click on the "Get PointCast Connections" icon. This downloads the channel-configuration file and immediately subscribes you.

To search the Connections directory, right-click on the Connections channel, select Personalize the Connections Channel, and click the Add button. This takes you to the Connections directory (see Figure 12-11). Just browse through the categories and select a channel to subscribe yourself.

***NOTE:** By default, you initially are subscribed to three connections: the PointCast Viewpoints Channel, Fidelity Investments, and the PC Financial Network (see Figure 12-12).*

12.8.2 Viewing Connections Articles

To view your individual connections, click the Connections Channel on the control bar, select a channel tab, and select an article. Note that the control bar is reserved for premium channels; currently, no facility exists for placing individual connections separately on the control bar.

12.8.3 Connection Properties

Each connection has its own update schedule and a number of individual properties. To view the connection properties, follow the directions for per-

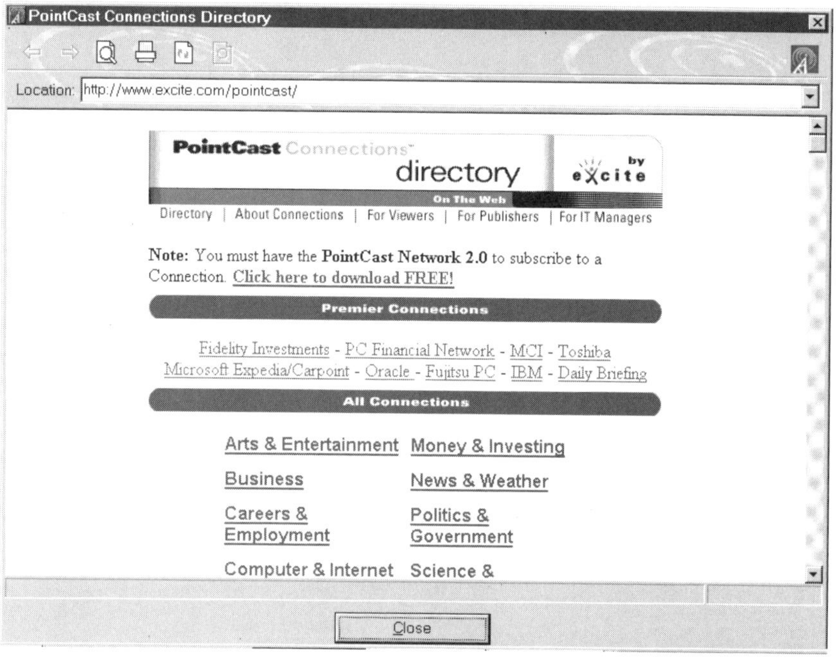

Figure 12-11 The PointCast/Excite Connections directory.

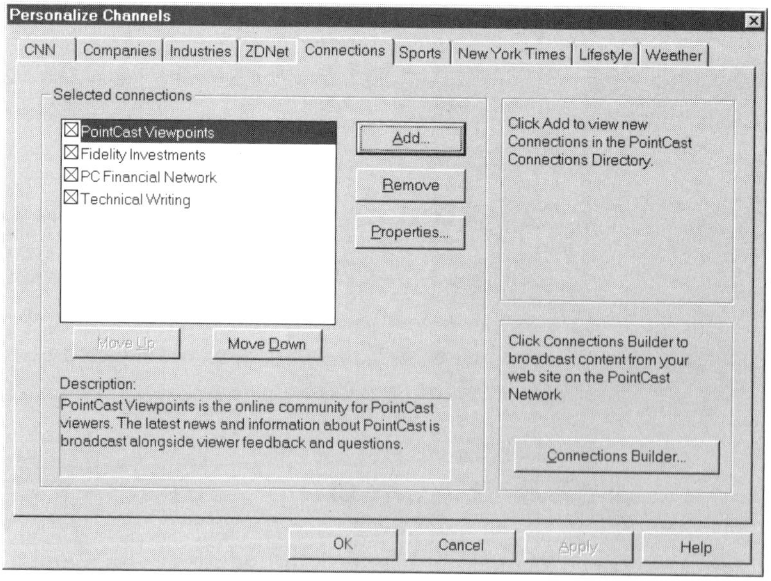

Figure 12-12 Adding and removing connections.

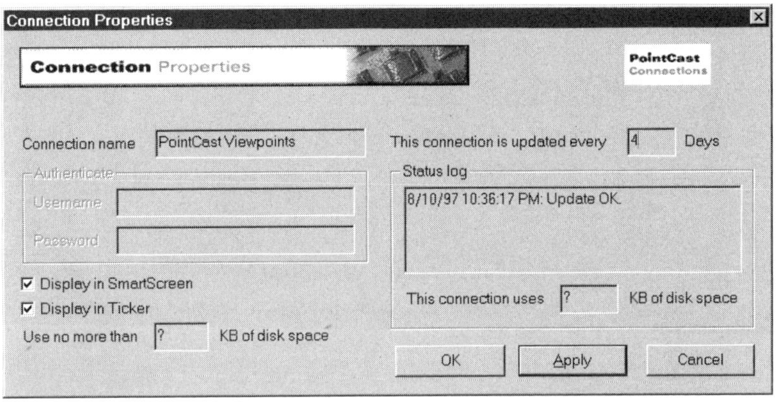

Figure 12-13 Setting connection properties. Each connection has its own update schedule and Status log. If your connection is restricted to paying subscribers, your username and password are saved here.

sonalizing the Connections channel, select a channel, and click the Properties button.

The update schedule is listed in the top right corner of the dialog box and is set initially by the content provider. A Status log indicates the date and time of the last update, along with any error messages.

In the Connection Properties dialog box, you also can elect to display the connection in the SmartScreen and/or the ticker. And, finally, if the connection requires a username and password, you can enter it here (see Figure 12-13).

SUMMARY

PointCast 2.0 is a significant software upgrade; it is one of the easiest and most reliable push technology applications on the market today. PointCast 2.0 features include native 32-bit support for faster performance on Windows 95/NT; improved bandwidth use; tight integration with Microsoft Internet Explorer 3.0 and 4.0; single-channel updates; a completely customizable screen ticker; enhanced 90-day stock-price charts; and a new user interface for marking news articles as read, unread, or protected. By far, however, the greatest new feature of PointCast 2.0 is the PointCast Connections Network, which enables viewers to subscribe to hundreds—perhaps thousands—of new channels.

To get started with PointCast 2.0, the best option is to install the software and just click Update All. You immediately begin to receive your first batch of news and information. PointCast channels are completely customizable, as are the PointCast SmartScreen screen saver and screen ticker.

Online Resources

- PointCast 2.0 Windows 95/NT Users Guide **http://www.pointcast.com/support/pcn/help/2.0/new**. A short guide to using PointCast 2.0.
- PointCast 2.0 Windows 95/NT FAQ **http://www.pointcast.com/support/pcn/pcn20/20faqs**. What are the symptoms of a possible firewall problem? How do I connect to PointCast with America Online? Can I track quotations for companies listed on foreign stock exchanges? What about companies that are not traded publicly? Check out the FAQ.

CHAPTER 13

Creating PointCast Channels

This chapter provides a thorough overview of creating your own PointCast channels. To ease the process of channel creation, PointCast has created two free development programs:

PointCast Connections Builder: Creates and maintains channels

PointCast Studio: Creates custom animations and screen savers

The PointCast software engineers spent a considerable amount of time and effort making these two development programs both flexible and user friendly. In fact, these two programs combine to create the most flexible, robust, and easy-to-use platform in the industry for developing Webcasting channels.

When using the Connections Builder, you do not have to write a single line of code. In fact, you can create an entirely new channel simply by following a three-step wizard. After you complete the wizard, you can add or delete new articles to or from your channel simply by pointing-and-clicking.

Using PointCast Studio, you easily can create full-screen animations in minutes. Among the many animation effects you can create are flying text, animated corporate logos, and animated bar graphs. You also can choose from more than a dozen built-in transition effects, such as dissolve, venetian blinds, and automatic scaling.

This chapter covers the creation of new channels with the Connections Builder. Chapter 14, "Creating PointCast Animations," covers PointCast Studio. For both these chapters, it is highly recommended that you first install the necessary software and follow along onscreen as you read. All the necessary software and sample programs are included on the CD-ROM at the back of this book.

13.1 Getting Started

13.1.1 Installing the PointCast Connections Builder

Every copy of the PointCast 2.0 client software includes a copy of the PointCast Connections Builder. If you haven't already installed the PointCast 2.0 client, you can install it from the CD-ROM at the back of this book or download a copy from `http://www.pointcast.com`.

13.1.2 Before You Begin

The next few sections guide you through the PointCast channel-creation process. But, before you begin, it is helpful to organize a few preliminary items:

Set up your Web server. PointCast works by retrieving specified files and articles from your existing Web server. And, to completely test your channel, you will need access privileges to add new files to your Web server; make sure that you have these access privileges before proceeding. PointCast works with any standard Web server, including the Microsoft *Internet Information Server* (IIS) and the Netscape SuiteSpot product line.

Organize your articles. Before you start working with the Connections Builder, it is recommended that you organize a few sample articles from your existing Web site. For now, just write down the URLs for two or three sample HTML pages from your existing Web site. This might include press releases, news updates, technical reports, or product information. If you don't have any articles, take the time out now to create two or three dummy HTML pages.

TIP: *During the development of your channel, you might find it tedious to work off your existing Web site, because you constantly will need to transfer files from your local hard drive to your Web site. To help ease the development and testing process, you might want to consider installing a personal Web server, such as O'Reilly's WebSite Server 1.1 or Microsoft's Personal Web Server. You then can thoroughly test your channel on your local machine. When everything is working, you can reconfigure your settings and transfer everything over to your real Web site.*

13.2 Creating PointCast Channels

13.2.1 The Connections Wizard

You can create a new channel manually by using the Connections Builder, or you can use the built-in Connections Wizard. The Connections Wizard guides you through a simple three-step process. Each of the steps is covered in detail in this section, but here is a quick overview:

1. **Select and define your articles.** Each PointCast channel consists of a set of articles. Articles can be HTML documents or PointCast animations. You identify the location of each article and set a

number of properties. You can determine the location and palette for each animation, for example, or decide whether your articles should appear in the user's Channel Viewer or the SmartScreen screen saver.

2. **Name and describe your connection.** Each PointCast channel must have a name and a short description. The channel name appears on a tab in the user's Channel Viewer. The description appears when the user subscribes to your channel and in the PointCast Connections directory.
3. **Configure your connection.** Users can subscribe to your PointCast channel by visiting your existing Web site and downloading your channel configuration or CDF file. This last step requests the location of your configuration file and enables you to set the schedule for automatic channel updates. During this final step, you also can register your channel with PointCast and receive a *Recreational Software Advisory Council* (RSAC) content rating.

13.2.2 Launching the Connections Builder

To run the Connections Builder, choose Programs | PointCast | Connections Builder from your Windows Start menu.

To run the Connections Wizard, select the Create a New PointCast Connection File option and make sure that Using Connections Wizard is selected. Then click OK.

13.2.3 Step 1: Select and Define Your Articles

In step 1, you add the individual articles that constitute your channel (see Figure 13-1). For now, you can use the sample HTML pages you gathered from your existing Web site.

For each article, you need to enter a set of properties:

Title: The title that will appear in the PointCast 2.0 Channel Viewer.

URL: The exact URL location of your HTML article.

Type: Each article can be an HTML page or a PointCast animation. For now, just check HTML for all your pages. Using the PointCast Studio,

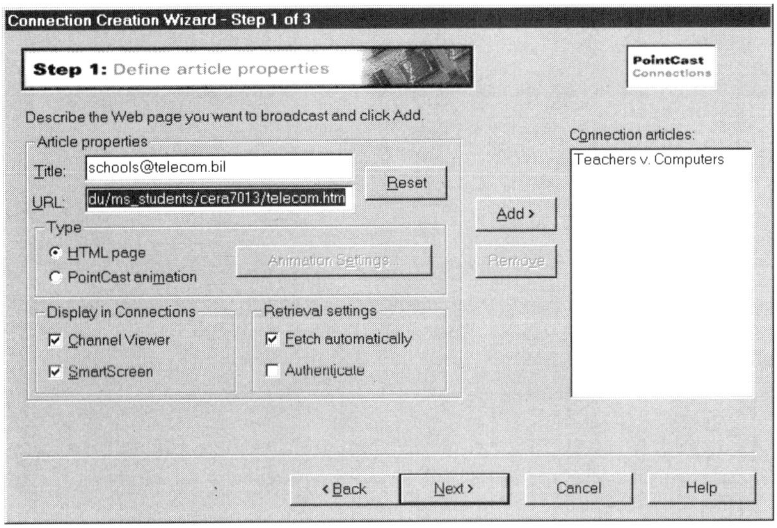

Figure 13-1
Step 1: Selecting and defining your articles.

you easily can create animations for your channel; we will return to this topic in Chapter 14, "Creating PointCast Animations."

Display in Connections: You have the option of displaying your article in the PointCast Channel Viewer and/or the PointCast SmartScreen screen saver. The decision is based largely on the type of content you are delivering. You might decide to place all your HTML articles in the Channel Viewer, for example, and create special animations that appear only in the PointCast SmartScreen.

Authenticate (retrieval settings): If you are planning to charge for your channel, you can password protect your articles using PointCast's built-in support for standard HTTP authentication. If you select the Authenticate option, PointCast guarantees that content is delivered to only paying customers with a valid username and password.

Fetch Automatically (retrieval settings): When this option is selected, PointCast automatically downloads the article or animation and places a copy on the user's local hard drive. Otherwise, PointCast waits for the user to select the article and then downloads its contents. To get the speed benefits of local caching, it is recommended that you always select this option; automatic retrieval is mandatory for all animations.

Standard HTTP Authentication

PointCast 2.0 supports standard HTTP authentication. This means that you can password protect individual articles or entire directories in the same manner that you password protect your existing Web site. This password protection enables content providers to charge for content or to restrict content to a specific group of individuals.

To password protect an article, you first must set up the access controls for your Web server and place the article in a password-protected directory. When adding the article to your channel, you then select the Authenticate option in the Retrieval settings.

The first time a user tries to subscribe to your channel, that person is prompted for a username and password (see Figure 13-2). PointCast saves this username and password and uses it to automatically retrieve any subsequent articles for the channel.

If the user has a valid username and password, the articles appear in the Channel Viewer. Otherwise, the article title and a security key icon appear (see Figure 13-3). For failed logon attempts, the article content consists of the HTTP 401 failed logon response message. You might want to alter this HTTP 401 message response to include specific instructions on subscribing to your channel and obtaining a valid username and password.

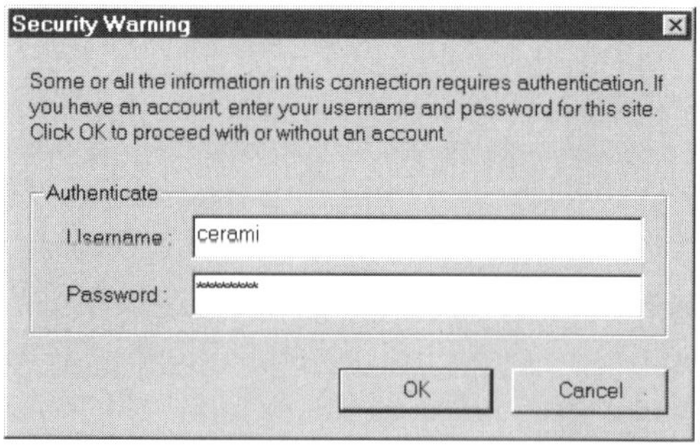

Figure 13-2 If you password protect any articles in your channel, PointCast prompts new users for a username and password. PointCast saves this information and uses it to automatically retrieve any subsequent articles for the channel.

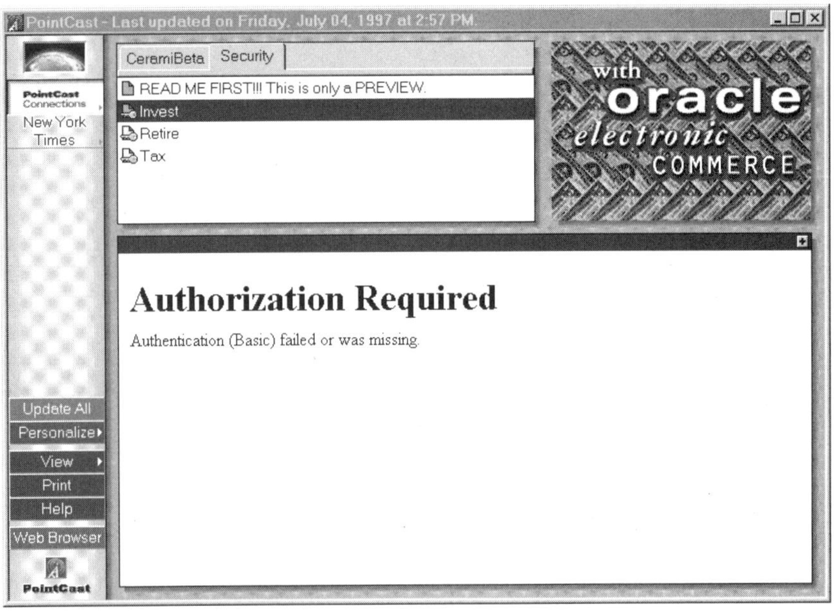

Figure 13-3 If a subscriber does not have a valid username and password, only the article title appears, along with a security key icon.

For each article, enter the given settings and click the Add button. You can add as many articles as you want, but PointCast recommends that you include three to five articles, and no more than eight. When you are finished, go to step 2.

13.2.4 Step 2: Name and Describe Your Connection

In step 2, you enter the name and description of your channel (see Figure 13-4). Each channel has both a title *and* a name. The title is restricted to 30 characters and appears in users' configuration menus when they choose to personalize their connections. The name is restricted to 10 characters and appears on the tab of the Connection Channel Viewer.

Each channel also has a brief description and a URL pointer for a longer description. The brief description appears when the user subscribes to your channel and in the channel-configuration menu.

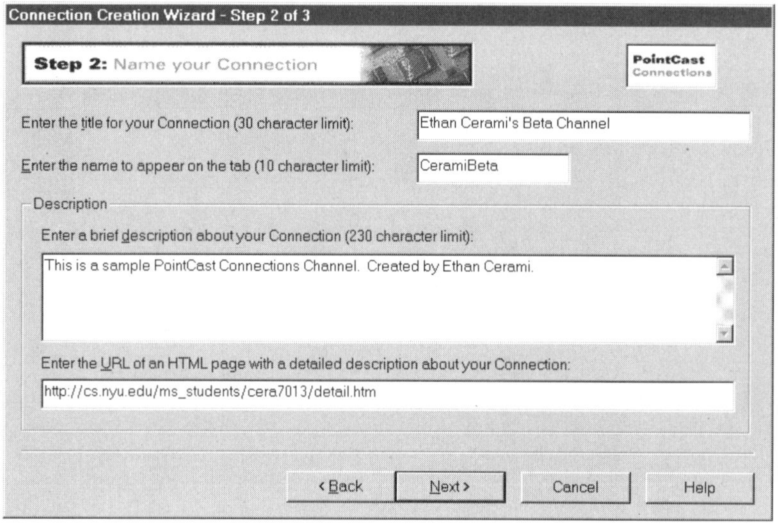

Figure 13-4 Step 2: Naming and describing your articles.

If you choose to list your channel in the PointCast Connections directory (see section 13.4.3, "The PointCast/Excite Connections Directory"), your channel title and brief description are listed, along with a hyperlink to the specified URL for more detailed information.

13.2.5 Step 3: Configure Your Connection

In step 3, you set the URL location of your channel and the schedule for channel updates (see Figure 13-5). The first Location box specifies the URL location of your PointCast configuration file. Not surprisingly, the configuration file is actually a *Channel Definition Format* (CDF) file. As you proceed through each step in the Connections Wizard, the Connections Builder creates a customized CDF file for your channel. With the Connections Builder, there is no need to write your own CDF files or even to understand CDF!

For the location of your CDF file, enter its "future" URL location on your existing Web server. Make sure that the file ends with the `.cdf` extension. After you complete the Connections Wizard, you need to remember to transfer this file to your Web site via FTP. Users resident on your Web site can download your CDF file and automatically subscribe to your channel.

The next step is to register your channel.

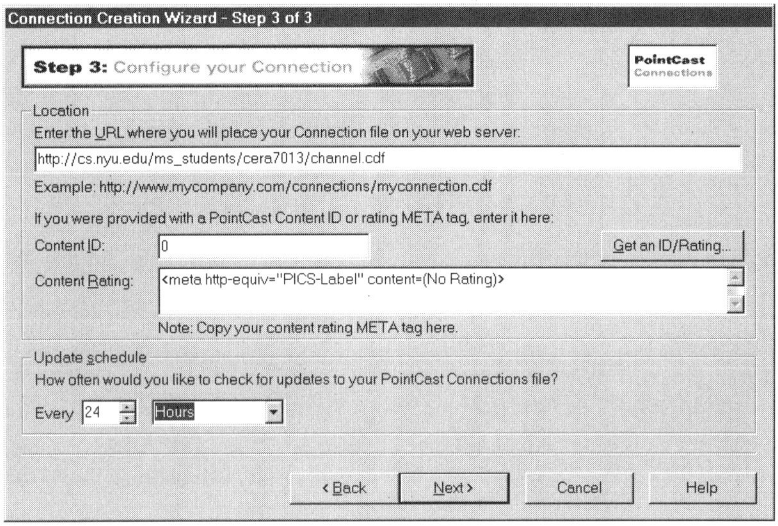

Figure 13-5
Step 3: Configuring your channel.

To take full advantage of the PointCast Connections Network, it is highly recommended that you register your channel with PointCast. It also is highly recommended that you receive an RSAC content rating. PointCast does not exercise any editorial control over the content of channels, but with the PointCast Administration tools, companies can choose to block certain violent, sexual, or vulgar content or to block any unrated content.

To ensure that your channel is not blocked, you must receive both a PointCast content ID and an RSAC rating. After you complete the development of your channel and commit to creating a PointCast Connections channel, you can return to the registration and content-rating process (see section 13.4, "Registering Your Channel"). If you are just developing and testing a channel, you safely can skip these settings for now.

The final step in creating your channel is to set an update schedule. You can choose to have your channel updated as frequently as every six hours or as infrequently as every 31 days. Try to be realistic about how often you plan to update your content.

After you click Finish, you are prompted to save your configuration files. Choose to save your files to your local hard drive. At this point, you might want to check out these automatically generated files with a text editor or Web browser.

You will notice that PointCast has created two files and one graphics file:

[name].cdf: An automatically generated CDF file (see Listing 13-1).

[name]_jump.html: An automatically generated HTML file that gives users instructions on subscribing to your channel and getting the PointCast 2.0 client program (see Figure 13-6). Of course, you can customize the file to fit your needs and then copy it to your Web site (see section 13.2.7, "Setting Up Your Web Site").

Listing 13-1
A Sample CDF File Generated by the PointCast Connections Builder. Note that this sample uses an earlier and now outdated version of CDF.

```
<CHANNEL

    Title = "CeramiBeta
    "LongName = "Ethan Cerami's Beta Channel"
    Abstract = "This is a sample PointCast Connections
         Channel.
    Created by Ethan Cerami.
    "InfoURI ="http://cs.nyu.edu/ms_students/cera7013/
         details.htm"
    SELF = "http://cs.nyu.edu/ms_students/cera7013/
         channel.cdf"
    ContentID = "0"
    Ratings = "(No Rating)"
    Frequency = "24"
    Authenticate = "No"
    >
    <ITEM
        Title = "schools@telecom.bill"
        HREF = "http://cs.nyu.edu/ms_students/cera7013/
             telecom.htm"
        Type = "HTML"
        Show = "Channel,SmartScreen"
        Precache = "Yes"
        Authenticate = "No"
        >
    </ITEM>
    <ITEM
        Title = "Computers v. Teachers"
        HREF = "http://cs.nyu.edu/ms_students/cera7013/
             teacher.htm"
        Type = "HTML"
        Show = "Channel,SmartScreen"
        Precache = "Yes"
        Authenticate = "No"
        >
    </ITEM>
</CHANNEL>
```

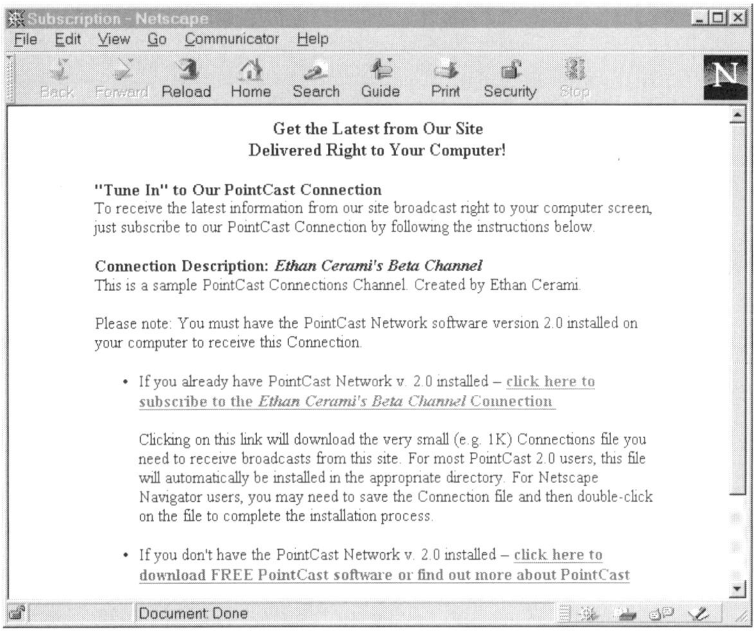

Figure 13-6 The Connections Wizard creates a custom HTML page to help users subscribe to your channel and/or download the PointCast 2.0 client.

`connections.gif`: A small icon that advertises the PointCast Connections Network. You can use the icon to advertise for your specific channel (see section 13.2.7, "Setting Up Your Web Site").

13.2.6 Testing Your Channel

Immediately after saving your configuration files, you are presented with the Connections Control Panel. This is the main user interface for modifying your channel and article settings. It is also the main interface for creating new channels if you want to simply skip the Connections Wizard (see Figure 13-7).

Now that you have created your first PointCast channel, you need to test it to make sure that it works.

To test your channel, click the Preview Connection icon or choose Preview from the File menu. PointCast retrieves your previously saved CDF file from your hard drive and creates a temporary subscription to your channel.

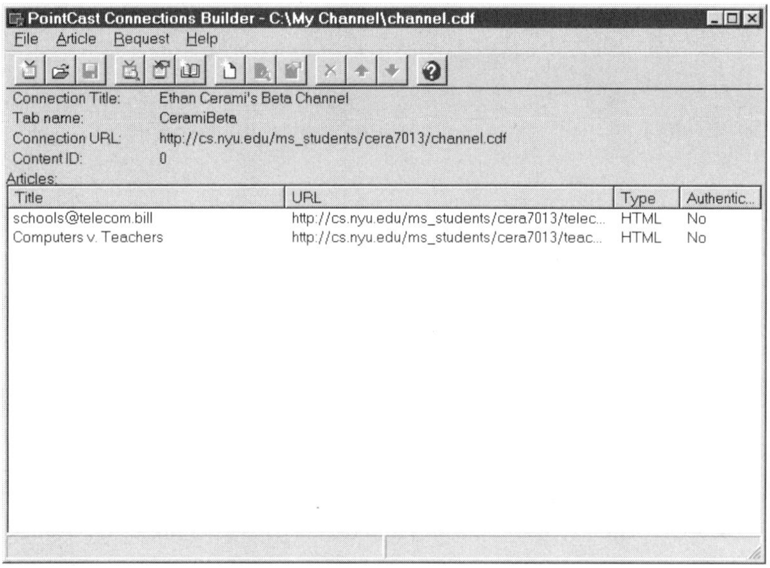

Figure 13-7 The main Connections Builder interface enables you to easily add, delete, modify, and preview channel contents.

Click the Add Connection button to confirm the temporary subscription, and your PointCast client software is launched with a new channel tab devoted to your channel. PointCast then connects to the Internet and downloads the associated articles. If all goes well, PointCast displays your articles in your Channel Viewer (see Figure 13-8). If you have marked your articles as SmartScreen items, you should confirm that your articles appear on both the screen saver and the screen ticker (see Figure 13-9).

If your articles do not appear in the Channel Viewer, first check to make sure that you have entered the correct URL addresses and try updating the channel again. If this doesn't work, test to make sure that your Web server is working properly by accessing the articles via your regular Web browser.

Along with your channel articles, you will notice a READ ME FIRST! article. This article includes a few tips on making sure that your connection is working. It also includes a button for removing your temporary subscription. After you preview your channel, click the Remove button. It is important to remove your subscription, because you can preview only one channel at a time.

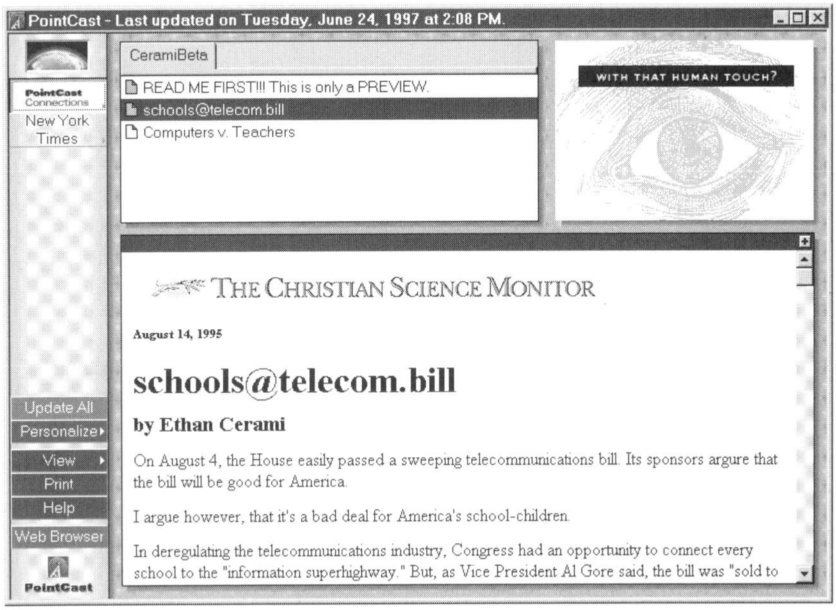

Figure 13-8 Testing your channel. By previewing your connection, PointCast creates a temporary subscription and downloads your channel's contents. If all goes well, you see your articles in the Channel Viewer.

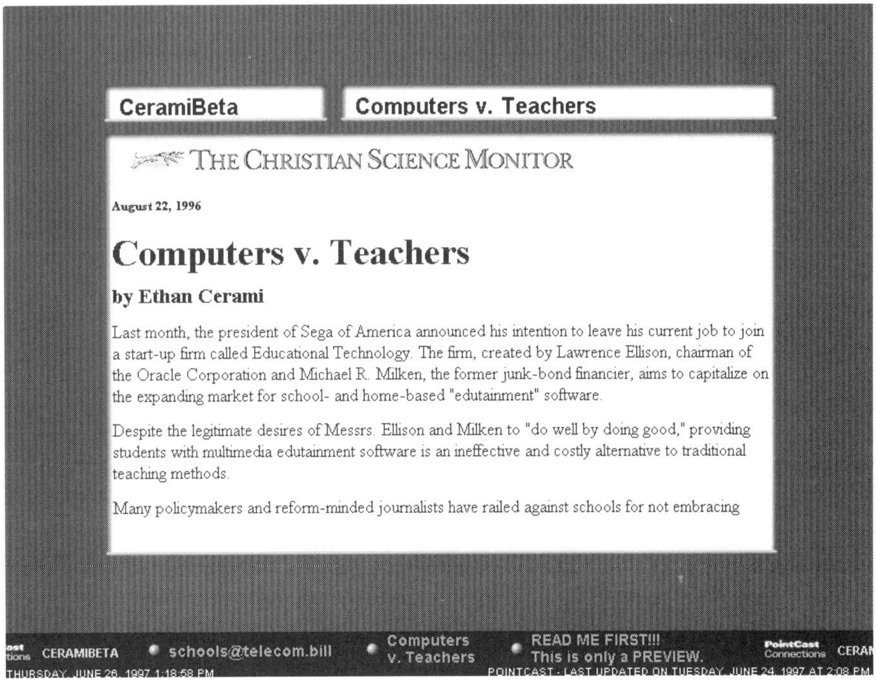

Figure 13-9 Your articles can appear in PointCast's SmartScreen screen saver and screen ticker.

13.2.7 Setting Up Your Web Site

After you set up and test your PointCast channel, the last step is to set up your Web site so that users automatically can subscribe to your channel via their regular Web browsers. At a very minimum, this requires that you transfer your CDF configuration file from your local hard drive to your Web server. After the CDF file is resident on your Web server, you just need to provide links to the file. By clicking on these links, users automatically download the CDF file, and PointCast makes an immediate subscription.

PointCast does have a few specific suggestions on setting up your Web site; feel free to follow these suggestions at your discretion.

The first suggestion is that you use the PointCast Connections icon on your heavy traffic Web pages. As noted earlier, the PointCast icon is generated by the Connections Wizard and placed in the same directory as your CDF configuration file. PointCast recommends that you link the Connections icon to your custom `[name]_jump.html` page. For users with PointCast 2.0 already installed, this provides a simple way to subscribe to your channel. For users who do not have PointCast installed, it provides a quick link to PointCast's download site and a subsequent link back to your site. Figure 13-10 shows PointCast's suggestion for setting up your Web site.

After you set up your Web site, make sure that you test your channel again. In particular, try subscribing to your channel via the `jump.html` page and try doing this with both Netscape Navigator and Internet Explorer. In both cases, PointCast should run automatically and complete the subscription process.

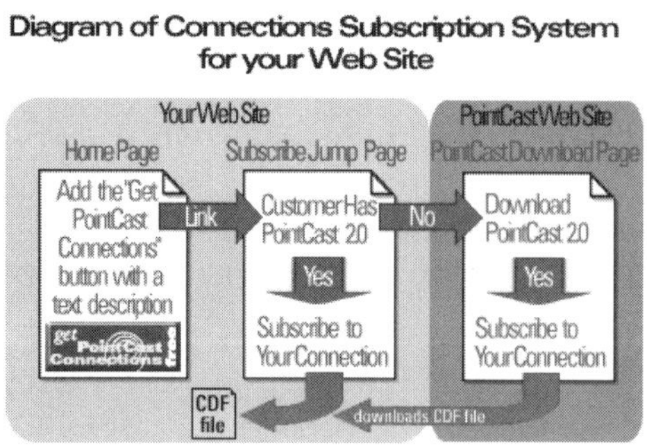

Figure 13-10 PointCast recommends a simple directory structure for attracting new users to your channel.

In some cases, Netscape Navigator may require that you first download the CDF file to your hard drive and then double-click on the file to complete the subscription process. If this turns out to be the case, you might need to add the following MIME type to your Web server:

MIME Type	Associated Extension
`application/x-pcn-connection`	`.cdf`, `.pcc`

13.3 Managing Your Channel

13.3.1 Working with the Connections Builder

As you continue to provide new content for your channel, you can manually modify your CDF configuration file. It's much easier to use the Connections Builder, though. Table 13-1 lists the major functions provided by the Connections Builder.

Remember! *After you modify your connection configuration (CDF file), remember to transfer the updated file to your Web server via FTP.*

13.3.2 Managing the Size of Your Channel

To preserve bandwidth, each PointCast Connection channel initially is limited to 150K of information. Users can increase this figure, but because you have no assurance that all your subscribers will do so, your entire channel never should exceed 150K at any one time. This 150K figure is calculated by adding all your PointCast animations and HTML pages plus all your inline graphics images.

TIP: *If your channel exceeds 150K, and you find yourself pressed for size, one common method for minimizing the size of a channel is to reference the same image in multiple HTML articles.*

Table 13-1

Connections Builder Functions

Icon	Button Name	Function
	Create New Connection	Creates a new channel with the three-step Connections Wizard.
	Open Existing Connection	Opens an existing CDF file.
	Save Connection to File	Saves your current channel configuration to a CDF format file. After you save your file to your local hard drive, remember to transfer it to your Web site via FTP.
	Preview Connection	Launches the PointCast 2.0 client software and creates a temporary subscription to your channel. Use this option to test your channel before releasing it to the public.
	Display Connection Properties	Displays the current configuration options for your channel. From this dialog box, you can do the following: ■ Change your channel title, name, and description ■ Set the URL location of your CDF file ■ Set the URL location of your information link, which provides a more detailed description of your channel ■ Request a PointCast content ID and RSAC rating ■ Set the update schedule for your channel
	Request Directory Listing	Submits your channel title, description, and URL to the PointCast/Excite Connections directory. You can choose to categorize your channel in any one of nine categories: Business, Companies, Education and Reference, Entertainment, Industries, Lifestyle, News, Money, and Sports.

Table 13-1

Connections Builder Functions

Icon	Button Name	Function
	Create New Article	Adds a new HTML document or PointCast animation to your channel. For each article, you must set a number of parameters: ■ Title: The title appears in the user's Channel Viewer. ■ URL: Specifies the exact URL location of your article on your existing Web site. ■ Type: each article can be an HTML document or a PointCast animation (**.anm**) file. ■ Display in Connection: The document or animation can appear in the Channel Viewer and/or the PointCast SmartScreen. ■ Authenticate: Each article can be password protected via standard HTTP authentication. ■ Fetch Automatically: Tells PointCast to download the article's contents and store them to the user's local hard drive (recommended).
	Display Article Properties	Displays an editable dialog box with settings for the currently selected article. Settings include Title, URL, Type, Display, and Retrieval options.
	Delete Article	Deletes the currently selected article from your channel. This does not actually delete the article from your existing Web site.
 	Change Order of Articles	You can choose the exact order of your articles and place newer articles near the top of the list. Just choose an article from the current list and click the up- or down-arrow icons.
	Display Help	The PointCast online help manual is detailed and well-written.

13.3.3 Formatting Article Contents

During installation of the PointCast 2.0 client software, users have the option of viewing article contents with the internal PointCast browser or Internet Explorer. Most users opt to use the internal browser. The PointCast browser does not provide the same functionality as Internet Explorer or Netscape Navigator, however.

Specifically, the PointCast browser supports HTML 3.2, but it does *not* provide support for Java, JavaScript, VBScript, ActiveX, or frames. This is one serious disadvantage of PointCast, and you should make sure that you test each HTML article in the PointCast browser to ensure browser compatibility. PointCast also recommends that if you are using frames that you broadcast the pages within the frames instead of the frames themselves. If your site includes ActiveX, JavaScript, or Java components, PointCast recommends that you place these components on supporting Web pages and include links to these pages from your article.

13.4 Registering Your Channel

13.4.1 Registering with PointCast

After you create your channel and commit to providing a PointCast Connections channel, the final step is to register it with PointCast. Registration is not required, but you do get several benefits, including free usage reports on your PointCast subscribers and updates on new PointCast products.

To register your channel, launch the Connections Builder and choose Content/ID Rating from the Request menu. Your default browser opens with a short HTML registration questionnaire.

13.4.2 RSAC Rating

As you complete the PointCast registration form, you will notice that PointCast also recommends that you obtain an RSAC content rating. The *Recreational Software Advisory Council* (RSAC) is an independent, not-for-profit organization with the goal of providing an objective content rating system for the Internet. If you have used Microsoft Internet Explorer

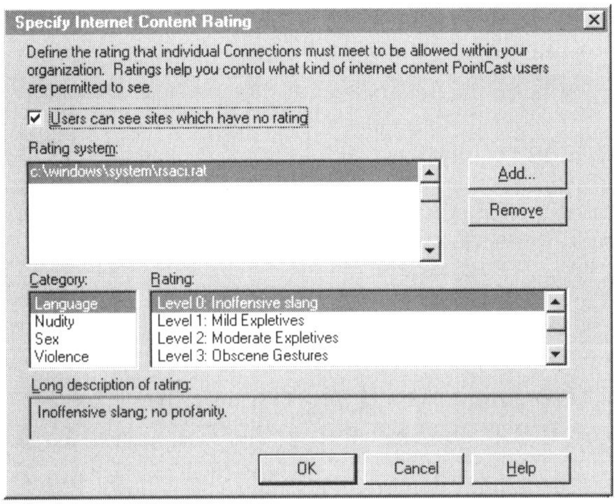

Figure 13-11 The PointCast Administration tool enables companies to block out any offensive or unrated material. To ensure that your channel is not blocked and reaches the largest possible audience, it is highly recommended that you obtain an RSAC rating.

3.0 or higher, you might have noticed that the RSAC rating system is used to provide parents with a method of filtering out sexual, vulgar, or violent Web content.

Obtaining an RSAC rating is optional, but the PointCast Administration tools enable companies to block out potentially offensive material or any unrated or unregistered material (see Figure 13-11). Hence, to ensure that your channel reaches the largest possible audience, it is highly recommended that you receive both a PointCast content ID *and* an RSAC content rating.

Fortunately, getting an RSAC rating is quite simple, and you can just follow the link from the main PointCast registration form. In a novel twist on content rating, RSAC also allows Web site managers to rate their own content.

You simply fill out a series of questionnaires concerning your content, and RSAC returns a computer-generated rating for your Web site or Web channel. You could lie, of course, but RSAC patrols the Web in search of violators! Companies that post fraudulent ratings can be held liable for fraud.

TIP: *You can use the RSAC rating process to rate individual HTML articles, hierarchical directories, or entire Web sites. If your entire Web site (or PointCast channel) contains the same type of content and is likely to receive the same content rating, it makes the most sense to rate the entire Web site at once.*

After you complete the online questionnaire, PointCast returns a content ID, and RSAC returns an automatically generated meta-tag. For example, here's the meta-tag for my CeramiBeta channel:

```
<META http-equiv="PICS-Label" content='(PICS-1.1
"http://www.rsac.org/ratingsv01.html" l gen true
comment "RSACi North America Server" by
"cera7013@cs.nyu.edu" for
"http://cs.nyu.edu/ms_students/cera7013" on
"1997.06.26T12:38-0500" r (n 0 s 0 v 0 l 0))'>
```

After you receive your content ID and RSAC meta-tag, you need to update your channel with the proper settings. Choose Properties from the File menu, and the Channel Properties dialog box appears (see Figure 13-12). Just type your content ID and cut and paste your RSAC meta-tag.

13.4.3 The PointCast/Excite Connections Directory

The PointCast Connections directory is a comprehensive directory of all registered PointCast channels. The directory is managed by Excite, Inc.

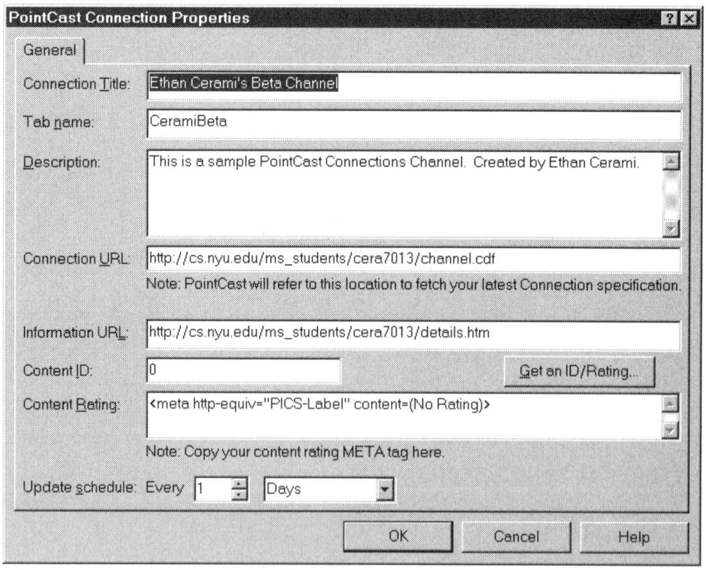

Figure 13-12 Setting PointCast channel properties. You easily can modify the name, description, and update schedule for your channel.

and is viewable in the PointCast 2.0 client or any Web browser at **`http://www.excite.com/pointcast`**. If you are hoping to attract new subscribers, this is probably one of the best places to list your new channel.

To list your channel in the Connections directory, choose Directory Listing from the Request menu. You are asked to confirm your channel title and description and to select a category listing. You currently can choose to list your channel in any one of nine categories: Business, Companies, Education and Reference, Entertainment, Industries, Lifestyle, News, Money, and Sports.

SUMMARY

The PointCast Connections Builder provides a flexible and easy-to-use interface for creating new PointCast Connections channels. The Connections Wizard provides an even easier interface for creating new channels in three simple steps. In each case, the Connections Builder creates a custom *Channel Definition Format* (CDF) file.

Each PointCast channel consists of a set of HTML documents and animations. To preserve bandwidth, each channel is restricted to 150K. And, to provide cross-browser support, note that the internal PointCast browser does support HTML 3.2 but does not support Java, JavaScript, VBScript, or frames.

After your channel is configured, users can subscribe to your channel by visiting your existing Web site. To gain maximum exposure for your channel, it is recommended that you register with PointCast and receive an RSAC content rating. By registering with PointCast, you can receive a free listing in the PointCast/ Excite Connections directory and free valuable reports concerning your subscriber audience.

Online Resources

- PointCast Connections FAQ
  `http://www.pointcast.com/support/connections/faqs/`.
  What should I do if my connection doesn't update properly? How frequently can I broadcast new connection information? What is the difference between broadcasting information with the PointCast Corporate Broadcast Manager (the next generation of I-Server) and PointCast connections? Check the FAQ.
- Connections Support KnowledgeBase
  `http://pioneer.pointcast.com/support/connections/know.html`.
  You can search the PointCast KnowledgeBase for information or specific questions on the PointCast 2.0 client or creating new channels.

CHAPTER 14

Creating PointCast Animations

The PointCast Studio enables you to create sophisticated PointCast animations quickly and easily. These animations can help draw significant attention to your Connections channel and can give your channel a professional and highly polished look. Your animations can also form an important supplement to your current set of HTML articles and help draw subscribers to your most important news and information. Even corporate broadcasters can create custom animations to keep employees abreast of the latest company developments and provide links back to the corporate intranet.

Each animation you create can be displayed in the user's Channel Viewer and/or the PointCast SmartScreen. Either way, your animations are likely to catch the eye of most subscribers, and you probably will want to invest the time to maximize the leverage of each animation. This chapter will help you do just that.

To help you get started as quickly as possible, this chapter is divided into two tutorials. Each tutorial explores a sample animation for a fictional news channel, known as the *Global Business News* (GBN) Network. As you read through each tutorial, it is recommended that you sit down at your computer and try it out. PointCast Studio is a straightforward application, but there is no substitution for hands-on practice. So dig in!

14.1 Getting Started

14.1.1 Installing PointCast Studio

Currently, PointCast Studio is available for Windows 95/NT; it is included on the CD-ROM at the end of this book. The Studio software includes a number of complete animations and animation templates. The tutorials presented in this chapter also are included on the CD-ROM in the `Contents/Chapter 14` directory.

14.1.2 Multimedia Development: Key Concepts

If you have done any work in multimedia development, you can think of PointCast Studio as a slimmed-down version of Macromedia Directory. In both these programs, you first select a cast of *actors*. These actors can be graphics of GIF files, text strings, or merely rectangular shapes. After you select your actors, you can set up your *stage*. The stage is a rectangular section of the screen where you can view your cast in action and preview the progress of your animation.

The progress of your animation is controlled by a *timeline*. The timeline resembles a musical score that determines the exact properties of each actor at each particular moment in time. Your first actor could consist of a text string with the name of your company, for example. At 1.0 second, the actor might be located at location (10, 20)—10 pixels to the right and 20 pixels from the top. At 2.0 seconds, your actor might be located at (50, 100)—50 pixels to the right and 100 pixels from the top.

By manipulating each actor on the timeline, you can create very sophisticated and visually enticing animations. And, much like Macromedia Director, Studio includes a number of built-in transition effects for high-impact animations. You easily can create an animation in which your corporate logo slowly dissolves into the background, for example, or your latest news headlines quickly zoom into place.

14.2 The Studio Interface

14.2.1 Orienting Yourself to the Studio Interface

Before we begin the tutorials, it will be useful to orient yourself to the main Studio user interface. The main interface consists of three parts: the Cast list, the timeline, and the stage (see Figure 14-1).

14.2.2 The Cast List

The Cast list includes a complete listing of all your actors. These actors can consist of graphics files, text strings, shapes, or even other PointCast animations. The actors are listed left to right, and each actor is identified with a text label. Notice that a small thumbnail sketch of each graphics actor is included.

The Cast list includes its own scrollbar so that you can peruse through your entire list of actors (see Figure 14-2).

14.2.3 The Timeline

The timeline includes a list of each actor at each particular moment in time. The y axis shows the progress of time in one-second intervals; you

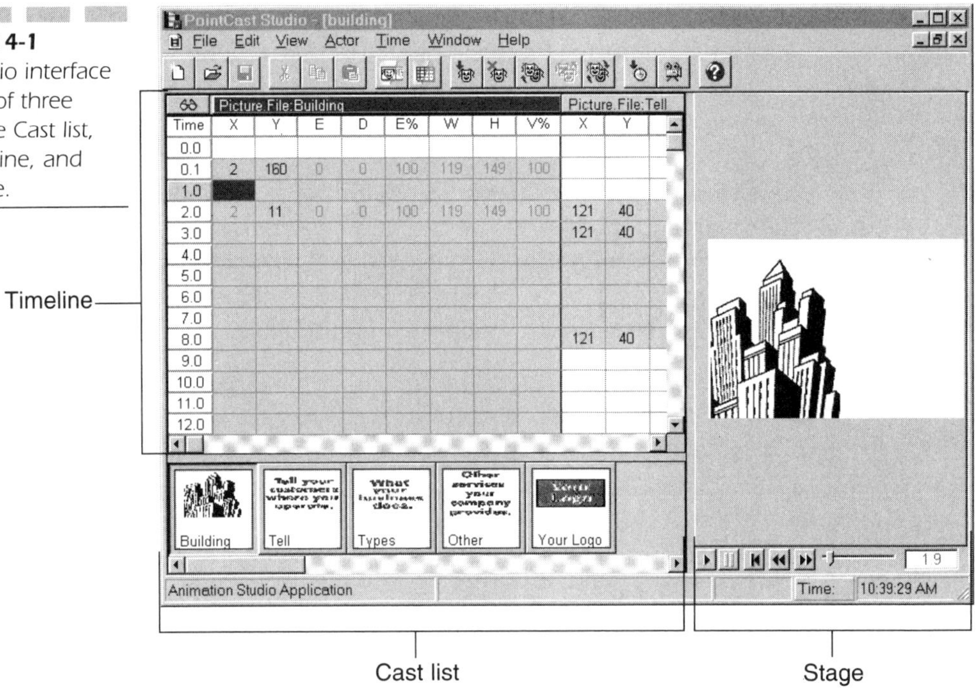

Figure 14-1 The Studio interface consists of three parts: the Cast list, the timeline, and the stage.

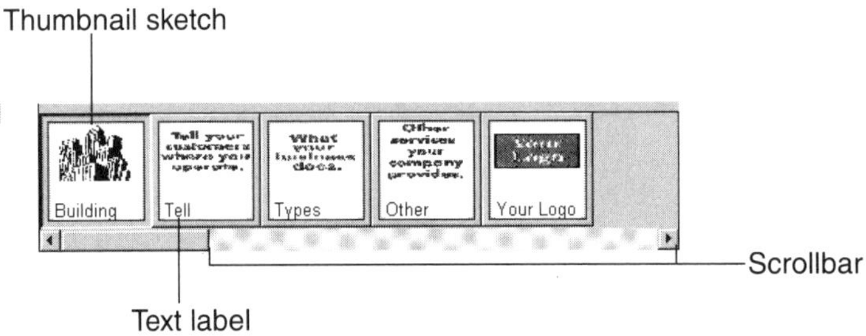

Figure 14-2 The Cast list includes all your current actors. Actors can include graphics, text strings, shapes, or other PointCast animations.

can think of each time row as one frame in a filmstrip animation. The x axis represents the entire list of actors.

At first, the timeline can be quite confusing, because each actor has a large set of parameters. The building graphic in Figure 14-3, for example, includes eight parameter settings: X, Y, E, D, E%, W, H, and V%. This list might appear alarmingly complicated, but rest assured that each one will be demystified shortly.

The timeline also includes its own vertical scrollbar for moving backward and forward in time and its own horizontal scrollbar for examining all the current actors.

14.2.4 The Stage

The stage or preview window displays the progress of your animation. The stage acts very much like a film screen, displaying each frame of your animation in rapid succession to create the effect of rapid animation (see Figure 14-4). You can use the preview window to view and test all the elements of your animation, including the placement of actors, transitional

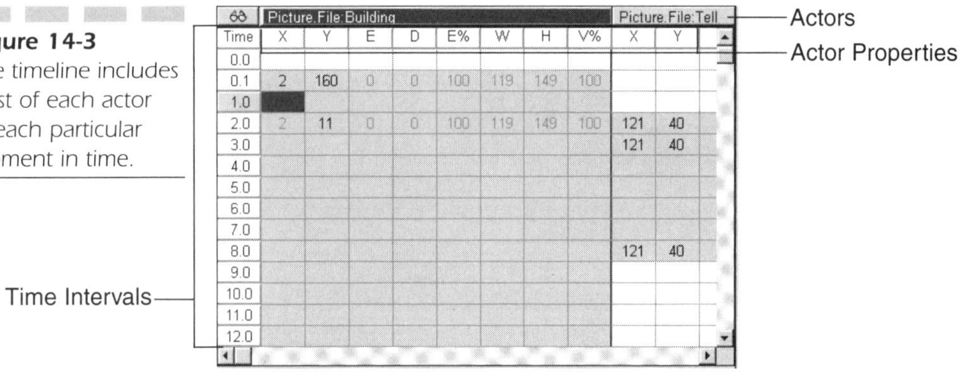

Figure 14-3 The timeline includes a list of each actor at each particular moment in time.

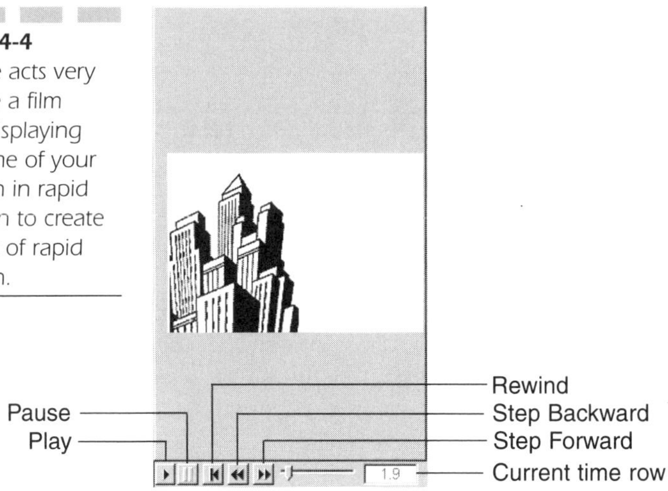

Figure 14-4 The stage acts very much like a film screen, displaying each frame of your animation in rapid succession to create the effect of rapid animation.

effects, and movement. You also can manipulate actors directly on the stage by pointing, clicking, and dragging.

With the preview window, you can play your animation from start to finish, just as it would appear in the user's Channel Viewer or SmartScreen. Or, you can advance or rewind one frame at a time to obtain a fine-grained view of your animation. To support this functionality, the preview window includes VCR-like controls for playing, pausing, rewinding, and stepping forward and backward. The lower right corner indicates the currently displayed time row.

Depending on the size of your animation, the preview window may display a scaled or minimized stage view. In addition to the preview window, Studio supports a full-screen preview mode, which is described in section 14.3.8, "Previewing Your Animation."

14.3 Tutorial 1: Flying Text Animation

14.3.1 Overview

Now that you are oriented to the Studio interface, the next step is to try out a few examples. This first tutorial demonstrates an example of flying text. Specifically, we will create two text strings. The first string will slide down from the top of the stage, and the second string will slide in from the left. This is an extremely simple example, but it will do an excellent job of introducing several key Studio concepts.

14.3.2 Creating a New Animation

To create the flying text example, you need to start with a clean slate:

1. Choose New from the File menu.
2. Select Blank Animation and click OK. You see the New Animation Settings dialog box (see Figure 14-5).
3. In the New Animation Settings dialog box, you can set a number of global parameters:

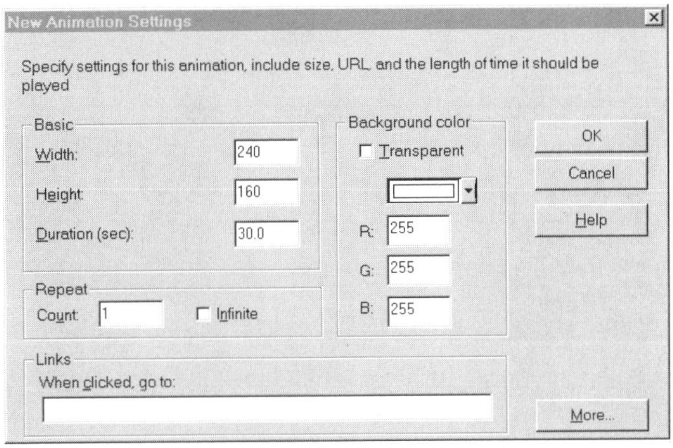

Figure 14-5
The New Animation Settings dialog box. For each new animation, you can set a stage width, height, background color, and URL link.

Width — The width, in pixels, of your animation.

Height — The height, in pixels, of your animation.

Duration — The total duration of your animation, in seconds. At first, this may be an estimate of how long you think the animation will last. As you finalize your work, you can shrink or expand the duration as needed.

Background Color — The solid background color of your stage. You can choose from a graphical palette or enter a specific RGB (Red, Green, Blue) value. (If you are planning to embed your animation within another animation, you also have the option of creating a transparent background. See section 14.6.2, "Embedded Animations," for additional information.)

Repeat — You can choose to have your animation repeat itself any number of times or repeat itself infinitely.

Links — PointCast animations support embedded URL links. Each actor can have its own URL link, but if you want one default link for your entire animation, you can enter it here.

More Options — If you click the More button, you see an additional series of settings. These settings pertain to you only if you are planning to embed this animation inside another one. (Embedded animations are discussed in section 14.6.2.)

Settings for Tutorial 1

For our first tutorial, we will create a small, short animation with the following settings:

Width	240 pixels
Height	160 pixels
Duration	5.0 seconds
Repeat	1
Background	Light Gray
Red	201
Green	203
Blue	215

TIP: *Studio comes bundled with a series of professional templates that you can modify for your own use. To preview and open an existing template, choose New from the File menu and select Template.*

14.3.3 What Exactly Is an Actor?

After you set up your main animation parameters, Studio displays the Insert Actor dialog box (see Figure 14-6). In this screen, you can create any number of actors for your animation. But, before we do so, it might help to better clarify the exact meaning of *actor*.

An *actor* is any single entity that appears in your animation. PointCast currently supports four main types of actors:

Picture — This can be any GIF or JPEG image. PointCast currently does not support animated GIFs (GIF89a), but it does support simple GIF filmstrips, which are described in section 14.6.1, "GIF Filmstrips."

Text — Any text string or sentence. Each text actor can have its own font, point size, style, and color.

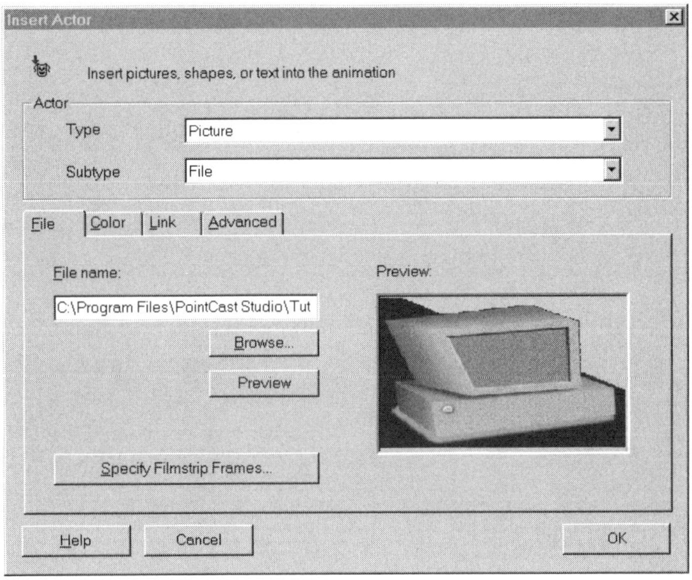

Figure 14-6
The Insert Actor dialog box. Studio currently supports four main types of actors: text strings, pictures, rectangular shapes, and other PointCast animations.

Shape — PointCast currently supports only rectangular shapes. Each rectangle can have its own size, and by manipulating its on-stage dimensions, you can exploit rectangle shapes to create animated pointers and bar graphs (see section 14.4.9, "Line Effects," for additional information).

Movie — A movie can represent another PointCast animation or a Macromedia Flash animation. By embedding animations, you can create very sophisticated screen saver animations (see section 14.6.2 for additional information).

NOTE: *As you create new actors, you may notice several other types of actors from the pull-down menu. In particular, you may notice HTML, Chart, Quote, and Cityforecast actors. These are known as* dynamic *actors and are designed* only *for PointCast corporate channels supported by Corporate Broadcast Manager. Dynamic actors are beyond the scope of this chapter, but additional information is available on the PointCast Web site at* **`www.pointcast.com`**.

14.3.4 Creating Text Actors

For our example, we will create two text actors: one title and one subtitle. In the Insert Actor dialog box, follow these steps:

1. Choose Text from the Type pull-down menu.
2. Choose String from the Subtype pull-down menu.
3. For each text actor, you can set a large number of parameters:

Dimensions	Total width and height, in pixels, of your text string. Depending on the length of your string and the point size you choose, you might need to adjust your dimensions to ensure that your text string is not truncated arbitrarily. This is mostly an issue of trial and error.
Text Face	Each text string can have its own font, and you can choose from a listing of all the fonts currently installed on your machine. Picking a font can get a little tricky, because you have no real assurance that your subscribers will share the same set of fonts. If PointCast encounters a font that is not installed on the user's machine, it attempts a close font substitution. In certain cases, this may cause your animation to behave erratically. The most common method of avoiding this problem is to pick very commonly used fonts, such as Arial, Courier, MS Serif, or Times Roman.
Point Size and Style	Each actor can have its own point size and style (bold or italic).
Truncation	If your text string does not fit within your preset dimensions, it may be cut off arbitrarily, often in mid-sentence. To prevent this unseemly truncation, you can select to truncate with ellipses. This option finds the last fully displayed word and places ellipses after it. The headline "Mars probe begins survey of rocks and soil," for example, might become "Mars probe begins survey . . . "

Alignment	You can choose to align your text to the left, right, or center.
Text String	The actual text of your string.
Color	You can choose a foreground and background color. You also can select a transparent background so that your string can effortlessly glide over but not obscure other onstage actors (see section 14.4.5, "Working with Transparency").
Link	Each text string can have its own URL link. URLs should include the http:\\ prefix, i.e., **`http:\\www.xyz.com`**.
Label	If you click on the Advanced tab, you see a complete summary of your text settings, including width, height, font name, and point size. At the bottom of this list, you see an option for Label. This label appears in the Cast list to help you quickly identify actors.

TIP: *If you absolutely must ensure the correct font for your text, the best approach is to convert your text into GIF images and insert them as picture actors.*

Settings for Tutorial 1

For our flying text example, we will create two text actors with the following settings:

	Text Actor 1	**Text Actor 2**
Text	GBN Channel Guide	We cover your World!
Width	170 pixels	150 pixels
Height	20 pixels	20 pixels
Font	Times New Roman	Times New Roman
Point Size	10	8
Text Color	Black	Black

After you create your two text actors, confirm that they appear in the Cast list (see Figure 14-7).

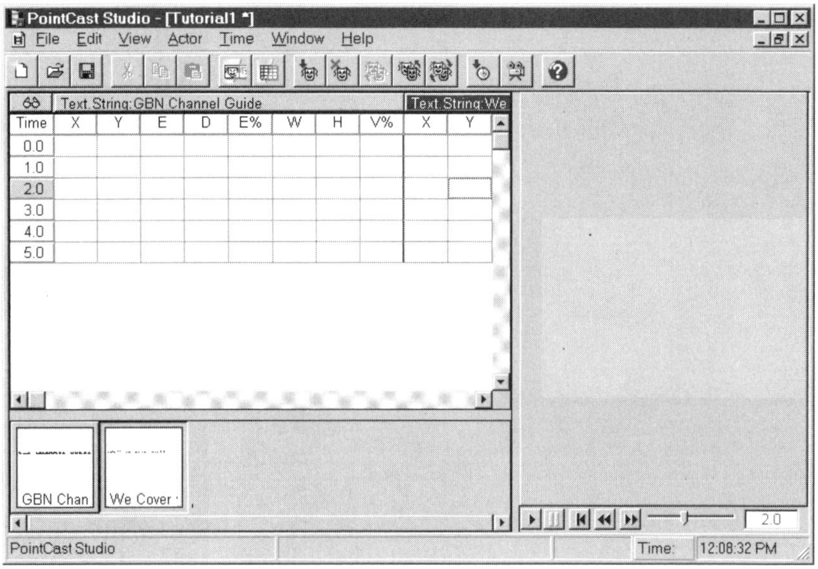

Figure 14-7
Tutorial 1 setup—we now have two text strings and an empty timeline.

14.3.5 Time Marks Defined

The timeline provides a snapshot of each actor at each particular moment in time. Again, the y axis represents the progress of time, and the x axis represents your complete list of actors.

For each moment in time, you can set a time mark that defines a set of unique properties. These properties can include the actor's position, height, width, visibility, or transition effect. Note that each column in the timeline represents a different property.

You can set eight main properties for each time mark. We will return to each of these in detail, but for now, here is a quick overview:

Abbreviation	Property	Description
X	X Position	Horizontal position of the actor, in pixels.
Y	Y Position	Vertical position of the actor, in pixels.
E	Effect	The special visual effect applied to the actor. This is a number between 0 and 6, indicating one of six possible Studio effects: wipes, doors, peeks, blinds, scale, and dissolve (0 is reserved for no effect).

Abbreviation	Property	Description
D	Direction	Direction from which the visual effect appears. This is a number between 0 and 10, indicating one of 11 possible direction options.
E%	Effect Percentage	Percent to which the effect has been applied to the actor (between 0 and 100).
W	Width	Width of the actor, in pixels.
H	Height	Height of the actor, in pixels.
V%	Visibility Percent	Degree of opacity of the actor, in percent (between 0 and 100). 0 percent opacity indicates that the actor is invisible.

14.3.6 Modifying the Timeline View

For our first tutorial, we will be setting only the location of our two text strings. To simplify things, we can choose to view only the x,y position and hide the other six properties.

To view only the x,y position, follow these steps:

1. Choose Timeline from the View menu.
2. Select Position Only. You now should see both actors on the timeline and separate columns for the X and Y positions (see Figure 14-8).

There are four options for the timeline view. Depending on your programming needs, you may find yourself switching between these four views:

Common Details	Lists the eight most commonly used properties: X Position, Y Position, Effect, Direction, Effect Percentage, Width, Height, and Visibility Percentage.
All Details	Lists the same properties as Common Details plus five others for cropping images and displaying filmstrip animations: Crop X, Crop Y, Crop Width, Crop Height, and Frame Number.
Position Only	X and Y position.
Effects and Position	X Position, Y Position, Effect, and Effect Percentage.

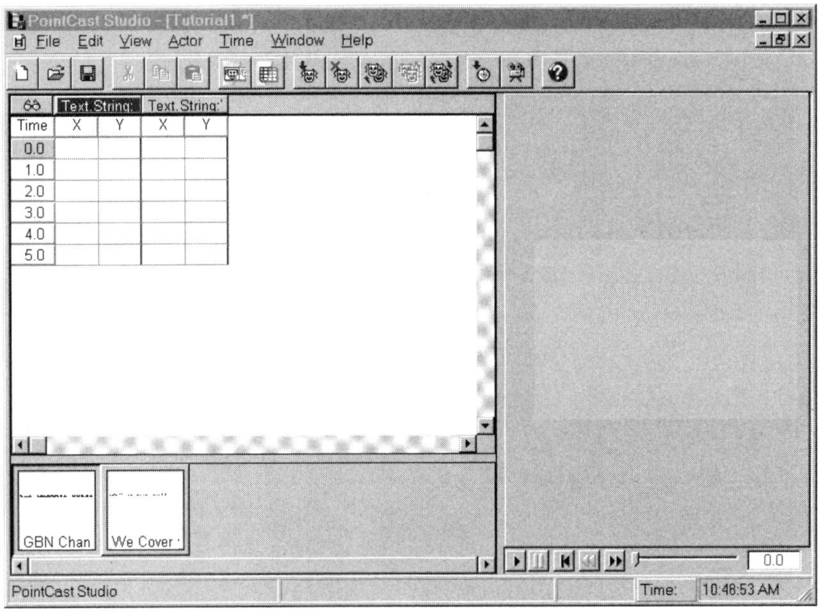

Figure 14-8
The x,y timeline view. Studio supports four options for viewing the timeline: Common Details, All Details, Position Only, and Position and Effect.

14.3.7 Using the Mark Editor

To create a time mark, you can type directly into the timeline, but it often is easier to use the built-in Mark Editor. With the Mark Editor, you easily can set every single property for any actor at any particular moment in time.

For example, to set the location of our title string actor with the Mark Editor, follow these steps:

1. Select the title actor in the Cast list.
2. Click on 0.0 in the timeline.
3. Choose Mark Editor from the View menu. The Mark Editor dialog box appears (see Figure 14-9). You will notice three tabs: Position and Effect, Size, and Frame. Under the Position and Effect settings, you can set the actor's exact location and special transition effect. The location represents coordinates in an x,y grid, where

the position (0,0) represents the upper left-hand corner of the stage (shown here).

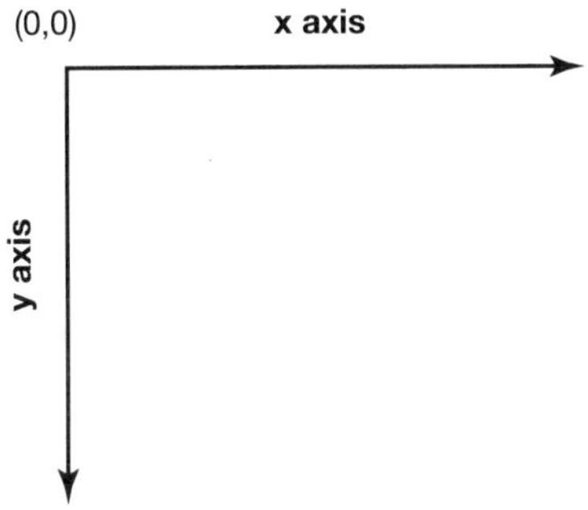

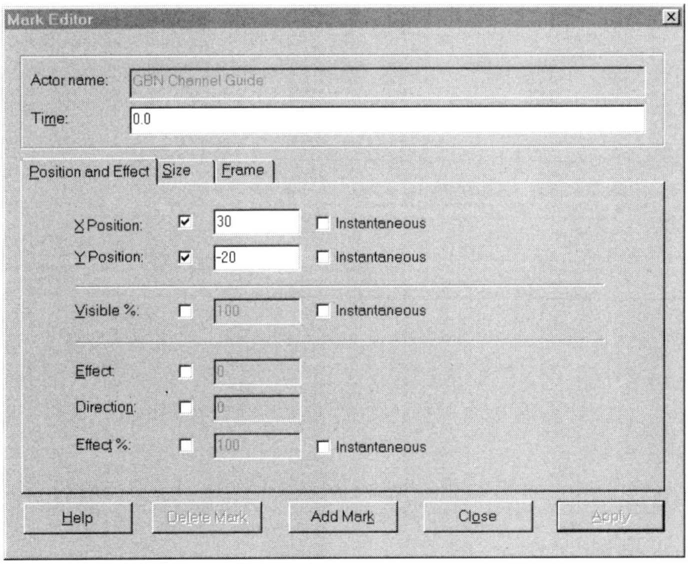

Figure 14-9 The Mark Editor. You can create time marks by typing directly into the timeline or by using the Mark Editor. The Mark Editor includes three tabs for settings: Position and Effect, Size, and Frame.

4. As a simple experiment, select the title actor and set its X position to 10 and its Y position to 10. Then click Add Mark. If you temporarily move your Mark Editor, you now see your text string on the stage in the preview window.

5. For our animation, we want the title text to slide in from the top and the subtitle text to fly in from the left. Hence, our first frame (Time: 0.0) will place each text string just slightly offstage—with the title text just above and the subtitle text just off to the left. Our second frame (Time: 2.0) will place each text in the center of the stage. Using your Mark Editor, set the following properties:

	Text String: GBN Channel Guide		Text String: We cover your World!	
Time	**X**	**Y**	**X**	**Y**
0.0	37	–20	–125	80
2.0	37	48	58	80

6. Note that at Time 0.0, our Title string is located at vertical position –20. At Time 2.0, it is located at vertical position 48. Given two unique positions in time, Studio automatically creates a smooth animation between the two. It basically takes your two points and extrapolates how far and fast your actor needs to move; it also calculates a smooth set of animation frames.

TIP: *You can set an actor's position by manipulating it directly onstage. Just point, click, and drag.*

14.3.8 Previewing Your Animation

Now that you have entered all your time marks, you are ready to preview your animation. To view your animation in the preview window, click the Play button. To preview your animation in full-screen mode, choose Preview from the View menu, or click the movie projector icon on the right-hand side of your toolbar. You now should see the title slide in from the top and the subtitle slide in from the left (see Figure 14-10).

14.3.9 Adding a URL

As you experiment with the flying text example, you might want to add a URL link to the entire animation or to each text string.

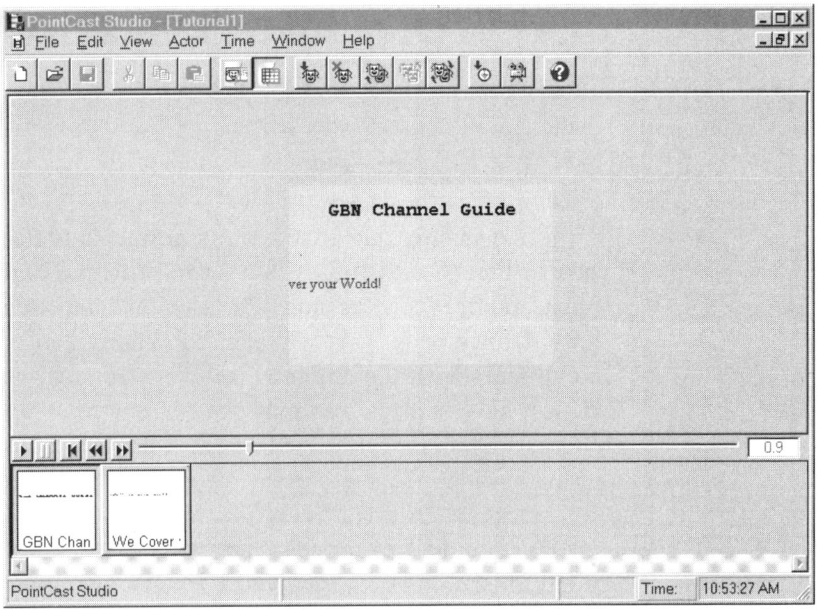

Figure 14-10 Tutorial 1 in action. Time: 0.9 seconds. The title slides in from the top, and the subtitle slides in from the left.

To set a default link for the entire animation, follow these steps:

1. Choose Animation Settings from the File Menu.
2. Enter your URL at the bottom of the dialog box.

To set a link for an actor, follow these steps:

1. Double-click on the actor in the Cast list.
2. Select the Link tab.

Note that actor links always take precedence over the default animation link.

TIP: *Studio provides an elegant method of testing embedded URL links. If you preview your animation in full-screen mode, you can click anywhere on the animation. If the selected actor or animation has an associated link, PointCast pauses the animation and displays the URL in a dialog box.*

14.4 Tutorial 2: Creating Transition Effects

14.4.1 Overview

Flying text is only one of the many animation effects you easily can create with PointCast Studio. Our second tutorial explores Studio's built-in transition effects. Transition effects enable you to draw attention to an actor's entrance or exit from stage. You easily can create a corporate logo that appears with the built-in dissolve effect, for example. The dissolve effect first selects a few random pixels from your logo and paints these on the stage. The effect then selects and paints additional pixels, and your logo transitions from a highly diffuse rendering to a very crisp, focused graphics image. Alternatively, you could use the built-in scale effect, and your logo would first appear as a tiny thumbnail image and gradually scale to its full size.

Studio currently supports six built-in transition effects. Any one of these effects is likely to create dramatic and eye-catching animations. And, as you create more animations and study other examples, you will note that transition effects are the most commonly used tools for creating high-impact advertisements and screen savers.

14.4.2 Creating Picture Actors

For the second tutorial, you will need to create a new animation and insert three picture actors. The picture images are included on the CD-ROM in the **Contents/Chapter14/Images** directory.

For this example, we will try experimenting with a larger stage. So, set the following parameters:

Width	600
Height	400
Color	White
Duration	15.0 seconds

To insert your picture actors, follow these steps:

1. Choose Insert Actor from the Actor menu.
2. Choose Picture from the Type pull-down menu.
3. Choose File from the Subtype pull-down menu.
4. On the File tab, you can browse through and preview your GIF and JPEG image files. Click the Browse button, and open the `Content/Chapter14/Images` folder.
5. For your first actor, select the `gbnlogo.gif` file. This is a sample corporate logo for our fictional news channel.
6. For your second actor, select the `comp.gif` image. This is an artist's rendition of a desktop computer.
7. For your third actor, select the `granite.gif` image. This is an image of a granite texture that we will use as a background to our animation.

TIP: *You can insert graphics images by dragging image files from the Windows interface and dropping them onto the Studio Cast list.*

14.4.3 Working with Layers

Your Studio screen now should look like Figure 14-11. In your Cast list, you should see the logo image, the computer image, and the granite image, listed from left to right.

The order of your Cast list is quite important. Each actor occupies a specific layer in your animation. The leftmost actor in your Cast list occupies the bottom layer. As you move from left to right, your actors occupy successively higher layers. The rightmost actor occupies the top layer.

To better understand the concept of layers, you can think of your animation as a paper collage. Actors on the left of the Cast list are the first ones to be pasted into the collage. As you continue to add more actors to the stage, these new actors are pasted on top of the other actors and actually may obscure them.

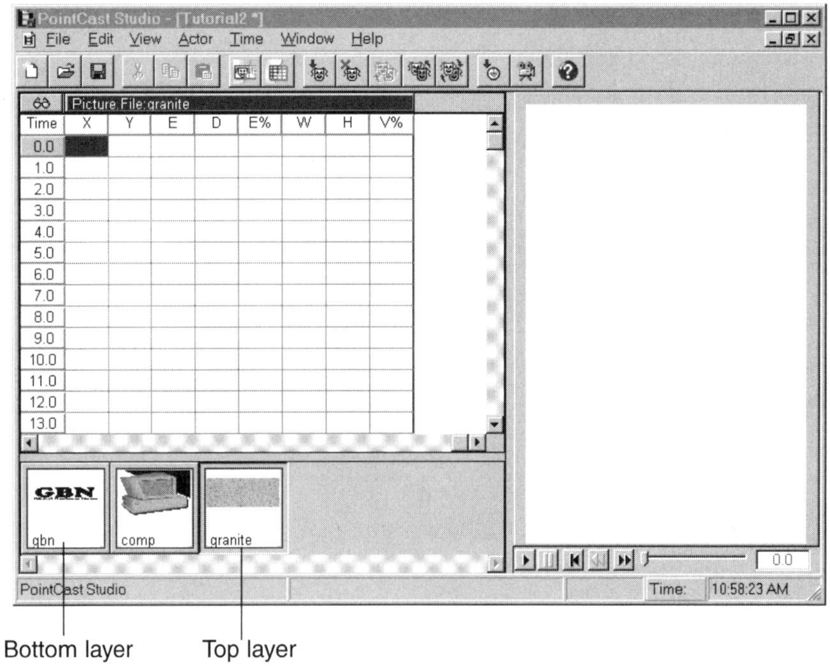

Figure 14-11
The Cast list determines the layer ordering of your actors. As you move from left to right, actors move from the bottom to top layer. Here, the granite actor occupies the top-level layer.

Try the following experiment. Set the x,y position of the computer image to (0,0) at time 0.0. You should see the computer image in the upper left-hand corner of your stage. Now, set the x,y position of your granite image to (0,0) at time 0.0.

You now see only a single granite image, and your computer image has completely disappeared. This occurs because the granite image exists to the right of the computer image in the Cast list and therefore occupies a higher layer in the animation. The computer image therefore is actually still onstage, but it is completely obscured by the granite image!

14.4.4 Reordering Layers

After you insert all your actors, you easily can reorder the layer hierarchy. Studio provides two options for this: You can set up the entire layer order at once, or you can choose to move individual actors up or down in the layer hierarchy.

To set the entire layer arrangement at once, follow these steps:

1. Choose Arrange from the Actor menu.
2. Choose All from the Arrange submenu. The Reorder Actors dialog box appears (see Figure 14-12). The actors are listed from top layer to bottom layer. Each actor includes several details, including a file size, a URL link, and a thumbnail sketch.
3. Select an actor.
4. Click Move Up or Move Down.

Continue to reorder your actors until you are satisfied, and click OK when you are done.

Alternatively, you can move individual actors up or down in the layer hierarchy by following these steps:

1. Select an actor in the Cast list.
2. Choose Arrange from the Actor menu.
3. Choose Bring Forward from the Arrange submenu to move the actor up one layer. Or, choose Send Backward from the Arrange submenu to move the actor down one layer.

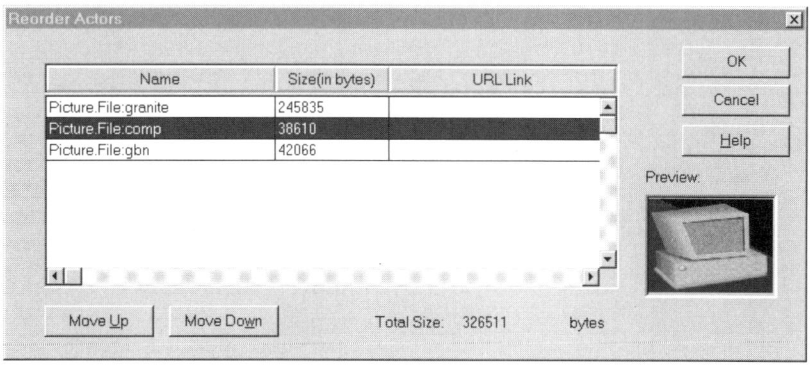

Figure 14-12 The Reorder Actors dialog box. Here, actors are listed from top layer to bottom layer. You easily can reorder them by moving each actor up or down.

Layer Order for Tutorial 2

By ordering or shuffling your actors into different layers, you can create several important visual effects. The most common effect is to create a textured background for your entire animation. You may recall that the general animation settings enable you only to select solid background colors, but you can create textured backgrounds by creating textured image actors and gluing them to the bottom layer.

For our second tutorial, we want to use the granite image as our background texture. To set this up, follow these steps:

1. Select the granite image.
2. Choose Send Backward twice from the Arrange submenu until the image occupies the bottom layer.

The granite image now occupies the bottom layer, and you should see your computer image again in the upper left-hand corner of the stage.

14.4.5 Working with Transparency

Because of the nature of layers, top-layer actors tend to completely obscure bottom-layer actors. To prevent this from occurring and to provide seamless layering of text and graphics actors, Studio offers the option of transparent backgrounds. When a text or graphics actor is set to transparent, the background image or color disappears and is replaced by the actor below it. Returning to our collage analogy, transparency is similar to taking a family photograph and cutting out the entire background, leaving only a cutout of the family.

In Studio, the transparency color is determined by the top-left pixel in your picture or text actor. The `gbnlogo.gif` actor, for example, has a dark-blue pixel in the top-left corner. When set to transparent, every dark-blue pixel is removed and replaced with the granite texture below. See Figures 14-13 and 14-14 for examples.

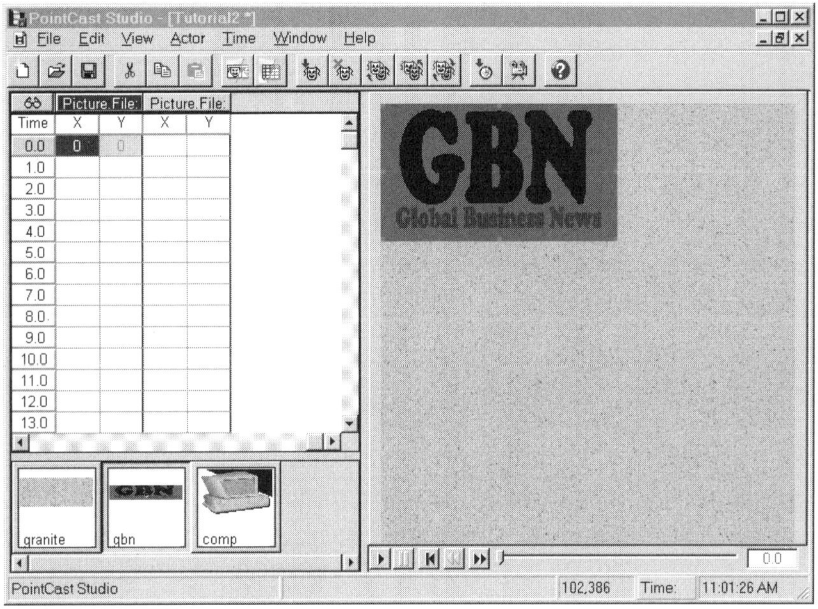

Figure 14-13 The GBN logo image actor is set to non-transparent. The granite background is obscured completely.

Figure 14-14 The GBN image actor is set to trans-parent. The granite background shows through, and images can be layered seam-lessly on top of one another.

Setting Transparency

To set an actor's background to transparent, follow these steps:

1. Double-click on the actor in the Cast list.
2. Select the Color tab.
3. Select Transparent.
4. Click OK.

Transparencies for Tutorial 2

For our second example, set the following transparencies:

granite.gif	Nontransparent. The granite texture is set to nontransparent because it occupies the bottom layer.
comp.gif	Transparent.
gbnlogo.gif	Transparent.

14.4.6 Transition Effects Defined

Now that we have set up our layering and transparencies, we are ready to apply the PointCast transition effects. Studio currently supports six built-in transition effects, which are listed in Table 14-1.

Each transition effect can appear from any of 10 directions. This includes eight compass directions (left, right, top right, bottom left, and so on), plus directions emanating from the center or edges of an image. The scale effect can appear from the upper left-hand corner, for example; the thumbnail image zooms into place by expanding downward and to the right. Or, the scale effect can appear from the center; the thumbnail image scales into place by expanding in all directions. Table 14-2 lists the direction codes.

Table 14-1

Transition Effects

Index	Name	Description	Direction
0	No Effect	No Effect	None
1	Wipe	Image appears from any direction as if wiped by a cloth.	All compass directions plus center and edges
2	Doors	Image appears through an opening door. The door can open horizontally from left and right or vertically from top and bottom.	Left (horizontal door) Top (vertical door)
3	Peek	Image slides into place from any direction. This provides the same effect as changing an actor's position over time.	All compass directions
4	Blinds	Image appears through an opening venetian blind. The blinds can be horizontal or vertical.	Left and Right(vertical blinds) Top and Bottom(horizontal blinds)
5	Scale	Image zooms into position or zooms out and disappears. For zoom-in, image first appears as a tiny thumbnail image and scales gradually to its full size. You can get a similar effect by changing an actor's width and height over time.	All compass directions plus center
6	Dissolve	Image gradually appears onstage or dissolves into the background.	All compass directions plus no movement, center, and edges

14.4.7 The Effect Wizard

Fortunately, there is no reason to memorize all the transition-effect and direction codes listed in Tables 14-1 and 14-2. You might need to refer to these tables when reading your timeline, though.

When creating transition effects, the best option is to use the Studio Effect Wizard. The Effect Wizard guides you through the creation of effects quickly and painlessly.

Table 14-2

Direction Codes

Index	Direction
0	No movement
1	From left
2	From top left
3	From top
4	From top right
5	From right
6	From bottom right
7	From bottom
8	From bottom left
9	From center
10	From edges

To use the Effect Wizard, follow these steps:

1. Select an actor in the Cast list.
2. Choose Effect Wizard from the Actor menu.
3. Select an effect.
4. Select a direction and click the Next button.
5. Select your time frame. Set the Start and Finish time rows for your effect.
6. Select the visibility of your actor. You can choose to create an actor entrance by showing the actor at the end of the effect. Or, you can create an actor exit by showing the actor at the beginning of the effect.

TIP: *To display direction icons (instead of index values) in the timeline, choose Options from the View menu. Then select Show Direction as Icon.*

Transition Effects for Tutorial 2

For our tutorial, we will create a number of transition effects. First, the GBN logo will appear onscreen with a dissolve effect from the top-left corner (see Figure 14-15). It then will minimize and move to the upper left-hand corner of the stage. While the logo is scaling, the computer image will appear at the upper right corner of the stage via a venetian-blind effect (see Figure 14-16).

To get started, you first need to place the granite background and the logo onstage:

1. Select the granite actor in the Cast list.
2. Select time row 0.0 and set the x,y position to (0,0).
3. Select the logo actor in the Cast list.
4. Select time row 0.0 and set the x,y position to (134,134)—the center of the stage.

You now are ready to create your transition effects:

1. Select the GBN logo actor in the Cast list.
2. Choose Effect Wizard from the Actor menu.
3. Choose Dissolve from the Effect pull-down menu.
4. Choose Top-Left from the Direction pull-down menu and click Next.
5. Set the Start time row to 0.0.
6. Set the End time row to 1.0.
7. Make the actor visible at the end of the effect and click Next.
8. Click Finish.
9. Preview your animation.

To create the zoom-out logo effect, follow these steps:

1. Create a scale effect from the top left between time 3.0 and 4.0. Make sure that the actor is visible at the beginning of the effect.
2. Try previewing your animation, and you will notice that the logo minimizes and disappears completely.
3. To minimize the logo only partially, you can manually set the Effect percent anywhere between 0 and 100. To move the logo to the upper-left corner, you simply can change its position.
4. To finalize the logo effect at time 4.0, set the x,y position to (0,5) and the Effect percent to 45.

The venetian-blind effect for the computer image is left for you as an exercise.

Figure 14-15 Tutorial 2 in action. Time: 0.4. The Dissolve effect in action.

Figure 14-16 Tutorial 2 in action. Time: 3.5. The logo scales to the upper left corner while the computer image appears via the venetian-blind effect.

14.4.8 Time Warping

If you are not happy with the speed of your animation, you easily can expand or contract time, otherwise known as *time warping*. With time warping, you select a range of time rows and enter a warp or multiplier factor. Studio takes care of the rest by inserting or deleting the necessary time rows. To double the length of your opening dissolve effect, for example, follow these steps:

1. Choose Expand/Collapse Time from the Time menu.
2. Set the Start row to 0.0.
3. Set the End row to 1.0.
4. Set the warp factor to 2. This doubles the length of your sequence. (When collapsing time, a warp factor of 2 shrinks your sequence in half.)
5. Select Expand Time and click OK.

TIP: *If you want more fine-grained control over your animation, Studio can support time rows down to one-tenth second. Just choose Timeline from the View menu and choose Time Settings.*

14.4.9 Line Effects

Before we end our second tutorial, we'll explore one last transition effect. In addition to text and picture actors, PointCast supports shape actors. Currently, PointCast supports only rectangle shape actors, but you actually may be surprised at the number of effects you can achieve with just this one shape.

Each rectangular shape can occupy a specific location and a specific width and height at any moment in time. By changing a rectangle's height or width, it is possible to create animated lines and sophisticated bar graphs.

We could add an animated underline to the GBN logo, for example. All you need to do is create a new shape actor and set the right coordinates:

1. Choose Insert Actor from the Actor menu.
2. Choose Shape from the Type pull-down menu.

3. Choose Rectangle from the Subtype pull-down menu (rectangles currently are the only supported shape).
4. Choose a color and click OK.
5. At time 1.0, set the position to (130, 265); set the width to 0 and the height to 5.
6. At time 2.0, set the position to (130,265); set the width to 350 and the height to 5.
7. Preview your animation. You should see the line grow in size from 0 pixels to 350 pixels wide (see Figure 14-17).

14.5 Adding Animations to Channels

14.5.1 Saving Animation Files

Studio provides two options for saving animation files:

Option 1: Images are directly embedded in your animation, and your animation (`.anm`) file is saved as a binary file.

Option 2: Images are stored in a separate directory, and your animation (`.anm`) file is saved as a readable text file. Images are stored in a directory with the same name as your animation file (without the `.anm` extension).

During channel development, it is recommended that you choose the first option and keep your images in a separate directory. That way, if your animation file is accidentally corrupted, you won't lose all your graphics images as well. As you get ready to transfer your animations to your Web server and start delivering your channel, it is recommended that you choose the second option. By embedding images, you cut down on the total number of file transfers and increase the speed of channel updates.

If you choose to keep your images separate, your animation is saved as a simple text file (see Listing 14-1 for the animation file for Tutorial 1). You can manually modify this text file or create automated scripts to create new animations on-the-fly.

Figure 14-17 Adding an animated line. Time: 1.4 seconds. With rectangle shape actors, it is easy to create animated lines and sophisticated bar graphs. Here, the gray line is growing from a width of 0 to 350 pixels in width.

Listing 14-1 Animation File from Tutorial #1

```
<MOVIE
    Width=240
    Height=160
    TimeInterval=100
    Duration=50
    Background=201,203,215
    Frames=PreStart:0,Start:0,PostEnd:30,End:30
    Size=5400
>
    <ACTOR
        Mask=TRUE
        Italic=FALSE
        Weight=Bold
        Width=170
        Height=20
        TextColor=0,0,0
        BackgroundColor=0,102,255
        FaceName="Times New Roman Special G2"
        Family=Modern
        PointSize=10
        Text="SVC News Channel"
        Truncate=TRUE
        Align=Left
        Label="SVC News Channel"
        Type=Text.String
    >
```

Continues

Listing 14-1.
Continued.

```
        <MARK  T=0 X=30 Y=-20>
        <MARK  T=20 Y=40 E=Dissolve D=N E%=100>
    </ACTOR>
    <ACTOR
        Mask=TRUE
        Italic=FALSE
        Weight=Normal
        Width=100
        Height=20
        TextColor=21,21,24
        BackgroundColor=255,255,255
        FaceName="Times New Roman"
        Family=Modern
        PointSize=8
        Text="24 Hours a Day!"
        Truncate=FALSE
        Align=Left
        Label="24 Hours a Day!"
        Type=Text.String
    >
        <MARK  T=0 X=-95 Y=63>
        <MARK  T=20 X=70 Y=69 E=Doors D=L E%=100>
    </ACTOR>
</MOVIE>
```

As you get ready to make your channel publicly available, PointCast offers the option of saving *lean* animation files. Lean animation files remove unnecessary palette information and all actor labels in an effort to create smaller, bandwidth-friendly animations.

To create a lean animation file, follow these steps:

1. Choose Advanced Settings from the File menu.
2. Select the File Save option for removing palette and label information and click OK.
3. Choose Save from the File menu.

PointCast claims that lean files can save significant amounts of memory. But PointCast may have overstated its case here. The entire animation file for tutorial 2, for example takes up 121 K. When saved as a lean file, it takes up 119 K, which is a savings of 2 K.

14.5.2 Adding Animation Articles

After you complete, test, and save your animation file, you need to add the animation to your channel configuration (CDF) file. It is easiest if you use the Connections Builder (fully described in Chapter 13). But before you modify your CDF file, remember to transfer your animation files to your Web site. (If you have chosen to keep your images in a separate directory, you also must transfer over the entire image subdirectory.)

Within the Connections Builder, you can add animations by choosing New from the Article menu. For each animation, you can set a number of general article parameters plus several specific animation properties:

General Article Properties	
Title	Title of your animation.
URL	Exact URL location of your animation file on your existing Web site. The file must have an `.anm` extension.
Type	Select PointCast Animation.
Display in Connections	You can display your animation in the Channel Viewer and/or the PointCast SmartScreen.

Retrieval and authentication options are covered in Chapter 13.

Animation Properties	
Alignment	You can align your animation to the left, right, or center.
Stretch to Fit	You can automatically stretch your animation to fit the enclosing frame.
Background Palette	You can use the default Windows palette or a customized palette created with your animation. In nearly all cases, it is recommended that you stick with the Windows palette.
Animation Repeat	You can choose to repeat your animation a set number of times or infinitely.

14.6 Advanced Topics

14.6.1 GIF Filmstrips

In addition to static graphics images, Studio supports filmstrip GIFs (not to be confused with GIF89a animated GIFs). *Filmstrip GIFs* are single graphics images divided into multiple frames (see Figure 14-18). By rapidly flipping through each frame, you can embed rather sophisticated animations that otherwise would not be possible with Studio's other built-in animation features.

Each filmstrip GIF is divided into a set number of rows and columns, and frames are numbered from left to right, top to bottom. The top left image in Figure 14-18 is considered frame 1, and the bottom right image is considered frame 12.

To embed a filmstrip GIF, you first need to insert your image as a regular picture actor and then set its frame parameters (located under Advanced Settings):

FramesX	Total number of columns in your image.
FramesY	Total number of rows in your image.

After you set your frame parameters, you can set your GIF in motion by flipping through each frame. You can do this by selecting a moment in time, setting the frame number to 1, selecting a later moment in time, and setting the frame number to its maximum. It's easiest to set frame numbers with the Mark Editor (see Figure 14-19).

To animate the rotating Earth depicted in Figure 14-18, all you need to do is set the frame number to 1 at time row 0.0, and set the frame number to 12 at time row 1.0. (The Earth filmstrip GIF is included in Tutorial 3 on the CD-ROM with this book.)

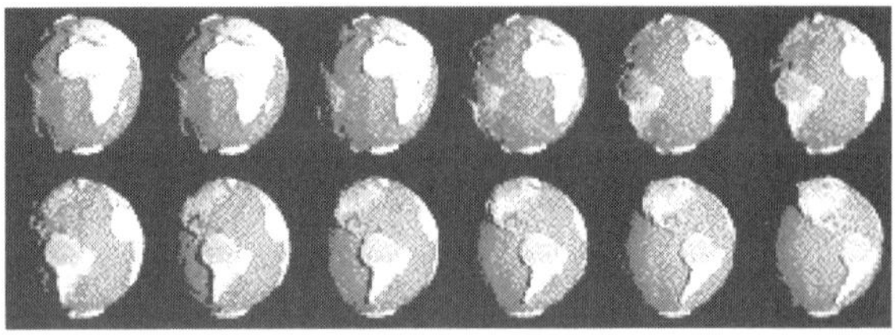

Figure 14-18
A 12-frame filmstrip GIF depicting a one-quarter rotation of the Earth. Frames are numbered left to right, top to bottom.

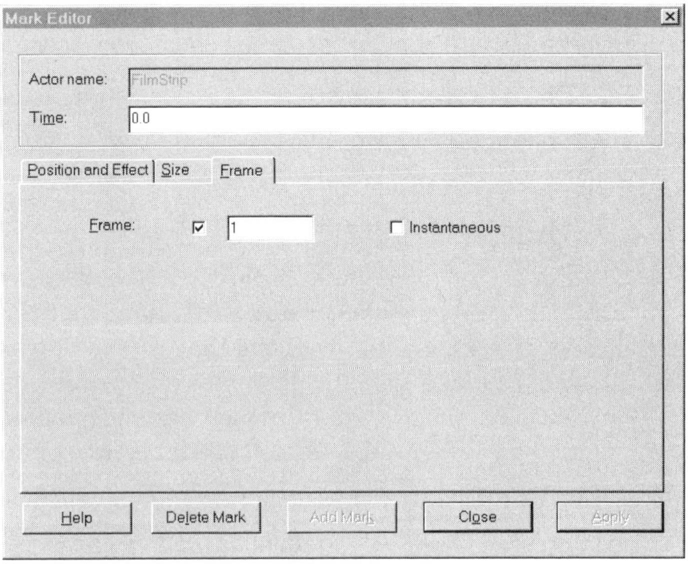

Figure 14-19 Setting the current frame with the Mark Editor. The Mark Editor is the easiest tool for working with filmstrip GIFs.

14.6.2 Embedded Animations

In addition to embedded filmstrip GIFs, Studio supports embedded PointCast animations. This capability enables you to embed multiple animations within one parent animation.

To embed an animation, you first need to set the frame parameters of the embedded or child animation. There are four main frames:

PreStart	Time row displayed just prior to the start of your animation.
Start	Time row when your animation begins (usually 0.0).
Stop	Time row when your animation ends.
PostStop	Time row displayed just after the end of your animation.

To set your frame parameters, follow these steps:

1. Choose Animation Settings from the File menu.
2. Click the More button.
3. Enter your frame settings in the pull-down list.
4. Click OK.

After you create the child animation, you can work on the parent animation. Within the parent animation, follow these steps:

1. Choose Insert Actor from the Actor menu.
2. Choose Movie from the Type pull-down menu.
3. Choose PointCast from the Subtype pull-down menu.
4. Enter the filename and click OK.

After embedded animations are inserted, they are very similar to filmstrip GIFs. You can display any particular frame (PreStart, Start, End, or PostEnd). And, if you choose one time row as Start and another time row as End, Studio automatically cycles through all the intervening frames and displays the full PointCast animation. You easily can embed the animation from Tutorial 1 inside Tutorial 2, for example (see Figure 14-20).

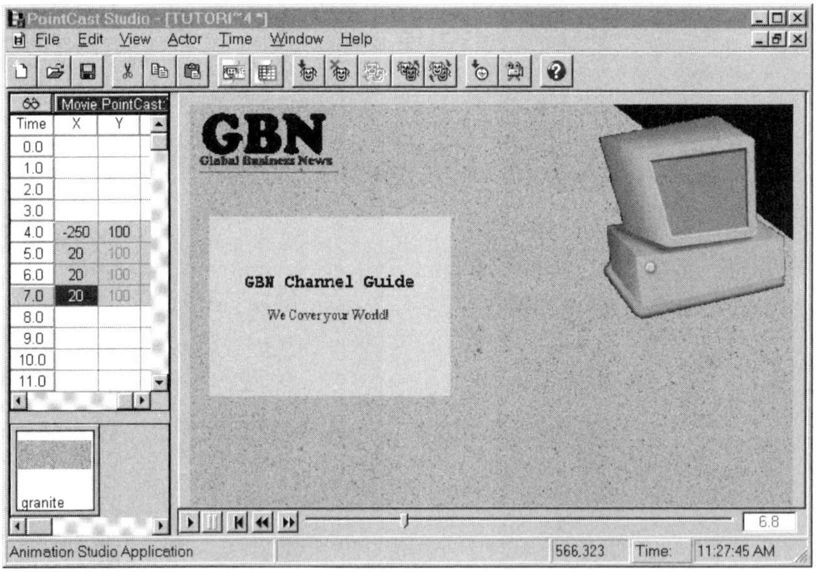

Figure 14-20 Studio supports embedded animations. Here, the animation from Tutorial 1 is embedded inside the animation from Tutorial 2.

SUMMARY

PointCast Studio is a straightforward application for creating high-impact PointCast animations. Studio works on the basic multimedia principles of actors, stages, and timelines. Actors represent single entities that can appear in your animation, such as graphics images or text strings. The stage is a window where you can preview your animation in action. And the timeline resembles a musical score that determines the exact properties of each actor at each particular moment in time.

Studio supports four main types of actors: images, text strings, rectangular shapes, and other PointCast animations. By typing directly into the timeline or by using the Mark Editor, you can set any of a number of actor parameters. The main parameters include Position, Width, Height, Visibility, Applied Transition Effect, and Percentage of Applied Transition Effect.

Studio also includes six built-in transition effects: wipe, doors, blinds, dissolve, scale, and peak. You easily can create transition effects with the built-in Effect Wizard. Studio also includes support for animated filmstrip GIFs and embedded animations.

After you create your animations, you can use the Connections Builder to embed them into your channel's contents.

Online Resource

- **`//www.pointcast.com/products/studio/`**.
  Describes the main features of Studio, along with detailed descriptions of actors, timelines, time marks, and visual effects.

PART V

Marimba's Castanet

CHAPTER 15

Introduction to Castanet

Marimba, Inc. is one of the hottest new software companies around. The company was founded by four defectors from the original Java development team at Sun Microsystems. Marimba's technical roots therefore are quite strong, and although Marimba has existed for less than two years, its products already have caused quite a stir.

The Castanet architecture introduced by Marimba takes push to an entirely new level, enabling the automatic delivery of both content *and* software applications. With Castanet, users simply subscribe to channels, and the Castanet Tuner downloads the full software application and installs a copy on the user's hard drive. At specified intervals set by the channel publisher, the tuner automatically checks for any new data or software upgrades and reinstalls the software. The software application therefore is always up to date and available to the end user, even when not connected to the Internet.

To get a quick understanding of what Castanet means, imagine this scenario. When the Pathfinder mission recently landed on Mars, the Jet Propulsion Laboratory Web site turned into one of the hottest spots on the Internet. Users from around the world downloaded the latest photographs from Pathfinder, and thousands of students went online to get background information on the mission. Now, imagine creating a channel that automatically pushes new photographs and new scientific data directly to scientists, schools, and the general public. Sounds good so far, right?

Now imagine giving every subscriber to your channel first-hand experience of what it would be like to navigate the Pathfinder across the Mars terrain. Build an entire software application that enables the end user to automatically receive new scientific data and take control of a virtual Pathfinder, complete with a full Control Panel, 3D images, and contour maps. Discover a small bug in the program and automatically push the software upgrade to all your subscribers. What have you got? A Castanet channel.

Although you might think this scenario sounds far-fetched, it's not. The *Jet Propulsion Laboratory* (JPL) already has created a Castanet application called the *Web Interface for Telescience* (WITs). Using the WITs software and the Castanet architecture, JPL is planning to enable remote scientists to participate in future Mars missions from their home institutions. The entire WITs program is expected to be used in the 2001, 2003, and 2005 missions to Mars. In the meantime, however, JPL has released a public version of the WITs software, enabling the end user to climb into the cockpit of a virtual Pathfinder (see Figure 15-1). The result is the automatic delivery of educational applications across the Internet.

Figure 15-1 The Web Interface for Telescience (WITs), from the Jet Propulsion Laboratory. Take a spin around Mars.

15.1 Castanet 101

Castanet enables the automatic delivery, installation, and updating of Java applications and content across the Internet and intranets. At its core, the Castanet architecture is composed of two main software components: the Castanet Tuner and the Castanet Transmitter. These two specialized software applications create a robust, secure, and scaleable infrastructure for delivering both software and data.

15.1.1 The Castanet Tuner

Castanet Tuners are client applications that can receive, install, and execute Java application channels. Tuners enable you to look for new channels, subscribe to channels, launch channel applications, or manually update channel contents (see Figure 15-2).

Much like every other push application, the Tuner follows a preset schedule and periodically polls the Castanet Transmitter for new information. If new information is available, the Tuner downloads only the updated information, enabling very quick and efficient network transactions. To ensure the integrity of each application, software upgrades also are performed *atomically*—that is, the Tuner attempts a reinstallation of software only when all the parts have been fully downloaded, and if the network fails during an update, the Tuner rolls back to the previously saved version.

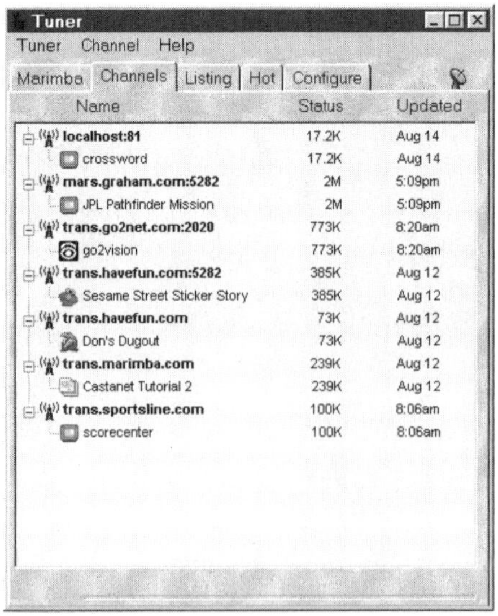

Figure 15-2 The Castanet Tuner manages, executes, and updates all your subscribed channels. The Tuner is easy to use and is available for Windows 95, Windows NT 4.0, Macintosh, and Solaris 2.5.

The Tuner is fully customizable for home users with modems or corporate users with direct Internet connections. And, users can customize the update schedule to receive updates as often as they want.

Castanet Tuner 1.1 is easy to use and currently is available free of charge for Windows 95, Windows NT 4.0, Macintosh, and Solaris 2.5 systems (the Windows 95/NT version is available on the CD-ROM that accompanies this book). The full Castanet Tuner also is available within Netscape's Netcaster product, making it available on 17 platforms supported by Netscape.

NOTE: *The Castanet Tuner is its own channel and checks for software upgrades once a week. Users therefore are always ensured that they are running the most up-to-date version of software.*

15.1.2 The Castanet Transmitter

Castanet Transmitters are server applications for distributing software and updated data to Castanet Tuners. Each Transmitter holds data for a certain number of channels and listens for Tuner requests on a specified TCP/IP port.

Transmitters are similar to regular HTTP servers, with two important differences. First, Transmitters negotiate with each Tuner to send *differential* updates—that is, only data updated since the last transmission is sent. This negotiation occurs with an elaborate checksum comparison of each Java class file and each Java resource file, including images, sounds, and data files. For small changes to large files, Transmitters even can send just the edited section along with specific editing commands instead of sending the entire file.

Second, Transmitters send all the data at once in one TCP connection. HTTP 1.0 Servers require separate TCP connections for each image or class file, and the overhead associated with each connection can be considerable. With one connection, Castanet updates are faster and use bandwidth much more efficiently.

Castanet Transmitter 1.1 is available for Windows 95, Windows NT 4.0, and Solaris 2.5 systems. The Transmitter can run as a standalone application or as an extension to popular HTTP Servers. But Marimba makes money by selling Transmitters; they aren't free! Check the Marimba Web site for the latest price quotes. Evaluation copies of the Castanet Transmitter are available for free, and a copy of the Windows 95/NT version is available on the CD-ROM at the end of the book. Note that the evaluation Transmitter enables you to publish up to three channels to three individual subscribers and is available for development purposes only.

15.1.3 How It Works

With just one Tuner and one Transmitter, Castanet is ready to go. Here is how it works.

The user requests a list of available channels. The Tuner relays the request to the Transmitter, and the Transmitter sends the list of channels. The user then subscribes to a channel, and the Tuner downloads a copy of the Java software and installs it on the user's hard drive (see Figure 15-3).

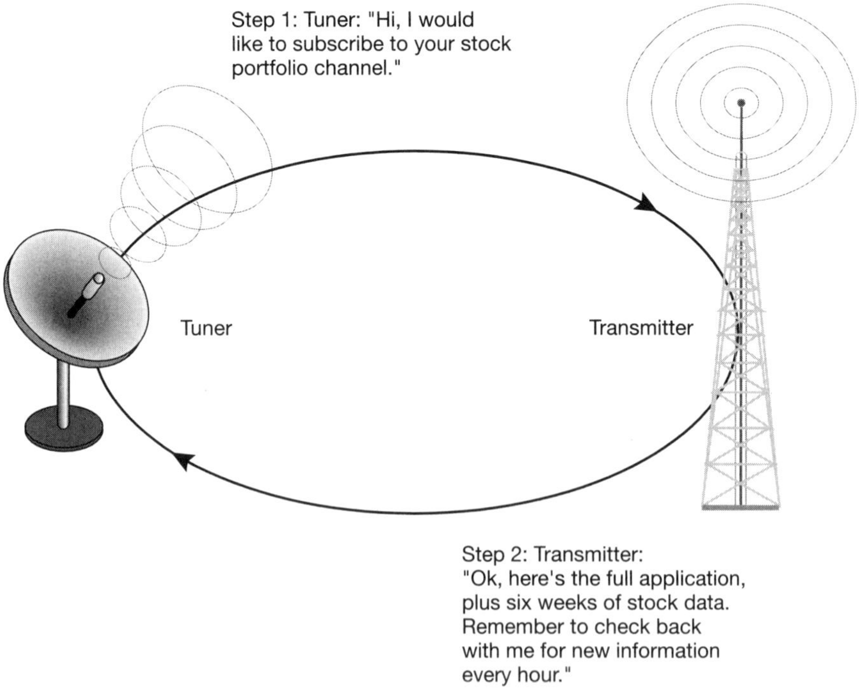

Figure 15-3 Subscribing to Castanet channels. Users initiate channel subscriptions with the Castanet Tuner. The Tuner downloads the software application from the Castanet Transmitter and installs it on the user's hard drive.

In addition to just the software, the Transmitter sends a Properties file. Among other things, this file includes a recommended schedule for channel updates (frequently—less than five minutes—to daily to weekly).

Following the suggested schedule, the Tuner periodically polls the Transmitter for new information. The new information might include news headlines, which are displayed automatically to the user, or new software components, which add to the program's functionality (see Figure 15-4). Each update is performed efficiently and differentially.

15.2 Castanet Channels

So, you have a Tuner, a Transmitter, and a sophisticated update mechanism. But what exactly can you deliver? Castanet supports four main types of channels: HTML channels, applet channels, presentation channels, and application channels.

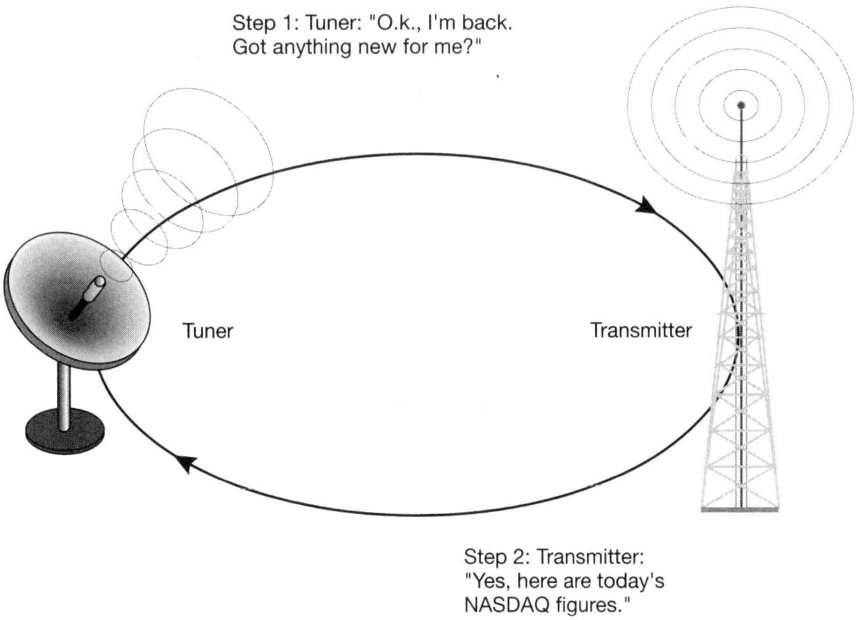

Figure 15-4 Channel updates. The Tuner follows a recommended schedule set by the channel developer and periodically polls the transmitter for new information. If new information is available, the data is differentially downloaded—that is, only files that have changed since the last update are downloaded.

15.2.1 HTML Channels

HTML channels represent an entire collection or directory of HTML pages. When a user first subscribes to the channel, the first page, usually `index.html`, is downloaded and passed to the user's default Web browser. If the user follows any links off the first page, those pages are downloaded.

After a few minutes, the Tuner downloads the entire HTML channel and stores a copy on the user's hard drive. The HTML documents therefore are always available, even when the user is not connected to the Internet. And, because HTML channel updates occur with Castanet's update technology, channel updates are both fast and efficient.

HTML channels are most similar to the Web-crawl capabilities provided by Netscape Netcaster and Microsoft Active Channels. Castanet uses a different approach, however, which enables you to transmit entire directories of HTML documents, circumventing the need to Web crawl any of these documents. Note that HTML channels do not follow the *Channel Definition Format* (CDF) officially endorsed by Microsoft.

15.2.2 Applet Channels

Applet channels are Java applets that are downloaded and updated automatically. In most cases, you can take any existing applet (Marimba actually calls these *legacy* applets!) and, with little or no changes to your source code, publish it as a Castanet channel. Because the applet is stored locally, users don't have to wait for lengthy downloads each time they want to work with your applet.

15.2.3 Presentation Channels

Presentation channels are user interfaces created with Marimba's Bongo software program. So what is Bongo? Bongo is a software application that enables programmers and nonprogrammers alike to easily create *graphical user interfaces* (GUIs) for Java applications and presentations. Developers simply can point-and-click to add a new button, for example. Or

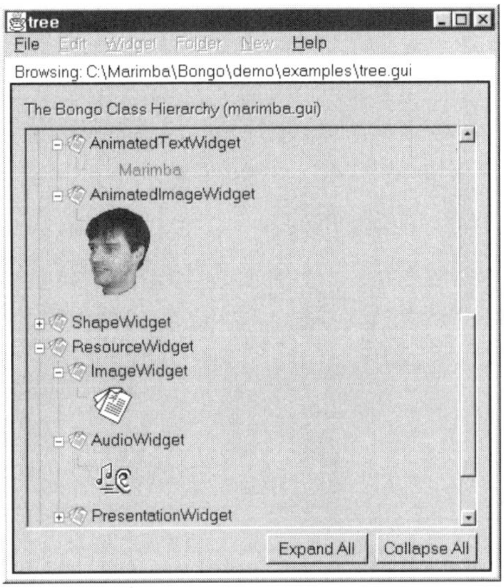

Figure 15-5 Marimba's Bongo software enables programmers and nonprogrammers to create Java GUI interfaces simply by pointing and clicking. Here is just a sampling of some of the widgets provided by Bongo.

they can choose from a large library of widgets, including scrollbars, drop-down menus, and animated text boxes (see Figure 15-5).

As you continue to develop your own Castanet channels, it is highly recommended that you check out Bongo. Many programmers have complained of Java's often complex *Abstract Windowing Toolkit* (AWT) for creating GUIs. In particular, many programmers have griped about Java's often confusing Layout Managers (anyone who has worked with Java's Grid Bag Layout Manager knows exactly what I'm talking about!). So check out Bongo and save yourself lots of programming aggravation! Evaluation copies and tutorials are available at the Marimba Web site at **`http://www.marimba.com`**.

15.2.4 Application Channels

To get the full effect of all of Castanet's many features, you will want to create an application channel. Application channels are secure Java programs that can receive automatic information updates or actually update themselves.

To ensure security, application channels are restricted to many of the same security restrictions as regular applets. But there is one exception to these restrictions: Application channels are able to read from and write to one specific directory on the user's hard drive. This capability enables a new generation of Java applications that finally can circumvent the applet security "sandbox" and thereby create persistent data.

Examples of commercially available application channels follow:

CBS SportsLine Score Center	Displays constantly updated sports scores (see Figure 15-6)
COREL Office for Java	Provides a full suite of productivity applications written entirely in Java
go2vision	Displays constantly updated news headlines, sports scores, and stock quotes
HotWired talk.com channel	Provides real-time chat rooms for hundreds of simultaneous users
MapQuest Channel	Provides an interactive atlas and listings of millions of businesses and places of interest throughout the world
Net It Now!	Publishes desktop documents across an intranet without the use of browser plug-ins
Pencil Me In	Enables enterprise-wide calendaring and scheduling
Sesame Street Sticker Channel	From the Children's Television Workshop (see Figure 15-7)
Wall Street Web	Monitors stocks, bonds, and mutual funds
Web Interface for Telescience (WITs)	Program from the Jet Propulsion Laboratory (described earlier in this chapter)

Figure 15-6
The CBS SportsLine Score Center provides a constantly updated list of sports scores from your favorite teams.

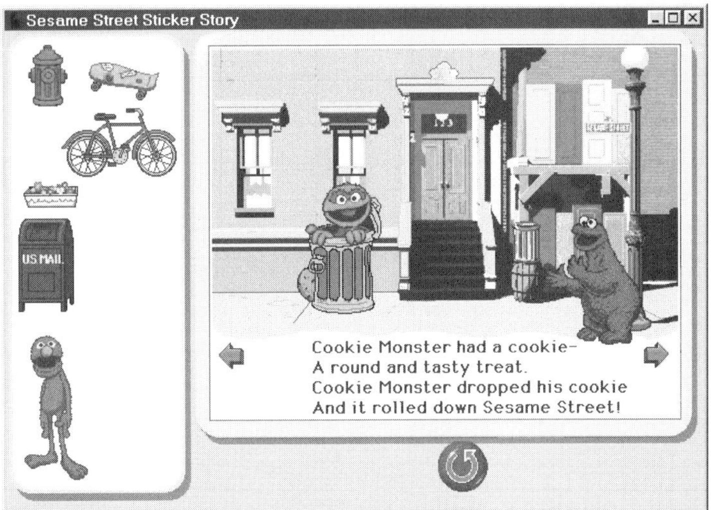

Figure 15-7
The Sesame Street Sticker Channel, from the Children's Television Workshop. Now where is that cookie, anyway?

15.3 Castanet Plug-Ins

Application channels can be customized and personalized for each subscriber through the use of Castanet plug-ins. Each channel can have its own plug-in, and the plug-in is housed on the Castanet Transmitter. You therefore can think of a Castanet plug-in as an extra component of software that plugs into the Transmitter to provide extra functionality, much like browser plug-ins provide added functionality for viewing different types of Web documents.

Each time a Tuner polls the Transmitter for new information, the tuner also sends a log file and profile data (see Figure 15-8). The log file could contain any record of user activity the channel developer wants to track. The application might track the specific advertisements that each user follows, for example, or it might compile a list of the most popular news categories or even store the results of an online survey.

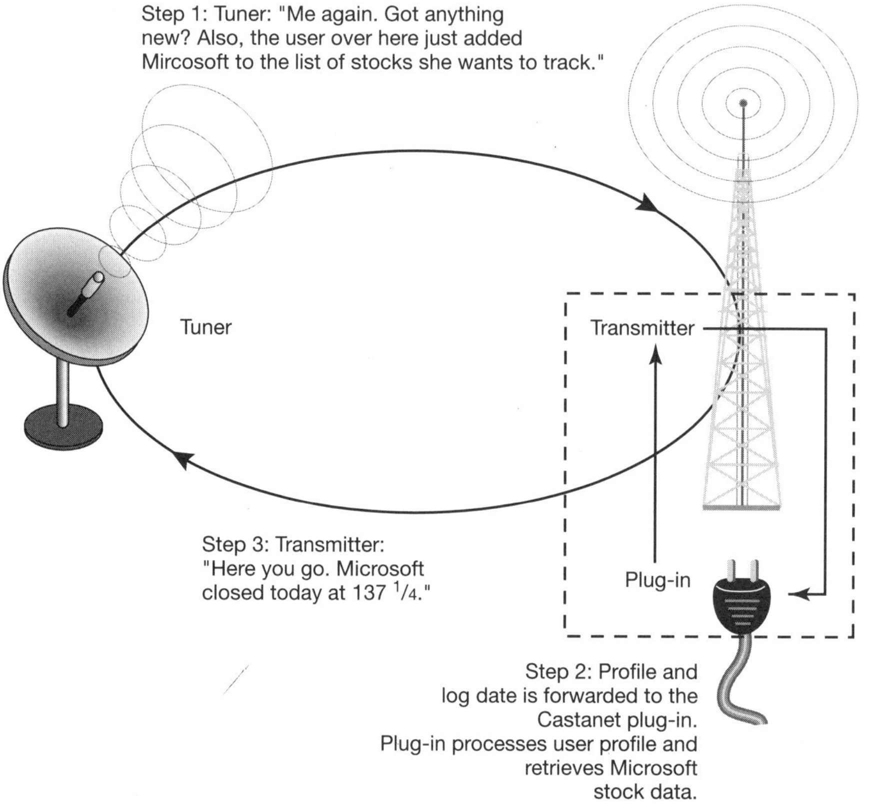

Figure 15-8
Castanet plug-ins. Each time a Tuner requests a channel update, it also sends its log and profile data. Plug-ins represent separate Java or C++ applications that can be used to record user feedback or customize the channel experience.

The profile data includes specific options and preferences set by the user. This might include demographic information, a list of news topics the user is interested in, or perhaps a list of stock symbols the user wants to track.

Plug-ins represent separate Java or C++ applications that can store and process both log and profile data. The plug-in might just save the logging information to the Transmitter hard drive, for example, or it might use the data to send back dynamic results. For an online survey, the results could be compiled automatically and sent back. Or, for advertisements, you could send back more detailed product information or information about similar products.

With profile data, you can personalize and customize both the content and the application. For a financial application, for example, you could send a bar chart program along with historical data for specific companies the user is tracking.

Processing user feedback is key to raising advertising revenue, and customized channels are key to retaining subscribers. Plug-ins give you the maximum flexibility to do both.

15.4 The Castanet Publisher

As a channel developer, you need one additional piece of software: Castanet Publisher. Castanet Publisher enables developers to efficiently copy over their Java applications from their local hard drives to the Castanet Transmitter. Much like Tuner updates, updates to the Transmitter via the Publisher are differential; only files that have changed since the last update are copied over. After channel contents are copied over, they are available immediately to all subscribers (see Figure 15-9).

The Publisher and Transmitter include several levels of security to ensure that only registered developers with security clearance can publish to the Transmitter. As is described in later chapters, you will need to use Castanet Publisher to test and debug your channels.

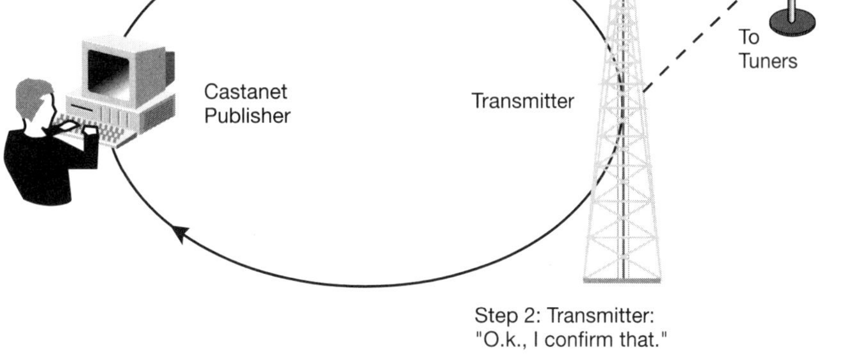

Figure 15-9 Castanet Publisher enables developers to efficiently copy their programs and data to the Castanet Transmitter. This enables many developers to publish to the same channel while ensuring an adequate level of security. After the updated channel is published, it is available immediately to all subscribers.

15.5 Scaling to Millions

With hundreds of Castanet Tuners inside your organization, you need a more efficient method of controlling tuner updates. And, with thousands of potential subscribers across the Internet, you need more than one Transmitter to handle the load. To solve both these problems, Castanet offers two additional software components: the Castanet Proxy Server and the Castanet Repeater. Together, these components can scale to reach thousands and even millions of subscribers.

15.5.1 The Castanet Proxy Server

The Castanet Proxy Server enables companies to efficiently manage Castanet traffic traveling through the corporate firewall. Without a Proxy Server, each Tuner makes requests directly to a Transmitter located somewhere on the Internet. Each Tuner can make the same request, and the updated information is relayed through the corporate firewall any number of times.

Tuner requests are sent to the Proxy Server, and the Proxy Server relays the request to the Transmitter. For each request, the Transmitter processes the channel plug-in to ensure personalization and customization; it returns a list of updated files but does not include the files themselves. If the Proxy Server already has the necessary files cached, they are sent immediately to the Tuner. Otherwise, the Proxy Server downloads and caches the new updated information and then forwards it to the Tuner (see Figure 15-10). This significantly reduces Castanet traffic through the firewall while ensuring the complete customizability of channels. The Proxy Server also maintains a single open connection to the Transmitter to eliminate the overhead associated with each TCP connection.

15.5.2 The Castanet Repeater

Castanet Repeaters enable organizations to distribute and balance requests for Tuner updates among several Transmitters. These Repeaters could be located in the same location as the original Transmitter or geographically dispersed throughout the world.

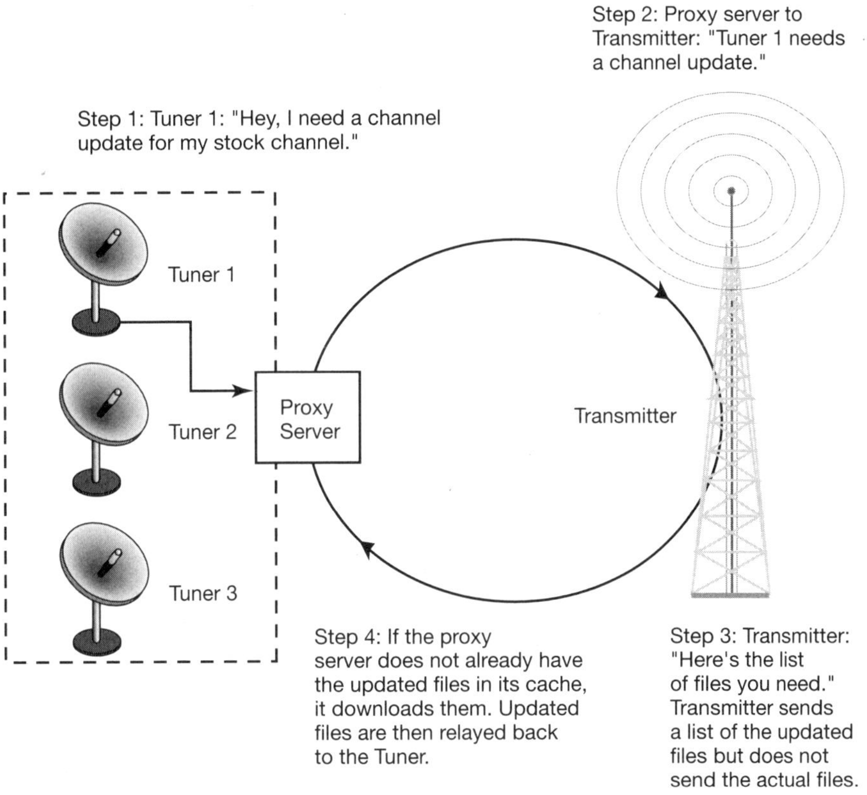

Figure 15-10
The Castanet Proxy Server handles Castanet traffic traveling though the corporate firewall. This makes for quicker updates and more efficient use of network bandwidth.

When a main Transmitter receives a Tuner request, the Transmitter can handle it or forward the request to a Repeater. Forwarding of Transmitter requests can be round-robin or based on time zone, sending the request to the Transmitter geographically closest to the requesting Tuner (see Figure 15-11). If the forwarding Repeater is down, the Tuner returns to the original Transmitter and requests the address of a substitute Repeater. When a developer updates or publishes a new channel, the updated information is propagated to the entire list of repeaters.

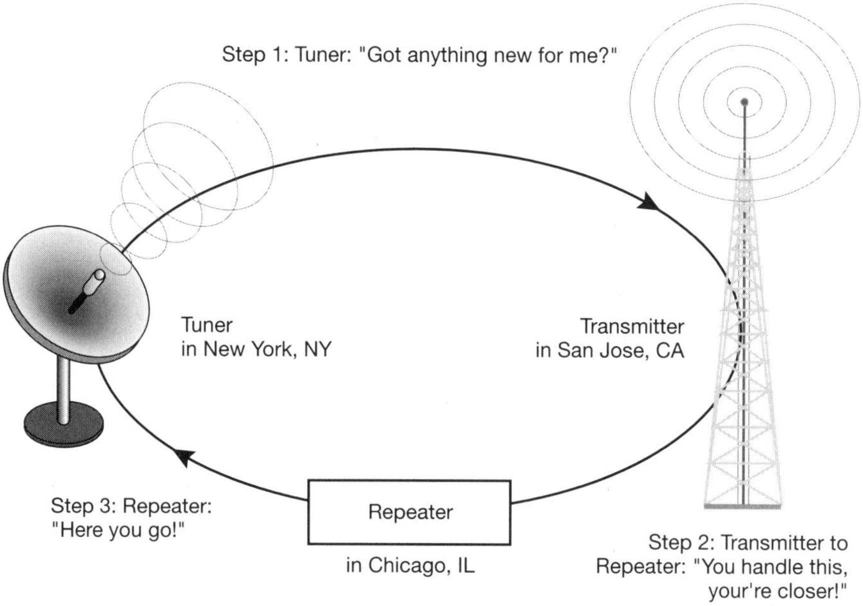

Figure 15-11 The Castanet Repeater enables an organization to distribute the load associated with multiple Tuner requests to multiple Transmitters. This enables the Castanet architecture to efficiently scale to an audience of millions. Repeaters remain entirely invisible to the end user.

Repeaters are completely invisible to the end user and enable the Castanet architecture to reach a potential audience of millions.

15.6 Assessing Castanet

15.6.1 Strengths

Castanet represents an entirely new infrastructure for software and content delivery. The infrastructure is cross-platform, efficient, completely customizable, secure, and scaleable. Here are Castanet's strengths:

Content and software. With Castanet, you can deliver news headlines or a customizable ticker for displaying those headlines. The application is merging with the content, and Castanet offers the greatest flexibility in delivering both.

Wide distribution through Netscape Netcaster. When Castanet was introduced, many skeptics wondered how many users would take the time to download and install a separate push application. Lots of people actually did, but the Castanet Tuner now is embedded directly into Netscape Netcaster, which widens the potential audience of Castanet subscribers to many millions.

Real Java applications. The current batch of Java applets suffers from two important drawbacks. First, the applet is downloaded each time the user visits the Web page. This often can be a lengthy process. Second, applets are restricted to a security "sandbox," which certainly is good for security but bad for creating full-blown Java applications. (Note: Netscape Communicator 4.0 and Internet Explorer 4.0 do allow a certain relaxation of security restrictions for signed applets.) Castanet solves both these problems: Applications are stored locally on the user's hard drive and are available immediately, whether online of offline. Also, application channels have the capability to read from and write to one directory on the user's hard drive, enabling Java applications to maintain persistent data.

Cross-platform. Castanet is built on Java. And Java is cross-platform, meaning that you can run Castanet just as easily on Windows 95/NT, Macintosh, or UNIX.

Customization. You can use Castanet plug-ins to customize each Castanet channel to record user feedback or personalize the channel content. Plug-ins are separate Java or C++ applications and therefore are completely customizable by the channel developer.

Efficient update mechanism. The entire Castanet architecture is designed to minimize bandwidth use as much as possible. Channel updates are performed within a single TCP connection and are performed differentially, ensuring that each Tuner downloads only what is new. The Castanet Proxy Server enables efficient bandwidth use within corporations, and the Castanet Repeaters can ensure rapid updates by distributing the network load among a number of Transmitters.

Scalability. With Castanet Proxy Servers and Repeaters, the Castanet architecture is capable of scaling to thousands and even millions of users.

Security. Each Castanet channel includes all the security measures of Java, including byte-code verification and a modified security sandbox similar to regular Java applets. The Castanet architecture also includes several built-in levels of security to ensure that only certain developers with security clearance can publish or modify channel contents.

15.6.2 Weaknesses

Castanet does have several disadvantages or weaknesses, however:

Development costs. Most push applications require developers to understand JavaScript, HTML, or the *Channel Definition Format* (CDF). Castanet requires a thorough understanding of Java and a much more extensive learning curve than other push platforms. The downsides associated with developing Castanet channels usually are longer development cycles and higher costs.

Java can be slow. Java sometimes can be twice as slow as native applications written in C or C++. The security and portability of Java therefore involve serious performance tradeoffs, even with the best Just-In-Time compilers.

15.7 Moving Beyond Java

In August, 1997, Castanet announced the availability of Castanet UpdateNow. UpdateNow is similar to Castanet, because it automatically distributes, installs, and updates software applications. But UpdateNow works with both Java applications and native code applications written in C, C++, and Microsoft Visual Basic.

One week after the release of UpdateNow, Marimba also reported that it was collaborating with Microsoft on Internet standards for describing software applications. The standard, the *Open Software Description* (OSD), currently is under review by the World Wide Web Consortium.

Much like CDF, OSD is an application language written in *Extensible Markup Language* (XML), but OSD is intended to enable developers to describe software components and their interdependencies. These software applications could be written in Java, C, C++, or Visual Basic. After the standardization process is complete, Marimba plans on including OSD within the Castanet architecture.

Both these initiatives represent a pragmatic strategy by Marimba to move away from a Java-only platform and to focus further on gaining corporate customers.

SUMMARY

Castanet enables the automatic delivery, installation, and updating of Java applications across the Internet and intranets. This capability enables channel providers to push both content and software applications.

The Castanet architecture is composed primarily of Tuners and Transmitters. Tuners are client applications that manage, launch, and update channel contents. Transmitters are server applications that distribute content and software updates. These two core components are supplemented with Castanet Publisher for publishing channel contents to the Transmitter, Castanet plug-ins for customizing and personalizing channels, the Castanet Proxy Server for managing Castanet traffic in large organizations, and Castanet Repeaters for distributing Tuner updates among several Transmitters.

Currently, Castanet supports four main types of channels: HTML channels, which essentially are directories of HTML documents; applet channels, which are regular Java applets stored locally on the user's hard drive; presentation channels, which are short tutorials or animations created with Marimba's Bongo GUI development software; and application channels, which are Java programs that can receive automatic updates and read from and write to one specific directory on the user's hard drive.

The Castanet architecture is robust, scaleable, secure, and completely customizable. On the downside, it requires a long learning curve, and is dependent on the speed (often slow) of Java. Marimba currently is moving beyond its Java-only platform strategy and is moving toward collaboration with Microsoft on the *Open Software Description* (OSD).

Online Resources

- Castanet White Paper **http://www.marimba.com/datasheets/castanet-wp.html**. What does Castanet mean for you? Where is Castanet going? Check out this recently updated white paper on the Castanet architecture.
- The Open Software Description (OSD) **http://www.marimba.com/osd/**. Over the next few months, new information regarding OSD is sure to appear. Check here for the latest updates and FAQ.

CHAPTER 16

Using the Castanet Tuner

The Castanet Tuner enables you to subscribe to, launch, and update Castanet channels. Currently, the Castanet Tuner is in Version 1.1 and includes a number of performance and feature enhancements over Version 1.0:

- Support for Java 1.1. The tuner now includes the latest *Java runtime environment* (JRE) 1.1.2 from Sun Microsystems. This includes an optimized Java Virtual Machine and all the necessary Java core class files.
- Simpler installation.
- Incremental HTML channels. In Version 1.0, the entire HTML channel had to be downloaded before you could view any of it. In contrast, Version 1.1 now includes incremental HTML channels, which enable you to view HTML pages as they are downloaded.

- Online/Offline mode. The Tuner now includes a specific toggle switch for working online or offline so that you can more easily use your Castanet channels when not connected to the Internet.
- Feedback can be disabled. You now can disable three specific feedback options. This is more or less akin to disabling cookies in your Web browser; you can prevent the recording of any of your habits or personal preferences, but you lose out on the customization provided by Castanet plug-ins.

16.1 Installation

16.1.1 Supported Platforms

Currently, the Castanet Tuner is available for Windows 95, Windows NT 4.0, Macintosh, and Solaris 2.5 systems. The Castanet Tuner also is included in Netscape's Netcaster, making it available on all 17 platforms supported by Netscape.

16.1.2 Hardware Requirements for Windows 95/NT

The hardware requirements for installing the Tuner on Windows 95/NT 4.0 follow:

- At least 16M of RAM
- At least 10M free disk space
- An Internet connection (modem or direct)

16.1.3 Installing the Tuner

The CD-ROM that accompanies this book includes a Windows 95/NT version of the Castanet Tuner. If you have a different platform, free downloads are available from the Marimba Web site at `http:\\www.marimba.com`.

The Castanet Tuner is a self-extracting InstallShield file. Just double-click on the filename (`Tuner1_1.exe`) to begin installation and follow the onscreen instructions.

16.1.4 Adding the Tuner to the Windows Start Menu

To automatically start the Castanet Tuner each time you boot up your machine, you need to add the Tuner to the Windows Startup directory. Follow these steps:

1. Right-click on any empty area of the Windows taskbar.
2. Choose Properties.
3. Select the Start Menu Programs tab.
4. Under the Customize Start Menu options, click the Add button.
5. Click the Browse button to locate the Tuner executable. If you followed the typical installation, the file is located in `C:\Program Files\Marimba\Castanet Tuner\Tuner.exe`.
6. Click the Next button.
7. You have created a Windows shortcut to the Tuner. Now you need to place it in the Windows Startup directory. Double-click on the Startup directory.
8. Click Finish.

16.1.5 The nowin Option

To automatically launch the Tuner without actually opening its window, you need to set its command-line argument. When launched with the `nowin` option, the Tuner displays a quick splash screen and then runs in the background on the Windows taskbar, enabling the Tuner to receive automatic channel updates. Follow these steps:

1. Right-click on any empty area of the Windows taskbar.
2. Choose Properties.
3. Select the Start Menu Programs tab.

4. Under the Customize Start Menu options, click the Advanced button.
5. Open the Startup directory located under the Programs directory.
6. Right-click on the Tuner shortcut and choose Properties.
7. Click the Shortcut tab.
8. Under Target, you should see `C:\Program Files\Marimba\Castanet Tuner\Tuner.exe`. Append the target so that it now reads `C:\Program Files\Marimba\Castanet Tuner\Tuner.exe -nowin`.
9. Click OK.

16.1.6 Launching the Tuner

To manually launch the Castanet Tuner, click the Windows Start button and choose the Castanet Tuner.

16.2 The Tuner Interface

The Tuner interface is composed of five tabbed pages. Before we begin a discussion of subscribing to channels, let's take a quick tour of each Tuner page.

16.2.1 The Marimba Page

The Marimba page is an About page that describes the Castanet Tuner. The page lists the current version of software, the date the version was officially released, and the date the Tuner software was last updated (see Figure 16-1). The Tuner is itself a Castanet channel and checks the main Marimba Transmitter once a week to download any new software upgrades or new channel listings.

16.2.2 The Channels Page

The Channels page lists all your currently subscribed and unsubscribed channels (see Figure 16-2). Each channel includes four columns of information:

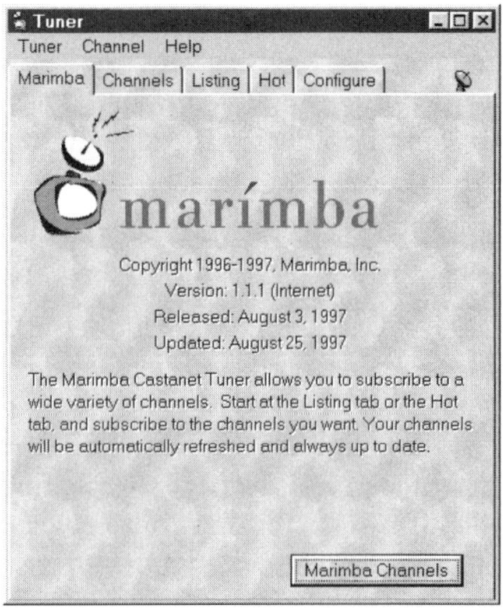

Figure 16-1
The Marimba page lists the current version of software, the date the version was officially released, and the date the Tuner software was last updated.

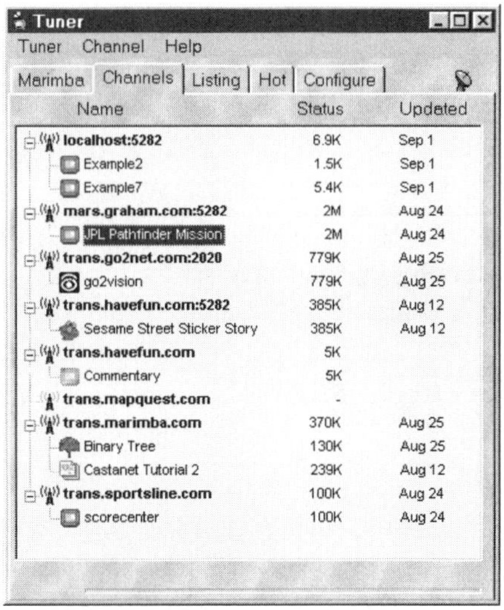

Figure 16-2
The Channels page lists all your currently subscribed and unsubscribed channels.

Column 1 — Indicates the name of the Transmitter. Each Transmitter can host multiple channels.

Column 2 — Indicates the name of the channel and whether you currently are subscribed to that channel. Unsubscribed channels are grayed out.

Column 3	Indicates the channel status. During channel updates, a small progress bar appears indicating the percentage of downloading completed. When downloading is complete, the column indicates the size (in kilobytes or megabytes) of the channel contents.
Column 4	Indicates when the channel was last updated. If any errors occur during updating, they are reported here.

16.2.3 The Listing Page

The Listing page includes a complete list of channels hosted by individual Castanet Transmitters on the Internet or your intranet (see Figure 16-3).

16.2.4 The Hot Page

The Hot page lists a half dozen premium Castanet channels (see Figure 16-4). Each time the Castanet Tuner is updated, the Hot page is updated with new listings.

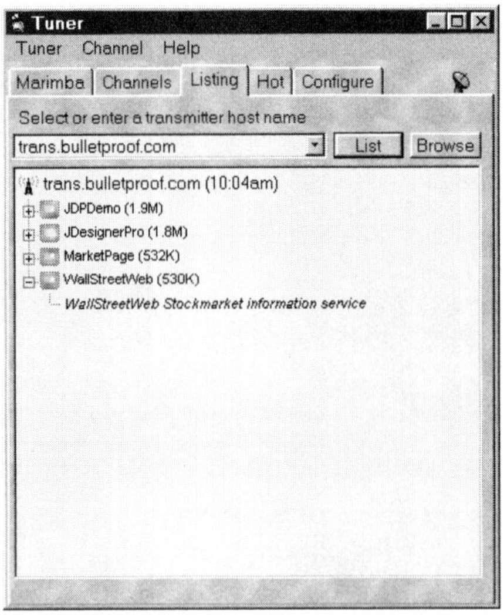

Figure 16-3 The Listing page includes a complete list of channels hosted by individual Castanet Transmitters. To get a short description of each channel, click on the plus (+) sign.

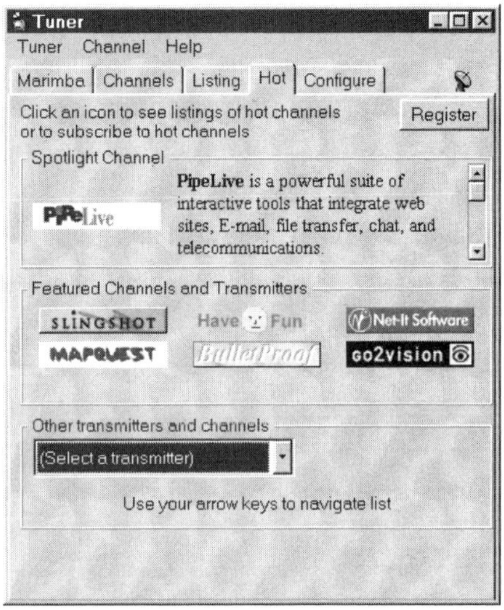

Figure 16-4
The Hot page includes a rotating list of premium Castanet channels. Check here first when looking for new channels.

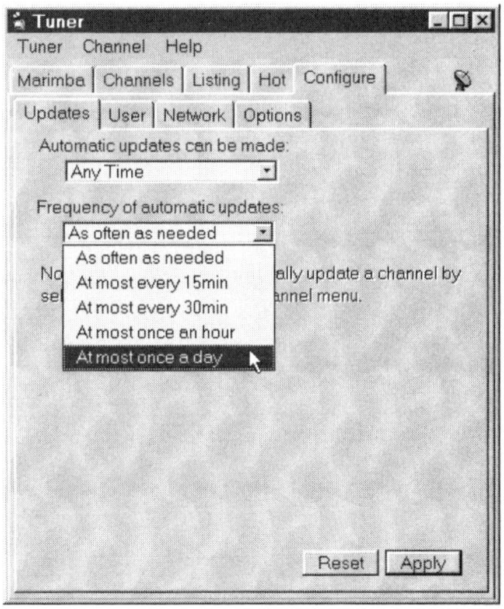

Figure 16-5
The Configure page. The Castanet Tuner is fully customizable for home users with modems and corporate users with direct Internet connections.

16.2.5 The Configure Page

The Configure page enables you to configure the network, update, and user options provided by the Tuner (see Figure 16-5).

16.3 Working with Channels

16.3.1 Subscribing to Channels

After you are oriented to the basic interface, you are ready to start subscribing to channels.

The best place to start is the Marimba site itself. The Marimba Transmitter hosts a number of small, simple channels that you can subscribe to just to make sure your Tuner is working properly. To subscribe to a Marimba channel, follow these steps:

1. Launch the Tuner and click on the Marimba page.
2. Click the Marimba Channels button.

The Tuner connects to the main Marimba Transmitter, downloads a listing of available channels, and switches to the Listing page (see Figure 16-6).

In the Listing page, you now see a complete list of available channels. Note that in the Host Name text box, you see **trans.marimba.com**. Most Castanet Transmitter names begin with the **trans** prefix instead of the regular **www** prefix normally associated with Web servers.

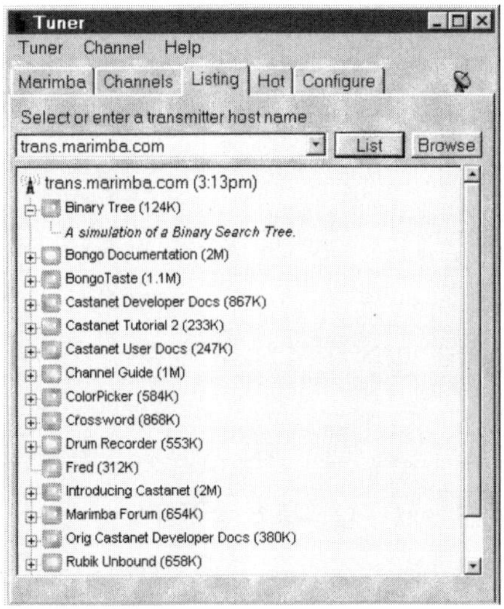

Figure 16-6 The Marimba channels. Marimba hosts more than a dozen of its own channels. Try subscribing to one of these to make sure your Tuner is set up correctly.

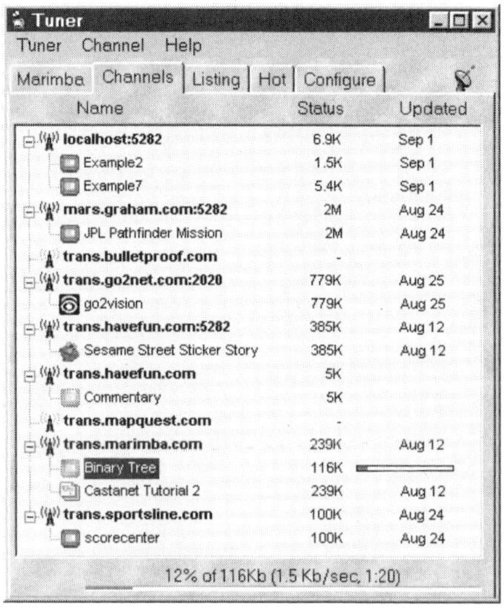

Figure 16-7 As soon as you subscribe to a channel, the Tuner downloads its contents. The progress bar to the right of the channel name indicates the percentage downloaded.

To get a description of a channel, just click on the plus (+) sign to the left of the channel name. To subscribe, just double-click on the channel name.

When you subscribe to a channel, the Tuner switches to the Channels page and begins downloading immediately. You should see a small progress bar to the right of the channel name (see Figure 16-7). This bar indicates the percentage of downloading complete. You also should see red beams streaming into the satellite dish icon at the upper right of the Tuner. A similar animation is displayed in the Windows taskbar so that you can monitor channel updates while working on other applications.

When the channel is fully downloaded, it is launched on your desktop (see Figure 16-8).

16.3.2 Launching Channels

After you download a channel, you can run it at any time, even when you are not connected to the Internet. Just click on the Channels page and double-click on the channel.

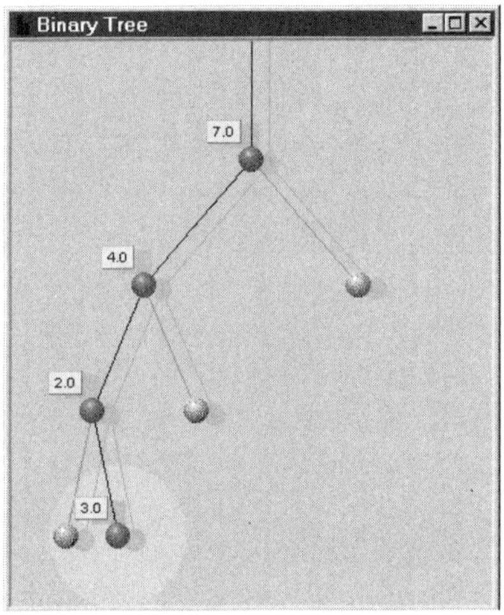

Figure 16-8 The Binary Tree channel. As soon as the channel is downloaded, the Tuner launches the application to the desktop.

16.3.3 Stopping Channels

To stop a channel, just click on the regular Windows close icon in the upper right-hand corner of the application window. Or, click on the Channels page and double-click again on the channel name.

16.3.4 Finding Channels

So where are the rest of the Castanet channels? Check out the Hot page. Remember that this page is a rotating list of premium Castanet channels. Just click any of the channel icons to subscribe. Or, you can scroll through the list of Transmitters for additional channels.

If you already know the name of the Transmitter, you can connect directly to it. Just click on the Listing page. In the Host Name text box, type the name of the host (usually beginning with the `trans` prefix) and press Enter. Most Transmitters are served off of port 80, but some are not. To connect to a port other than port 80, you must enter the hostname, followed by a colon (`:`), followed by the port number—for example, `trans.mapquest.com:5282`.

To get a refreshed listing of channels available on the selected Transmitter, click the List button. To view an HTML listing of available chan-

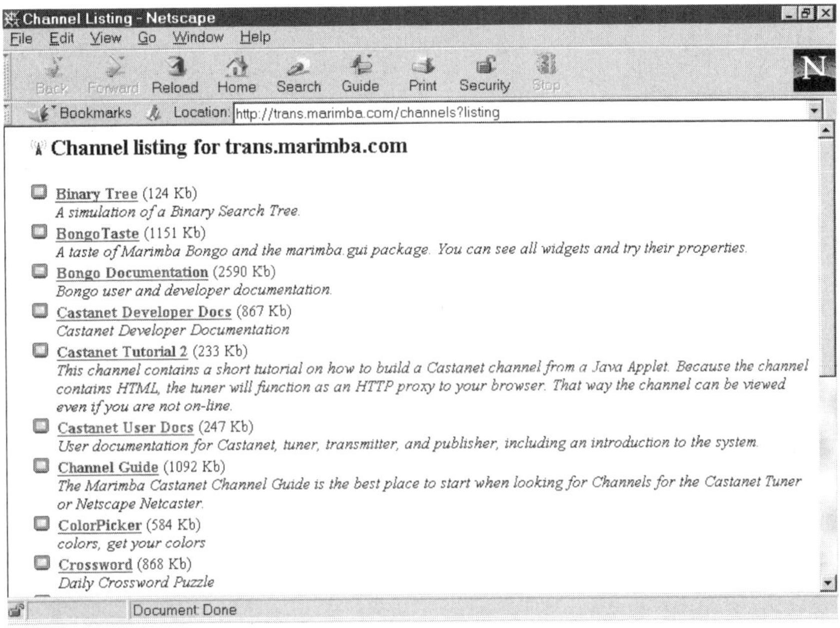

Figure 16-9 Browsing for channels. You can subscribe to new channels via the Tuner or your default Web browser.

nels, click the Browse button. This opens your default Web browser with a complete listing of channels and their descriptions (see Figure 16-9).

16.3.5 Subscribing to Channels via Your Web Browser

You also can find and subscribe to Castanet channels with your default Web browser. Another excellent starting point for finding channels is Marimba's channels directory at **`http:\\www.marimba.com\channels`** (see Figure 16-10).

If your browser is configured properly with the correct MIME type, you can just click on any of these channels. Your browser automatically launches the Castanet Tuner, and the Tuner immediately downloads the channel contents.

If you try to subscribe to a channel with your Web browser (particularly Internet Explorer), and the browser asks whether you want to save a file to the hard drive, you need to edit your MIME types to include Castanet

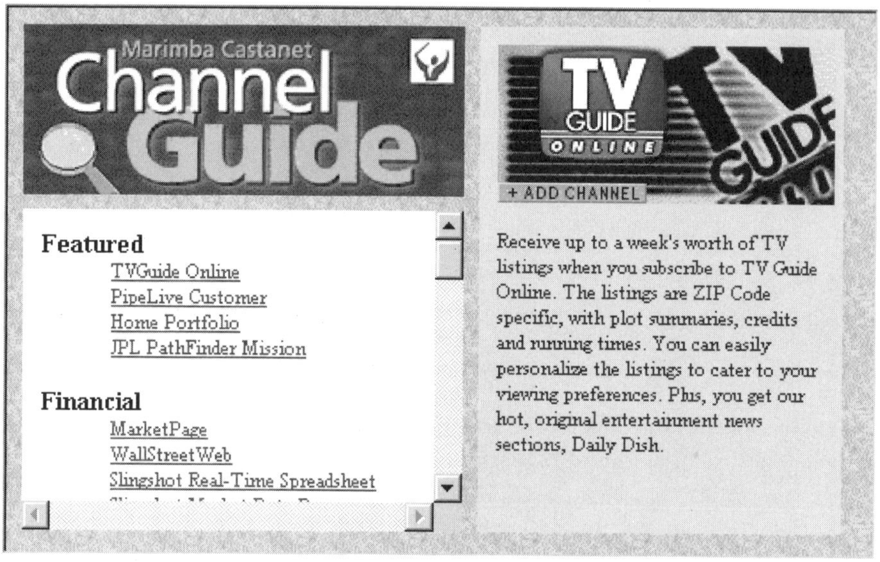

Figure 16-10 The Marimba channels directory. One-stop shopping for new channels.

files. The associated extension for channel files is **`.chn`**, the content type is **`application/marimba`**, and the path to the Tuner executable is, by default, **`C:\Program Files\Marimba\Castanet Tuner\Tuner.exe`**.

Note that if you are using the latest version of Netscape Navigator 4.0 with Netcaster, Netcaster is launched instead of your standalone Castanet Tuner.

16.3.6 Working with HTML Channels

HTML channels are entire collections or directories of HTML documents. In Version 1.0, users had to download the entire HTML channel before viewing any of its contents. In contrast, Version 1.1 now lets users view the HTML channel incrementally.

When you subscribe to an HTML channel, the Tuner downloads the first document (usually **`index.html`**) and passes this document to your default Web browser. If you click on any of the links in the first page, the Tuner downloads these links. But, after a few minutes, the Tuner proceeds to download the entire HTML channel. After the channel is downloaded, it is stored on your hard drive and therefore is always available —even when you are not connected to the Internet.

There is one catch, however: You must set up your Tuner as a Proxy Server for your Web browser. This enables the Tuner to intercept HTTP requests. If the request is related to an HTML channel, the Tuner retrieves the document from the user's hard drive and relays the document back to the browser. Otherwise, the Tuner simply forwards the request, and the Web browser operates as usual.

To set up your Tuner, you must set the Network Proxy options of your browser to point to 127.0.0.1 (local host), port 5283.

For Netscape Navigator 4.0, follow these steps:

1. Choose Preferences from the Edit menu.
2. Open the Advanced Category and select Proxies.
3. Select Manual Proxy Configuration and click View.
4. Under HTTP Server, enter `127.0.0.1`, port number `5283`.

For Internet Explorer 4.0, follow these steps:

1. Choose Options from the View menu.
2. Select the Connection tab.
3. Select the Connect Using a Proxy Server option.
4. For the Proxy Server address, enter `127.0.0.1`, port number `5283`.
5. Click Apply and then click OK.

Even if your Web browser already points to a corporate Proxy Server, this will work, because the Web browser points to the Castanet Tuner, and the Tuner, in turn, points back to the corporate Proxy Server.

NOTE: *If you set your browser to handle HTML channels, the Castanet Tuner must be running* at all times. *If you try to browse and the Tuner is not running, your browser hangs while it looks for a nonexistent Proxy Server, and you cannot download any Web pages!*

TIP: *If you get impatient and want the full channel to download as soon as possible, return to the Tuner and choose Download Remainder from the Channels menu.*

16.3.7 Creating Desktop Shortcuts (Windows Only)

If you are running Castanet on Windows 95 or Windows NT 4.0, you can create desktop shortcuts for each channel application. Click on the Channels page, select your channel, and choose Create Shortcut from the Channels menu.

Each channel you subscribe to is included in the Channels directory of the Windows Start menu (see Figure 16-11). Channels are organized by Transmitter.

16.3.8 Unsubscribing from Channels

To cancel your subscription to a channel, click on the Channels page. Select the channel and then choose Unsubscribe from the Channel menu. The channel name and icon now appear grayed out.

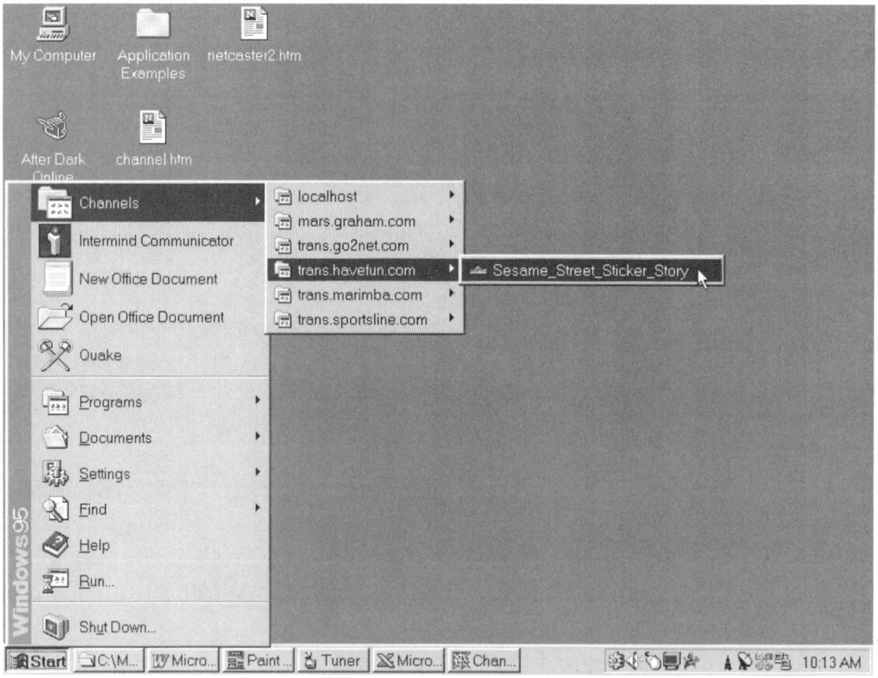

Figure 16-11 The Windows Start menu. Each Castanet channel is added to the Windows Start menu. You also have the option of creating desktop shortcuts for each channel.

When you unsubscribe from a channel, the Tuner deletes all the Java class files, including any Java resource files, such as images or sounds. The Tuner will not delete any preferences or persistent data you created with the channel application, though. When you unsubscribe from a calendar channel, for example, the Java files are deleted, but any persistent data, such as important appointments or engagements, are protected. That way, in case you resubscribe to the channel, your data still is available.

16.3.9 Removing Channels

To unsubscribe to a channel *and* delete all its persistent data, choose to remove it. Again, click on the Channels page, select the channel, and choose Remove from the Channels menu. This removes all Java files, plus any persistent data or user preferences, and removes the channel from the Channels page.

16.3.10 Displaying the Java Console

To display the Java console associated with each channel, choose Show Console from the Tuner menu. This is similar to the Java console provided by Web browsers and is absolutely essential for debugging purposes.

16.4 Updating Options

16.4.1 Automatic Channel Updates

When you subscribe to a channel, the Castanet Transmitter sends all the Java class files plus a Properties file. This file includes a recommended schedule for channel updates.

The Transmitter sends two schedules. The first tells the Tuner how often to check for updates while the channel is actually running on the desktop. This is called as the *Active Update schedule*.

The Active Update schedule usually is reserved for channels that receive and display constantly updated information. A sports ticker might have an Active Update schedule set to every 15 minutes, for example.

That way, when the ticker is running on your desktop, the Tuner checks for new scores fairly frequently and immediately displays them.

The second schedule tells the tuner how often to check for updates when the application channel is *not* running. This is called the *Inactive Update schedule*. The schedule generally is used to check for software upgrades or major new information. Depending on how the channel developer has set up the channel, the channel actually can launch itself if it receives new information or receives new information that the user may deem important. This varies from channel to channel.

This all sounds well and good, but how can you find the update schedule for a particular channel? The update schedule is included on the Channel Properties page. Click on the Channels page, select a channel, and choose Channel Properties from the Channel menu. You see detailed information on the channel, including the following:

- Hostname of the Transmitter
- Date the channel was first published
- Date the channel was last updated
- Date the Tuner last checked for an update
- Channel size
- Channel author and administrator

In the middle of the screen, you see the Active and Inactive Update schedules (see Figure 16-12). The schedules can vary from frequently (meaning less than every five minutes) all the way up to daily or weekly.

16.4.2 Limiting Automatic Updates

As much as possible, the Tuner attempts to follow the recommended schedule set by the channel provider. However, the user still has the last say in setting the frequency of updates. To set a customized schedule of updates, click the Configure page and then select the Updates tab.

On the Updates page, you have two settings (see Figure 16-13). The first setting lets you determine the general range of the update schedule. You can choose from Any Time, Between 9 a.m. – 5 p.m., Not Between 9 a.m. – 5 p.m., and Never (Manual Only).

The second setting lets you to determine the overall frequency of updates. You can choose from As Often As Needed, At Most Every 15 Minutes, At Most Every 30 Minutes, At Most Once an Hour, and At Most Once

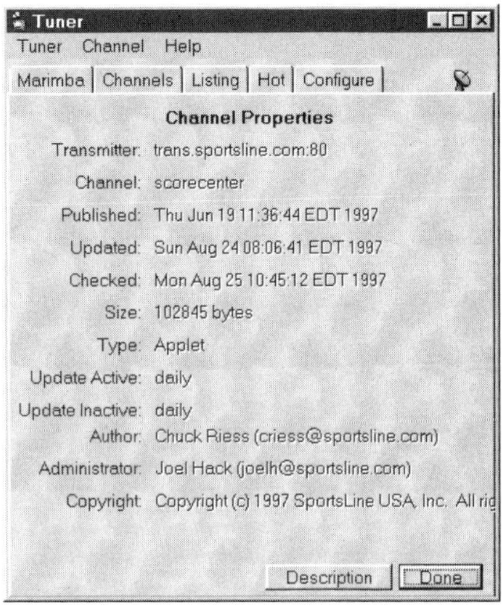

Figure 16-12 The Channel Properties page. Here, you can find the automatic Active and Inactive Update schedules.

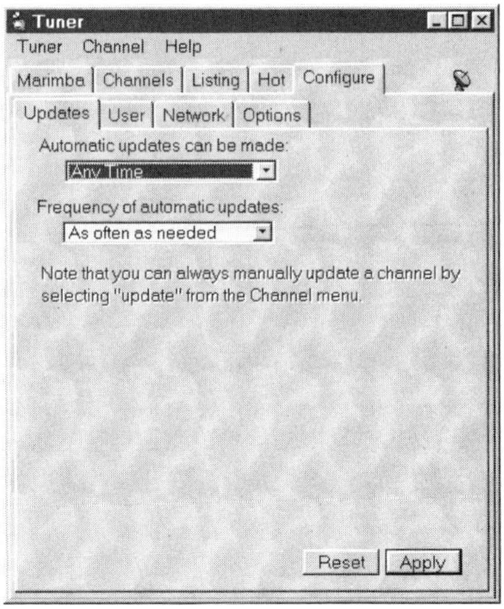

Figure 16-13 The Update Options page. As a user, you can limit the frequency of automatic updates.

a Day. Note that the channel cannot be updated more frequently than the schedule recommended by the channel provider.

After you set your update options, make sure that you click the Apply button.

If you are working from home and don't want any automatic updates, choose Never from the first drop-down menu.

16.4.3 Manually Updating Channels

You can choose to manually update a channel at any time. Just go to the Channels page, select the channel, and choose Update from the Channel menu.

16.4.4 Stopping Channel Updates

To cancel a channel update in progress, choose Cancel Transfers from the Tuner menu.

16.4.5 Working Offline

If you are working on a modem from home or a laptop on the road, you can elect to set the Tuner to offline mode. On the Tuner menu, you should see a checkmark next to the Online option. To go offline, just select the Online option (selecting the Online option toggles you back and forth between online and offline). When you are in offline mode, the Tuner does not attempt to make any network connections or update any channels unless you choose to do so manually.

16.4.6 Updating the Tuner

Once a week, the Tuner prompts you that it needs to be updated (see Figure 16-14). You can agree to the update or postpone it until a later time.

To manually update the Tuner, first quit any channel applications and then choose Update Tuner from the Tuner menu. If the Tuner downloads any updates, it automatically exits, installs the new components, and restarts itself.

16.5 Configuration Options

The Castanet Tuner is fully customizable to meet the needs of both home users with modem connections and corporate users with direct Internet

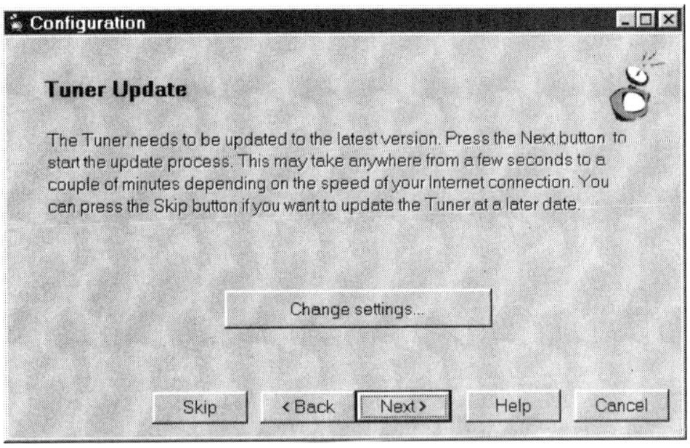

Figure 16-14
The Castanet Tuner is a Castanet channel and updates itself once a week.

connections. The Configure page has four sets of options, which are described in the following sections.

NOTE: *See Section 16.4.2, "Limiting Automatic Updates," for information about update options.*

USER OPTIONS This is optional user information that is sent to Marimba. Current fields include Name, E-mail Address, and Mailing Address. This information is sent only to Marimba and is not released to any channel providers.

NETWORK OPTIONS If your local area network has an HTTP Proxy Server or a Castanet Proxy Server, enter the information here. You must include the hostname and port number, as well as a username and password, if required. If you encounter any difficulties, contact your system administrator.

GENERAL OPTIONS

Connection options	You can set your Tuner to work with a modem or a direct Internet connection.
Windows options	You can elect to have new channels automatically added to the Windows Start menu.
CD-ROM options	Some channels are a hybrid CD-ROM/Web application. Bandwidth-intensive information,

	such as large images, are transferred from the CD-ROM, whereas dynamically updated data is transferred over the Web. To grant your channels access to the CD-ROM, toggle the CD-ROM option.
User Feedback options	There are three user feedback options: Tuner IDs, Log Files, and Profile Data. The Tuner ID uniquely identifies your Castanet Tuner and therefore is similar to a Web cookie. The log file includes a record of your online and offline activity within any given channel. Your profile data includes any preferences or options you set. You can disable any of these options, but this also disables the customization and personalization features provided by Castanet plug-ins.
Print options	Java 1.1 now supports printing. To grant your channels the right to print, toggle the Allow Printing option.

16.6 Exiting the Tuner

To close the onscreen Tuner window, click the close icon in the upper right-hand corner. Unlike in most applications, however, this does not really close the Tuner. It merely minimizes the application to the Windows taskbar so that the Tuner can continue any automatic updates in the background.

To really quit the Tuner, choose Quit from the Tuner menu.

SUMMARY

The Castanet Tuner enables you to subscribe to, launch, and automatically update Castanet channels. Version 1.1 has several performance and feature enhancements over Version 1.0, including support for Java 1.1, online and offline modes, incremental HTML channels, and the option to disable user feedback.

To get started with the Tuner (and to make sure everything is working), try subscribing to one of the demonstration channels hosted on the Marimba Transmitter (**trans.marimba.com**). Just open the Marimba page, click the Marimba Channels button, and double-click on any of the channels. The channel is automatically downloaded and launched.

Each Castanet channel follows its own update schedule, which is set by the channel developer. But, as the end user, you have the last word on the frequency of channel updates. These and other customization options are available on the Tuner's Configure page.

Online Resources

- Quick Start Tuner Guide **http://www.marimba.com/doc/Castanet_User_Docs/tuner/1.1/quickstart.html**. The essentials to using the Castanet Tuner.
- Castanet Tuner 1.1 FAQ **http://www.marimba.com/doc/Castanet_User_Docs/tuner/1.1/faq.html**
- Castanet Tuner 1.1 Release Notes **http://www.marimba.com/doc/Castanet_User_Docs/tuner/1.1/notes.html**. Is this a bug or a feature?

CHAPTER 17

Using the Castanet Transmitter and Publisher

The Castanet Transmitter is the server application that distributes Castanet channels. The Castanet Transmitter is highly optimized to deliver channel transmissions as quickly and efficiently as possible. It does this through two primary mechanisms.

First, all channel contents are sent in a single TCP connection, which eliminates the overhead of multiple TCP connections normally required for HTTP 1.0 Servers. Second, the Transmitter negotiates with each Tuner to send differential downloads. Each Tuner therefore is sent only files that have been changed since the last update.

Castanet Publisher, on the other hand, enables developers to quickly transfer Java class and data files from their local hard drives to the Castanet Transmitter. This enables multiple developers to publish to the same Transmitter while maintaining the necessary security precautions. Much like Tuner updates, publishing to the Transmitter is differential and therefore highly efficient. After the channel contents are published, they are available immediately to all subscribers.

Currently, both the Transmitter and Publisher are in Version 1.1. And, Version 1.1 of the Publisher now includes specific support for publishing to the Castanet Tuner built into Netscape Netcaster.

If you are planning on developing your own channels, it is essential to understand both the Transmitter and Publisher. Therefore, before moving on to the next few chapters on channel development, make sure that you read this chapter first.

17.1 Installation

17.1.1 Platforms Supported

Currently, Version 1.1 of the Castanet Transmitter and Publisher are available for Windows 95, Windows NT 4.0, and Solaris 2.5 systems.

17.1.2 Hardware Requirements

To run the Castanet Transmitter and Publisher on Windows 95/NT, you must have the following:

- At least 16M of RAM
- At least 10M of free disk space; additional disk space is needed for channels as they are published

17.1.3 Installing the Transmitter/Publisher

The Castanet Transmitter and Publisher come bundled together in a single, self-extracting InstallShield archive. An evaluation copy of the Windows 95/NT version is available on the CD-ROM that accompanies this book. Evaluation copies for other platforms are available at the Marimba Web site at **`http:\\www.marimba.com`**.

NOTE: *The evaluation copy of the Transmitter / Publisher enables you publish up to three channels to three individual subscribers and is for development purposes only. Check the Marimba site for the latest price quotes on purchasing full versions of the Transmitter.*

Before attempting to install the Transmitter/Publisher, make sure that you do the following:

- Uninstall any previous versions of the Castanet Transmitter.
- Exit any running Castanet applications. Make sure that you check the Windows taskbar to see whether the Tuner is running in the background.

Then double-click on the self-extracting file **`Trans.exe`** and follow the onscreen instructions.

17.2 Launching the Transmitter

You can launch the Transmitter from the Windows Start menu or from the command line (**`C:\Program Files\Marimba\Castanet Transmitter\Transmitter.exe`**).

17.3 Transmitter Configuration

When you first launch the Castanet Transmitter, you need to set the proper configuration parameters. You can set these parameters by flipping through the configuration pages provided by the Transmitter user interface (see Figure 17-1).

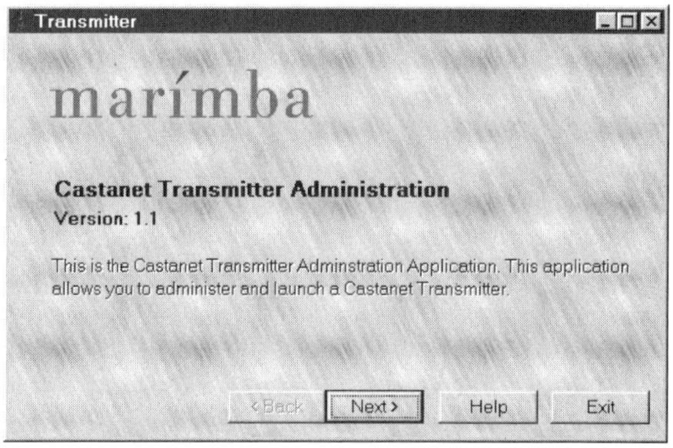

Figure 17-1 The Castanet Transmitter opening page. Keep clicking the Next button to fully configure your Transmitter.

17.3.1 Transmitter Channel Directory

First up, the Transmitter Channel directory (see Figure 17-2). This directory contains all the files pertaining to your individual channels, including the Java class files, plug-in programs, and any logging or profile data sent back from your subscribers. Unfortunately, there is no Browse button here, so you must enter the full pathname of your Channel directory. The Channel directory could be located in the **Marimba** directory or anywhere on your hard drive. If the directory does not exist, you are prompted to confirm its creation.

NOTE: *The Channel directory also can be located on a remote machine on your local network, but Marimba recommends a local directory for optimum performance.*

If you choose to uninstall the Transmitter at a later date, the Channel directory is not deleted. This enables you to easily upgrade to new versions of Transmitter software without losing your existing channels or settings.

17.3.2 Transmitter Hostname and Port

The next page asks you for the full domain name and port number of the Transmitter (see Figure 17-3). If you are planning to use the Transmitter for real delivery of applications across the Internet, you must include the

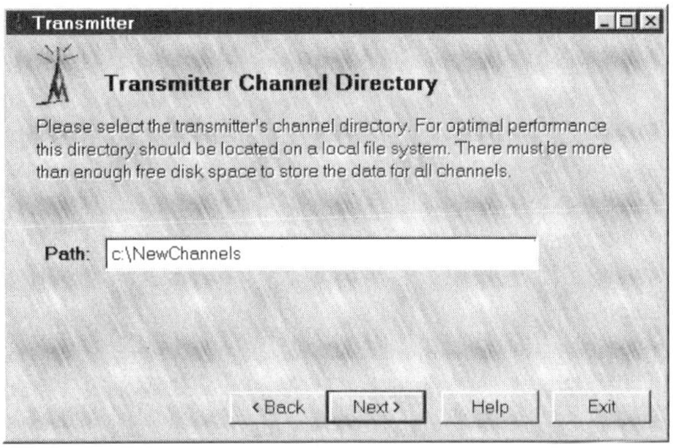

Figure 17-2 Transmitter configuration, step 1: The Transmitter Channel directory.

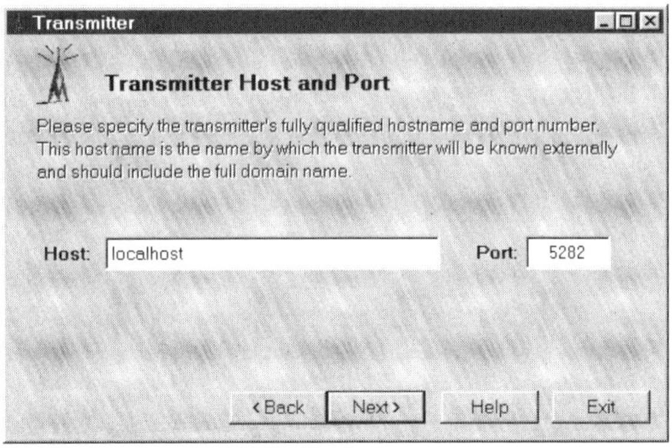

Figure 17-3 Transmitter configuration, step 2: Hostname and port number.

full domain name of your machine here. If you are planning to use the Transmitter for development purposes only, set the hostname to `localhost`. This enables you to download and debug channel applications entirely on your local machine.

If your current machine already is running a Web server, make sure to pick a port number other than 80 (port 80 is reserved for HTTP Servers).

17.3.3 Transmitter Access

The Transmitter Access page enables Castanet's built-in security mechanism (see Figure 17-4). To password protect your Transmitter, enter the password here. Each time you use Castanet Publisher to publish new chan-

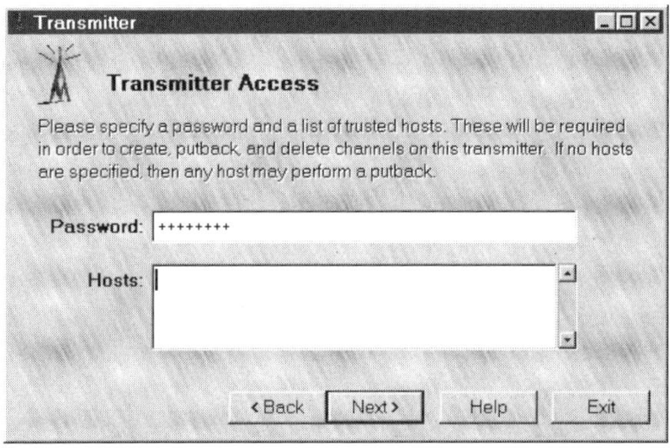

Figure 17-4 Transmitter configuration, step 3: Transmitter access and password protection.

nels or to modify old channels, you are asked to enter this password. If you do not want to password protect your channel, leave this field blank.

As an extra measure of security, you can enter a list of trusted hosts. Enter the full domain names of trusted hosts here, or leave this section blank to accept requests from any host.

17.3.4 Publish Notifications

Each time a new channel is published or updated, you can direct the Transmitter to send e-mail to the specified e-mail address (see Figure 17-5). As a default, the Transmitter sends these updates to Marimba so that it can be aware of new channels. If you do not want e-mail notification, leave the E-Mail Address field blank.

17.3.5 Advanced Settings

After you complete the Transmitter configuration, you can launch it by clicking the Launch button (see Figure 17-6).

Or, you can opt to configure the Transmitter's Advanced settings:

Transmitter Concurrency: Each time a Transmitter receives a Tuner request, the request is assigned to a thread process. This enables the Transmitter to handle multiple Tuner requests simultaneously. To optimize the performance of the Transmitter, you can set the maximum number of available threads. This can be a tricky issue, though.

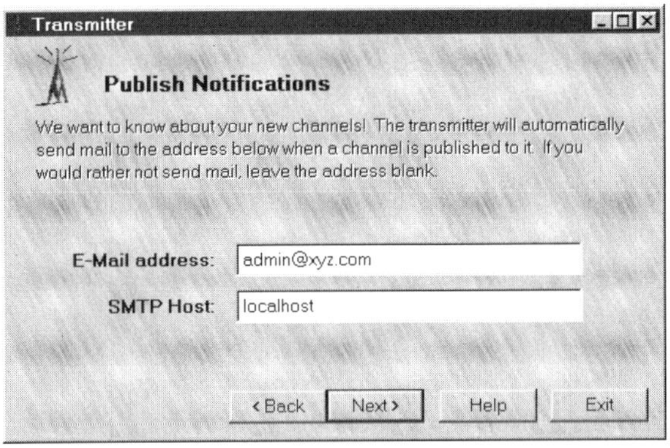

Figure 17-5 Transmitter configuration, step 4: E-mail notification.

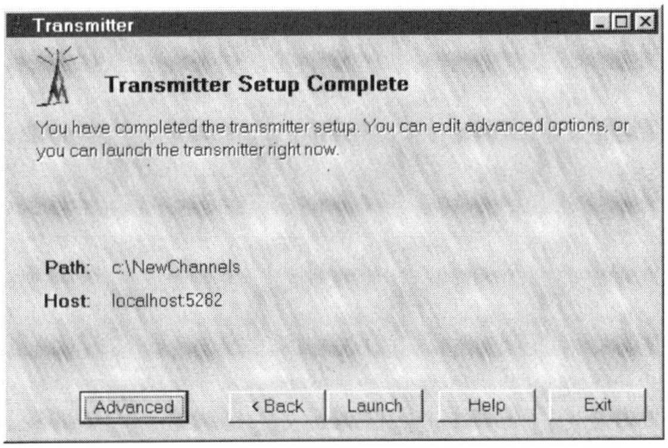

Figure 17-6 Transmitter configuration, step 5: Launch. After you complete the standard configuration, you can launch the Transmitter. Or, click the Advanced button to set the Threads and Cache options.

If you have too few threads, you cannot handle many requests at once. And, if you have too many threads, they may swamp your system and actually slow performance. The optimum number of threads depends on both your hardware and overall traffic patterns, and you have to be willing to experiment a bit. When in doubt, keep the default settings, especially if you are using the Transmitter only for development purposes.

Transmitter Cache: Each Transmitter has a memory cache and a disk cache. If you want to further optimize the performance of your Transmitter, consider increasing these cache limits. But make sure to test the performance. And, again, when in doubt, keep the default values, especially if you are using the Transmitter only for development purposes.

17.3.6 The Properties File

After you complete the Transmitter configuration, the Transmitter stores your settings in the **properties.txt** file. This file is located in the Channels directory you set up in section 17.3.1. If you want to change these settings at any time, you can use the Transmitter interface, or your can manually edit the **properties.txt** file. Listing 17-1 shows a sample **properties.txt** file.

NOTE: *Do not attempt to manually modify the Transmitter password. This is an encrypted string that must be set via the Transmitter GUI interface.*

17.3.7 The License Agreement

As noted earlier in this chapter, the evaluation copy of the Castanet Transmitter enables you to publish only three channels to three unique subscribers. If you try to publish a new channel and the Transmitter refuses, check the license agreement. Just click the View License button on the last page of the Transmitter setup. The license tells you the maximum number of channels, the number of actual channels, the maximum number of users, and the number of actual users (see Figure 17-7).

17.4 Using the Castanet Publisher

You now have your Transmitter fully configured and running. But is it really working? To test the Transmitter, you need to give it a real channel.

Listing 17-1 A sample **properties.txt** file.

```
#Transmitter Properties
server.cachesize=32
server.host=localhost
server.maxthreads=32
server.memdisk=4
server.password=V3lvbWluZyE=
server.port=5282
server.putback.mailto=
server.smtphost=localhost
server.trustedhosts=localhost/127.0.0.1
```

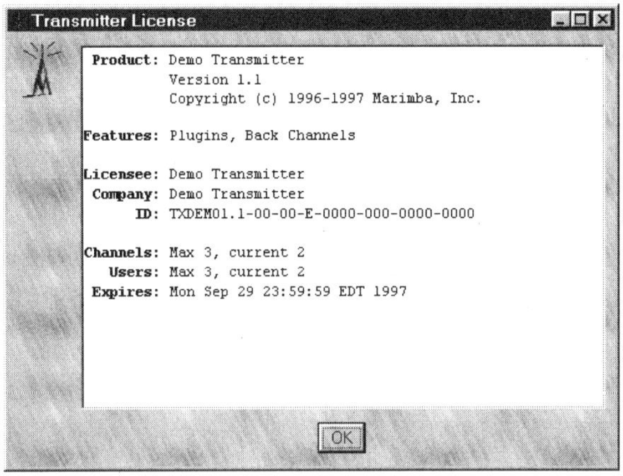

Figure 17-7 The Transmitter license agreement.

In other words, you need to publish a new channel with Castanet Publisher. After the Transmitter has a channel, you can use your Tuner to test the Transmitter. Hang in there. We are very close!

NOTE: *The next section is your introduction to Castanet Publisher. More details on Publisher are provided in Chapters 18 and 19.*

17.4.1 Launching Publisher

First, launch Castanet Publisher. Publisher is included in the **`Castanet Transmitter`** directory on the Windows Start menu.

17.4.2 Publishing a Sample Channel

Fortunately, the evaluation copy of the Castanet Transmitter includes several sample channels. Let's publish one of these channels just to make sure everything is working.

When you launch Publisher, you see the introductory screen (see Figure 17-8). Click the Channels button to get started. You now should see a blank screen called Channels under Development (see Figure 17-9). As you continue to add new channels, you will see them listed here.

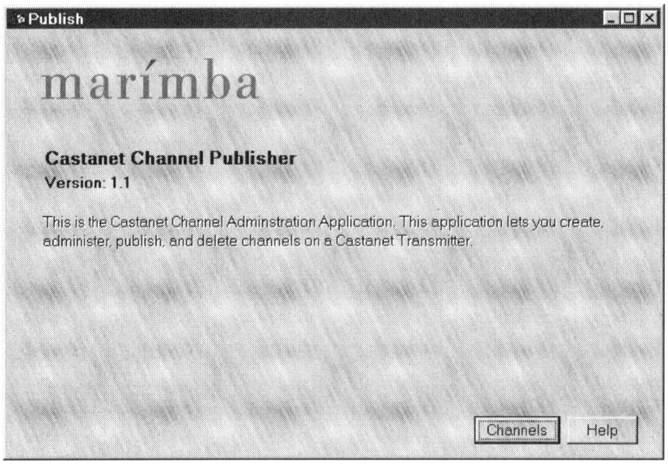

Figure 17-8
The Castanet Publisher, the official gateway to your Transmitter.

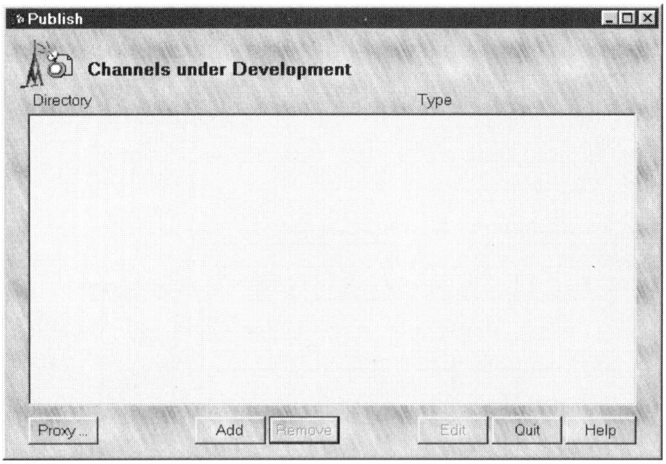

Figure 17-9
The Channels under Development screen.

Click the Add button to add a new channel. Then enter the full pathname of your channel's directory. Again, unfortunately, there is no Browse button, so you have to enter the entire pathname. In the latest Transmitter release, the sample channels are included in the **`Publisher`** subdirectory under the **`developers`** subdirectory—**`c:\Program Files\Marimba\Castanet Publisher\developers\channels\`**. If you cannot find the channels here, look around (previous releases install the channels in the **Castanet Transmitter** directory).

The sample channels directory includes six sample channels. For now, we will pick the Crossword channel, so enter the full pathname of the crossword directory: **c:\Program Files\Marimba\Castanet Publisher\developers \channels\Crossword**. Then click the Add button.

You now should see the Channels under Development page again with your channel listed at the top (see Figure 17-10). Now click the Edit button to set the channel properties. You will see the main interface for configuring all of the many parameters associated with channels (see Figure 17-11).

Each sample channel includes its own **properties.txt** file (not to be confused with the Transmitter's **properties.txt** file). This file includes parameters for the channel, and you will notice that each of the configuration pages already is populated with settings. To publish the channel correctly, you want to keep most of these settings. In Chapters 18 and 19, we will return to the exact meaning of each of these parameters.

For now, just make sure that the Transmitter page options are correct. In particular, be sure to enter the right hostname (usually, **localhost**) and the right port number. Also, make sure that you have entered the correct password. Leave all the other settings as they are.

When you are finished, click the Apply button. Then click the Publish button. The files are copied over to the Transmitter, and you should re-

Figure 17-10
Viewing your sample channel name on the Channels under Development screen.

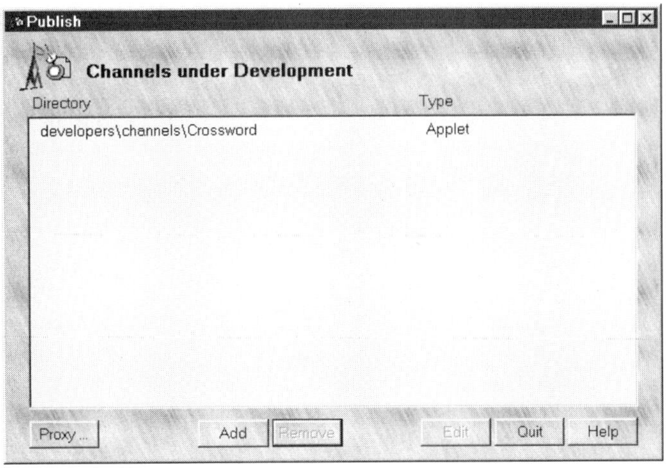

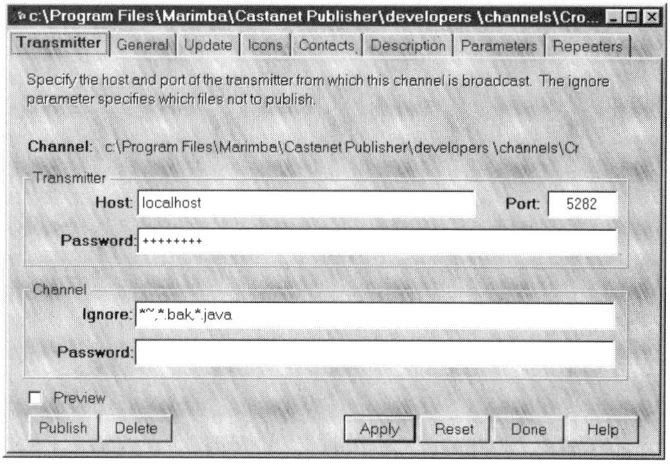

Figure 17-11 The Castanet Publisher configuration options. You can set a wide range of properties for each channel. For now, just make sure that the Transmitter options are correct.

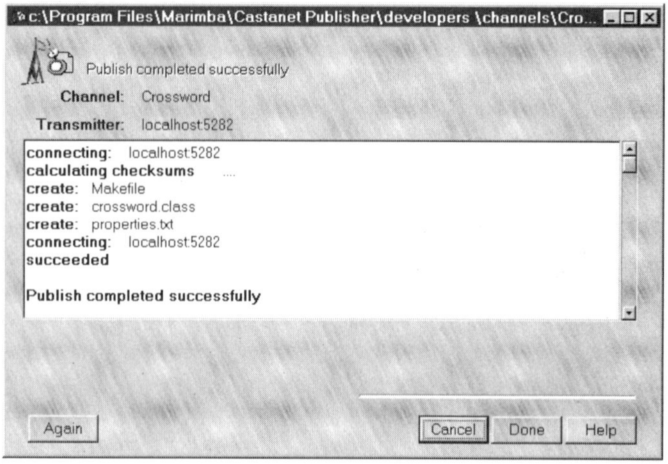

Figure 17-12 The Castanet Publisher. Success!

ceive a confirmation of success (see Figure 17-12). If any errors have occurred, they are reported here.

If you have any errors in the publication of your channel, make sure that the Transmitter is running. And, make sure that you have entered the correct hostname, port number, and password.

To exit the Publisher, click the Done button (this button is a bit of a misnomer and actually should be labeled `Back`) until you return to the starting page; then click Quit.

17.4.3 Testing the Transmitter

Your transmitter now is ready to serve a single Castanet channel. To test the entire system, launch your Castanet Tuner and click the Listing page.

In the Hostname field, enter the name of your Castanet Transmitter. If your Transmitter is not running on port 80, you must remember to specify the correct port—for example, `localhost:5282`. Then click List. The Crossword channel now appears (see Figure 17-13). Just double-click to subscribe.

If the channel downloads and executes properly, everything is set up correctly and you are ready to start developing your own channels (see Figure 17-14).

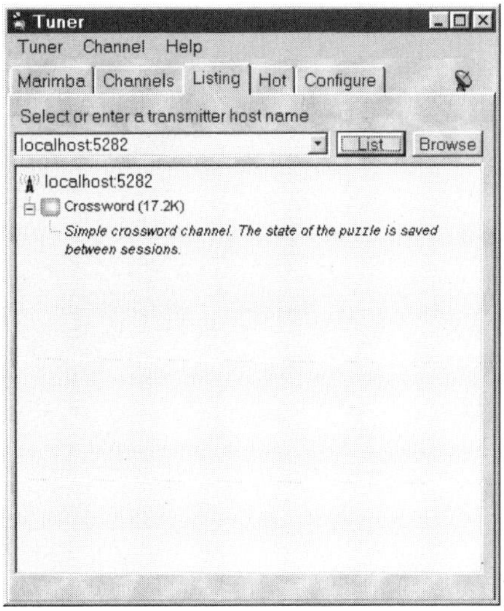

Figure 17-13
The Castanet Tuner. Use the Tuner to test your Transmitter. You should see at least one channel listed here.

Figure 17-14 The Crossword channel. If you see this, everything is working properly.

SUMMARY

If you are serious about developing your own Castanet channels, you have to start with a thorough understanding of the Castanet Transmitter and Publisher. Working with these two programs is essential to developing and debugging your own channels. So take the time now to work with these applications.

The Castanet Transmitter distributes channels and channel updates to Castanet Tuners. The Transmitter is relatively easy to set up and can be set up on your local machine so that you can develop and debug channels entirely on one machine.

Castanet Publisher enables developers to copy over their Java class files and other data from their local hard drives to Castanet Publisher. Even if you have your Tuner, Publisher, and Transmitter on the same machine (for development purposes, of course), there is no other way to publish your channel. This chapter covered just the basics of using the Publisher—just enough to enable you to test the Transmitter. The next chapter covers the Publisher in much greater detail.

Online Resources

- The Castanet Transmitter, The Big Picture **http://www.marimba.com/doc/Castanet_User_Docs/transmitter/1.1/bigpicture.html**
- The Castanet Transmitter, Quick Start Guide **http://www.marimba.com/doc/Castanet_User_Docs/transmitter/1.1/quickstart.html#arguments**
- Castanet Transmitter 1.1 Release Notes **http://www.marimba.com/doc/Castanet_User_Docs/transmitter/1.1/notes.html**
- The Castanet Publisher, Quick Start Guide **http://www.marimba.com/doc/Castanet_User_Docs/publisher/1.1/quickstart.html**

CHAPTER 18

Creating HTML and Applet Channels

You now should have your Castanet Tuner and Castanet Transmitter up and running. And you have had at least one chance to interact briefly with Castanet Publisher. Hopefully, all has gone smoothly so far, and you are ready to take the plunge in creating your first real Castanet channels.

HTML channels are the easiest to build, so we will begin our discussion there. After that, we will progress to applet channels. The next chapter will move on to full-blown application channels, which take full advantage of the Castanet architecture. Along the way, we will explore all the publishing options supported by Castanet Publisher.

18.1 HTML Channels

18.1.1 HTML Channels Defined

HTML channels are collections or directories of HTML pages transferred via the Castanet architecture. Like other Castanet channels, HTML channels are updated periodically on a schedule set by the channel developer. The update schedule can be very frequent (every hour, for example), daily, or weekly. This ensures that end users always have the most up-to-date information.

HTML channels are stored on the user's hard drive and therefore are always available, whether online or offline. And, because HTML channels take advantage of Castanet's efficient automatic updating mechanism, channels can be updated frequently, quickly, and efficiently. The update mechanism is considerably faster and more efficient than the Web-crawling technique used by Netscape Netcaster.

The Castanet architecture is designed mainly for the efficient transfer of files, but it is not designed for displaying HTML pages. To view HTML channels, end users therefore must use the Castanet Tuner with their default Web browser. Users must set their Castanet Tuner to act as a Proxy Server for their Web browser. This enables the Web browser to access the files previously stored by the Castanet Tuner.

Unfortunately, this might be a little too much to ask for the basic end user, and it adds a layer of complexity to the viewing of HTML channels. The user also must remember to leave the Tuner running at all times in order to browse the Web. But remember that most users will not be using the standalone Castanet Tuner. Most users will be using the Castanet Tuner embedded inside Netscape Netcaster, and the Tuner inside Netcaster is integrated seamlessly with the Netscape Navigator browser. No special configuration is required, and viewing HTML channels is as easy as viewing an HTML page. This makes things considerably easier and significantly expands the potential audience for HTML channels.

In addition to the efficient updating mechanism provided by Castanet, HTML channels provide an efficient mechanism for logging user activity. By including a few short HTML-like tags in your documents, you can direct the Castanet Tuner to record specific user activity and to relay this information back to the Castanet Transmitter.

18.1.2 Incremental HTML Channels Defined

In the original Castanet Tuner, the entire HTML channel had to be downloaded before you could view any of it. With Castanet Tuner 1.1, and the Castanet Tuner embedded in Netcaster, you now can view your HTML channels incrementally. This gives the impression of a much faster response time.

If the first page of your HTML channel is `index.html`, your channel is considered an incremental HTML channel. Otherwise, it's a regular HTML channel that is downloaded in its entirety. If you are delivering an incremental channel, the Tuner first retrieves the `index.html` page. If the user then clicks on any subsequent links, the Tuner downloads these pages. After a few minutes, the Tuner proceeds to download the entire channel contents and stores these files on the user's hard drive.

18.1.3 Creating Your HTML Documents

The first step in creating your HTML channel is to create your HTML documents. You could reuse existing content from your current Web site or create new channel-specific content. Either way, this is just regular HTML. Nothing new here.

Because your HTML content will be parsed by a separate browser (or, in the case of Netcaster, your content will be parsed by Netscape Navigator), your HTML channel can include anything that might appear on a regular Web page. You therefore can take full advantage of frames, images, JavaScript, and dynamic HTML. You also can embed your own Java applets, or if you are writing specifically for Internet Explorer, you even can include your own ActiveX controls.

18.1.4 Creating Your HTML Channel Directory

With regular Web sites, you simply take your HTML documents and place them somewhere in the root directory of your Web server. With HTML channels, however, you first create a base channel directory on your local hard drive. Anything in this directory, including any subdirectories, is considered part of the channel. You then transfer this directory to the Castanet Transmitter via Castanet Publisher. Any time you want to make changes to your HTML documents, you modify them in your local directory and republish them with Publisher.

18.2 A Sample HTML Channel

18.2.1 The Castanet Tuner Help Channel

With this background information in hand, let's try creating a sample HTML channel. And, instead of creating an entirely new set of HTML documents, let's just use the HTML documents provided by the Castanet Tuner. The goal is to take the existing help documents concerning the Castanet Tuner and repackage them as an HTML channel. That way, users always can stay on top of the latest developments and receive the most up-to-date help documentation.

If you followed the standard Tuner installation, the Tuner help documents are installed in `C:\Program Files\Marimba\Castanet Tuner\lib\doc\tuner`. If you cannot find these documents, try taking another set of HTML documents—perhaps from your existing Web site.

18.2.2 Publishing HTML Channels

After you identify the base directory for your HTML channel, you are ready to transfer the files over via Castanet Publisher. To get started, make sure that the Transmitter is running, and then launch Castanet Publisher.

On the opening screen, click the Channels button. Then click the Add button to add your HTML channel. For the directory, enter the full pathname of the Tuner help documentation: `c:\Program Files\Marimba\Castanet Tuner\lib\docs\tuner\`. Then click the Add button.

NOTE: *The Add and Create buttons on the Directory page can be a bit misleading. Because you are creating a new channel, you might think to click the Create button. The Create button is reserved for creating new directories on your hard drive, though.*

Now that you have added your channel to thc list in the Channels under Development screen, you are ready to set the channel properties. Click the Edit button to proceed. Each of the channel properties is explained in the following sections.

18.2.3 Transmitter Properties

The Transmitter Properties page tells Publisher where to publish your channel (see Figure 18-1). You can publish to multiple Transmitters, so make sure these settings are correct:

Host — The full Internet domain name of your Transmitter. If you are publishing to a Transmitter on the same machine, enter `localhost` here.

Port — The Transmitter listens for Publisher and Tuner requests on this TCP port. Make sure that you have the right port number, and make sure that you are not accidentally connecting to a Web server (port 80) running on the same machine as the Transmitter.

Password — This is the same password you set during the initial configuration of your Transmitter (see Chapter 17).

In addition to these options, you will notice two more settings in the Channel options:

Ignore — If you have specific directories or files that you do *not* want to publish to the Transmitter, you can enter them here. Most of the time, this is reserved for publishing

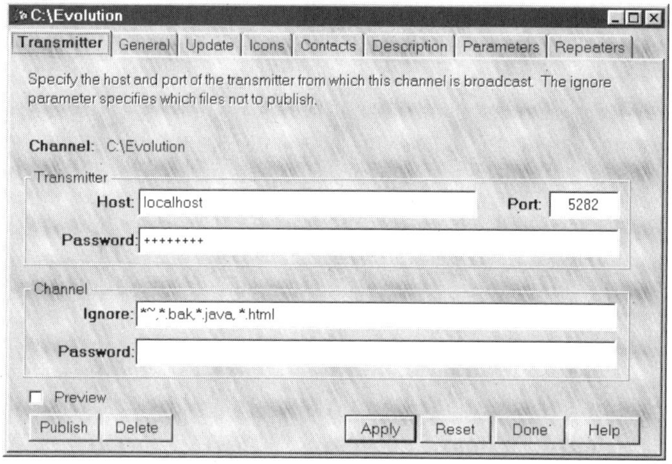

Figure 18-1 The Transmitter Properties page.

applet and application channels. You can choose not to publish any files ending in **`.java`** or **`.bak`**, for example, to prevent the wholesale distribution of your source files (a good idea!). If you want to block certain directories from being published, enter the relative pathname followed by a slash. To prevent the distribution of the image directory of our sample channel, for example, enter **`image\`**. This blocks any files in the **`image`** directory, as well as any subdirectories. Make sure that you do not block the transfer of **`*.txt`** files, however. To successfully publish your channel, Publisher must transfer the **`properties.txt`** file (which contains all the properties you now are setting!).

Password — Another password? Yes, each Transmitter has a unique password. And each Channel also can have a unique password. If you are publishing your channel for the first time and want to add an extra layer of security, enter a password here. Then, each time you try to update the channel, this password is required.

18.2.4 General Properties

The General Properties page describes several of the most important characteristics of your channel (see Figure 18-2). Depending on what type of channel you are creating (HTML, applet, presentation, or application), the settings can vary considerably.

For now, we will focus only on generic properties common to all channels and the specific properties associated with HTML channels:

Name	All channels must have a name. The name appears on the list of available channels distributed by the Transmitter. It also appears on the Channels page of the Castanet Tuner.
Type	You can choose from HTML, Applet, Presentation, or Application. For now, choose HTML.
Classpath	If your HTML channel includes any Java applets, and those applets require access to special Java packages (such as the Bongo.zip package for GUIs), enter them here. For most HTML channels, you can ignore this setting.
Index Page	The Index page is the first page retrieved by the Tuner when the user initially subscribes to the channel. If the Index page is **`index.html`**, this is considered an incremental HTML channel.

Figure 18-2
The General Properties page. HTML channel settings.

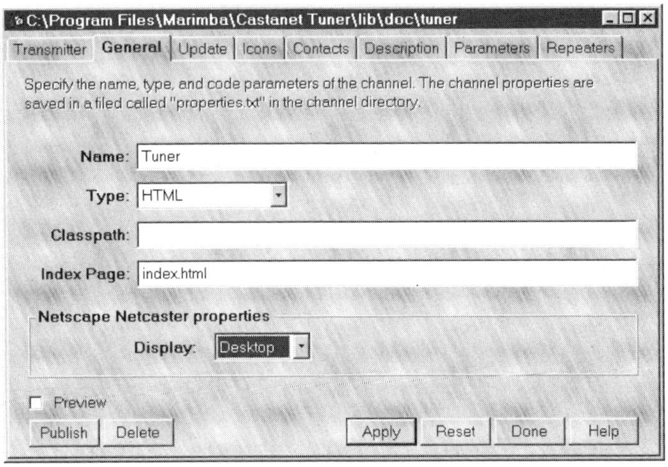

Netscape Netcaster Properties	If you are planning on distributing HTML channels to Netcaster subscribers (and you should be), there are several options to support Netscape Navigator Webtops. Webtops are full-screen Web pages attached to the bottom application layer of the user's operating system. This provides an always visible and fully immersive Web experience. There are three options for displaying your HTML channels in Netcaster: Desktop — A Netscape Webtop. Fullscreen — A full-screen Navigator window. Window — A regular Navigator window.

18.2.5 Update Properties

Each channel follows its own update schedule, as shown on the Update Properties page (see Figure 18-3). And, as detailed in Chapter 16, section 16.4.1, "Automatic Channel Updates," each channel actually follows two update schedules. The *Active Update schedule* determines the frequency of updates while the channel is active or running on the user's desktop. The *Inactive Update schedule* determines the frequency of updates while the channel is *not* running.

HTML channels are never really considered active in the same sense as applet, presentation, and application channels. If you are creating an HTML channel, you therefore only need to set the inactive update frequency. This property determines the overall frequency of updates. The options are Never, Hourly, Daily, and Weekly. The user always can override this setting. (For now, disregard the Data Available Action option; we will return to it in section 18.4.4.)

18.2.6 Icon Properties

Each channel can have its own set of icons. Four types of icons are available on the Icon Properties page (see Figure 18-4):

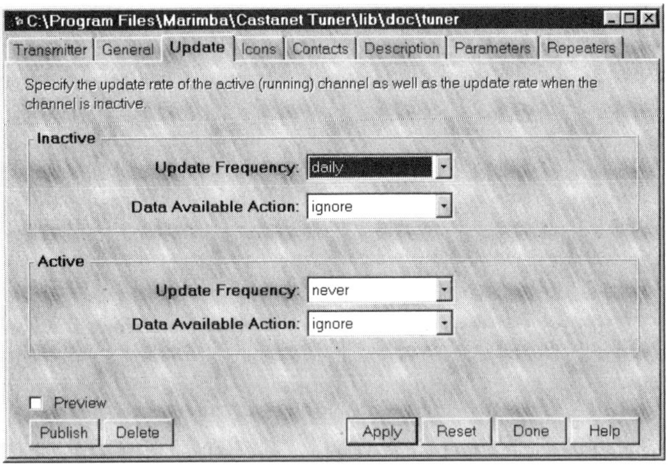

Figure 18-3 The Update Properties page.

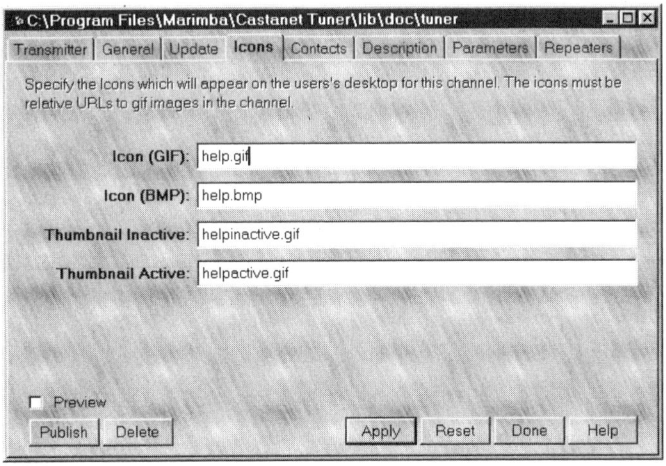

Figure 18-4 The Icon Properties page.

Icon (GIF) — A 64×64-bit desktop icon in GIF format. This is used on all platforms except Windows.

Icon (BMP) — A 64×64-bit desktop icon in Windows BMP format. This icon is used for desktop shortcuts in Windows 95/NT 4.0 (described in section 16.3.7, "Creating Desktop Shortcuts").

Thumbnail Inactive	A 16×16 GIF or JPEG image displayed on the Channels page of the Castanet Tuner. The Inactive icon appears if the user is subscribed to the channel but the channel currently is not running.
Thumbnail Active	A 16×16 GIF or JPEG image that indicates the channel is running.

Each of these icons must be placed inside your channel's base directory. Pathnames are relative to this base directory. If no icons are specified, the Tuner uses the default icons.

18.2.7 Contacts

If you want to specify an author or administrative contact for your channel, you can enter it here. This can be a full name or e-mail address. This information appears in the Channel Properties page of the Castanet Tuner.

18.2.8 Description

Your channel description goes here, as does any copyright information you want to enter. The channel description appears along with the Transmitter's list of available channels and on the Channel Description page of the Castanet Tuner.

18.2.9 Testing Your Channel

After you complete all your settings, click the Publish button to transfer your files to the Transmitter. You receive a confirmation of the process or a listing of specific errors. Then fire up your Tuner and try subscribing to your channel.

18.3 HTML Logging Capabilities

With the inclusion of a few simple HTML-like tags, you easily can add sophisticated logging capabilities to your HTML channels. These logging capabilities can track the links each user follows or even keep a running tab on which advertisements are displayed. Logging data is stored temporarily on the user's hard drive, and each time the channel is scheduled for its automatic update, the Tuner transfers the data directly to the Transmitter. This enables channel developers to track user behavior whether they are online or offline.

After data is transferred to the Transmitter, it is appended to the channel's log file or processed by a customized Castanet plug-in, if one exists.

Note that the end user always can opt to disable the logging and feedback functions through the Options page of the Castanet Tuner (or the Options dialog box provided by Netcaster).

18.3.1 The Log Tag

To track user activity, you simply add the Castanet **<?log=>** tag to your existing HTML documents. The Log tag always is preceded by a question mark (**?**) and usually is embedded inside an HTML Anchor **<A>** tag. To track user interest in your new products, for example, you could use this code:

```
<A HREF="?log=products/widget.htm">Check out our latest
     widget</A>
```

When the user follows the **widget** link, the event is recorded in the user's log file.

If you want to include more descriptive log entries, you can precede the URL address with a description. For example, you could write this:

```
<A HREF="?log=ClickedOnWidgets,products/widget.htm"><Check
     out our latest widget</A>
```

Don't forget the comma!

Finally, you also can include Log tags within Image tags. For example, the following line records that the widget ad was displayed to the user:

```
<IMG SRC="?log=WidgetAdDisplayed,images/widgetAd.gif">
```

18.3.2 The Channel Log File

Each channel gets its own log file (by default, each log file is named after the channel and ends with a **.log** extension). All log files are located in the **logs** subdirectory of the Transmitter Channel directory (this is the directory you identified when you configured the Transmitter).

The following is the log file generated from the previous tags:

```
127.0.0.1 - w94vahgps34n [28/Aug/1997:15:05:42 -0400] "GET
     WidgetAdDisplayed HTTP/1.0" 200 0
127.0.0.1 - w94vahgps34n [28/Aug/1997:15:06:10 -0400] "GET
     WidgetAdDisplayed HTTP/1.0" 200 0
127.0.0.1 - w94vahgps34n [28/Aug/1997:15:06:16 -0400] "GET
     ClickedOnWidgets HTTP/1.0" 200 0
127.0.0.1 - w94vahgps34n [28/Aug/1997:15:06:18 -0400] "GET
     WidgetAdDisplayed @cx:HTTP/1.0" 200 0
```

The first column of the log file displays the IP address of the subscribed Tuner, and the second column identifies the unique Tuner ID. The third column records the date and time, and the last column records the actual event and protocol.

From this data, we can see that we had only one subscriber. But the subscriber saw our widget ad a total of three times and actually followed the link for additional information on the product.

TIP: *If you are just interested in processing user feedback like this, you might want to consider writing a simple PERL script that periodically parses the log file and dumps new data into a database. If you are a PERL wizard, this can be substantially easier than creating your own Castanet plug-in.*

18.4 Applet Channels

18.4.1 Sample Applet Channel

If you already have an existing Java applet, you easily can repackage it as a Castanet applet channel. And, 95 percent of the time, you can repackage your applet with little or no change to your existing source code.

To create an applet channel, first identify the Java applet you want to deliver. If you don't have one, you can use my Evolution applet on the CD-ROM accompanying this book. This is a relatively simple applet that demonstrates some of the very basic principles of genetic algorithms. It also demonstrates some very basic principles of Java GUI and layout development.

Before we publish the Evolution applet, let's consider changes to the source code.

18.4.2 Modifying Your Applet Source Code

There are only two instances when you must modify your applet source code. First, check to see whether your applet makes any calls to the browser's `showStatus` method. If your applet is running on a Web browser, the `showStatus` method displays a message in the browser's message or status line. But, if you run your applet on the Castanet Tuner, the message actually is displayed on the Tuner's Java console. Most users do not have this window open, though. Therefore, if the message is critical to the functioning of your program, consider delivering the message directly to the applet (perhaps use the `drawString` method or add your own Status text field). Otherwise, you safely can ignore the problem.

Second, check to see whether your applet makes any calls to the `getCodeBase()` or `getDocumentBase()` method. These calls generally are used for retrieving images or sounds or making live connections back to the server. If you are running your applet on a Web browser, either of these methods returns a URL of this form: `http://host:port/directory`. If you run the same applet on the Castanet Tuner, though, the URL is in this form: `tuner://host:port/directory`.

Each time a user subscribes to your channel, all the associated resource files, including images and sounds, are transferred over and stored on the user's hard drive. In fact, everything in your base channel directory is transferred over. The `tuner://` prefix therefore tells the Tuner to immediately retrieve the associated files from the hard drive instead of making additional network connections back to the Transmitter.

If your applet is using `getCodeBase` or `getDocumentBase` to subsequently retrieve files that exist in your base channel directory, no changes to the source code are necessary. But, if you are using either of these methods to retrieve other files or make live connections back to the Transmitter, you must modify your code. Specifically, you have to parse out the `tuner:\\` string and replace it with the `http:\\` string so that the Tuner knows to forward your request back to the Transmitter.

Fortunately, my Evolution applet does not make any calls to `showStatus`, and it doesn't make any live connections back to the server. So it's all ready to go and can be used without any modifications to the source code. To publish the channel, launch Castanet Publisher and follow the property guidelines in the next sections.

18.4.3 General Properties

To execute your Castanet applet, you need to provide runtime parameters similar to those provided by a Web browser. Most of the parameters on the General Properties page are related directly to the attributes associated with the HTML applet tag (see Figure 18-5).

The parameters on the General Properties page follow:

Type	Applet
Classpath	If your applet requires any special libraries, such as the `Bongo.zip` package, you can include them here.
Code	This is your main class file executed when the channel is launched. Simply include the name of the class file without the `.class` extension. This is identical to the `CODE` attribute of the HTML Applet tag.
Codebase	If your applet does not reside on the root level of your base directory, you can include a relative path here. This is identical to the `CODEBASE` attribute of the HTML Applet tag.

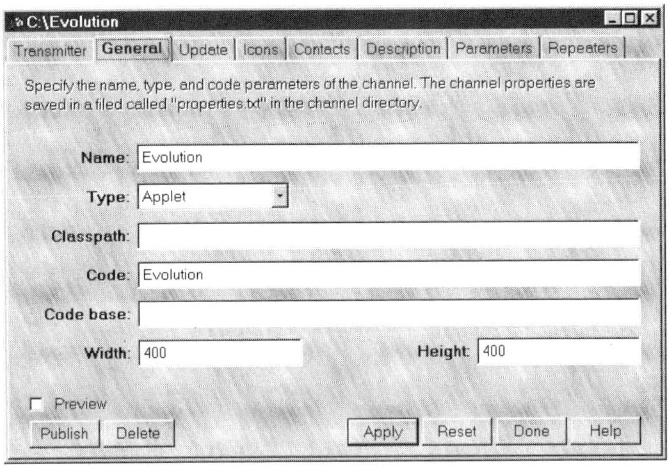

Figure 18-5 The General Properties page—applet channel settings.

Width — Width in pixels of your applet.

Height — Height in pixels of your applet.

18.4.4 Update Properties

In comparison to HTML channels, you have much more flexibility in setting the update properties of applet channels.

When your channel receives an automatic channel update, the Tuner can direct the channel to take several possible courses of action. This is known as the *data available action*. For *inactive* applications, three courses of action (or options) are possible:

`ignore` — Installs the channel update to the user's hard drive and waits for the user to restart the channel. After the channel is restarted, it uses all the updated data and/or updated software components.

`start` — Installs the channel update to the user's hard drive and launches the applet, presentation, or application channel.

`notify` — Wakes up the inactive application, tells it that new data is available, and lets the application decide on a course of action. Primarily reserved for application channels. We will return to this option in the next chapter.

For *active* channels, three data available actions (or options) are possible:

`ignore` Installs the channel update to the user's hard drive. However, it lets the user continue to work with the current version of software. When the user exits and restarts the channel, the new data and/or software components are used.

`restart` Restarts the applet, presentation, or application channel.

`install` Primarily reserved for application channels. When new data arrives, the Tuner installs the data to the user's hard drive and notifies the application channel. The application channel then can retrieve and display the new information without restarting. This option is used primarily for real-time or live updates and is explored in greater detail in the next chapter.

NOTE: *Although the* `notify` *and* `install` *options are reserved primarily for application channels, it is possible to use these data available actions for applets. However, this requires that you significantly modify your existing source code. And I don't really consider it a useful option. If you really want your applets to take full advantage of the Castanet architecture, it is best to rewrite your entire code as an application channel (see Chapter 19).*

Table 18-1 presents a list of valid data available actions for each type of Castanet channel.

18.4.5 Applet Parameters

If your applet requires a set of parameters, you must enter them on the Parameters page (see Figure 18-6). Enter the parameters in `parameter=value` pairs, one per line. The Evolution applet, for example, requires you to set the number of columns and rows:

```
rows=5
columns=5
```

Table 18-1 Update Schedule Options

	HTML Channels	Applet Channels	Presentation Channels	Application Channels
Inactive schedule	never, hourly, daily, weekly	never, hourly, daily, weekly	never, hourly, daily, weekly	never, hourly, daily, weekly
Data Available Action options	ignore	ignore, start, notify	ignore, start	ignore, start, notify
Active Schedule	N/A*	never	never	never
		frequently	frequently	frequently
		5 minutes	5 minutes	5 minutes
		10 minutes	10 minutes	10 minutes
		15 minutes	15 minutes	15 minutes
		30 minutes	30 minutes	30 minutes
		45 minutes	45 minutes	45 minutes
		hourly	hourly	hourly
		daily	daily	daily
		weekly	weekly	weekly
Data Available Action options	N/A*	ignore, restart, install	ignore, restart	ignore, restart, install

*HTML channels are not considered active in the same sense as applet, presentation, and application channels. Therefore, there is no active schedule for HTML channels.

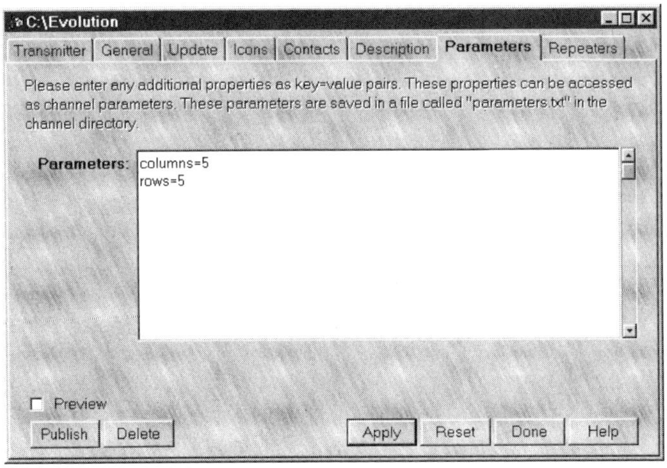

Figure 18-6 The Parameters page.

18.4.6 Testing Your Applet Channel

After you set all the channel properties, publish the channel. Then launch your Tuner and try subscribing to the applet. If all goes well, you should see my Evolution applet (see Figure 18-7).

Figure 18-7
The Evolution applet—genetic algorithms in a box.

What the Evolution Applet Does

The Evolution applet is a spin-off of an idea proposed by the biologist Richard Dawkins. The applet begins with 25 squares. Each square contains a small picture of one or two lines. Click on a square, and the selected picture is copied over to the upper left corner of the applet. This picture then is mutated 24 times, and the offspring appear in the 24 remaining squares. Mutations could include the addition of new lines, the deletion of current lines, or the changing of line angles. Keep clicking on boxes, and you continue to create new generations of more complicated pictures. And, occasionally, you actually generate meaningful pictures (I once had a flower magically appear!).

Source: The Evolution applet was first proposed by Professor Jonathan Amsterdam, New York University.

18.5 Publisher Options

Now that you have had an opportunity to work with Castanet Publisher, you should be aware of several of its additional features. These additional features include previewing channel updates, publishing hidden channels, and executing Publisher from the command line.

18.5.1 Previewing Channel Updates

Each time you republish a channel, Publisher only sends differential updates to the Transmitter. If you want to determine which files will be transferred but do not want to actually transfer those files, you can preview the channel update. Just select the Preview option (located directly above the Publish button), and then publish your channel. Publisher displays its usual success/failure message with the list of updated files, followed by the message `Publish Completed Successfully (no changes)` (see Figure 18-8).

18.5.2 Hidden Channels

If you want to test your channel but do not want to advertise its existence, you can create a hidden channel. The Hidden option is located on the

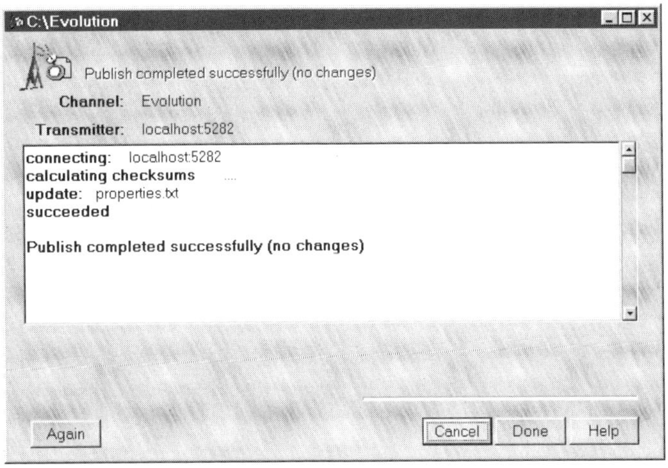

Figure 18-8 Previewing channel updates. Publisher lists the files to be transferred but does not actually transfer them.

Description Properties page of Castanet Publisher (see Figure 18-9). Hidden channels are not included in the list of available channels distributed by the Transmitter, but users and developers still can subscribe to the channel if they know its exact name. To subscribe, choose New Channel from the Tuner menu and enter the exact host and channel name (see Figure 18-10).

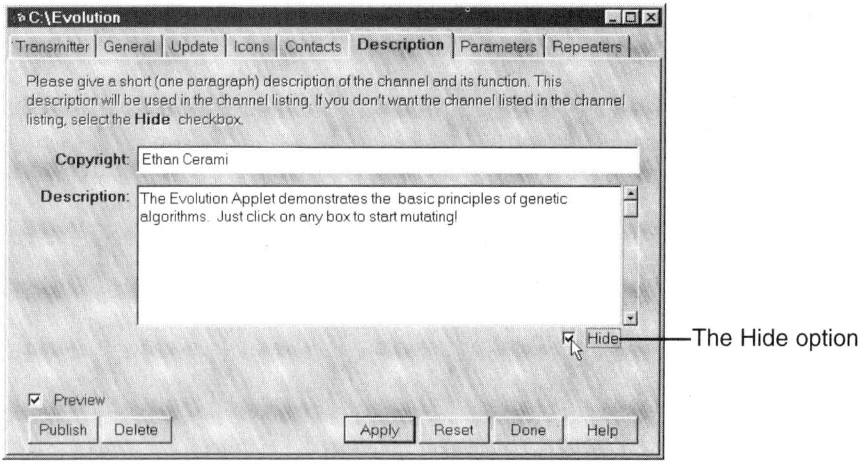

Figure 18-9 The Hide option is located on the Description Properties page.

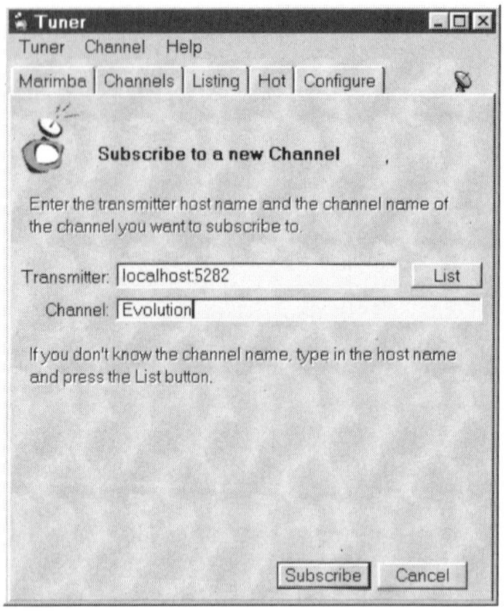

Figure 18-10 To subscribe to a hidden channel, choose New Channel from the Tuner menu and enter the exact channel name.

18.5.3 Running Publisher from the Command Line

In addition to using the Publisher GUI interface, you can use the command-line interface. This is useful particularly if you are creating an automated script that periodically adds new information to your channels.

The command-line executable **`publish.exe`** is located in the **`commands\`** directory of Castanet Publisher. To use it correctly, you must specify the base directory (**`-d`** argument) of your channel:

```
c:\publish -d directory
```

As long as you use the **`-d`** option, Publisher automatically reads your channel's **`properties.txt`** file. This file contains all your channel settings, including the Transmitter name and password. For example, the following line publishes the Evolution applet (assuming that the channel resides in **`c:\Evolution`**):

```
C:\publish -d c:\Evolution
```

The command-line arguments for **`publish.exe`** follow:

`-add` ***`destinationpath sourcepath`***	Copies the files or directories specified in *sourcepath* to the *destinationpath* on the Transmitter.
`-channel` ***`channelname`***	Specifies the name of the channel to be published or deleted; an alternative to the **`-d`** argument.
`-d` ***`basedirname`***	Specifies the base directory of the channel to be published or deleted.
`-delete`	Deletes the channel.
`-ignore` ***`suffix-list`***	Does not copy these files over to the Transmitter.
`-n`	Lists the files that would be copied to the Transmitter but

	does not actually copy them. This is the same as the Preview option described in section 18.5.1.
`-q`	Specifies Quiet mode. Does not display the filenames as they are copied over.
`-password password`	Overrides the password specified in the channel's properties.txt file.
`-proxy hostname[:port][password]`	Specifies the Proxy Server to receive the channel update. Specifies the password if one is required.
`-transmitter` ***`hostname[:port]`***	Overrides the name and port number of the Transmitter specified in the channel's **`properties.txt`** file.

SUMMARY

HTML channels are collections or directories of HTML documents. The HTML documents can, in turn, contain dynamic HTML, JavaScript, Java applets, or ActiveX controls. To create an HTML channel, first create your HTML pages. Then publish them to the Transmitter via Castanet Publisher. Castanet enables sophisticated logging capabilities for tracking user behavior online and offline.

Applet channels are regular Java applets that have been repackaged as channels. Most of the time, you easily can create applet channels with little or no changes to your existing code.

Each channel follows an Active Update schedule and an Inactive Update schedule. Each time a Tuner receives a channel update, it can follow one of several courses of action known as the data available action. Different schedules and actions are available for each type of Castanet channel. Consult Table 18-1 for an overview of the differences.

Online Resource

- From Applet To Channel, Step by Step
  `http://www.marimba.com/doc/Castanet_Developer_Docs/current/index.html`. Quick tutorial on repackaging your legacy applets as Castanet applet channels.

CHAPTER 19

Creating Application Channels

Application channels take full advantage of the Castanet architecture. You can create stock tickers, headline news applications, games, groupware applications, and even full-scale productivity applications. And, each of these channels can receive real-time information updates and actually can store persistent data on the user's hard drive. The possibilities are limitless, and the market for Castanet applications is likely to grow enormously in the near future.

This chapter explores the steps necessary for creating and deploying application channels. We will begin with a series of very simple sample applications. The goal of these examples is to present key concepts in their most elementary forms, enabling you to quickly grasp new concepts. We then will move on to more complicated sample applications and finally end the chapter with a full-scale application channel capable of delivering real-time news headlines to a scrolling screen ticker.

19.1 Getting Started

19.1.1 Prerequisites

To build application channels, you must know Java. Specifically, you should be familiar with a few key concepts:

- The general principles of Java's object-oriented facilities, including inheritance and method overriding
- The concept of interfaces and the particulars of implementing them
- The steps necessary for building applets

If you do not know Java, or if any of these concepts seem unfamiliar to you, you should take the time now to learn them. The stronger your knowledge of Java, the faster you will understand the concepts presented in this chapter.

19.1.2 Working with the JDK

To compile your Java application channels, you need a Java 1.0 or 1.1 compiler. You can use any of the commercially available compilers, including Microsoft Visual J++ or Symantec Café. Or, you can use the freely available *Java Development Kit* (JDK) from Sun Microsystems.

19.1.3 Setting the CLASSPATH Variable

To compile properly, application channels must have access to the Marimba API. The API is contained in a series of compressed zip files (do not unzip them!) that were installed during the installation of your Castanet Transmitter.

To indicate the location of the Marimba API files, you must set your **CLASSPATH** variable. When your program is compiled, the compiler searches the **CLASSPATH** directory for any additional packages or libraries. If the compiler fails to find the Marimba API, it returns with a series of errors.

The current version of the Castanet Transmitter installs the Marimba API files in the **Castanet Publisher** directory. If you followed the typical installation, the files will be located in this directory:

```
C:\Program Files\Marimba\Castanet Publisher\developers\
     compiling
```

Here, you see three zip files:

channel.zip	The Marimba API for creating application channels. This includes the application interface, the Marimba FastIO package, plus a number of miscellaneous utilities.
bongo.zip	The Marimba API for creating Bongo presentations and applications.
plugin.zip	The Marimba API for creating Castanet plug-ins.

Depending on your programming needs, you need to add any one or all of these zip files to your **class** path. The examples presented in this chapter only require access to the **channel.zip** file, though.

If you are using a commercially available compiler, check the documentation on setting the **CLASSPATH** variable. If you are using the JDK on Windows 95/NT, you need to set the **CLASSPATH** variable in your **autoexec.bat** file, which is located on drive C.

To set the **CLASSPATH** variable, type **SET CLASSPATH=** followed by an absolute pathname. Separate each zip file with a semicolon.

Here, for example, is my **CLASSPATH** variable.

```
SET CLASSPATH=C:\Program Files\Marimba\Castanet
     Publisher\developers\compiling\channel.zip;C:\
     Program Files\Marimba\Castanet Publisher\developers\
     compiling \bongo.zip
```

19.2 The Application Interface

19.2.1 Applets versus Application Channels

Creating application channels is enormously similar to creating applets. To create a Java applet, you first must extend the Applet class. You then can override any of the applet methods, including **init**, **start**, and **stop**. Listing 19-1, for example, is a simple applet that draws a circle to the screen and overrides the **init**, **start**, and **stop** methods (see Figure 19-1).

Listing 19-1
A sample applet.

```
/* <applet code="Circle" width=200 height=200></applet>*/

import java.awt.*;
import java.applet.*;

public class Circle extends Applet {

      public void init () {
            System.out.println ("Initializing...");
      }

      public void start () {
            System.out.println ("Starting...");
      }

      public void stop () {
            System.out.println ("Stopping...");
      }

      public void paint (Graphics g) {
            g.drawOval (25,25,50,50);
      }
}
```

Figure 19-1
A sample applet.

In contrast, to create an application channel, you extend a class provided by the Marimba API. Creating application channels therefore is as easy as creating applets, and the more you know about creating applets, the better off you are.

19.2.2 The Application Interface

So, which Marimba class do you extend to create a channel? Not so fast.

The Marimba API first includes an *interface* for creating application channels. An interface represents a broad skeletal outline of what a class should do but gives no hint whatsoever on implementation. I like to think of interfaces as the ideal boss. Your boss tells you that you must succeed in achieving a specific set of goals: "I don't care how you get it done, just get it done!" You therefore have complete flexibility with your time and resources, and you can do whatever you want as long as you get the job done.

Interfaces work the same way. An interface tells a class that it *must* implement a series of methods. But the interface does not tell the class *how* to implement those methods.

The application interface provided by Marimba requires that you implement four specific methods (see Listing 19-2):

`setContext()` When your application is launched, the Castanet Tuner calls this method first. **`setContext`** gives your application a sense of its runtime environment. You can think of this as the equivalent of a channel passport: It tells you application who it is and where it is living, and it outlines its special privileges and responsibilities.

`start()` Next, the Tuner calls the **`start()`** method. The **`start()`** method includes all your program initialization and is called only once. It therefore is similar to the **`init()`** applet method.

`handleEvent()` **`handleEvent`** is used to process channel updates. When you receive a channel update, for example, you can choose to restart the application or immediately install and display the new information.

`stop()` Clean up your program and get ready to exit. Use this method to close any open connections or stop any running threads. This is equivalent to the **`stop()`** applet method.

Listing 19-2
The Application Interface

```
public interface Application {

      //  Give the channel a sense of its runtime
      //  environment
      void setContext (ApplicationContext context);

      //  Initialize the Channel
      void start();

      //  Handle Channel Updates
      boolean handleEvent (Event evt);

      //  Stop the channel:  perform any clean-up
      void stop();

}
```

19.2.3 Hello, World!

No programming example would be complete without a Hello, World! application (and this chapter has several of them). Listing 19-3 shows a sample application that implements the application interface and writes **`Hello, World!`** to the Java console of the Castanet Tuner.

Here are a few details to note:

- In line 4, we import the **`marimba.channel`** package. This enables us to access the application interface.
- We have implemented all four methods required by the application interface.
- The **`setContext`**, **`start`**, and **`stop`** methods display short, informative messages. All calls to **`System.out.println`** are displayed in the Java console of the Castanet Tuner.

19.2.4 Publishing the Hello World Example

If you can successfully compile the Hello World example, your **`CLASSPATH`** variable is set correctly and you will be able to compile all the examples in this chapter. Otherwise, check section 19.1.3, "Setting the **`CLASSPATH`** Variable," again or consult the online documentation accompanying your compiler (the JDK, for example, includes a README file with useful information regarding **`CLASSPATH`** variables).

Listing 19-3
Hello, World!
Version 1.0

```
//     Example Application Channel: HelloWorld!

import java.awt.*;
import marimba.channel.*;

public class HelloWorld implements Application {

        //    Set Application Context
        public void setContext (ApplicationContext ctx) {
                System.out.println ("Setting Context...");
        }

        //  Initialize Channel
        public void start () {
                System.out.println ("Hello World!");
        }

        //  Stop Channel
        public void stop () {
                System.out.println ("Stopping...");
        }

        //  Handle channel updates
        public boolean handleEvent (Event evt) {
                return true;
        }
}
```

Unfortunately, you cannot run your example from the command line. To run your program, you first need to publish it to the Castanet Transmitter and then use your Castanet Tuner to subscribe to the channel.

To publish your channel, launch Castanet Publisher and follow the same steps required for publishing applet or HTML channels. In particular, note the following:

- Remember to include the full absolute path to the `HelloWorld` directory.
- On the Transmitter page, make sure to enter the correct hostname, port number, and any password, if required.
- On the General page, set the type to `Application`. And, in the `Main` class, enter `HelloWorld`. The `Main` class must implement the application interface and always is launched first.

After you successfully publish the channel, use your Castanet Tuner to subscribe to the channel. Then open the Java console window and launch the channel (see Figure 19-2).

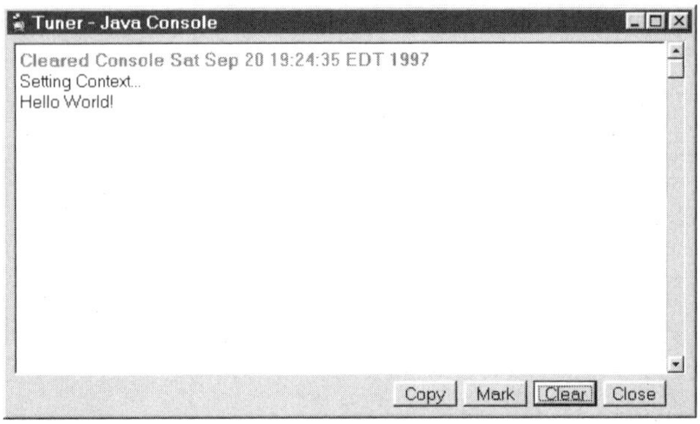

Figure 19-2 Hello, World! Version 1.0.

19.2.5 The Channel Development Process

Now that you have your first channel up and running, let's take a moment to discuss the channel-development process. When compiling standalone Java applications or Java applets, you always have the option of running your program from the command line. To run standalone applications, you can use the **java** command, for example, and for applets, you always can use the JDK applet viewer. Unfortunately, no such options exist for channel applications.

This results in a longer, more complicated debugging process. Here, in a nutshell, are the steps required for developing, testing, and debugging channels:

1. Write you application channel and compile it.
2. Publish the channel to the Transmitter.
3. Subscribe to the channel with the Castanet Tuner.
4. Run the channel and test it. Check for bugs.
5. Edit you application channel and recompile it.
6. Republish the channel to the Transmitter.
7. Using the Castanet Tuner, manually update the channel.
8. Go back to step 4 and repeat.

Unfortunately, this can become a rather arduous and tiresome process. But it currently is the only method of testing and debugging channels. If you are developing a rather sophisticated application channel, your best option is to first create a standalone Java application. You then can run and debug the application from the command line. Once the application is working, you then can rework your application into an application channel. Then continue debugging.

The final example in this chapter is a scrolling ticker channel application. To ease the channel development, I first created a standalone Java application that displays a single scrolling line of text. I therefore was easily able to debug the graphical layout and the scrolling animation simply by running it from the command line. Once I had the animation in working order, I transformed the application into an application channel by implementing the application interface. Breaking your channel development into these two distinct phases can save you lots of time and aggravation.

19.2.6 Hello, World! Version 2.0

Before we proceed any further, let us modify our first example application so that it is slightly more useful. This time, instead of displaying to the Java console, we'll create a small frame window and display **`Hello, World!`** in it (see Figure 19-3). Listing 19-4 extends the **`Frame`** class provided by the Java *Abstract Windowing Toolkit* (AWT) and implements the application interface.

Here are the main highlights of the example in Listing 19-4:

- The **`setContext`** method stores a copy of the **`ApplicationContext`**. The **`ApplicationContext`** gives the channel access to the Castanet Tuner and is explored in detail in later sections. To take full advantage of the Castanet architecture, you always should store a local copy of the **`ApplicationContext`**.
- The start method sets the frame size, adds a single label, and displays the frame window.

19.3 The `ApplicationFrame` Class

19.3.1 The `ApplicationFrame` Class Defined

You can choose to create your applications from scratch by implementing the application interface, or you can choose to use Marimba's **`ApplicationFrame`**

Listing 19-4
Hello, World!
Version 2.0

```
//     Example Application Channel: HelloWorld!,
//     Version 2.0
//     Extends Frame, Implements Application

import java.awt.*;
import marimba.channel.*;

public class HelloWorld extends Frame implements
Application {
      private ApplicationContext context;

      //    Set Application Context
      public void setContext (ApplicationContext
     context) {
            context = context;
            System.out.println ("Setting Context....");
      }

      //  Initialize Channel
      public void start () {
            this.setSize (200,100);
            Font font = new Font ("Helvetica",
            Font.BOLD, 20);
            Label msg = new Label ("Hello World!");
            msg.setFont (font);
            msg.setAlignment (Label.CENTER);
            this.add (msg);
            this.show();
      }

      //  Stop Channel
      public void stop () {
            System.out.println ("Stopping...");
      }

      //  Handle channel updates
      public boolean handleEvent (Event evt) {
            return true;
      }
}
```

class. The **ApplicationFrame** class provided by Marimba extends the **Frame** class provided by the AWT and implements the application interface with a number of default implementations. It therefore is very similar to our example in Listing 19-4.

The **ApplicationFrame** class makes programming considerably easier and makes application channels as easy as applets. Listing 19-5 contains an outline of the **ApplicationFrame** class.

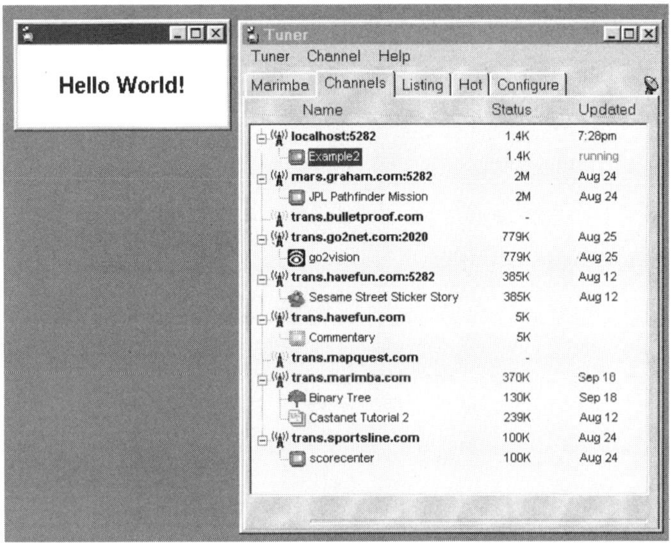

Figure 19-3 Hello, World! Version 2.0.

19.3.2 Hello, World! Version 3.0

Here then is our final Hello, World! example. This time, we extend the **`ApplicationFrame`** and override the **`start()`** method, as shown in Listing 19-6.

This is more typical of the application channels you will create. And, you now can see that application channels are extremely similar to applets. Therein lies the true simplicity of Castanet.

NOTE: *If you are creating channels that use the Bongo software library, Marimba also provides the* **`ApplicationPlayerFrame`** *class. Extend this class instead of* **`ApplicationFrame`** *if your application uses of any Bongo GUI elements or presentations.*

19.4 The Application Context

19.4.1 The Application Context Defined

We have now alluded several times to the *application context*. The application context is very similar to the applet context normally associated with regular Java applets.

Listing 19-5
An Outline of the **ApplicationFrame** Class

```
package marimba.channel;

import java.awt.*;

public class ApplicationFrame extends Frame implements
      Application {

      protected ApplicationContext context;

      //  Save the ApplicationContext
      public void setContext(ApplicationContext context) {
            this.context = context;
      }

      //  Show the Frame
      public void start() {
            show();
      }

      //  Destroy the channel, hide and dispose the frame
      public void stop() {
            hide();
            dispose();
      }

      //  Handle Channel Updates
      public boolean handleEvent(Event evt) {
      ...
      ...
      }
}
```

The *applet context* enables the applet to communicate with the Web browser that is hosting it. You can use the applet context to retrieve images or audio files, for example, to display messages in the browser's status box (**showStatus**), or to open a specified URL page (**showDocument**).

In much the same manner, the application context enables the application channel to communicate with the Castanet Tuner that is hosting it. In contrast to Web browsers, though, the Castanet Tuner enables much greater functionality. You can use the **ApplicationContext** to read or write from a specified directory on the user's hard drive, for example, or you can use it to direct automatic updates and installations.

Listing 19-6
Hello, World!
Version 3.0

```
//     Example Application Channel: HelloWorld!, Version 3.0
//     Extends ApplicationFrame

import java.awt.*;
import marimba.channel.*;

public class HelloWorld extends ApplicationFrame {

        //  Initialize Channel
        public void start () {
                this.setSize (200,100);
                Font font = new Font ("Helvetica",
                Font.BOLD, 20);
                Label msg = new Label ("Hello World!");
                msg.setFont (font);
                msg.setAlignment (Label.CENTER);
                this.add (msg);
                this.show();
        }
}
```

19.4.2 Application Context Methods

The application context includes a great number of public methods that enable access to the Castanet Tuner. Here, for your reference, is a listing of the most important methods. We will return to the specifics of some of these methods in sections 19.5 and 19.6 when we discuss the storing of persistent data. For a complete listing of the **`ApplicationContext`** API, consult Appendix A, "Marimba Castanet API."

`public URL getBase()` Gets the base URL of this channel. Used primarily to retrieve image and data files.

`public String getChannelName()` Gets the name of this channel.

`public String getChannelStatus (String channelName)` Gets the status of a channel on this Transmitter. The status will be **`unsubscribed`**, **`subscribed`**, or **`running`**.

`public URL getDataBase()` Gets the URL for the data directory of this channel. This is the only directory where the channel can store persistent data.

`public String getDataDirectory()` Gets the data directory string of this channel. This is the only directory where the channel can store persistent data.

`public String getParameter()` Gets an application parameter. The application parameters are specified in the **`properties.txt`** file associated with each channel. Parameters are case-insensitive.

`public Updates getPendingUpdates()` Gets the update report for this channel. Returns **`null`** if there are no existing updates of any kind.

`public String getServerName()` Gets the name of the server of this channel. The server name is of the form **`hostname:port`**.

`public void installData (String dir)` Requests the installation of all or part of new channel data. Pass an empty string to install the entire channel.

`public long publishTime()` Returns the time at which this version of the channel was published.

`public void restart()` Restarts the application.

`public void update()` Requests a channel update.

`public long updateTime()` Returns the time the channel was last updated with new data.

19.4.3 Example Application

The application context is extremely simple to use. Listing 19-7 displays runtime information concerning the channel and its host Tuner (see Figure 19-4).

This example refers to several important methods that we will revisit in the next two sections. First, note the **`getDataDirectory()`** method. This method returns an absolute path to the channel's data directory. With the modified Castanet security sandbox, channels can read from and write to this directory only. All other directories are strictly off limits.

Second, the **`getBase()`** method returns a URL to the channel's base directory. You can use this URL to retrieve image or data files that were downloaded along with your Java class files. This is the equivalent of the applet **`getDocumentBase()`** method, except that the Tuner retrieves these

Listing 19-7
Example Application Context

```
//     Basic Application Channel
//     Extends ApplicationFrame
//     Displays ApplicationContext Data to the Java Console

import java.awt.*;
import java.util.*;
import marimba.channel.*;

public class BasicChannel extends ApplicationFrame {

  //  Initialize Channel
  public void start () {
    String name = context.getChannelName();
    System.out.println ("Channel Name:  "+name);
    System.out.println ("Channel Status:"+context.
         getChannelStatus(name));
    System.out.println ("Data Directory:
         "+context.getDataDirectory());
    System.out.println ("Base URL:  "+context.getBase());
    System.out.println ("Last Updated:
         "+new Date(context.updateTime()));
    System.out.println ("Active Update Schedule:
         "+context.getParameter
           ("update.active"));
    System.out.println ("InActive Update Schedule:
         "+context.getParameter
       ("update.inactive"));
    }
}
```

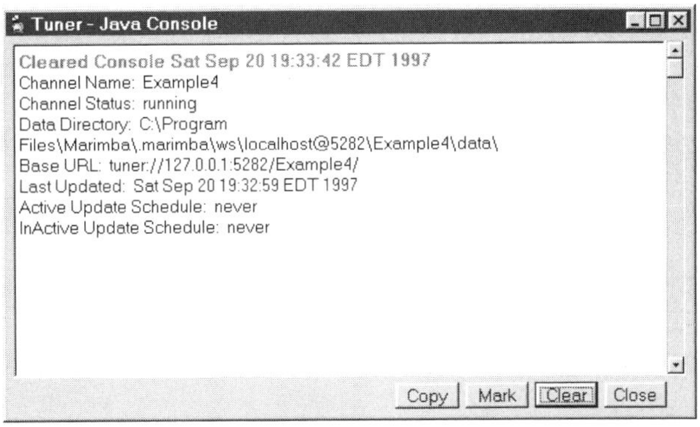

Figure 19-4
Output: Using the application context.

files from the user's hard drive and does not actually make a connection back to the Transmitter.

Finally, note the use of **getParameter**. This is the equivalent of the **getParameter** method normally associated with applets. But this **getParameter** enables you to access any channel settings. These channel settings reside in the **properties.txt** file that is generated when you publish your channel. Here, we query the properties file for the Active and Inactive Update schedules.

19.5 Storing Persistent Data

One of the great advantages of Castanet application channels is the capability to store persistent data to the user's hard drive. This enables you to create full-scale applications that can save state between executions. And, not only does Marimba provide this extra functionality, but it also includes a series of classes for easier and faster I/O access.

19.5.1 The Marimba Fast I/O Classes

The Marimba library includes two classes for fast input and output. The **FastInputStream** class enables you to read data. The **FastOutputStream** class enables you to write data. Both these classes are similar to the **BufferedInputStream** provided by the Java API, but they provide faster I/O access and actually are considerably easier to use.

An overview of the Fast I/O API follows. For the complete API, consult Appendix A.

Before we proceed in using the Marimba fast I/O classes, however, let us clarify a potential source of confusion.

19.5.2 The Base Channel Directory versus the Data Directory

Each time you subscribe to a channel, the Castanet Tuner downloads an entire directory of contents. From now on, we will refer to this directory as the *base channel directory* or simply the *base directory*. This base

FastInputStream

Constructors

`FastInputStream(byte[])`	Creates a stream that reads from a buffer.
`FastInputStream(byte[], int, int)`	Creates a stream that reads from a buffer.
`FastInputStream(File)`	Opens a file.
`FastInputStream(InputStream)`	Combines two streams.
`FastInputStream(InputStream, int)`	Combines two streams given a buffer size.
`FastInputStream(RandomAccessFile)`	Accesses a `RandomAccessFile`.
`FastInputStream(String)`	Opens a file.

Main Methods

`public void close() throws IOException`	Closes `FastInputStream`.
`public boolean getError()`	Returns `True` if there has been a read error. I/O errors are not reported during reads. Instead, they are reported when the stream is closed.
`public int read(byte[], int, int)`	
`public boolean readBoolean()`	
`public byte readByte()`	
`public char readChar()`	
`public double readDouble()`	
`public float readFloat()`	
`public void readFully(byte[])`	
`public void readFully(byte[], int, int)`	
`public int readInt()`	
`public String readLine()`	

(Continues)

`public long readLong()`

`public short readShort()`

`public int readUnsignedByte()`

`public int readUnsignedShort()`

`public String readUTF()`

FastOutputStream

Constructors

`FastOutputStream(byte[])`	Creates a memory output stream with a given size.
`FastOutputStream(File)`	Opens a file for writing.
`FastOutputStream(int)`	Creates a memory output stream with a given size.
`FastOutputStream(OutputStream)`	Combines two streams.
`FastOutputStream(OutputStream, int)`	Combines two streams given a buffer size.
`FastOutputStream(RandomAccessFile)`	Opens using a **`RandomAccessFile`**.
`FastOutputStream(String)`	Opens a file for writing.

Main Methods

`public void close() throws IOException`	Closes **`FastOutputStream`**.
`public boolean getError()`	Returns **`True`** if there has been a write error. I/O errors are not reported during writes. Instead, they are reported when you flush or close the stream.

`public final void print(char)`

`public final void print(long)`

`public final void print(String)`

```
public final void println()
public final void println(char)
public final void println(long)
public final void println(String)
public final void write(byte[], int, int)
public final void write(int)
public final void writeBoolean(boolean)
public final void writeByte(int)
writeBytes(String)
writeChar(int)
writeChars(String)
writeDouble(double)
writeFloat(float)
writeInt(int)
writeLong(long)
writeShort(int)
writeUTF(String)
```

directory includes everything needed to make your application run, including all of your Java class files, image files, sound clips, and various data files. When your channel is updated with new information, the new information also is installed here.

Your application channel can retrieve or read any of these files. But, when you direct the Tuner to retrieve these files, it simply retrieves them from the user's hard drive and does not need to make any network connections back to the Transmitter. These files therefore represent one set of files the application can retrieve from the user's hard drive. But remember that your application can only read these files. It cannot modify them in any way. And it cannot create new files in the base directory.

In contrast to the base channel directory, each channel also gets a data directory. This is where you store persistent data. Your application has privileges to read, modify, or create new files in the data directory. The data directory is the second method by which you access data from the user's hard drive.

Even though both the base channel directory and the data directory exist on the same hard drive, they are accessed in different ways. Understanding these differences is crucial.

19.5.3 Reading Files from the Base Channel Directory

To retrieve a file from the base channel directory, you *must* access it with the URL received from the application context **getBase()** method. The following code, for example, opens the **data.txt** file in the base directory and reads one line of data:

```
URL datafile = new URL(context.getBase(), "data.txt");
FastInputStream in = new FastInputStream
      (datafile.openStream());
String text = in.readLine();
```

Here, you can see that we are using the **FastInputStream** and the **readLine** method to read a single line of text from the data file.

19.5.4 Reading from and Writing to the Data Directory

To read from or write to a file in the data directory, you can use the URL provided by the application context **getDataBase** method or the file path provided by the **getDataDirectory** method. Here, for example, we read the **hiscore.dat** file and store the high score in memory:

```
File datafile = new File (context.getDataDirectory(),
      "hiscore.dat");
FastInputStream in = new FastInputStream (datafile);
int hiscore = in.readInt();
```

If the user ends up beating the high score, we simply use **FastOutputStream** to write the new high score back out to the **hiscore.dat** file.

19.5.5 Example Application

To further illustrate these points, the example in Listing 19-8 uses both the base channel directory and the data directory. When you publish this channel, make sure to include a **data.txt** file in your base channel directory. The file should include a single line of text or a single sentence.

The application first opens the **data.txt** file from the channel base directory and extracts the single sentence. It then takes this sentence and stores it on the user's hard drive in a file called **storage.txt**. The application also prints the full pathname of the data directory so that you can manually verify that the **storage.txt** file exists and contains the correct message.

It is important to note that your application must be prepared to catch the **IOException**. This is standard for all of Java's I/O classes. If you are creating a new URL to access the base directory, you also must remember to catch the **MalformedURLException**. The exception handling in this code simply prints a stack trace to the Java console.

Listing 19-8
Handling Persistent Data

```
//     Basic Application Channel
//     Extends ApplicationFrame
//     Reads Data file from the Channel's Base URL
//     Then Writes Data out to local data directory

import java.awt.*;
import java.io.*;
import java.net.*;
import marimba.channel.*;
import marimba.io.*;

public class BasicChannel extends ApplicationFrame {

    //  Initialize Channel
    public void start () {
        String text = read_url("data.txt");
        write_file (text, "storage.txt");
    }

    //  To read files in the channel base directory,
    //  you must use URL addresses formed with
    //  context.getBase()
    private String read_url (String filename) {
        String text = null;
        try {
            System.out.println ("BaseURL:  "+context.
            getBase());
            URL data = new URL(context.getBase(), filename);
            FastInputStream in = new FastInputStream
            (data.openStream());
            text = in.readLine();
            System.out.println ("Retrieving Text:  "+text);
            in.close();
        }
```

(Continues)

Listing 19-8
Continued

```
        catch (MalformedURLException e) {
            e.printStackTrace();
        }
        catch (IOException e) {
            e.printStackTrace();
        }
        finally {
            return text;
        }
    }

    //  Write to file in data directory
    private void write_file (String text, String filename) {
        try {
            System.out.println ("Data Directory:
            "+context.getDataDirectory());
            File datafile = new File (context.getDataDirec-
            tory(),filename);
            FastOutputStream out = new FastOutputStream
            (datafile);
            System.out.println ("Writing out text:  "+text);
            out.writeChars (text);
            out.close();
        } catch (IOException e) {
            e.printStackTrace();
        }
    }
}
```

19.6 Handling Updates

We now are edging closer to creating full application channels. Our next hurdle is understanding Castanet's channel-update mechanisms.

19.6.1 The Update Events

Java is an event-driven programming language. At any point in time, it could handle any number of events. A user might click a button, an animation timer might go off, or a user simply might hold down the Shift key. To process any of these events, you must include specific event handlers in your code.

The Castanet Tuner generates its own events to signal the arrival of new data or new channel updates. In fact, it generates four specific channel-update events. Understanding the differences between these events is crucial to creating dynamic application channels.

As much as possible, the Castanet Tuner attempts to follow the update schedule recommended by the channel provider. But the exact steps followed by the Tuner during channel updates depends largely on whether the application being updating is active or inactive.

19.6.2 Handling Active Channel Updates

Let's first examine what happens when the application being updated is active and running on the user's desktop.

Each time the Tuner initiates a channel update, it first sends a warning signal, known as the **`DATA_UPDATE_EVENT`**:

`DATA_UPDATE_EVENT` tells the currently active application that an update is *about* to occur. Most commonly, you will want to catch this event only if you are creating sophisticated Castanet plug-ins. You can catch the event, for example, and direct the application to immediately save any logging or profile data so that the information is automatically relayed back to the Castanet Transmitter. If you are not creating any plug-ins, you can safely ignore this event.

The Tuner then proceeds to check the Transmitter for new information. If there is no new information, the Tuner goes back to sleep and waits for the next update interval. But, if there is new data, the Tuner stores the updated channel files to a temporary directory and sends a **`DATA_AVAILABLE_EVENT`**.

`DATA_AVAILABLE_EVENT` tells the currently active application that a new channel update has arrived. The Tuner awaits your instructions on how to proceed.

When you receive a **`DATA_AVAILABLE_EVENT`**, your application has three basic options:

1. You simply can ignore the event. The next time the user launches the application, the Tuner installs and uses the newly updated channel. But, for now, it sticks with the currently running version.
2. You can restart your application by calling the application context **`restart()`** method (see section 19.4.2, "Application Context Methods").

This directs the Tuner to stop the channel, install the channel update, and then restart the channel. If you are planning to follow this option, it is usually a good idea to give the user the option or at least some warning.

3. You can keep your channel running but install the new data by calling the application context `installData()` method. This directs the Tuner to install the new data to the base channel directory, where your application can access the new information. This is the preferred method of handling dynamic updates.

If you choose the third option, the Tuner installs the channel update and sends one last event: `DATA_INSTALLED_EVENT`.

`DATA_INSTALLED_EVENT` tells the currently active application that the new channel update has been installed successfully. After the application is installed, it can access the new channel data.

Handling Active Channel Updates

1. The Tuner sends a `DATA_UPDATE_EVENT`. This tells the application that an update is about to occur. Direct your application to save any profile or logging information.
2. The Tuner checks the Transmitter for new information. If no new information is available, the Tuner goes back to sleep and waits until the next update interval.
3. If new information is available, the Tuner sends the `DATA_AVAILABLE_EVENT`. This tells the application that new information is available. The Tuner waits for your application's instructions.

   An active application channel has three basic options for handling a `DATA_AVAILABLE_EVENT`:

   - Ignore it. Use the updated channel the next time around.
   - Restart the application. Call `ctx.restart()`.
   - Keep the application running and install the data now. Call `ctx.installData()`.

4. If the application follows the third option, the Tuner installs the new channel update. When the update is installed successfully, the Tuner sends the `DATA_INSTALLED_EVENT`.

19.6.3 Handling Inactive Channel Updates

If the application channel being updated is inactive, the Tuner follows a different course of action.

First, because the application is inactive, there is no need to give it advanced warning and therefore no need to send the `DATA_UPDATE_EVENT`. Second, the Tuner checks the Transmitter. If new information is available, the Tuner installs the data to the user's hard drive. It then wakes up a small part of the application channel (the Tuner basically launches just enough of the application to call its event-handler routines, but it refrains from calling the application's `start()` method). The Tuner then sends a `DATA_NOTIFY_EVENT`.

`DATA_NOTIFY_EVENT` tells the application that a new channel update has arrived and has been installed. If the event handler returns `True`, the Tuner launches the channel by calling its `start()` method. Otherwise, the Tuner closes the channel by calling its `stop()` method.

The `DATA_NOTIFY_EVENT` gives developers and users the capability to inspect new data before making a decision on whether to launch the channel. As an elaborate example, this might be useful for a sophisticated stock-analysis channel. The user makes a specific request to be notified if Company XYZ's stock falls below 70. When the new data arrives, the Tuner sends the `DATA_NOTIFY_EVENT`. The application wakes up and inspects the new data. If the price is above 70, it returns `False` and goes back to sleep. But, if the price is below 70, it returns `True` and the channel is launched, immediately displaying the alarming news.

Handling Inactive Channel Updates

1. The Tuner checks the Transmitter for new information. If no new information is available, the Tuner goes back to sleep and waits until the next update interval.
2. If new information is available, the Tuner installs the channel update, wakes up the application, and sends the `DATA_NOTIFY_EVENT`.
3. The application has a chance to inspect the data. If the application's event handler returns `True`, the Tuner calls the application's `start()` method. Otherwise, the Tuner calls the application's `stop()` method.

19.6.4 The `ApplicationFrame` `notifyAvailable()` and `notifyInstall()` Methods

Once you understand the differences between the various update events, all you need to do is catch the events by implementing the application interface **`handleEvent()`** method. Listing 19-9, for example, handles three channel-update events.

Most of the time, however, it is much easier to use the event handlers built right into the **`ApplicationFrame`** class. Listing 19-10 includes the event handling methods from the **`ApplicationFrame`** source code. Take a look at the listing before we examine it in detail.

Note the following in Listing 19-10:

- By default, the **`ApplicationFrame`** handles the **`DATA_AVAILABLE_EVENT`** and **`DATA_INSTALLED_EVENT`**. It will not handle the **`DATA_NOTIFY_EVENT`** or the **`DATA_UPDATE_EVENT`**, however. You will have to override this method to provide handling for these methods.
- When the **`ApplicationFrame`** receives a **`DATA_AVAILABLE_EVENT`**, the **`notifyAvailable()`** method is called. The **`notifyAvailable()`** method checks the channel's publishing properties to determine a course of action. These are the channel properties that were set with Castanet Publisher. If the channel's data available action (known here as **`update.action`**) is set to **`restart`**, the **`ApplicationContext restart()`** method is called. If, on the other hand, the channel's data available action is set to **`install`**, the **`ApplicationContext installData()`** method is called. Passing an empty string to the **`installData()`** method directs the Tuner to install all the updated channel files. If you want an easy way of handling the **`DATA_AVAILABLE_EVENT`**, the best option is simply to override the **`notifyAvailable()`** method.
- When the **`ApplicationFrame`** receives a **`DATA_INSTALLED_EVENT`**, the **`notifyInstall()`** method is called. This method does not actually do anything, but it does provide a code stub for catching the **`DATA_INSTALLED_EVENT`**. Simply override the **`notifyInstall()`** method in your own code.

Listing 19-9
Handling Channel-Update Events

```
//  Handle Channel Updates
public boolean handleEvent(Event evt) {
switch (evt.id) {
      case DATA_UPDATE_EVENT:
            saveLog();
            return true;
      case DATA_AVAILABLE_EVENT:
            installUpdate();
            return true;
      case DATA_INSTALLED_EVENT:
            displayNewData();
            return true;
      }
…
}
```

Listing 19-10
Source Code for the **`ApplicationFrame`** Class

```
    public void notifyAvailable(String dir) {
        if ("restart".equals(context.getParameter("update.action"))) {
            context.restart();
        } else if ("install".equals(context.getParameter("update.action")))
       {
            context.installData("");
        }
    }

    public void notifyInstall(String dir) {

    }

    public boolean handleEvent(Event evt) {
        switch (evt.id) {
          case DATA_AVAILABLE_EVENT:
            notifyAvailable((String)evt.arg);
            return true;

          case DATA_INSTALLED_EVENT:
            notifyInstall((String)evt.arg);
            return true;

          case Event.WINDOW_DESTROY:
            context.stop();
            return true;
        }
        return super.handleEvent(evt);
        }
}
```

The most interesting factor to notice here is that these update handlers are built right into *any* application that extends the **ApplicationFrame**. For example, recall that the example in Listing 19-8 reads a single line of text from the **data.txt** file and outputs this string to the Java Tuner console and to an output file. Now, try this:

1. First, publish the channel. But, this time, make sure that the Active Update Frequency option is set to Frequently and that the Active Data Available Action option is set to Restart.
2. Subscribe to the channel and leave it running.
3. Edit the **data.txt** file in your developer directory.
4. Republish your channel.
5. Wait a few minutes, and the channel updates itself. When the channel is updated, the **ApplicationFrame notifyAvailable()** method is called. This method checks the channel's publishing options and immediately restarts the application. And, once restarted, the Application displays the newly updated data text. It's as simple as that!

19.6.5 Example Application Channel

Let's now move onto a simple application channel that really takes advantage of the Castanet update architecture and really takes advantage of the **ApplicationFrame** event handlers.

The example in Listing 19-11 provides a very simple headline news application. It is actually a precursor to the scrolling ticker case study presented in section 19.7.

Before explaining the code, let's first examine what it does. When the channel is launched, it opens a **data.txt** file in the channel base directory. The data file contains a single news headline that is displayed immediately to the Java Tuner console. Most of this functionality is identical to the example in Listing 19-8.

The channel then simply sits and waits for a channel update. But, this time, instead of restarting the application, the channel handles the update dynamically and immediately displays the new headline to the user in the Java console (see Figure 19-5).

Take a look at the code before we examine it in detail.

Listing 19-11 Headline News Channel, Version 1.0

```
//      Headline News Channel, Version 1.0
//      Extends ApplicationFrame
//  Displays Updated data to the Tuner Console

import java.awt.*;
import java.io.*;
import java.net.*;
import java.util.*;
import marimba.channel.*;
import marimba.io.*;

public class HeadlineNews extends ApplicationFrame {

   //  Initialize Channel
   public void start () {
        String text = getData("data.txt");
        System.out.println ("News:  "+text);
   }

   //  Process Channel Updates
   //  New Data is now available.  Install the data.
   public void notifyAvailable (String dir) {
        System.out.println ("New Data Available.");

        // Print list of updated files
        // Depending on the list of files, you can choose to
        // install or restart the application.
        Updates update = context.getPendingUpdates();
        Enumeration files = update.getUpdates();
        while (files.hasMoreElements()) {
             String filename = (String) files.nextElement();
             System.out.println ("updated files:  "+filename);
        }
        context.installData ("");
   }

   //  Process Channel Updates
   //  New data is now installed.  Read new data from
   //  data.txt file.
   public void notifyInstall (String dir) {
        System.out.println ("New Data Installed.");
        String text = getData ("data.txt");
        System.out.println ("Updated News: "+text);
   }

   //  Get News Headline from data.txt file
   //  Must use context.getBase() method
   private String getData (String filename) {
        String text = null;
        try {
```

Continues

Listing 19-11 Continued

```
            URL data = new URL(context.getBase(), filename);
            FastInputStream in = new FastInputStream
            (data.openStream());
            text = in.readLine();
            in.close();
        }
        catch (MalformedURLException e) {
            e.printStackTrace();
        }
        catch (IOException e) {
            e.printStackTrace();
        }
        finally {
            return text;
        }
    }
}
```

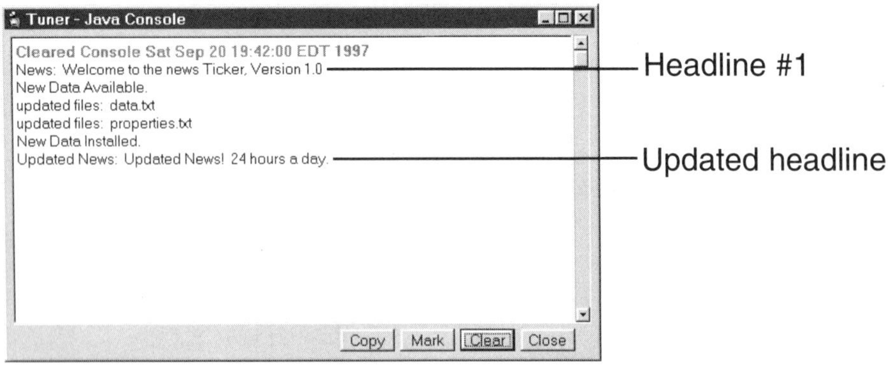

Figure 19-5 Headline News Ticker, Version 1.0

As you examine the code in Listing 19-11, note the following:

- First, the **getData()** method reads in a single line of text from the **data.txt** file. By now, the **FastInputStream** should look familiar.
- Second, we have overridden the **ApplicationFrame notifyAvailable()** method. Take a close look at this method, and you will notice that we have referenced the **ApplicationContext getPendingUpdates()** method. This method returns a Castanet **Update** object, which can

be queried for a list of pending updates. Specifically, the **`Update`** object has three public methods:

`public Enumeration getDeletes()`

Returns the enumeration of all the deletions that are pending or **`null`** if there are none.

`public Enumeration getCreates()`

Returns the enumeration of all the creations that are pending or **`null`** if there are none.

`public Enumeration getUpdates()`

Returns the enumeration of all the updates that are pending or **`null`** if there are none.

Here, we query the **`Update`** object for a list of the updated files and display them to Java Tuner console. We then call the **`ApplicationContext installData()`** method. Note that **`installData`** again is called with an empty string, directing the Tuner to install *all* of the newly updated channel files.

At times, however, it might be necessary to specifically check each of the updated, deleted, and newly created files and then selectively install only some of them. This is why the **`Update`** object can be important. If the channel developer publishes a new **`data.txt`** file, for example, the best option is to explicitly install just the data file: **`ctx.installData`** (**`data.txt`**). But what happens if the developer has updated the **`HeadlineNews.class`** file instead? The best option, in this case, is to simply call the application context **`restart()`** method and start over with a newly updated application.

- The third and final point to note about Listing 19-11 is that we have overridden the **`notifyInstall()`** method. When the new data has been installed successfully, we again call the **`getData()`** method to retrieve and display the new headline.

Try the example. Then, after you have the channel running, try editing the **`data.txt`** file and then republish the channel. Confirm that the new headline does indeed appear in the Java console.

19.7 Case Study: Headline News Ticker

We now are ready to examine a fully functional (and hopefully useful!) application channel. The Headline News Channel builds on the example in Listing 19-11 to provide an animated scrolling ticker on the user's desktop (see Figure 19-6).

The program itself is not much more complicated than our last example. In fact, the program uses much of the same structure provided by all the previous examples. Take a look at Listing 19-12 before we examine it in detail.

Again, the actual headline is stored in the **data.txt** file of the base channel directory. If you modify this file and republish your channel, the news ticker immediately displays the new headline. Now, note the following:

- First, we have defined two classes here. The **HeadlineNews** class handles the channel updates. The **Scroller** class handles the on-screen scrolling animation.
- The **Scroller** class really has nothing to do with the Castanet architecture. It merely paints the scrolling text with a separate animation thread and a double buffering graphics technique for smoother animation. As far as the **Headline** class is concerned, the only important method is the **setText()** method, which sets the currently displayed headlines. As noted in section 19.2.5, "The Channel Development Process," I first created the **Scroller** class as a standalone application. After I got the scroller working, I integrated it with the **HeadlineNews** class.
- The **HeadlineNews** class extends the **ApplicationFrame** class and overrides the **start()**, **notifyAvailable()**, and **notifyInstall()** methods.

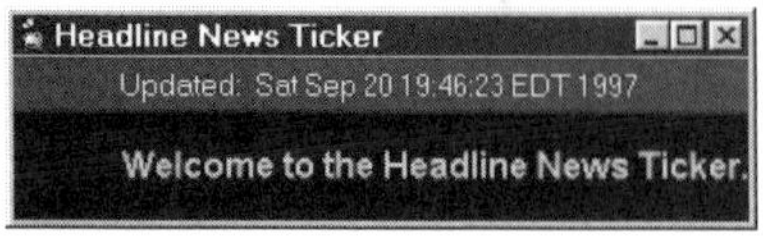

Figure 19-6
Headline News Ticker, Version 2.0

Listing 19-12
Headline News Channel, Version 2.0

```
//       Headline News Channel, Version 2.0
//       Extends ApplicationFrame
//   Displays Updated data in Scrolling Ticker
//   Created by Ethan Cerami, 1997

import java.awt.*;
import java.io.*;
import java.net.*;
import java.util.*;
import marimba.channel.*;
import marimba.io.*;

public class HeadlineNews extends ApplicationFrame {
   private Label header;
   private Scroller scroller;

   // Initialize Channel Frame
   // Use Borderlayout and add Scrolling Panel
   public void start () {
      String text = getData("data.txt");
      System.out.println ("News:  "+text);

      this.setSize (350,100);
      this.setTitle ("Headline News Ticker");
      this.setLayout (new BorderLayout());
      header = new Label ("Updated:  "+(new  Date (context.updateTime())));
      header.setBackground (Color.blue);
      header.setForeground (Color.white);
      header.setAlignment (Label.CENTER);

      scroller = new Scroller (text, 16, 20);
      this.add ("North", header);
      this.add ("Center", scroller);
      this.show();
      scroller.start();
}

   // Process Channel Updates
   // New Data is now available.  Install the data.
   public void notifyAvailable (String dir) {
      System.out.println ("New Data Available ->  Installing Data.");
      context.installData ("");
   }

   // Process Channel Updates
   // New data is now installed.  Read new data from
   // data.txt file.
   public void notifyInstall (String dir) {
      System.out.println ("New Data Installed ->  Updating Ticker");
      header.setText ("Updated:  "+(new Date (context.updateTime())));
      scroller.setText (getData ("data.txt"));
   }
```

Continues

Listing 19-12
Continued.

```
    // Get News Headline from data.txt file
    // Must use context.getBase() method
    private String getData (String filename) {
        String text = null;
        try {
            URL data = new URL(context. getBase(), filename);
            FastInputStream in = new FastInputStream (data.openStream());
            text = in.readLine();
            in.close();
        }
        catch (MalformedURLException e) {
            e.printStackTrace();
        }
        catch (IOException e) {
            e.printStackTrace();
        }
        finally {
            return text;
        }
    }
}

// Scroller Class is responsible for scrolling the
// current news headline.
class Scroller extends Panel implements Runnable{
    private String text;
    private String newtext;
    private int stringwidth;
    private Dimension d;
    private Graphics offScreenGraphics;
    private Image offScreen;
    private int currentx, currenty;
    private Thread anim;
    private Font font;
    private int speed;

    /**  Constructor Function
    @param text = news text to appear in ticker
    @param fontsize = ticker font size
    @param speed = animation delay  */
    public Scroller (String text, int fontsize, int speed) {
        this.text = text;
        font = new Font ("Helvetica", Font.BOLD, fontsize);
        this.speed = speed;
        stringwidth = 0;
    }

    /**  Set new headline text
    @ param text is the new headline to appear in ticker */
```

Listing 19-12

```
public void setText (String text) {
   newtext = text;
}

/**  Paint Method  */
public void paint (Graphics g) {
   update (g);
}

/** Update Method:  Provides Double Buffering for /Smoother Animation  */
public void update (Graphics g) {

   //  Prepare for Double Buffering
   if (d==null) {
       d = this.getSize ();
       offScreen = createImage (d.width, d.height);
       offScreenGraphics = offScreen.getGraphics();
       currentx = d.width;
   }

   offScreenGraphics.setFont (font);

   //  Get width of current news headline and set currenty
   if (stringwidth == 0) {
       FontMetrics fm = offScreenGraphics. getFontMetrics();
       stringwidth = fm.stringWidth (text);
       currenty = (fm.getAscent() + (d.height - (fm.getAscent() +
       fm.getDescent()))/2);
   }

   offScreenGraphics.setColor (Color.black);
   offScreenGraphics.fillRect (0,0,d.width, d.height);
   offScreenGraphics.setColor (Color.green);

   offScreenGraphics.drawString (text, currentx,currenty);
   g.drawImage (offScreen, 0,0, null);
}

/** Start Method:  Start Thread Animation */
public void start () {
   anim = new Thread (this);
   anim.start();
}

/** Stop Method:  Stop Thread Animation */
public void stop () {
    anim.stop();
}
```

Continues

Listing 19-12
Continued.

```
    /** Run Method:  Scroll Ticker;  check boundaries */
    public void run () {
         anim.setPriority (Thread.MIN_PRIORITY);
         while (true) {
              repaint();
              //  Perform automatic wrap-around
              //  and smooth transition for new headline
              if (currentx < 0-stringwidth) {
                   currentx = d.width;
                   if (newtext!=null) {
                        text = newtext;
                        newtext = null;
                        stringwidth =0;
                   }
              }
              else currentx-;
              try { anim.sleep (speed);
              } catch (InterruptedException e) {
              }
         }
    }
}
```

- The **`start()`** method initializes the scroller with the values retrieved from the **`getData`** method. It then lays out the frame with the AWT **`BorderLayout`** Manager. The header of the ticker also is set to display the date and time of the last updates. For this, we use the application context **`updateTime()`** method.
- When a channel update occurs, the Tuner sends the **`DATA_AVAILABLE_EVENT`**, immediately triggering the **`notifyAvailable()`** method. We choose to install the entire channel update by calling **`installData()`** with an empty string.
- After the Tuner successfully installs the new data, it sends the **`DATA_INSTALLED_EVENT`**, immediately triggering the **`notifyInstall()`** method. Here, we set the new update time and update the scroller with the string returned from the **`getData()`** method.

Online Resource

- Castanet Developer Documentation, Channel Development: The Big Picture
  `http://www.marimba.com/doc/Castanet_Developer_Docs/current/channeldev.html`. Ten concise pages on developing your own application channels. Special emphasis on handling update events.

Appendix A

Marimba Castanet API

The complete Marimba Castanet API is available online at **http://www.marimba.com/doc/**.

A.1 Package `marimba.channel`

A.1.1 Interface `marimba.channel.Application`

This is the application interface for the Marimba Tuner. A class that implements this interface can act as an application in the context of the Tuner.

```
public interface Application extends Object {

    // Constants
    public final static int DATA_UPDATE_EVENT;
    public final static int DATA_AVAILABLE_EVENT;
    public final static int DATA_INSTALLED_EVENT;
    public final static int DATA_NOTIFY_EVENT;

    // Public Instance Methods
    public abstract void setContext(ApplicationContext);
    public abstract void start();
    public abstract void stop();
    public abstract boolean handleEvent(Event evt);
}
```

A.1.2 Interface marimba.channel.ApplicationContext

This provides the context for an application. It is the interface of the application to the Tuner.

```
public interface ApplicationContext extends Object {

        // Public Instance Methods
        public abstract URL getBase();
        public abstract URL getCodeBase();
        public abstract URL getDataBase();
        public abstract boolean channelFileExists(String
                path);
        public abstract String[] listChannelDirectory(String
                directory);
        public abstract String getDataDirectory();
        public abstract Updates getPendingUpdates();
        public abstract String getChannelDirectory();
        public abstract String getServerName();
        public abstract String getChannelName();
        public abstract String getParameter(String nm);
        public abstract void installData(String dir);
        public abstract boolean appendLog(byte data[]);
        public abstract boolean appendLog(String data);
        public abstract byte[] getProfile();
        public abstract boolean setProfile(byte data[]);
        public abstract long publishTime();
        public abstract long updateTime();
        public abstract void restart();
        public abstract void stop();
        public abstract void update();
        public abstract void startChannel(String serverName,
                String channelName);
        public abstract void subscribeChannel(String
                serverName, String channelName);
        public abstract void unsubscribeChannel(String
                channelName);
        public abstract void removeChannel(String
                channelName);
        public abstract String[] listChannels();
        public abstract String getChannelStatus(String
                channelName);
        public abstract AudioClip getAudioClip(URL url);
        public abstract Image getImage(URL url);
        public abstract void showDocument(URL url);
        public abstract void showDocument(URL url, String
                frame);
        public abstract void showDocument(String url);
        public abstract void showDocument(String url, String
                frame);
        public abstract void showStatus(String msg);
}
```

A.1.3 Class `marimba.channel.ApplicationFrame`

A helper class for creating channel applications. This class creates, shows, and destroys an AWT frame as the base frame of the application.

```
public class ApplicationFrame extends Frame implements
        Application {

        //  Public Constructor
        public ApplicationFrame()

        //  Public Instance Methods
        public void setContext(ApplicationContext context);
        public ApplicationContext getContext();
        public void stop();
        public void notifyAvailable(String dir);
        public void notifyInstall(String dir);
        public boolean handleEvent(Event evt);
}
```

A.1.4 Class `marimba.channel.ApplicationPlayerFrame`

A presentation player for channels built with Bongo.

```
public class ApplicationPlayerFrame extends PlayerFrame
        implements Application {

        // Public Constructor
        public ApplicationPlayerFrame();

        //  Protected Instance Variable
        protected ApplicationContext context;

        // Public Instance Methods
        public void setContext(ApplicationContext context);
        public ApplicationContext getContext();
        public void stop();
        public void notifyAvailable(String dir);
        public void notifyInstall(String dir);
        public boolean handleEvent(Event evt);
}
```

A.1.5 Class `marimba.channel.Updates`

This class generates a list of pending updates, creates, and deletes that would be performed if all the changes for the specified channel were installed right now.

```
public class Updates extends Object {

        //  Public Constructor
        public Updates(Vector updates, Vector creates,
              Vector deletes)

        // Public Instance Methods
        public Enumeration getDeletes();
        public Enumeration getCreates();
        public Enumeration getUpdates();
}
```

A.2 Package `marimba.io`

A.2.1 Class `marimba.io.FastInputStream`

A fast, unsynchronized buffered input stream. This stream combines a lot of the functionality of `BufferedInputStream`, `ByteArrayInputStream`, and `DataInputStream`.

```
public class FastInputStream extends FilterInputStream
implements DataInput {

        //  Public Constructors
        public FastInputStream(String file) throws
              IOException;
        public FastInputStream(File file) throws IOException;
        public FastInputStream(RandomAccessFile in);
        public FastInputStream(InputStream in);
        public FastInputStream(InputStream in, int size);
        public FastInputStream(byte buf[]);
        public FastInputStream(byte buf[], int off, int
              len);

        //  Protected Instance Variables
        protected byte buf[];
        protected int count;
        protected int count;
        protected int markpos;

        //  Public Instance Methods
        public boolean getError();
        public boolean backup(int n);
        public int read();
        public int read(byte b[], int off, int len);
        public long skip(long n);
        public int available() throws IOException;
        public void close() throws IOException;
        public void readFully(byte b[]);
        public void readFully(byte b[], int off, int len);
        public int skipBytes(int n);
```

```
        public boolean readBoolean();
        public byte readByte();
        public int readUnsignedByte();
        public short readShort();
        public int readUnsignedShort();
        public char readChar();
        public int readInt();
        public long readLong();
        public float readFloat();
        public double readDouble();
        public String readLine();
        public String readUTF();
        public PropertyObject readObject();
        public boolean markSupported();
        public void mark(int limit);
        public void reset();
        public void seek(long p) throws IOException;
        public long getFilePointer() throws IOException;
}
```

A.2.2 Class `marimba.io.FastOutputStream`

A fast, unsynchronized buffered output stream. This stream combines the functionality of `DataOutputStream`, `PrintStream`, and `BufferedOutputStream`.

```
public class FastOutputStream extends FilterOutputStream
implements DataOutput {

        // Public Constructors
        public FastOutputStream(String file) throws
              IOException;
        public FastOutputStream(File file) throws
              IOException;
        public FastOutputStream(RandomAccessFile file) throws
              IOException;
        public FastOutputStream(OutputStream out);
        public FastOutputStream(OutputStream out, int size);
        public FastOutputStream();
        public FastOutputStream(int size);
        public FastOutputStream(byte buf[]);

        // Protected Instance Variables
        protected byte buf[];
        protected int count;

        //  Public Instance Variables
        public OutputStream out;

        //  Public Instance Methods
        public boolean getError();
        public final void write(int b);
        public final void write(byte b[], int off, int len);
        public final void flush() throws IOException;
        public void close() throws IOException;
```

```
        public void justClose();
        public int size();
        public byte[] getByteArray();
        public byte[] toByteArray();
        public String toString();
        public final void writeBoolean(boolean v);
        public final void writeByte(int v);
        public final void writeChar(int v);
        public final void writeInt(int v);
        public final void writeLong(long v);
        public final void writeFloat(float v);
        public final void writeDouble(double v);
        public final void writeBytes(String s) throws
               IOException;
        public final void writeChars(String s) throws
               IOException;
        public final void writeUTF(String str);
        public final void writeObject(PropertyObject obj);
        public final void print(char ch);
        public final void println(char ch);
        public final void print(String str);
        public final void println(String str);
        public final void print(Object obj);
        public final void println(Object obj);
        public final void print(long n);
        public final void println(long n);
        public final void println();
        public void seek(long p) throws IOException;
        public long getFilePointer() throws IOException;
}
```

Index

C

D

J

K

L

M

R

S

U

V

W

X

Y

Z

ABOUT THE AUTHOR

Ethan Cerami is an Associate in the Research and Development division of Cognitive Communications, L.L.C., a firm specializing in Intranet development for Fortune 500 companies. He is also currently completing his masters degree in computer science at New York University, where he teaches undergraduate courses in computer programming.

SOFTWARE AND INFORMATION LICENSE

The software and information on this diskette (collectively referred to as the "Product") are the property of The McGraw-Hill Companies, Inc. ("McGraw-Hill") and are protected by both United States copyright law and international copyright treaty provision. You must treat this Product just like a book, except that you may copy it into a computer to be used and you may make archival copies of the Products for the sole purpose of backing up our software and protecting your investment from loss.

By saying "just like a book," McGraw-Hill means, for example, that the Product may be used by any number of people and may be freely moved from one computer location to another, so long as there is no possibility of the Product (or any part of the Product) being used at one location or on one computer while it is being used at another. Just a book cannot be read by two different people in two different places at the same time, neither can the Product be used by two different people in two different places at the same time (unless, of course, McGraw-Hill's rights are being violated).

McGraw-Hill reserves the right to alter or modify the contents of the Product at any time.

This agreement is effective until terminated. The Agreement will terminate automatically without notice if you fail to comply with any provisions of this Agreement. In the event of termination by reason of your breach, you will destroy or erase all copies of the Product installed on any computer system or made for backup purposes and shall expunge the Product from your data storage facilities.

LIMITED WARRANTY

McGraw-Hill warrants the physical diskette(s) enclosed herein to be free of defects in materials and workmanship for a period of sixty days from the purchase date. If McGraw-Hill receives written notification within the warranty period of defects in materials or workmanship, and such notification is determined by McGraw-Hill to be correct, McGraw-Hill will replace the defective diskette(s). Send request to:

Customer Service
McGraw-Hill
Gahanna Industrial Park
860 Taylor Station Road
Blacklick, OH 43004-9615

The entire and exclusive liability and remedy for breach of this Limited Warranty shall be limited to replacement of defective diskette(s) and shall not include or extend any claim for or right to cover any other damages, including but not limited to, loss of profit, data, or use of the software, or special, incidental, or consequential damages or other similar claims, even if McGraw-Hill has been specifically advised as to the possibility of such damages. In no event will McGraw-Hill's liability for any damages to you or any other person ever exceed the lower of suggested list price or actual price paid for the license to use the Product, regardless of any form of the claim.

THE McGRAW-HILL COMPANIES, INC. SPECIFICALLY DISCLAIMS ALL OTHER WARRANTIES, EXPRESS OR IMPLIED, INCLUDING BUT NOT LIMITED TO, ANY IMPLIED WARRANTY OF MERCHANTABILITY OR FITNESS FOR A PARTICULAR PURPOSE. Specifically, McGraw-Hill makes no representation or warranty that the Product is fit for any particular purpose and any implied warranty of merchantability is limited to the sixty day duration of the Limited Warranty covering the physical diskette(s) only (and not the software or information) and is otherwise expressly and specifically disclaimed.

This Limited Warranty gives you specific legal rights; you may have others which may vary from state to state. Some states do not allow the exclusion of incidental or consequential damages, or the limitation on how long an implied warranty lasts, so some of the above may not apply to you.

This Agreement constitutes the entire agreement between the parties relating to use of the Product. The terms of any purchase order shall have no effect on the terms of this Agreement. Failure of McGraw-Hill to insist at any time on strict compliance with this Agreement shall not constitute a waiver of any rights under this Agreement. This Agreement shall be construed and governed in accordance with the laws of New York. If any provision of this Agreement is held to be contrary to law, that provision will be enforced to the maximum extent permissible and the remaining provisions will remain in force and effect.